Adaptive Governance

Global Environmental Accord: Strategies for Sustainability and Institutional Innovation
Nazli Choucri, series editor

A complete list of books published in the Global Environmental Accord series appears at the back of this book.

Adaptive Governance

The Dynamics of Atlantic Fisheries Management

D. G. Webster

The MIT Press
Cambridge, Massachusetts
London, England

© 2009 Massachusetts Institute of Technology

For information about special quantity discounts, please email special_sales@ mitpress.mit.edu

This book was set in Sabon on 3B2 by Asco Typesetters, Hong Kong.
Printed on recycled paper and bound in the United States of America.

Library of Congress Cataloging-in-Publication Data

Webster, D. G., 1975–
Adaptive governance : the dynamics of Atlantic fisheries management / D. G. Webster.
    p.   cm. — (Global environmental accord)
Includes bibliographical references.
ISBN 978-0-262-23270-8 (hardcover : alk. paper) — ISBN 978-0-262-73192-8 (pbk. : alk. paper) 1. Fishery management. 2. Fishery policy.
3. Intergovernmental cooperation. I. Title.
SH328.W43   2008
338.3'727—dc22   2008017103

10   9   8   7   6   5   4   3   2   1

In memory of Bob Friedheim, who introduced me to the study of global environmental issues, and Hayward Alker, who told me that I had to write this book.

Contents

Series Foreword

A new recognition of profound interconnections between social and natural systems is challenging conventional constructs and the policy predispositions informed by them. Our current intellectual challenge is to develop the analytical and theoretical underpinnings of an understanding of the relationship between the social and the natural systems. Our policy challenge is to identify and implement effective decision-making approaches to managing the global environment.

The series Global Environmental Accord: Strategies for Sustainability and Institutional Innovation adopts an integrated perspective on national, international, cross-border, and cross-jurisdictional problems, priorities, and purposes. It examines the sources and the consequences of social transactions as these relate to environmental conditions and concerns. Our goal is to make a contribution to both intellectual and policy endeavors.

Nazli Choucri

Foreword

Adaptive Governance: The Dynamics of Atlantic Fisheries Management sheds light on an important aspect of international environmental governance that has largely escaped the attention of analysts bent on understanding the roles that environmental and resource regimes play both in causing problems and in addressing issues that arise in a variety of settings. In the early years, students of environmental governance focused on processes of regime formation, seeking to explain why regimes form to address some problems but not others. Subsequent analyses have dealt with the effectiveness of regimes in altering behavior or solving problems. Now attention is shifting to a search for understanding the ways in which regimes change over time. Largely overlooked in research dealing with these issues are a series of questions regarding the ongoing management activities that consume the lion's share of the time and energy of those involved with individual regimes as they go about the business of applying the provisions of these institutional arrangements to day-to-day concerns. How well do decision-making procedures work in addressing routine matters? Are there identifiable patterns in the results that flow from the use of these procedures on an ongoing basis? Can decisions about routine matters trigger processes that lead to major institutional changes? Can we identify the factors that account for variance in these terms?

Analysts have addressed questions of this sort in other issue areas. There are, for example, a number of studies that delve into such matters with regard to the operation of the World Trade Organization. However, sustained empirical studies of the day-to-day operation of environmental and resource regimes are few and scattered. Now, D. G. Webster has taken direct aim at this topic in the realm of international environmental governance. Grounding her work in an in-depth assessment of the operation of the International Convention for the Conservation of Atlantic Tunas (ICCAT), she explores the selection of management measures pertaining to a number of highly migratory species—mainly tunas, swordfish, and marlins—that fall under the jurisdiction of this convention. A close examination reveals that there is considerable variance in the management measures that ICCAT has adopted both in dealing with different species and in dealing with the same species over time. What accounts for this variance across a universe of cases involving the management of highly migratory species that seem quite similar? This is the sort of challenge that warms the heart of researchers in the social sciences who are on the lookout for opportunities to conduct natural experiments. There is significant variance in the dependent variable. Yet many aspects of the relevant setting remain constant by virtue of the fact that they pertain to a single management regime that has not experienced any dramatic or watershed changes in its constitutive provisions since its formation in 1966.

Confronted with this puzzle, Webster goes to work to develop an explanatory framework capable of accounting for the observed variance in the selection of management measures across species and time. Because the voting members of this regime are states, she focuses on the behavior of states, treating them for the most part as unitary actors that have relatively well-defined interests regarding the management of highly migratory species. And because the regime focuses on the pursuit of maximum sustainable yields from harvested species, she concentrates on decisions pertaining to the setting of allowable harvest levels and related matters on a species-by-species basis. Those interested in the rise of ecosystem-based management as an alternative to maximum sustainable yield in framing issues of governance and intrigued by the growing role of various nonstate actors in environmental governance may be impatient with this concentrated effort to explain the behavior of the regime created under the terms of ICCAT. Nevertheless, this regime is representative of a sizable number of environmental governance systems now in operation. Whatever our preferences and hopes for the future, it is surely important to enhance our ability to explain outcomes under the conditions prevailing today.

To explain variance in the choice of management measures affecting highly migratory species, Webster develops what she calls a "vulnerability response framework." This framework seeks to classify states interested in the harvest of specific species into categories (e.g., highly

vulnerable, gradually vulnerable, and so forth) based largely on considerations of economic flexibility and competitiveness. The resultant vulnerability matrix for each species provides a method for assessing the
bargaining strength of the key players and a line of reasoning in which
movements toward or away from strong management measures are
expected to reflect the preferences of the player(s) with the greatest bargaining strength in the relevant arena. A series of chapters apply this
framework to the selection of management measures for individual
species under ICCAT's jurisdiction with results that accord well with
observed outcomes.

As Webster herself makes clear, this line of analysis has significant limitations. The engine that drives the model is in some ways underspecified.
The categories differentiating among levels of vulnerability are hard to
operationalize with regard to specific species. The number of cases is
too small to support claims of a statistical nature. And since the management measures selected with regard to individual species are known at
the outset, there is a danger that interpretations developed for specific
cases will be adjusted—if only unintentionally—to generate the "right"
answers. Still, Webster has taken a significant step forward in generating
expectations about the selection of management measures, and she offers
a number of helpful suggestions to those who may be interested in developing this mode of analysis further. As a point of departure for additional work in this field, this book has much to offer.

It is important to be clear about several larger limitations of this study
as well. It is tempting to see links between the selection of management
measures and the condition of various stocks of highly migratory species,
and such links may well occur in individual cases. An analysis that focuses on variance in the selection of management measures can detect
pressures for significant changes in the status quo. However, it cannot
provide unambiguous evidence regarding the role of a regime in maintaining species or stocks of individual species in a healthy condition.
The range of biophysical and socioeconomic drivers operating simultaneously and likely to have some impact on the condition of a species is too
great to allow us to identify precise links of this sort. Beyond this lies the
question of generalizability. Webster's account of the vulnerability response framework and its capacity to explain variance in the selection
of management measures rests on a close encounter with a single regime.
This is not a defect in the argument that she presents in this book. Still, it
is pertinent to ask whether the analysis is capable of explaining variance

in the selection of management measures in other fisheries management regimes and ultimately in a broader range of environmental and resource regimes operating at the international or transnational level today. This will be a challenge for those who find the vulnerability response framework attractive and wish to explore the extent to which it can be transported to other settings.

These observations about the limits of Webster's argument are important, but they must not be allowed to obscure or diminish the significance of her achievements. Although the effort to explain variance in the day-to-day operations of environmental governance systems is clearly important, mainstream work in this field has largely ignored this matter. Webster rightly calls our attention to this fact and proceeds to develop an analytic tool capable of explaining this variance. Whatever its fate in the long run, her work constitutes a prominent contribution to our understanding of this important phenomenon. Analysts interested in this topic in the future will have to reckon with Webster's contribution, whether they conclude that some alternative is needed or simply seek to flesh out the vulnerability response framework and to sharpen it for application to a range of specific cases. In either case, her work will have played a significant role in the ongoing effort to improve our understanding of environmental governance.

Oran R. Young
Santa Barbara, California
December 2007

Preface

This book is the culmination of many years of work on the problem of global environmental governance generally and the process of international fisheries management specifically. Even so, it is a beginning rather than an ending. While the ideas underlying the framework of vulnerability response have an intuitive appeal in many arenas, they are operationalized here only in the realm of international fisheries management. Furthermore, the cases themselves are drawn from a single regime, the International Commission for the Conservation of Atlantic Tunas (ICCAT). While comparison among multiple regimes would certainly be useful, the path of my research led to a choice between expansion to other management institutions or the inclusion of the last two cases, which cover Atlantic bluefin tuna. Because this species is so important economically and biologically, and in the development of tuna management world-wide, I chose the latter option. Plans for additional cases from other fisheries regimes and the development of more formal computational techniques are already under way, and it is my great hope that the ideas presented here will lead to much more expansive research into other forms of human response to environmental change and resultant patterns of adaptive governance.

Readers who would like to explore the data used in this analysis can find it at http://mitpress.mit.edu/adaptive_governance.

Acknowledgments

This book would not have been possible without the advice and assistance of many people. First my thanks go to the Offield Family Foundation, Paxson Offield, and the University of Southern California's Wrigley Institute for Environmental Studies for their consistent support of my research. The Alice C. Tyler Charitable Trust and John C. Tyler Trust, the Haynes Foundation, the Rose Hills Foundation, and the Florence and A. Leroy Webster Trust also provided much-appreciated funding.

On the academic side, I am grateful to John Elliot, Anthony F. Michaels, Robert Friedheim, and Linwood Pendleton for starting my research off in the right direction and to Timur Kuran and Hayward Alker for seeing it through to the end. These mentors challenged me to go beyond conventional perspectives in economics and international relations and helped me to bridge many of the gaps between the two. I am also indebted to Oran Young and two anonymous reviewers for their excellent insights on my initial manuscript. Their comments helped me to streamline my writing and the overall organization of this book.

When I first started this project, I had no idea how deeply I would be drawn into the world of international fisheries management. It is a complicated business, but I had exceptional guidance from scientists like John Graves, Gary Sakagawa, Michael Hinton, Victor R. Restrepo, Peter Miyake, and John Mark Dean, as well as decision makers such as Robin Allen, David Ardill, David Balton, Raleigh Schmitten, Masanori Miyahara, Peter S. C. Ho, John Spencer, Kim Blankenbecker, Alan Gray, and Xavier Vant. Many representatives of interest group also took the time to explain their positions to me. These include David Wilmont, who—along with John Graves—got me into my first ICCAT meeting, Ellen Peel, Helen Bours, Nelson Beideman, Richard Ruis, Robert Hayes, and Susan Singh-Renton. Special appreciation goes to Russell Dunn and

David Kerstetter for helping me through that first meeting, along with many others, and Philomena Seidita for her assistance with the labyrinth of ICCAT documents.

On a more personal note, I'd like to thank Julie Brown, Farideh Mota-medi, and Cindy Locken for their technological and moral support, and my parents, Ronald and Sandra K. Webster, for their unwavering faith in my abilities.

Adaptive Governance

1

Adaptive Governance

Progress is an ambiguous phenomenon. It has driven humanity's prosperity, yet it also comes with unintended effects, such as resource depletion, ecosystem disruptions, and climate change. Coping with these problems is a struggle in itself, one that depends on the coordinated actions of many individuals. Furthermore, while there are those who voluntarily eschew the comforts of consumerism, there are considerable numbers of people who are vested in the current economic system. For these individuals—whether they are producers, consumers, and/or decision makers—dealing with the side effects of progress is costly. Because so few are willing to sacrifice their way of life, early warnings of potentially catastrophic events can go unheeded for decades as "progress" rolls on (Rosenau 1993, 258).

For instance, in fisheries, progress has meant bigger, faster boats, more efficient capture techniques, and a wider availability of fish for human consumption—as well as profits, jobs, and other economic benefits. At the same time, the rapid expansion of fishing effort in the past century has caused major concern regarding the long-term viability of living marine resources, whether or not they are commercially valuable. To their detriment, fishers and governments alike have been unable to curtail excess fishing effort in many areas in spite of strong scientific and economic evidence of overexploitation. Recent collapses of important fisheries like Pacific anchoveta and the North Atlantic groundfishes, which include cod, haddock, plaice, and halibut, have shown how acute such failures can be. On the other hand, as Hilborn, Orensanz, and Parma (2005) point out, some other important fisheries, like north Pacific halibut, have been well managed.

What is even more interesting is that almost every documented example of sustainable fisheries management has occurred, not by design

Figure 1.1
Pivotal cycle in common-pool resource management.

alone, but through an adaptive process. That is, the most effective measures are not born whole in the heads of managers, but are usually the result of trial and error. Certainly, design is involved, as the huge body of literature on fisheries management shows. However, observation suggests that fishers and managers learn by first trying and failing with measures that are less costly but also less effective before they become willing to accept the sacrifices required for successful regulation. The same can be said of the international institutions that govern shared and high-seas fisheries. The rules and norms of decision making may seem frustratingly static for long periods, but change does occur as fishing countries are forced to cope with the troubles that arise under open access.

Figure 1.1 shows how the ideal-type or pure form of adaptive fisheries governance might work in the international arena. On the left-hand side of the figure, the usual downward spiral associated with open access has been expanded to include political responses to the costs of resource depletion. This is the preliminary metastable state. Management is ineffective, but—at least at the international level—the system seems static. However, underneath this element, pressure is building from the "bottom up." As the resource gets smaller and smaller, fishers face growing competition, and policy makers are more and more dissatisfied with the status quo. If periodic release of this pressure occurs through partial management interventions, then the system might persist for a long time. It might even shift gradually into the effective management cycle pictured on the right-hand side of the figure. However, rapid change is also possible, including the sudden collapse of the regime or the stock(s) in its jurisdiction.

In fact, the simplicity of figure 1.1 is quite deceptive. There are many different microlevel interactions and context-specific elements that control the strength and flow of this macrolevel system (Schelling 1978; Putnam 1988). Actors may be affected or respond at different rates, creating different levels of aggregate concern. Options often depend on available technologies and institutional precedents, so the potential for change is limited at any given point in time. Complex dynamics and stochastic elements can also distort the causal links that are depicted so clearly in the figure, creating a pattern of "one step forward, two steps back, then maybe a couple of steps sideways." In fact, the only certainty is that the system will always be in flux, and that for every action there will be a reaction—sometimes equal, sometimes amplified by feedbacks, and sometimes nullified by exogenous forces.

All of this makes it quite difficult to understand adaptive governance. The *vulnerability response* framework developed in this book is a meso-level perspective that falls between the thin approaches of economic and game theory-based work and a thick approach, which relies heavily on detailed case descriptions (Young 2002). It will guide the development of predictions regarding the evolution of countries' policy positions that can then be tested using cases from the International Commission for the Conservation of Atlantic Tunas (ICCAT, pronounced ī-kat), which manages highly migratory fish species in the Atlantic. This analysis is an important first step toward understanding adaptive governance in international fisheries. Collective decisions on management are not predicted, but are reported in the cases so that emergent patterns of collective outcomes can be identified in the final chapter.

After a brief background on the politics and economics of highly migratory species (HMS) in section 1.1, the rest of this chapter outlines some important innovations in the international management of these valuable and beleaguered fish. As described in sections 1.2 and 1.3, the most important of these innovations was developed by ICCAT. Several of the stocks that are managed by the Commission have been severely depleted, but ICCAT has also developed new management tools that include specific allocation of access rights and international monitoring and enforcement mechanisms. Furthermore, there has been some intriguing variation in the application of these measures that needs to be explained. Finally, section 1.4 elaborates on the need for a combined perspective in order to explore both the static and dynamic aspects of adaptive management in the HMS context.

1.1   The HMS Context

Highly migratory species are some of the Earth's most important renewable resources and present some of the most complicated practical issues for sustainable use. As top end predators, they play a key role in the marine ecosystem, ensuring that populations of smaller fish do not exceed the carrying capacity of the oceans (Berkes et al. 2006). In addition, the commercial value of these species is quite large and is distributed across many fleets. More than 150 countries and "fishing entities" harbor fleets targeting HMS stocks, supplying the world with almost half a million tons of fish per year (FAO 2007b).[1] Furthermore, half of all HMS harvests are traded internationally at an export value of over US $5 billion, surpassed among fish products only by shrimp and groundfish (FAO 2006).

These aggregate statistics conceal some variations among the species. Adult tunas, especially bluefin and bigeye, are prized by sushi and sashimi connoisseurs and can bring very high prices for quality fish. Juvenile and small tunas are packaged and sold in large quantities at low prices. Swordfish, which is also commercially targeted, is consumed mainly in high-end restaurants in the United States and Europe. There are some less prolific highly migratory species that command low prices, including several stocks of billfish. Some, like white marlin, are only caught incidentally; these stocks are *by-catch*, rather than targeted species, in commercial fishing operations (Majkowski 2005; FAO 2007c).

As might be expected, growing demand for highly migratory species has precipitated considerable expansion of the fishing industry targeting these stocks. This in turn has resulted in the depletion of many of these fisheries. Of the twenty-four major market tunas, thirteen are estimated to be overexploited, six are fully exploited, and only four are moderately exploited (De Leiva Moreno and Majkowski 2005). Of the six stocks of swordfish in the major oceans, at least two are thought to be moderately overexploited and the rest are at full exploitation. Several by-catch stocks, including white marlin and Atlantic blue marlin, are also heavily depleted (IATTC 2006; ICCAT 2007a; IOTC 2005).

It is generally believed that the overexploitation of targeted stocks is due to the common pool nature of high seas fishing, which is open to

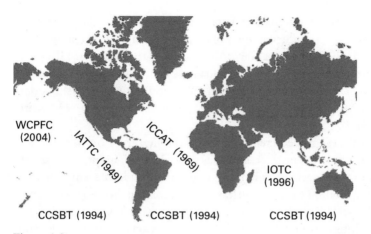

Figure 1.2
Map of regional fisheries organizations with jurisdiction over HMS. IATTC,
Inter-American Tropical Tuna Commission, began activities in 1949; ICCAT, International Commission for the Conservation of Atlantic Tunas, began activities
in 1969; CCSBT, Commission for the Conservation of Southern Bluefin Tuna,
began activities in 1994; IOTC, Indian Ocean Tuna Commission, took over
activities from the Indo-Pacific Tuna Development and Management Program
(IPTP, 1982) in 1996; WCPFC, Western and Central Pacific Fisheries Commission, began activities in 2004.

fleets from around the world. The scale of these fisheries precludes collective action by individuals and no single country has jurisdiction over
highly migratory species, so international cooperation is required if these
stocks are to be maintained at either biologically or economically optimal levels. Recognizing this, fishing countries have signed agreements
establishing several multilateral commissions, or regional fisheries management organizations (RFMOs), which meet annually to negotiate
international management measures (see figure 1.2 for a map of tuna-
related RFMOs).[2] The ultimate goals of these commissions vary somewhat, but the target of most is to maintain highly migratory stocks at
some benchmark level of harvest, usually maximum sustainable yield
(MSY; Sydnes 2001).

As the numbers on overexploitation show, these commissions have not
been completely successful at meeting their goals. There has been little
public outcry regarding these failures, largely because tunas and tunalike
species are not charismatic, at least not on the level of dolphins, turtles,
and whales. Movements by noncommercial interest groups have had

minimal impacts on international management because they just don't have the capacity to influence the policy process on a large enough scale (DeSombre 1999; Webster 2006). Alternatively, the range of HMS fisheries undermines the power of coastal states, which has proved pivotal to the sometimes successful management of straddling and transboundary stocks (Hannesson 1997; Peterson 1995; Stokke, Anderson, and Mirovitskaya 1999).

Because of these impediments, much of the literature on these organizations is quite pessimistic regarding the RFMOs' ability to manage highly migratory species.[3] For many years it did indeed seem that these international bodies were powerless to prevent the overexploitation of many of the world's most important HMS stocks. However, in the mid-1990s, the International Commission for the Conservation of Atlantic Tunas began adopting strong management measures that both conformed to scientific advice and that were monitored and enforced at the international level. Although these measures were not uniformly applied, nor were they successful in all instances, they have been partially linked to the rebuilding of some stocks (ICCAT 1995–2007b: 2005, 58, 125). Thus, an explanation is required for the overarching issue—the negotiation of management innovations in spite of multiple barriers to cooperation—as well as for the underlying irregularities in the timing, application, and effectiveness of those measures.

1.2   Depletion and Rebuilding of Atlantic Highly Migratory Species

Among the five HMS regional fisheries bodies, the stocks managed by the International Commission for the Conservation of Atlantic Tunas are the most depleted. Historically some of the most heavily fished stocks on the planet, Atlantic tunas and tuna-like species were still plentiful when the commission first met in 1969. This continued throughout the 1970s, and members of ICCAT's Standing Committee on Research and Statistics (SCRS) made few management recommendations.[4] However, in the 1980s, larger fleets, more advanced fishing technologies, and high demand for fish products led to steep reductions in the abundance of several stocks. Tracing these changes in their research, the SCRS began suggesting that the commission should either freeze or reduce fishing pressure on about half the stocks in their jurisdiction. In spite of these warnings, six of the twelve major Atlantic HMS stocks were assessed as overfished by the mid-1990s (ICCAT 1971–1994: 1994, 204; 1995–2007b: 1995, 170; 1996, 46, 53; 1997, 34; 1998, 29).

Table 1.1 lists the current status and utilization of those stocks as estimated by the SCRS in their most recent assessments. All of these scientific evaluations are based on the concept of maximum sustainable yield. This is the idea that a particular stock, or group of fish that is both biologically and geographically capable of reproduction can be fished at some constant average rate that maximizes current catches without reducing the potential for future harvests. The level of MSY depends on several factors, but two of the most important are the size of the stock, or its biomass, and its overall growth rate. There are two major components that can be evaluated by using this method. One is the level of fishing effort (F_{MSY}), which is associated with *overfishing*, or the process of taking out more than the MSY level of harvest. The other is the size of the stock (B_{MSY}), which can be *underfished* if it is too large to allow significant population growth or *overfished* if it is too small to support harvests at or above MSY (Clark 1990).

As a management benchmark, MSY has many drawbacks. For instance, it is based on the premise that the sole purpose of management is commercial exploitation. Also, by focusing on a single stock it simplifies a highly complex system and thereby ignores potential ecosystem effects of fishing. A pertinent example is the territorial expansion of the large and very predatory Humbolt squid (*Dosidicus gigas*) in recent years (Zeidberg and Robison 2007). If this top predator is biologically successful, the tunas that remain may have a harder time finding food, reducing their overall growth rate. This would reduce the sustainable yield for these stocks but the change would not be captured in most MSY-based assessments for several years.[5] Finally, the use of this benchmark emphasizes direct effort or catch limits rather than more holistic approaches such as place-based management (Crowder et al. 2006).

In spite of these disadvantages, MSY dominates the dialogue in regional fisheries management organizations. The simplicity of the approach has a certain appeal for scientists, particularly in an area where first-hand data on abundance are difficult to collect. Decision makers have also embraced MSY, largely because of its focus on maximizing resource use over time. Management at MSY is the stated goal of ICCAT and several similar RFMOs. Other organizations use the term "optimal sustainable yield" in their agreements, but MSY remains the de facto

Table 1.1
Biomass Status and Utilization for Major Atlantic HMS Stocks

Atlantic stocks	Status relative to B_{MSY}	Utilization relative to F_{MSY}
Bigeye tuna	Rebuilt	Stable, previously overfishing
Eastern skipjack tuna	Not estimated, probably full/underfished	Not estimated, probably full
Western skipjack tuna	Not estimated, probably full/underfished	Not estimated, probably full
Yellowfin tuna	Full/slightly overfished	Full, increase in effort unsustainable
Eastern bluefin tuna[a]	Severely overfished	Overfishing still occurring
Western bluefin tuna[b]	Severely overfished	Overfishing still occurring
Northern albacore	Rebuilding, moderately overfished	Overfishing still occurring
Southern albacore	Underfished	Underfishing, increase effort sustainably
Northern swordfish	Rebuilt	Underfishing, previously overfishing
Southern swordfish	Underfished	Probably underfishing, can increase effort
Blue marlin	Severely overfished	Probably overfishing still occurring
White marlin	Severely overfished	Overfishing still occurring

B_{MSY} = biomass that supports maximum sustainable yield; Underfished = biomass > B_{MSY}; Full exploitation = biomass ≈ B_{MSY}; Moderately overfished = biomass ≥ 50% B_{MSY}; Severely overfished = biomass ≤ 50% B_{MSY}.
F_{MSY} = level of fishing mortality (F) that will keep harvests at maximum sustainable yield; Underfishing = fishing mortality < F_{MSY}; Stable = fishing morality is at F_{MSY}; Overfishing = fishing mortality > F_{MSY}.
[a] Spawning stock biomass; summary statistics relative to biomass 1970–74; includes Mediterranian.
[b] (SSB), recruitment MSY.
Source: Most recent estimate of B/B_{MSY} and F/F_{MSY} as recorded in ICCAT (2007a).

measure of stock abundance. Furthermore, it is the basis for the only available estimates of the size of fish stocks and the level of fishing effort for Atlantic highly migratory species, so it will be used throughout this text. In fact, one could say that MSY is in itself an institution, which may or may not evolve over time.

Turning back to the table, one can see that seven of the twelve major stocks that are managed by ICCAT have been classified as overfished at some time in the past two decades. Of these, four are severely over-exploited, including both eastern and western bluefin tunas as well as blue marlin and white marlin. Overfishing is still occurring for these stocks, so they are likely to continue to decline unless some factor changes in the near future. One other stock, northern albacore, is moderately overexploited. This is actually an improvement since it was thought to be severely overexploited as recently as 1997. Because overfishing has not stopped, the Atlantic stock of northern albacore is not likely to return to MSY levels of productivity and may even decline again.

On a more positive note, two of the stocks listed in the table have been rebuilt to MSY levels. Bigeye tuna and northern swordfish, both of which were found to be moderately overexploited in the late 1990s, are now estimated to be close to full exploitation. Moreover, fishing mortality—once well above the level that supports MSY—is now thought to be at sustainable levels. This reversal of fortunes is both exciting and intriguing, but it should be viewed with caution. Because of the complex nature of ocean ecosystems, it is virtually impossible to directly link ICCAT management to the rebuilding of particular stocks.[6] Even with lower fishing effort, stocks may not rebound because of poor environmental conditions, such as unfavorable temperatures or lack of prey species. Alternatively, a really good combination of events, such as perfect spawning conditions and abundant food supplies, could result in stock increases irrespective of changes in fishing pressure. These possibilities confound our ability to determine the causal role of ICCAT management in the observed changes in the size of bigeye and swordfish stocks.

Nonetheless, it is still possible to describe the management of these stocks as a qualified success, not because of the rebuilding per se, but because of the steps that the commission took to ensure that fishing effort was reduced to the levels recommended by its scientific committee. For many years, scientific advice was ignored or downplayed by members of the commission, and the measures that they adopted failed to match up with SCRS recommendations. This all changed prior to the rebuilding of these stocks. The commission set total allowable catch (TAC) levels in accordance with scientific advice and distributed the TAC among member and nonmember fishing countries, making enforcement easier. This also facilitated the adoption of the international enforcement mechanisms mentioned earlier. Because of these new measures, they were able to reduce legal fishing in the Atlantic and curtail illegal fishing as well. While it would be better if we could be certain of the impact of these measures on the stocks, their adoption was still quite an achievement in international cooperation.

1.3   Management Innovations at ICCAT

In fact, the measures adopted for bigeye and northern swordfish were part of a larger trend toward increased management for most of the Atlantic HMS stocks. As shown in figure 1.3, only a few regulations were adopted by the commission throughout the 1970s and 1980s. These included size limits on yellowfin, bigeye, and bluefin tunas and catch limits on western bluefin tuna. In contrast, from 1990 to 2003, ICCAT introduced catch limits for stocks of yellowfin, bluefin, albacore, and bigeye tunas, as well as swordfish and blue and white marlins. Time-

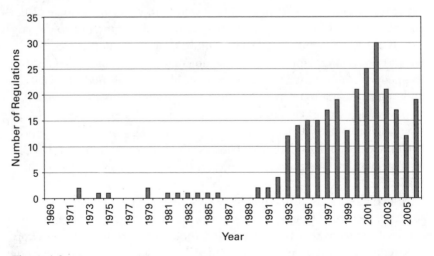

Figure 1.3
Number of ICCAT management measures adopted per year. Source: ICCAT 2007a.

area closures and capacity limits were also adopted for several of these stocks.[7] During this same period, it pioneered the use of international monitoring and enforcement mechanisms, such as statistical documents that enable tracking individual fish through various points of trade, and the multilateral implementation of sanctions on countries whose fleets were found to be fishing in contravention of ICCAT rules (ICCAT 2007a).

The management innovations of the 1990s reflect important changes in the regulation of Atlantic highly migratory species, and some less obvious alterations in the rules and norms by which the commission operates. Many of the measures that were adopted in this period would have been completely unacceptable to most ICCAT members in the 1970s. At that time, catch limits were not tenable because of disagreements between historical fishing countries like Japan, Spain, France, and the United States and developing countries like Brazil, Morocco, the Ivory Coast, and Senegal. The heart of this conflict was a disagreement over the distribution of access rights. Developing countries refused to accept limits that would inhibit the expansion of their fleets, while their counterparts insisted that historically dominant fleets should not have to reduce their own harvests to make room for new entrants when the stocks were already in trouble.

Tension between these interests still exists at ICCAT and in many other regional fisheries organizations, but sufficient rapprochement has taken place to permit agreement on both total allowable catch limits and national quota distributions. Moreover, the implicit acceptance of developing countries' rights that began in the 1980s was codified by the commission in 2001 with the adoption of the ICCAT Criteria for the Allocation of Fishing Possibilities. Officially recognizing the rights of developing coastal states, the criteria also give credence to the claims of historical fishing countries without establishing any set weighting system for the various elements on the list (ICCAT 2007a, oth. 01-25).[8] As of yet, neither norm has completely won out, and quotas continue to be determined by negotiation.

Although some vestiges of norm entrepreneurship, or the manipulation of norms for national gains, are evident in the divided state of affairs at ICCAT, the vague nature of the allocation criteria stems from much deeper international institutions.[9] Of particular importance is the norm of sovereignty, not just in legal or operational terms as per Litfin (1998a), but also in regard to acquisition. There is an accepted though unpublicized right of national governments to do whatever they can (diplomatically) to maximize their citizens' access to shared resources.[10] It was for the protection of this institution that safeguards such as the objection procedure—which allows members to opt out of particular management measures—were written into the original ICCAT convention. Similarly, the norm of decision by consensus, rather than de jure majority voting, has predominated over most of the commission's history. Until recently, reliance on domestic monitoring and enforcement mechanisms also ensured that countries could implement ICCAT recommendations based on their own national standards.

These sovereignty-protecting institutions undermine the impact of recent innovations. Decision by consensus gives individual countries inordinate power to block agreement on regulations that are detrimental to their domestic interests, including any trade measures used to ensure compliance by contracting parties.[11] Because of this system, ICCAT has mainly been successful at excluding nonmembers rather than directly enforcing cooperation internally. Considering that membership at ICCAT is still open to any country with an interest in fishing in the Atlantic, those wishing to avoid sanctions often apply for commission membership (ICCAT 1966, art. XIV, par. 1).[12] Other weaknesses in ICCAT institutions, like the objection procedure, are also persistent, but signs of change are evident, such as recent calls for majority voting on some proposals and criticisms of countries that have chosen to object to important management measures.

While such pressures build, the current decision-making procedures at ICCAT forestall the application of punitive measures to contracting parties. However, the adoption of stronger, multilateral monitoring and enforcement mechanisms has improved compliance somewhat. Also, contracting parties have agreed to serious cuts in their own harvests of some HMS stocks, which can be monitored via the newly developed trade-based systems. This makes noncompliance more risky than in the past, even if the worst punishment is international censure.

All in all, the recent actions taken by ICCAT suggest that as a collective body, fishing countries are giving up more now to obtain cooperative management than they were willing to give up in the past. Moreover, this willingness to pay is not limited to side payments, which are an accepted international institution, but also include measures that curtail access to international markets.[13] As DeSombre (2006) points out, this shift from physical to economic enforcement is a major step toward overcoming the daunting scale of monitoring and enforcing international agreements. While much has remained the same at the commission, these innovations are important changes that need to be more fully understood.

1.4 A Combined Perspective: Vulnerability Response

Several potential sources of change in international fisheries management have been identified in the literature. Broader trends in international politics are one causal factor, particularly the empowerment of developing countries in multilateral fora (Barrett 2001; Powell and DiMaggio 1991; Wendt 1999).[14] Alternatively, Haas and Haas (1995) have posited the importance of epistemic communities in such transitions, and it is possible that stronger management could have resulted from the consolidation and dissemination of knowledge regarding the state of HMS stocks in the Atlantic. Similarly, grassroots movements and international nongovernmental organizations have worked to protect some ICCAT species, although they have been less successful in this area than in others (Webster 2006).[15] Finally, game-theoretic economic models such as those summarized by Munro, Van Houtte, and Willmann (2004) suggest that exogenous shifts in economic incentives have altered management. This too has been observed, yet alone, none of these perspectives systematically explains adaptive governance at ICCAT.

What is needed is an approach that captures the underlying dynamics of fisheries economics but remains malleable in the face of institutional, scientific, and political variations. Furthermore, in order to understand recent adaptations in the governance of international fisheries, one must account for the ways in which countries actually respond to biological depletion and resultant domestic economic losses. It is well known that the complex nature of these fisheries obscures causal pathways, which leads to polarization and politicization of scientific advice (Ludwig, Hilborn, and Walters 1993). At the same time, management tends to be costly, both economically and politically. With the benefits so uncertain, few decision makers are willing to expend political capital or stretch bureaucratic budgets unless there is considerable pressure to do so (Hersoug 1996, 19).[16]

From a theoretical perspective, such behaviors resemble satisficing strategies, which are identified in the organizations literature, rather than the rationality assumptions of economics.[17] That is, countries are responding to costs as they manifest, rather than anticipating and avoiding those costs through optimal management. While this approach is less amenable to mathematical modeling, it is possible to develop midrange frameworks that direct predictions of satisficing behavior that are theoretically powerful and rigorous without abandoning important details that create temporal and cross-sectional variation in specific cases. This type of analysis also permits the incorporation of both political and economic decision parameters within the international context, much as advocated by Putnam (1988) in his discussion of two-level games.

In fact, switching to satisficing as the central decision mechanism adds several layers of complexity to the task of theorizing about adaptive governance in an international fisheries context. One must seek out patterns of change and interactions that occur at different levels of analysis, including the economics of the fishing industry, the politics of domestic agenda setting, and the relations of international negotiations. Each of these is further complicated by fluxes in biological and oceanographic systems. Nor can stochastic or exogenous elements be completely ignored. The vulnerability response framework presented in chapter 2 is designed to incorporate all of these elements in a coherent approach to an analysis of changes in countries' policy positions in the context of international fisheries management. This task is not as onerous as it sounds, largely because the framework draws on theoretical precepts from each of the perspectives discussed here, rather than attempting to repeat earlier work.

Once the framework is presented, it is tested in chapters 3 to 10, using case studies from ICCAT. Each case covers a specific stock that is managed by the commission and all represent important variations in bioeconomic parameters, such as price, geographic range, and biological productivity. Drawn from a single RFMO, institutional elements are fairly constant among the cases, at least in cross-section. While it would certainly be useful to expand the scope of the study to include stocks managed by other RFMOs, the intensive nature of analysis precluded such an endeavor at this time. However, as discussed in section 2.4, many of the most important metainstitutions in international fisheries management are shared among the RFMOs, so the results should be somewhat generalizable in that context.

The cases are divided into three parts to facilitate comparison among some of the most closely linked stocks. Each subset of cases is preceded by a short explanation of the links between the stocks covered and the bioeconomics of the fisheries targeting those stocks. First, part I covers tropical tunas, which may be targeted separately as adults but are usually caught together in the juvenile phase of their life cycle. The three chapters in this part deal with bigeye, yellowfin, and skipjack tunas, in that order. Next, part II contains the two cases of northern and southern swordfish in chapters 6 and 7, along with the case of blue marlin and white marlin in chapter 8. It is interesting that swordfish are frequently a by-catch for fleets targeting bigeye tuna, whereas marlins are a by-catch for fleets targeting either swordfish or bigeye tuna. Finally, part III includes the two stocks of Atlantic bluefin tuna, which are some of the most expensive and beleaguered fish in the sea.

Note that both the framework and the cases focus on national policy positions rather than adaptive governance as a complete theory of international fisheries management. The aggregation process—the way in which different national policy positions come together to operationalize international management or alter rules and norms of group decision making—is quite difficult to capture when we abandon the strictures of rational choice. Therefore, collective decisions are not predicted, but they are reported in the cases in order to explore the patterns of management that emerge from different systems. Largely encompassed in chapter 11, this analysis is only a preliminary step toward understanding adaptive international governance, but it is an important one.

2

The Vulnerability Response Framework

Consumers and conservationists, commercial and recreational fishermen, politicians, diplomats, and bureaucrats—all of these groups value highly migratory species for different reasons and therefore have diverse, often divergent, perspectives on fisheries management. Looking more closely, one can see that there are divisions within these clusters and overlaps as well. At the international level, such disparate demands on policy makers are complicated by concerns over the relative gains of other countries. No government wants to pay the costs of management if others refuse to take up their fair share of the burden. Of course, fairness itself is a relative concept and is often contested, adding yet another dimension to this complex issue area. All of these actors engage in adaptive governance, but in order to understand adaptation more generally, we need to parse out the most important agents and the patterns that their behavior creates.

Abstracting from the rich tapestry of interaction between interest groups and governments, this chapter presents a basic framework for exploring adaptive changes in national policy positions. Conceptual stand-ins for real countries, *states* are assumed to be unitary and independent actors in fisheries negotiations; all decisions are made by each state as a single entity, with no internal divisions and all of the power necessary to control its domestic fleets. At the same time, these states are assumed to respond to political pressures from the commercial fleets that carry their flag and operate in a particular fishery. By narrowly defining national policy preferences in this way, it is possible to capitalize on the concept of comparative advantage to predict which states are most vulnerable to the economic costs of overexploitation and will therefore be the first to prefer the political distribution of access rights.[1]

Thus, economic vulnerability can be used as an indicator for the range of national positions regarding international management and changes in those positions over time. However, states are not responding to vulnerability per se. Rather, they are responding to pressures from fishers who are losing out under open access, as described in section 2.1. Vulnerability, which is defined more narrowly in section 2.2, is simply an indicator that tells us which states will respond first, second, and so on. Because of this relationship, the approach described in this chapter is referred to as the vulnerability response framework. The formation of policy preferences from the response side of the framework is described in section 2.3, followed by the translation of those preferences into policy positions in section 2.4. Then the method of testing of the framework using cases from ICCAT is covered in section 2.5. Finally, section 2.6 briefly touches on the difficulties of aggregating national policy positions in such a complex area and explains how information reported in the cases is used to identify emergent patterns of adaptive governance at the international level.

2.1 Satisficing and Adaptive Governance

Before going on to explain how the vulnerability response framework works, it is important to note that this approach differs substantially from previous efforts in that decision makers, now reified as states, are assumed to be instrumentally rational yet bounded in their ability to maximize. Given the biological and economic uncertainties that abound in this large-scale, highly complex commons, satisficing is a more likely organizational outcome than optimizing (March and Olson 1998). As per Simon (1955), satisficing entails settling for some predetermined level of benefit. Whether individuals or organizations, satisficers only look for what is "good enough" and will end their search as soon as they have found it. March and Simon (1958; 1993) argue that organizations satisfice because of information costs and competing internal goals. This fits well with most descriptions of the national decision-making processes associated with international fisheries management.

The assumption of satisficing provides the underlying logic for the vulnerability response framework. Fishers' economic incentives to engage in political action—their escalating dissatisfaction with the status quo under open access—cause them to increasingly demand government protection. This in turn reduces job satisfaction and stability for decision makers, who then become dissatisfied and start to search for alternatives with higher levels of political benefits. In so doing, their options are limited by the availability of managerial resources, which are circumscribed by the political-economic importance of fisheries in the given state.[2] Therefore they are expected to choose the least costly but not necessarily the most effective option in order to reclaim their acceptable level of satisfaction. It is this dynamic interaction that creates the trial-and-error process associated with the ideal-type of adaptive governance. States try a cheap option, find that it doesn't work, and are left even more dissatisfied than before; escalation continues until a true solution is found or the fishery collapses, whichever comes first.

Unlike rational utility maximization, satisficing does not readily yield a neat, steady-state solution.[3] Some stability can exist; as long as the minimum net benefits requirement is met, the decision maker should remain satisfied with the status quo. On the other hand, if some component of the utility function changes, either in substance or definition, or the standard of satisfaction shifts, then a search for a better policy is initiated. The results of that search are heavily dependent on the structure of the organization, the knowledge and technological availability of alternatives, and, at times, pure chance. Furthermore, there is no "invisible hand" per se, no particular equilibrium force holding satisficing conditions in stasis. Markets are expected to shift, the political climate will change, entrepreneurs will rise up, and—most apropos in this context—resources will be depleted over time.

While it is more unruly than maximizing, satisficing has its analytical benefits as well. In many ways it is more realistic than optimizing and it is also more dynamic and malleable, emphasizing the causes of change in a system in addition to sources of continuity.[4] Moreover, the concept provides a means of incorporating both complexity and bounded rationality into models of the decision-making process (March and Simon 1993, 161–162). As will be shown, using a framework based on satisficing assumptions can still result in a limited number of causal elements, which can produce testable expectations. Here the focus is on a mid-range framework to guide predictions of changes in governmental concern as a stock is depleted over time. It is both cross-sectional, in that different categories of countries are expected to have different positions at any given point in time, and temporal, in that national policy positions are expected follow different courses over time.

2.2   The Economics of Vulnerability

Given the underlying condition of satisficing, we can expect that those states that are most vulnerable to the economics of overexploitation will be the first to search for alternatives to open access. What exactly does economic vulnerability entail, and which states will be most vulnerable? In international fisheries, when national positions parallel commercial fishing interests, economic vulnerability can be defined by a combination of two major characteristics for the domestic fleet targeting a stock: the costs of production (competitiveness) and the opportunity costs of alternative sources of revenue (flexibility). Note that these categories are quite similar to the characteristics of interdependence outlined by Keohane and Nye (1977), and can only be measured relative to other national fishing fleets. This parallel is intentional, but different terminology is used here, partly because it is more amenable to the topic of fisheries and partly to distinguish between a system-level attribute (interdependence as used by Keohane and Nye) and a state-level attribute (vulnerability as used in this text).[5]

Within any one country, the fishers targeting a stock of fish are usually asymmetric in regard to their costs of production. According to Clark (1990, 155–157) and Opsomer and Conrad (1994), such asymmetries cause less efficient fishers to lose market share under open access, negatively affecting net revenues and eventually forcing them out of the fishery. One can also assume that domestic fleets are clustered around a particular level of efficiency because of country-specific similarities in the prices of capital, labor, and other factors of production. When multiple countries have fleets targeting the same stock of fish using the same gear, as in the case of highly migratory species, then domestic fleets with high operating costs per unit of catch are not very competitive and, ceteris paribus, will be pushed out of the fishery. Alternatively, more efficient and therefore more competitive fleets should be able to benefit much longer from the shared resource (Opsomer and Conrad 1994).

In a fluid economy, where neither labor nor capital is "sticky," the private and social costs of a reduction in fleet size that is due to escalating international competition are negligible, and fishers would make few complaints. However, in most countries there are considerable barriers to the movement of fishers and fishing capital into other sectors of the economy. Owing to these constraints, individual fishers, fishing communities, and supporting industries must absorb heavy costs as compe-

		Competitiveness	
		Low	High
Flexibility	Low	Highly Vulnerable	Moderately Vulnerable
	High	Gradually Vulnerable	Mildly Vulnerable

Figure 2.1
Economic vulnerability matrix.

tition gets tougher. Diverting fishing effort to more abundant stocks or different sectors of the economy can mitigate some of the economic repercussions of competition, but there may be opportunity costs to such transitions that differ from fleet to fleet and country to country.[6] The relative ability to find substitutes—in this case, the flexibility to transfer fishing effort to alternative stocks—can be a major determinant of national policy positions (Barkin and DeSombre 2000).[7]

From this point, it is possible to create a simple vulnerability matrix that correlates crude proxies for competitiveness and flexibility with the timing and magnitude of competition faced by a domestic fishing fleet. Again, this measure is meaningful only in relative terms, so all fleets must be considered together. The simplest form for this matrix is illustrated in figure 2.1. Although it relies heavily on gross indicators of vulnerability, this 2 × 2 matrix demonstrates the most important facets of the concept. If more consistent and detailed data could be collected on some of the domestic sources of vulnerability, for instance the costs of production or willingness to exit the industry, then a more continuous measure of vulnerability could be developed.[8] Unfortunately such information is not currently available, and significant effort would be required to create even a cross-sectional database of these indicators. On the other hand, the simplicity of this approach also has its merits, particularly insofar as it allows a focus on specific threads within a highly complex issue area.

In a world where capital is distributed evenly, highly and gradually vulnerable countries would be pushed out of any international fishery rather quickly. There would be few limits on the expansion of more efficient fleets, and so they would be able to rapidly increase production while maintaining lower prices, easily winning the race for fish.

However, capital is not evenly distributed in our world, and so the story of international fisheries management is quite different.[9] Like many other industries, large-scale commercial fishing of tunas and tuna-like species originated in countries like the United States, Canada, France, Spain, and Japan, all of which had access to considerable capital for investment. Technological resources were also more available in these countries, facilitating the mechanization of commercial fishing. These system-level economic factors served to protect early fleets that would have otherwise been more vulnerable to competition because of high costs of labor and other inputs.[10]

Inevitably, this barrier to entry eroded. Owing to economic development, capital and technological know-how became more available in less vulnerable countries. At the same time, overcapitalization and economies of scale were reducing the costs of modern fishing vessels and gear. Typical of the tragedy of the commons, overcapitalization refers to suboptimal overallocation of capital to the capture of an open access resource. For fisheries, this generally means that fishers were always investing in newer, faster boats and better gear, flooding secondary markets with used but still quite serviceable equipment. Thus capital was becoming more widely available and capital goods were becoming cheaper, so fleets began to thrive in countries with relatively cheap input costs like South Korea, Taiwan, and Mexico (FAO 2007b).

By the late 1960s, historically dominant fleets were facing growing competition—both from each other and from more efficient new entrants. Nevertheless, production continued to increase for most fleets through the early 1990s. During this period, flexibility became more and more important as competition over traditional fishing grounds drove fleets to find new stocks to exploit. Here again, older fleets led the way with distant-water vessels that could cross the seas and new fish-finding technologies like radar and spotter planes. Even the giant factory ships, which cost millions of dollars, found their way into less expensive ports like Taipei and Manila throughout the 1980s. In addition to greater flexibility, distant-water vessels have huge capacity and can operate for months and even years without returning to land.[11] Countries like Taiwan and China are producing their own distant water vessels, further increasing their capacity to outcompete less efficient fleets.

Now that so many different stocks of fish are already exploited, competition is greater than ever before. Highly vulnerable fleets like those harbored by the United States and Canada (in the Atlantic) and Australia (in the Pacific) have been losing out doubly as both their landings and prices decline. Twists of history left these countries with heavily mechanized but short-range fleets targeting highly migratory species mostly within their 200-mile coastal zones.[12] In spite of their greater flexibility, gradually vulnerable fleets like the distant-water vessels flagged by Japan, Spain, and France have also been feeling the pinch of competition. They have run out of fresh alternatives and must work much harder for less return.

Even moderately vulnerable fleets from countries like Mexico, Brazil, and South Africa are worried about competition over highly migratory stocks, particularly because of the proximity of mildly vulnerable distant-water fleets from Taiwan, China, Thailand, and the Philippines. Fleets in both categories are growing, but the latter has much greater capacity to reduce stocks of highly migratory tunas and tuna-like species. In addition to highly competitive and flexible fleets targeting a particular stock, the mildly vulnerable category encompasses fleets that may capture a species even though they are not targeting it. These by-catch fleets are not even competing over the stock being managed, so they are not vulnerable in this context, but they can have a big impact, especially when their targeted stock is much larger and more prolific than the by-catch stock.

Finally, the mildly vulnerable classification even includes a large number of vessels that do not have a permanent home base and are widely known as illegal, unregulated, and unreported (IUU) fishers or sometimes flag of convenience fleets. Maritime law requires all vessels to exhibit the flag or symbol of their port state when they are at sea. In many countries, fishers must comply with various regulations, including labor, environmental, and resource management laws and pay fees in order to receive a flag. However, there are some small developing countries that have sold their flags rather cheaply and with no strings attached. These are known as providers of flags of convenience, which are sought after by some fishers in order to avoid more stringent regulations elsewhere. Other fleets use counterfeit flags to cover up unauthorized operations (FAO 2002, 65).

2.3   The Politics of Response

All of this increasing competition leads to dissatisfaction with the status quo, particularly among the more vulnerable fleets described here. This begins their search for alternatives, both economic and political. Indeed, the search for economic alternatives has driven much of the growth of the industry, as beleaguered fleets appropriated new technologies and searched for more plentiful fishing grounds. Such economic responses are already crudely captured by the attribute of flexibility in the model. Fishers also search for political alternatives when they face heavy international competition. In essence, they seek protections from their national governments, which in turn must balance the demands of fishers with those of many other constituencies. Also satisficing, states are expected to remain content with open access as long as their fleets are thriving, but will become increasingly dissatisfied as their fleets begin to feel the pinch of competition.[13]

Although the details may differ, these political responses can be expected to vary in predictable ways, depending on a state's economic vulnerability. First, because heavy competition and overexploitation tend to be correlated, we can expect that *governmental concern*—or the resources that decision makers are willing to expend in searching for and appropriating a better regime—will increase with signs of stock depletion. As scientists begin to point to declines in a stock of fish, we should expect to see the first political responses to economic competition.[14] This is a particularly useful relationship because detailed economic data on profits, or even fleet size, are unavailable for most countries. Moreover, it suggests that a state will select cheaper alternatives when overexploitation is first announced, hoping to find an easy solution, and will only choose more expensive policies if the status quo continues to deteriorate. Again, "cheap" refers to the political costs of an alternative, which may include expenditures of government resources, but largely depends on the popularity of a particular program among constituents.

Because of the global nature of fisheries for highly migratory species, political costs also include the use of diplomatic resources to attain cooperative policy solutions at the international level. As Barkin and DeSombre (2000) point out, these costs tend to predispose states to unilateral actions, but in this context decision makers will eventually seek to engage in multilateral negotiations. Domestic policies alone simply do not solve the underlying collective action problem associated with the governance of large-scale commons resources. The specific costs of negotiating international fisheries measures will be dealt with in the next section. Here, the main thing to understand is that multilateral management can benefit vulnerable countries in two ways. First, by reducing harvests

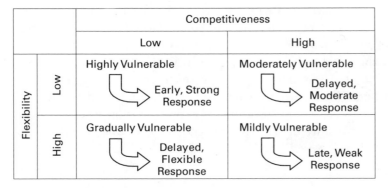

Figure 2.2
Vulnerability response matrix.

to more sustainable levels, multilateral management can increase the long-run net benefits derived from the resource. Second, multilateral management can make the allocation of those benefits a matter of political negotiation rather than economic competition (Barrett 2001).

Figure 2.2 illustrates the hypothesized relationship between political response and economic vulnerability for the categories of states found in figure 2.1. It follows from the satisficing assumption that highly vulnerable fleets will be the first to pressure their national governments for protections because they are the first to be pushed out of the fishery by escalating competition. As mentioned earlier, economic barriers to entry during the early stages of fishery development protected these vulnerable fleets so that they became relatively large and influential. Once those barriers are lowered by overcapitalization and economic development, these fleets will have trouble maintaining their position in the fishery without government assistance. At first, highly vulnerable states may respond to discontent among their fishers by applying domestic protections, such as subsidies, to keep their fleets going. However, as these notoriously ineffective measures become more and more expensive, international alternatives begin to look much better by comparison.[15]

Specifically, highly vulnerable states are expected to prefer the early adoption of strong management measures. "Early" means that they will begin to express a preference for management as soon as scientists advise a commission that a stock is depleted. Regulations that are in accordance with such scientific advice and include some type of enforcement mechanisms are considered to be "strong" management measures. Measures that fall short of scientific advice are "weak" management measures, and those that contain no monitoring and enforcement mechanisms are labeled as "unenforced" management measures. In terms of enforcement, there are three levels. In the parlance of ICCAT, the weakest are nonbinding *resolutions*, which encourage states to comply. Next are binding *recommendations*, which require states to comply and to monitor and enforce measures domestically. The third and strongest level of enforcement contains binding recommendations in combination with international monitoring and enforcement mechanisms. As mentioned in chapter 1, the latter were virtually nonexistent in fisheries until the 1990s and represent a major institutional shift at the international level.

While highly vulnerable states will always prefer strong measures, their willingness to pay for such regulations will be low at first but will increase as long as the fleets continue to suffer under growing competition. Gradually vulnerable countries will prefer strong management measures, too—eventually. In fact, there are only two major differences between the expected political responses for these categories. First, unlike their highly vulnerable counterparts, gradually vulnerable states will not become dissatisfied until their fleets have almost run out of options. That is, they are expected to prefer open access as long as alternative stocks are readily available—hence the "gradual" nature of their vulnerability—but will quickly switch to a protective mode once those alternatives are used up. To facilitate discussion, these will be referred to as "high-flex" and "low-flex" phases of response for gradually vulnerable countries. Second, in either phase, gradually vulnerable states will always look for a more malleable regulatory system than highly vulnerable states. Their need to accommodate distant-water fleets will dominate their perspective on the management of a single stock even when most of their alternatives have been exhausted.[16]

Moderately vulnerable states will also evince delayed concern regarding biological depletion, but for different reasons. Blocked from developing industrial fishing in the early stages, moderately vulnerable states have little reason to restrict the development of their fleets once they are provided with the opportunity. These are states whose fleets could continue to grow under open access even when stocks are moderately depleted and international competition is heavy. However, they can still feel the pinch of competition, particularly from gradually and mildly vulnerable fleets, with their exceptionally large capacity to exploit stocks on the high seas. Because of this, moderately vulnerable states are expected to show a moderated response that favors curtailment of distant-water fishing along with concessions for the expansion of coastal developing fleets.

Mildly vulnerable states are virtually immune from both international competition and concern over the disappearance of any one stock of fish. In this category, domestic fleets are either highly competitive and flexible or they do not directly target the stock in question. This leads to a slow political response and makes mildly vulnerable fishing states the least willing to switch from open access to any type of regulatory system.[17] Because distant water fleets usually have substantial harvesting capacity, they also have considerable ability to undermine management by refusing to comply with multilateral measures. Therefore, other, more vulnerable countries will need to provide considerable side payments or make serious threats in order to obtain their cooperation on strong international regulations. The necessity for a strong bargaining position is heightened in the case of by-catch countries, since they will be unwilling to give up any of their targeted catch to protect a species that is caught incidentally. This is all part of the strategic nature of international fisheries management, which is covered in the next section.

2.4 Power and Positioning

Translating the political responses of different states into predictions of policy positions requires some additional information on negotiation strategies in regional fisheries management organizations. Following examples such as Axelrod and Keohane (1985), Barrett (2001), Haas, Keohane, and Levy (1995) and Keohane and Nye (1977), it is possible to simplify the strategic setting in international fisheries management in order to get a clearer view of the links between political response and national policy positions. Three metainstitutions should be kept in mind: (1) international fisheries is a realm for diplomacy, not violence; (2) cooperation is not undertaken unless it seems to be in the best interests of states; and (3) most RFMOs operate on the basis of consensus, but majority voting is not unknown. In this section, these norms will be used to develop a method of separating the "true" policy positions of states from mere strategic maneuvers.

First, formal military engagement is not considered to be an appropriate strategy in this issue area. Except for a few minor warning shots in the 1980s, battles over highly migratory species have been purely diplomatic for at least a century (Juda 1996). This entails a plethora of tactics, including concessions, side payments, issue linkages, and even political or economic threats. Unfortunately, most of these interactions go on in secret and therefore cannot be documented. However, quite a bit can be deduced from actual records of stated policy positions, including statements and changes in proposed measures, defections by specific countries, and quota swaps among commission members. More information on available sources of data on policy positions is presented in section 2.5.

Second, all of the RFMOs share the de facto goal of management at maximum sustainable yield, but also the pervasive norm that national interests take precedence over environmental considerations. The result is a propensity to view scientific advice as a maximum rather than a minimum. Except for species that generate a loud public outcry, RFMO members seldom propose management measures that go beyond those recommended by the respective scientific committee. At the same time, when there is uncertainty regarding scientific advice—and there is always uncertainty—countries will generally use it to their advantage. Because science is viewed in this way, it can be used as a touchstone for evaluating policy positions; hence the requirement that "strong" policy positions match up with scientific advice. Without mechanisms to independently monitor and enforce such scientifically based measures, cheating could clearly benefit an individual state, and so this is the second requirement for the "strongest" policy positions. In the absence of international enforcement mechanisms, "stronger" policy positions are predicted, specifically proposals for binding rather than nonbinding resolutions. This rubric will facilitate the evaluation of policy positions and help to distinguish between rhetorical or tactical statements and a true preference for change.

Third, most RFMOs operate on the basis of consensus, even when majority voting is encoded in the original agreement. That is, any one country can block the adoption of a measure by refusing to either agree or abstain.[18] Even though this mechanism imparts considerable power to individual countries, consensus blocking is not undertaken lightly because it usually has substantial diplomatic ramifications. Most countries prefer to use an escape clause, like the objection procedure, which allows them to simply opt out of a particular measure rather than block it. This too is heavily frowned upon, predominantly by countries with a vested interest in a particular measure. Such "frowning" may be as light as a temporary snubbing or as heavy as the retraction of an economic aid package. Unfortunately, the more severe repercussions are seldom recorded in the official record of the RFMO, but there are other ways to explore such maneuvers. Early in ICCAT's history, several votes were held on management measures. As will be explained later, this makes adoption of measures easier because only a simple majority is necessary and no single member can prevent the acceptance of a proposal.

Within the vulnerability response framework, prediction of a particular state's strategy relative to a specific stock at a given point in time generally depends on: (1) a state's level of political response, (2) a state's diplomatic resources, and (3) the positions of other states at the negotiating table. The level of political response indicates the willingness to pay the costs of switching to strong management, as described in the previous section. Diplomatic resources are varied, but generally parallel the broader international scene. Economic and military powerhouses like the United States, Japan, and the EU, along with China and Russia, are most able to rely on pure influence in negotiations. "Emerging" or moderately developed countries like Brazil, Mexico, South Africa, South Korea, and Taiwan[19] can be considered at about midrange on the power scale, while smaller, poorer countries like Belize, Ghana, Senegal, and the Philippines have little individual clout. It is interesting to note that gradually vulnerable states, like Japan or members of the EU, often have better fisheries-specific connections and therefore may be able to outweigh the United States, which is usually in the highly vulnerable category.[20]

The last element in prediction is the hardest to pin down. Designed to improve our understanding of a dynamic process, the vulnerability response framework must capture the complex dance of drawn-out negotiations as well as expected changes in national policy preferences. Only in this way can what we observe—the policy positions of fishing countries—be linked to bioeconomic changes in the fisheries themselves. Given the wide array of negotiating tactics available to members of most RFMOs, exact national strategies or positions cannot be predicted. Nonetheless, general expectations can be drawn from knowledge of the negotiating environment and the bioeconomics of the stock at hand.[21] In order to facilitate this endeavor, one more matrix is introduced.

Figure 2.3 groups national strategies into four different categories that are only loosely related to the vulnerability response matrix. States in each vulnerability category may be expected to engage in one type of

		Secondary (tactical) Position	
		Change	Stasis
Primary Position	Change	Building Direct threats and/or sidepayments to attain a policy	Hostage Prevent adoption of some measure(s) until own policy accepted
	Stasis	Countermeasures Prevent adoption of some measure(s) by proposing alternative policy	Blocking Block consensus, object,or defect to prevent adoption of policy

Figure 2.3
Strategy matrix.

strategy more than others, but they may use alternative tactics when the opportunity arises. Note that the rows in figure 2.3 refer to a state's primary position, specifically whether or not they prefer some change or the status quo. The columns also cover stasis and change, but at the secondary level. This is definitely an oversimplification, but a useful one. It will help to separate the true positions of states, particularly vis-à-vis strong management, from negotiating tactics that are undertaken as a means to those ends. While the primary policy position is predicted by vulnerability response, secondary positions cannot be foreseen without substantial, situation-specific knowledge of the diplomatic setting. Generic expectations regarding the use of such tactics within RFMOs are provided here to show how tactics can be disentangled from positions.[22]

The upper left-hand box in figure 2.3 is referred to as *building*. Used mainly by states that strongly desire some change in policy at the RFMO level, this strategy entails the use of direct threats or side payments to other states in order to build a coalition on a proposal. If there is already substantial agreement on that policy, the state will not need to expend much effort to reach either a consensus or a simple majority.[23] If national interests are more divergent, then the state will have to be very powerful and willing to use that power in order to build a coalition on their policy position. Generally speaking, highly vulnerable countries are expected to engage in building more than any other strategy because they are most interested in guiding management away from open access and installing a strong management regime as well as a politically based allocation system.

As per the vulnerability response predictions, highly vulnerable states will not be willing to invest much in coalition building when stocks first start to decline, since competition is still fairly light. Assuming that sufficient diplomatic resources are available to them, highly vulnerable states will engage more and more powerfully as long as competition continues to escalate.[24] At the same time, the job of building a consensus (or coalition) around strong management measures should be getting easier. There are two reasons for this. First, as their alternatives are used up, gradually vulnerable countries are expected to begin to prefer strong (or at least stronger) management measures. This is the "low-flex" phase of their response. Some concessions may still be necessary to maintain as much flexibility as possible, but their positions will be much closer to those of highly vulnerable states. Second, as the stock declines, moderately vulnerable countries will also begin to experience the problems associated with fewer fish. This will trigger their interest in curtailing distant-water fleets and make it easier to obtain their cooperation.

In the opposite corner of the figure are purely defensive *blocking* strategies. These are used exclusively by countries that wish to prevent the adoption of a policy. Like building, blocking is easier when more countries share the same position and harder when the majority is on the other side. However, blocking under consensus decision making requires a willingness to accept the rancor of the rest of the commission, rather than the use of side payments or threats. Hypothetically, this strategy is available to states with few diplomatic resources as well as more powerful states, but in reality only powerful countries have chosen to block consensus on their own. The threat of blocking is used more often by moderately or mildly vulnerable states in order to obtain concessions and side payments for their cooperation. The usefulness of this tactic depends on the credibility of that threat. A single, small state could lose a great deal by blocking consensus, but a coalition of such states or a large, powerful state could distribute the burden of censure more widely and would therefore be more likely to carry out its threat if it is not appeased.

States can also block the adoption of a policy by building a coalition or a consensus around a *countermeasure*. This is represented in the lower left-hand corner of figure 2.3 and can include dilution of a recommendation (i.e., selecting a higher minimum size limit or total allowable catch) or substitution (i.e., proposing a minimum size limit or time-area closure instead of a catch limit). It is most commonly expected as a delaying tactic by gradually or moderately vulnerable states in the early phase of negotiations. By proposing a weak or poorly enforced measure, these less vulnerable states can prevent the adoption of stronger and more costly policies that are proposed by highly vulnerable states without engaging in the same level of brinkmanship required in a pure blocking strategy. As described earlier, the increasing competition that comes with open access and concomitant reductions in alternative stocks will eventually change the preferences of gradually and moderately vulnerable states. When this occurs, any countermeasures they propose are expected to be similar to the strong measures advocated by highly vulnerable states, with small differences to provide flexibility or economic development, respectively.

Even though vulnerability response predicts a near convergence in the policy preferences of these three types of states, the problem of who pays remains. When there is a split among fleets, countermeasures can also be used in attempts to shift the burden of management from one group to another. Typical dividing lines include historical versus developing countries, coastal versus distant-water countries, and longline versus purse seine countries, the latter being based on the type of gear favored by domestic fleets. No matter what the perceived grounds for contestation, highly vulnerable states and low-flex, gradually vulnerable states will eventually make the necessary concessions or side payments to obtain agreement. Being less competitive, their fleets will suffer most under status quo management and therefore they will become increasingly willing to accept the costs of change—even if it means making exemptions or transferring quotas to moderately and mildly vulnerable states. Other types of side payments or threats may also be used off the record, but changes in the visible elements of willingness to pay can substantiate the expected escalation of political response.

The last category in figure 2.3 is another hybrid. It entails the threat to block one measure as a means of building a consensus or coalition on a different measure, essentially taking the former *hostage* to attain the latter. Prediction of this strategy is trickier than the others because its availability depends on the entire range of policy positions at a given point in time. States would have to find a suitable proposal and determine that the repercussions of taking it hostage, which might include retaliation by other states, are worth the gains it would make elsewhere. Such specifics are well beyond the purview of this framework and most certainly cannot be predicted, but when evidence of such tactics is available, it is reported in the cases. This should provide a foundation for understanding how strategic factors can influence collective outcomes differently than driving forces such as vulnerability response.

Similar information will be provided for other parameters that are exogenous to vulnerability response, such as changes in bioeconomic conditions that could unexpectedly increase or decrease the level of competition in a fishery. There are many factors that dictate the rate of depletion in any fishery. Some are biological, such as the rate of reproduction or recruitment, years until sexual maturity, and the natural mortality rate. Others are economic, such as the capacity in a fishery, the costs of production, and the price for the catch. Changes in any of these elements and many others can affect the level of competition and therefore the level of governmental concern. For instance, a big increase in demand will initially raise the price for a certain type of fish, which will in turn create additional revenues for fishers in the short run. This will temporarily dampen political response, but as long as open access continues, competition will return and states will again search for alternatives. Retrospective application of the framework will generate more accurate predictions of policy positions by taking known changes in bioeconomic conditions into account.

2.5   Testing the Framework

One of the benefits of the approach described here is that it serves as a malleable framework for analysis in an issue area that is characterized by inherent complexity and a dearth of standardizable data. Using it, one can search for general patterns that otherwise might not be identified in a case-specific analysis. At this stage, testing is largely limited to developing expectations regarding temporal changes in primary policy positions, relative to the bioeconomic context. This entails classifying countries according to the vulnerability response matrix in order to predict the timing of changes in policy positions, and then testing those predictions against actual proposals or other official statements. Because aggregation, or collective decision making, at the RFMO is nonlinear and may depend heavily on tactical availability, negotiation skill, and other elements, adaptive management itself cannot be predicted from the framework at this time. However, information on collective outcomes will be provided in the cases in order to identify any emergent patterns of adaptive governance.

Because markets for these fishes are global and fishers are highly mobile, perfect separability does not exist, even at the level of a regime. Nonetheless, cases can be compiled on a stock-by-stock basis, reflecting the structure of the decision-making process and international norms that give countries with fleets targeting a stock greater legitimacy under the rubric of conservation for use. The tradeoff for this limitation is that some policy positions—particularly cross-stock shakedowns—will not be predicted, although they most certainly do occur. That said, where there are direct interactions between stocks, for instance when the exploitation of one stock affects the exploiters of another stock, efforts will be made to extend the analysis to include all countries that are involved.

Cases for testing are drawn from ICCAT. These eight studies fall into three categories as: Tropical Tunas, Billfishes, and Bluefin Tuna. Except for the marlins, which are covered in chapter 8, these cases are undertaken individually with reference to the larger management context as needed. There are two reasons for this approach. First, ICCAT scientific advice is provided separately for each stock. It is predicated on the concept of maximum sustainable yield, which is stock specific. As yet there is no application of an ecosystem or place-based approach to management.

Second and relatedly, the commission also manages stocks separately. Four different panels or subcommittees deal with different sets of stocks. Panel 1 includes tropical tunas, Panel 2 covers bluefin tuna, Panel 3 deals mainly with albacore tuna (*Thunnus alalunga*) and Panel 4 has jurisdiction over billfish as well as other ancillary species.[25] Panel membership depends on interest in fishing the stock and country-specific fees. Decisions made in each panel must then be approved by the full commission. Marlins are an exception to the single-stock approach because these stocks are usually discussed and regulated together, even though scientists evaluate them separately.

It is important to remember that although official management decisions are made separately for different stocks, negotiations are not limited in the same way. Countries can make cross-stock threats and side payments. They can also hold up management of one stock to influence decisions on another. As noted earlier, indirect negotiating tactics will not be predicted using the framework, but will be reported if evidence is available. At a minimum, this will allow the measurement of obvious cross-stock interactions and help to determine the relative importance of tactics versus primary policy positions in the larger context of adaptive governance. The results of this theory-building exercise are analyzed in the conclusion.

Predictions of primary policy positions are based on the vulnerability response framework and knowledge regarding the dynamics of competition with the fishery for the stock covered in each case. Unfortunately, data on important indicators, such as costs of production, domestic consumption, and other elements that could be used to accurately trace trends in the profitability of national industries, are not available for many countries. In fact, there is too much variation and uncertainty to even build a statistically acceptable data set. For many countries, data on economic factors in fisheries are so scarce that specification of production functions for domestic fleets is not possible (Iudicello, Weber, and Wieland 1999, 64). Furthermore, estimates of biological benchmarks may differ among stocks and for the same stock over time, depending on the accuracy of parameters and the methods available. This variation is apparent in the reports of the scientific bodies associated with each regional fisheries organization. Also, there are complex and stochastic elements that further inhibit statistical predictions of harvest levels, prices, and even national decision making.

Nonetheless, the simple model described here can be used to derive historical expectations for the international action preferred by individual states as a highly migratory stock is reduced under open access. This can be done by using proxies to determine the economic vulnerabilities of the array of states involved in negotiating management of the stock. As long as the same proxies are used in a set of cases, the results should be comparable. Each of the cases in this book was completed using the level of economic development and distant-water capacity as proxies to place ICCAT members in the appropriate vulnerability category.

2.5.1 Determining Vulnerability

Economic vulnerability was tracked for each country during the entire period covered by the cases. This was necessary to encompass changes in domestic fishing fleets and national economies that have occurred since the first meeting of ICCAT in 1970 through to the 2006 meeting of the commission. Countries with fleets targeting the stock can be identified through ICCAT's official database of reported HMS harvests. The entry or exit of major fleets is also recorded by the commission's scientific body. Countries were placed in each matrix using two central proxies. Assuming that capital costs are less deterministic under over-capitalization, competitiveness was approximated using an indicator for operating costs, the purchasing power parity (PPP) equivalent of constant (2000) per capita gross domestic product (GDP; World Bank 2006). Although somewhat arbitrary, a threshold of international $15,000 was selected as the most reasonable break in the data.[26]

Distant water capacity was considered to be the most important differentiating factor and the central proxy for flexibility. The dichotomy between countries with distant-water fleets and those with only coastal fleets is well established in the literature (DeSombre 2005; Munro, Van Houtte, and Willmann 2004). General descriptions of fleet characteristics are readily available from ICCAT scientific reports and national reports to the commission. More important, national landings by area can be obtained from ICCAT's Reported Landings 1950–2005 Database (ICCAT 2007d). Countries with landings that occur only in areas adjacent to their coast are considered to have coastal fleets; those with landings in other areas are distant water. The United States and Canada were most frequently found in the highly vulnerable category because their Atlantic fleets are coastal and their costs of production are high. On the other hand, Japan and the European Community (EC; or its member countries prior to 1997)[27] are both home to distant water fleets, so they usually fit in the gradually vulnerable category. There were many countries in the moderately vulnerable category, mostly coastal states like Brazil, Venezuela, Morocco, and Ghana. With their distant-water fleets and relatively low costs of production, South Korea, Taiwan, and China were frequently classified as mildly vulnerable countries in the cases.

For the most part, all matrices for the same stock resemble each other, but there are some important breaks in the cases. For instance, in the yellowfin case, U.S. distant-water fleets permanently exited the fishery in the 1970s, but U.S. coastal fleets began targeting that stock in the 1980s, so the country would have been classified as gradually vulnerable in the earlier period but is now highly vulnerable (ICCAT 1971–1994: 1977, 76; 1990, 136). Similarly, most countries would fit into the same cost column over the entire existence of the commission. However, an important change in vulnerability classification involves countries like South Korea and Taiwan, which fall into the low-cost column when the proxy is averaged over time, but would be considered high cost if only recent data are considered. Although they can be classified as mildly vulnerable over much of the history of these fisheries, these countries are transitioning into the gradually vulnerable category (World Bank 2006; IMF 2006; Sahrhage and Lundbeck 1992, 192–193).

Another set of fleets that has been growing in recent years is not regulated by any particular country. It is labeled "not elsewhere included" (NEI) in the ICCAT database, but more often is referred to as illegal, unregulated, and unreported in international fisheries documents. These fleets are highly flexible and cost efficient, therefore they fit into the mildly vulnerable category. Similarly, a subcategory for by-catch countries was included under the mildly vulnerable classification. These countries harbor fleets that harvest a small percentage of the case stock while directly targeting some other stock. Countries whose fleets generate considerable by-catch of a focus stock are usually identified in both scientific assessments and the reports of the commission.

2.5.2 Predictions of State Behavior

Once a country's position in the matrix is determined, it can be used to predict the timing of changes in political response relative to the biological depletion of a stock. These predictions follow directly from the framework described in the previous sections and are based on the same set of assumptions. As long as competition is increasing under open access, governmental concern will be increasing as per the framework. Highly vulnerable states will start at higher levels of concern and move more quickly toward stronger management. This generally includes the proposal of binding recommendations that match scientific advice in the 1970s and 1980s (these are stronger than nonbinding resolutions) or the introduction of similar measures enforced by international mechanisms in the 1990s (truly strong measures with multiple sources of verification). Gradually vulnerable states will either block or propose countermeasures to strong management until their alternatives are used up. Moderately vulnerable states will do the same unless they are provided with room to develop their fleets. Mildly vulnerable states will resist throughout, but may acquiesce if faced with considerable threats or side payments.

As a part of the prediction process, information from the SCRS and the UN Food and Agriculture Organization is used to track changes in important underlying factors that might exogenously reduce or escalate competition. These data include information on the exit or entry of a large portion of a fishing fleet, a substantial and persistent change in the international price of a species, and the dissemination of new fishing technologies. Depending on the direction of the change, these indicators are used to predict either a reversal in political response (if competition diminishes) or an escalation (if competition increases). Data on global harvests by gradually vulnerable fleets are also monitored as an indicator of the availability of alternatives. Once these total catches peak, the relevant state will be considered as "low-flex," because all of its cheapest economic alternatives have been used up, and response predictions will be altered accordingly.

In order to simplify the analysis, policy preferences are limited to costly restrictions that are evaluated on two factors: conformance to scientific advice and international monitoring and enforcement provisions. As noted earlier, the strongest proposals will have both attributes, whereas weak proposals will fall short on one or both. Unenforced proposals are also considered to be weak because cheating is prevalent when fishing states police only themselves. Precedence, which is a frequently observed norm at the commission, is not considered in making predictions, but is noted in the cases. The same is true of any other linkages that cross outside of stock-specific case boundaries.

For the most part, weak proposals are cheaper than strong proposals, and will be preferred first by all but highly vulnerable states. As such, weak proposals are generally considered as countermeasures—a tactical choice that signals preference for the status quo, rather than substantive change. The specifics of these tactics are not predicted, but states that are expected to favor the status quo will also be expected to use either countermeasures or blocking. For states that are expected to favor change, like those in the highly vulnerable category, the framework predicts support for strong management measures. However, strong proposals may be "cheap" for a given state if the costs of management are to be borne by others. Even highly vulnerable states are expected to try to shift costs in this way at first, but together with low-flex, gradually vulnerable states, they will eventually take the burden on themselves.

To obtain their stated policies, countries that are members of the multilateral regional fisheries organizations can engage in common diplomatic tactics like those described in section 2.4 (Peterson 1995). They may also negotiate bilaterally or in groups, forming alliances with other countries to increase their power within a regime. All else being equal, states with similar interests are expected to form coalitions to improve their bargaining power. One example of this is the "Group of 18," a coalition of moderately vulnerable countries that worked together to alter the allocation criteria used by ICCAT.[28] At times wider geopolitical interests can intervene; for instance, Taiwan and China are both mildly vulnerable but are not expected to cooperate. Like any other international forum, the ability of a state or group of states to affect the international management of highly migratory species depends greatly on their collective capacity to utilize these mechanisms (Baldwin 1993).

2.5.3 Building the Cases

Predictions from the vulnerability response framework are compared with the actual policy positions of commission members by tracing changes in those positions against changes in scientific advice. The main criteria for successful prediction are: (1) Does the state favor either a change to strong management measures or maintenance of the status quo (including weak management measures) as predicted? (2) Does the state exhibit the expected course of governmental concern based on the degree of stock depletion?

Note that the answer to the second question requires that highly and low-flex, gradually vulnerable countries exhibit increasing willingness to pay for strong management. That is, they will give up more in terms of concessions and quota reallocation as the case stock is depleted over time. On the other hand, there should also be evidence that moderately and mildly vulnerable countries resisted strong management measures until their demands were met. For moderately vulnerable countries, relatively small concessions for fleet development should be sufficient, but mildly vulnerable countries should receive substantial side payments or heavy coercion.

Reports from ICCAT's Standing Committee on Research and Statistics, which are available on an annual basis, provide ample evidence on the biological status of most stocks relative to MSY, the management advice provided by scientists, and their evaluations of the effectiveness of measures already in place. This information can be used on a stock-by-stock basis to illuminate the fundamental vulnerability response pattern for each stock under ICCAT's purview. Although painstaking, the process is rather simple. After combing through the assessments for a given stock, one can create a timeline or history comparing the biological state of the stock with the recommendations and resolutions passed in association with it. Changes in statistical procedure or model assumptions may also be taken into account if they mitigate or exacerbate the biological depletion (and, by proxy, the level of competition) in any way. It is upon this gridwork that all other analyses are overlaid.

Most of the discernible aspects of national policy positions have been recorded in ICCAT's annual reports, which consist of the proceedings of meetings of the commission and its subcommittees, along with administrative and financial overviews. Published by the ICCAT secretariat every year, these volumes also compile the national reports on fisheries activities and management actions taken by member states. The annual reports are a fount of information that reveal the issues that are important to contracting parties, the proposals they make to deal with those problems, and the final measures adopted by the commission. Also, the financial reports provide information on members' contributions to the commission's budget, and the administrative reports give a concise review of the important events that occur during the year. In total, the annual reports chronicle ICCAT's collective response over its more than 30 years of HMS management.

While most of the knowledge used in the case studies is based on facts gathered from official documentation like the annual reports, insight into negotiating tactics and governmental concerns was also gained through more informal channels. They included personal observation of six of ICCAT's annual meetings, as well as one meeting of the Indian Ocean Tuna Commission (IOTC), a meeting of the Inter-American Tropical Tuna Commission (IATTC), and various other meetings related to management of these types of species.[29] Scrutinizing the proceedings of negotiations first-hand provided a more nuanced and deeper understanding of the relations among delegations, domestic interests, and institutions. These meetings also provided many opportunities to interview decision makers and collect qualitative data that extend beyond what could be perceived from outside the negotiations. These contacts added to the historical store of knowledge and filled in the somewhat dry timeline provided by documented sources with the expert opinions of people who were directly involved in past negotiations.[30]

Finally, internationally recognized databases on factors such as prices and trade in highly migratory species are used to monitor exogenous shifts in economic parameters. For instance, a jump in price will temporarily rejuvenate an overfished fishery, reducing competition because fishers receive higher revenues per unit of effort. This reprieve will be short lived because higher net revenues will draw more effort into the fishery, dissipating positive revenues, otherwise known as scarcity rent by resource economists, a second time. Examples of these databases include the UN Food and Agricultural Organization's Commodities Production and Trade 1976–2005 Database (FAO 2007c) and the FAO's Capture Production 1950–2005 Database (2007b). National databases such as the U.S. National Marine Fisheries Service Annual Commercial Landings Statistics Database (NMFS 2007) and the Eurostat Trade Since 1995 by CN8 Database (European Commission, 2007) are also useful.

2.6 Aggregation

Aggregation refers to the process by which national policy positions are amalgamated into international management measures. Predictions of aggregation patterns are particularly difficult in this context because cooperation cannot be linked with either political response or global power in an additive or linear manner. While many simplifying assumptions have been utilized to make the framework manageable, many more would be required to generate a formula to predict aggregation. There is a central driving force in the framework—competition—that seems to be pushing states toward strong management, but there are many intervening elements as well. For one thing, there is as yet no way to predict the tactical maneuvers of fishing states within the framework. Satisficing leads the dissatisfied to search for alternatives, but the setting and the searcher both determine the choice. Timing is problematic as well, particularly when so many exogenous forces can interrupt the dynamic of exploitation under open access.

Because of these complexities, the vulnerability framework cannot provide a full explanation of adaptive governance, but it can start us down a path of better understanding. Indeed, the compilation of the cases in this book is as much about building a theory of adaptive governance as testing the vulnerability response framework. As part of each case study, side payments, threats, and other tactics are reported on a country-by-country basis. Negotiations are traced as closely as possible using official documentation in order to show which countries are more successful within the ICCAT context and which strategies are more effective. These observations are linked to changes in the cooperative management measures that are adopted by the commission as well as any alterations in informal rules and norms. This process tracing will show where the vulnerability response frame work works well and where it works poorly, pointing out areas that need improvement or assumptions that should be relaxed.

In the concluding chapter, this detailed information is analyzed with a broader focus to identify any patterns of adaptive governance that emerge from the cases. In two of the cases, a transformative pattern is documented, which includes a transition from conflicts over costs to accord regarding strong management when more vulnerable countries finally agree to make the necessary concessions, threats, and side payments. Most of the other cases display less successful patterns. Mired in conflict for various reasons, ICCAT fails to adopt strong management in those cases. Finally, the marlins case, which covers two species that are not commercially targeted in the Atlantic, reaches a period of accord without generating strong management as per the definition proposed here. This outcome can be expected for such by-catch species whenever noncommercial interests are unable to exercise powerful and lasting influence over the commission. Because case selection was limited to only one of the RFMOs that deal with highly migratory species, these patterns are not highly generalizable, but expansion of the approach may lead to a more inclusive theory in the future.

Now that the framework has been presented, it is tested using eight case studies drawn from ICCAT. Owing to considerable overlap among the cases, they are presented in three parts. First, part I covers the tropical tunas. Highly abundant, these fishes often occur in mixed schools, although some are targeted individually. Chapter 3 shows how vulnerability response has led to belated but effective management of bigeye tuna (*Thunnus obesus*), which is sold for higher prices than the other tropical tunas. Chapters 4 and 5 then recount how responsive management has not yet occurred for the more abundant but lower-priced yellowfin tuna (*Thunnus albacares*) and skipjack tuna (*Katsuwonus pelamis*) fisheries. The skipjack case in chapter 5 is particularly interesting because this species is caught with juvenile yellowfin and bigeye. This cross-over provides an opportunity to delve into vulnerability response interactions in a truly mixed fishery.

Part II contains the three billfish cases. Like the bigeye case, the northern swordfish (*Xiphias gladius*) case presented in chapter 6 provides evidence linking vulnerability response to strong management. This contrasts with the southern swordfish (*Xiphias gladius*) case in chapter 7. At first, the case seems to contradict vulnerability response because strong management occurred with little biological depletion. However, further investigation reveals that ICCAT was not able to establish regulations that matched scientific advice until estimates of stock size and maximum sustainable yield were revised upward. The case of Atlantic blue marlin (*Makaira nigricans*) and white marlin (*Tetrapturus albidus*) is covered in chapter 8. As by-catch, marlins are not expected to generate much activity under vulnerability response. However, owing to lobbying efforts by noncommercial fishers, ICCAT has passed some measures to protect marlins. This provides an opportunity to explore the interactions among multiple interest groups and their impacts on adaptive governance.

Part III contains only two case studies, but these pertain to two of the most controversial stocks that are managed by ICCAT—western and eastern bluefin tuna. Chapter 9 shows how preemptive enclosure of the western stock of Atlantic bluefin tuna minimized the vulnerability of ICCAT members. Because of this, their response was only sufficient to slow down the overexploitation of the stock, rather than reversing it as in the northern swordfish and bigeye cases. The eastern stock of bluefin tuna, which is covered in chapter 10, is also overexploited, with little hope for recovery. The case study shows that the vulnerability response dynamic observed in previous cases was interrupted by the introduction of a new technology, which caused revenues to go up while the desire to manage the stock went down.

Finally, chapter 11 summarizes the findings from these cases. The explanatory capacity of the model is reviewed with particular focus on exceptions to the vulnerability response expectations. Then patterns of adaptive governance are identified. These include (1) the transformative pattern of vulnerability response that is documented in the bigeye and northern swordfish cases, (2) the interrupted patterns that show up in the yellowfin and eastern bluefin tuna cases, (3) the premature exclusion observed in the western bluefin case, (4) the pseudosuccessful pattern from the southern swordfish case, and (5) the glass-ceiling pattern found in the Atlantic marlins case along with various other by-catch-related case segments. Patterns 2–5 are variations on the transformative pattern, and the causes of these deviations are covered as well.

Tropical Tunas

Skipjack tuna
(*Katsuwonus pelamis*)

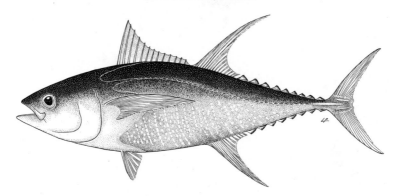

Yellowfin tuna
(*Thunnus albacares*)

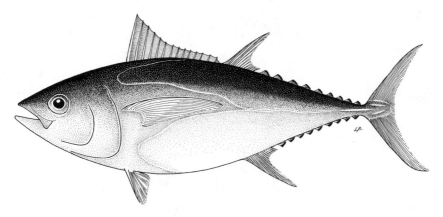

Bigeye tuna
(*Thunnus obesus*)

Source: United Nations Food and Agriculture Organization

I
Tropical Tunas

These cases cover three tropical tuna species in the Atlantic: yellowfin (*Thunnus albacares*), skipjack (*Katsuwonus pelamis*), and bigeye (*Thunnus obesus*).[1] From an analytical perspective, the tropical tunas need to be considered together because this is sometimes a mixed fishery in which different species are harvested at the same time, so there is not complete geopolitical or economic separability between the stocks. Nevertheless, each case poses its own inherently interesting set of problems and conundrums from a vulnerability response perspective. Whereas bigeye tuna could be labeled a classic case of vulnerability response, the yellowfin case is an example of biological rebuilding without serious management efforts. The skipjack fishery, which also captures large amounts of small yellowfin and bigeye, presents a situation where strategic considerations generated management measures even though there was no significant biological depletion of the primary target species.

Together, these three stocks account for around 60% of all Atlantic landings of highly migratory species (see figure I.1). Individually, skipjack is the smallest of the three species, maturing at between 42 and 52 cm and with a relatively short life span of 2–3 years (ICCAT 1995–2007b: 2004, 42). Uncertainty regarding the stock structure of skipjack has prevented scientists from estimating maximum sustainable yield, but ICCAT's Standing Committe on Research and Statistics has suggested that catches as high as 175,000 tons are unsustainable (ICCAT 1995–2007b: 1998, 37). Yellowfin tuna grow much larger than skipjack, reaching a maximum length of about 170 cm. The most recent estimates put MSY for yellowfin at about 148,000 tons (ICCAT 1995–2007b: 2004, 28). Bigeye is the largest of the three species, reaching lengths of over 200 cm. It is also the slowest to mature, taking about 3 years to reach spawning age at approximately 100 cm (ICCAT 1995–2007b:

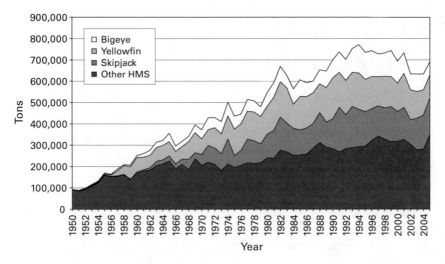

Figure I.1
Reported landings of tropical tunas relative to other HMS in the Atlantic. Source:
ICCAT 2007d.

2004, 34). Estimates of MSY for bigeye are much lower than for yellowfin, ranging from 79,000 to 105,000 tons. Thus, skipjack is the most
abundant of the three stocks in the Atlantic, followed closely by yellowfin and trailed considerably by bigeye.

Tropical tunas are important in value as well as volume. In 2000,
global catches of bigeye tuna were the most valuable of any marine species, bringing in revenues of about U.S. $3 billion. Yellowfin and skip-
jack were also significant, with total catches valued at U.S. $2 billion
and U.S. $1 billion, respectively (FAO 2002, 10). Figure I.2 shows the
estimated real value of Atlantic landings of tropical tunas from 1976 to
2001. At the beginning of the time series, bigeye is the least valuable of
three species, while yellowfin brings in the most revenue, followed closely
by skipjack. Because of growing demand, prices for bigeye tuna greatly
surpassed the other tropical tunas by the early 1990s. The per-unit value
of yellowfin has shown little increase, while prices for skipjack tuna actually declined, negating most gains from higher catches.[2]

There are three main fisheries for tropical tunas. Small tropical tunas
are usually targeted in mixed schools made up of skipjack, which never
gets very big, combined with young bigeye and yellowfin. This fishery
is dominated by purse seines, which supply canneries around the globe
(see figure I.3 for an illustration of purse seine operations). Schools of

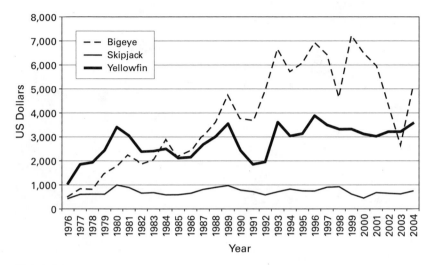

Figure I.2
Per-unit value of tropical tunas (global). Source: FAO 2007c.

medium-sized yellowfin may also be targeted for canning. On the other hand, adult bigeye and yellowfin are targeted by longlines for sale as sushi, sashimi, or tuna steaks in Japan, the United States, and other affluent countries (see figure II.3 in the introduction to part II for an illustration of longline operations). These are generally single-species fisheries, although there can be substantial by-catch of other species like turtles and marlins. Baitboats may also harvest either adults or juveniles of each species.[3]

Both baitboats and purse seines started using fish aggregating devices (FADs) in the early 1990s. Man-made floating objects with a global positioning system beacon on board, FADs attract schools of small tunas and make them easier to find than free-floating schools (FAO 2007a). This new technology increased the efficiency of fishing effort, enabling larger harvests, but it also increased the percentage of juvenile bigeye and yellowfin tuna in the overall catch (ICCAT 1971–1994: 1993, 130, 140). As will be seen in the cases, higher landings of small tunas negatively affected the growth of bigeye and yellowfin stocks and created competition between fleets targeting adults and those harvesting juveniles incidentally.

These and other issues are addressed in detail as the cases are used to test the vulnerability response framework. Since it is the most overfished and most regulated stock, bigeye is covered first to illustrate the

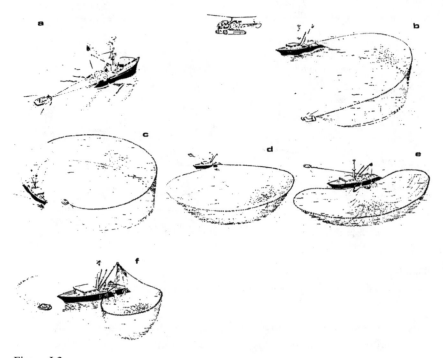

Figure I.3
Two-vessel deployment and operation of a large-scale tuna purse seine net. In large operations like this, the mother ship will frequently carry a small tender vessel and even a helicopter that is used for spotting schools of tuna. Upon location of a school, the tender vessel leaves the mother ship, towing a huge net, and circles the fish (a–c). Once the school is fully encircled, the bottom of the net is drawn or "pursed" shut (d) and the catch is hauled back onto the mother ship by heavy-duty winches (e–f). Source: United Nations Food and Agriculture Organization.

full journey from increasing economic competition to strong management response. Chapter 4 shows how vulnerability led to early regulation of yellowfin tuna—when the stock was thought to be much smaller than is known today—but has not generated a contemporary response even though the stock is now thought to be fully exploited. The third chapter in this part deals with the mixed fishery for small tunas, which mostly targets skipjack. It shows how strategic elements and changes in international norms can obscure political responses, causing national policy preferences to deviate from the expectations derived from the framework.

3

Bigeye Tuna

From the mid-1980s onward, bigeye tuna, the least prolific of the tropical tunas, was also the most valuable. During that period, fishing effort rocketed upward, as shown by the steep increase in landings from 1987 to 1994 (see figure 3.1). Fishing mortality, or the amount of fish killed in fishing operations, remained well above even the highest estimate of MSY from 1993 to 2000. As a result, the stock declined rapidly and competition increased dramatically. By 1996, biomass was estimated to be only 70% of the level that would produce maximum sustainable yield.[1] In the 1980s, twenty-five countries or fishing entities (i.e., the EC) were reporting bigeye landings. That number had increased to forty-one in the first decade of the twenty-first century. Harvest in the not elsewhere included category also increased from 338 tons in 1982 to a peak of 28,701 tons in 1999. Fisheries for bigeye tuna were getting more and more crowded while there were fewer and fewer fish to be found. Such heavy competition should evoke considerable political response, making this an excellent case for testing the framework.

Technical aspects of the Atlantic bigeye fishery have important impacts on the economic vulnerability of fishing states as well as the biological abundance of the stock. National fleets tend to be specialized in either longlines that target adult bigeye or surface gears (mainly two types of gear, purse seines and baitboats) that target schools of small tunas, which include juvenile bigeye (ICCAT 2007d). ICCAT member countries whose fleets directly target bigeye can be expected to follow the vulnerability patterns described in chapter 2. Countries whose fleets indirectly catch juvenile bigeye are not economically vulnerable to increasing competition over the species; they will behave as mildly vulnerable by-catch states. Without much vulnerability, by-catch countries have no

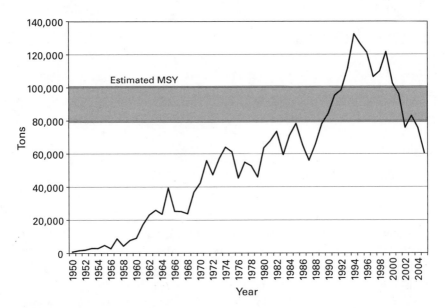

Figure 3.1
Reported landings and most recent estimate of MSY for Atlantic bigeye tuna.
Sources: ICCAT 2007d; 1995–2007b: 2006.

endogenous economic incentive to forgo harvests of skipjack and yellowfin in order to protect juvenile bigeye. This will make change difficult because of increased conflict over the distribution of the costs of regulation,
including expanded use of the countermeasures tactic in order to shift the
costs of management, and vehement objections from states that capture
bigeye only incidentally.

As with all of the cases, this one starts with the identification and classification of all countries with fleets harvesting bigeye tuna, as per subsection 2.5.1. Then the policy positions of these countries are predicted
using the vulnerability response framework. All this occurs in section
3.1. Sections 3.2 and 3.3 then describe the actual positions taken by
ICCAT members, as a test of the framework, as well as details of the
negotiations, which are used to refine and extend the framework. This
narrative is broken into two sections to highlight a major breakingpoint
in negotiations, when ICCAT members suddenly shifted from a long period of conflict to a period of relative accord. Findings from the cases are
summarized at the end of the chapter.

		Competitiveness	
		Low	High
Flexibility	Low	Highly Vulnerable Canada, Portugal (pre 1997), and USA	Moderately Vulnerable Brazil, Morocco, South Africa, etc.
	High	Gradually Vulnerable Japan (low-flex 1990)	Mildly Vulnerable China, Taiwan, and the Philippines By-catch: EC and Ghana

Figure 3.2
Vulnerability response matrix for bigeye tuna. A list ending in "etc." indicates that countries have been omitted from this summary for ease of reference. See table B.1 in appendix B for a full list.

3.1 Vulnerability Response Predictions

Figure 3.2 lists the countries in each vulnerability category for the Atlantic bigeye tuna fishery.[2] The impact of the dichotomy between surface and deepwater gears appears in the mildly vulnerable box, where the European Community (or France and Spain prior to their replacement by the EC in 1997) and Ghana are listed because bigeye is a by-catch of their surface fleets that target schools of small tunas. Even though their catches are incidental, these fleets can have a big impact on the bigeye stock. Prior to the price increase of the 1980s, members of the EC captured between 25 and 40% of annual landings of bigeye tuna. When harvests by longlines went up in response to greater demand, their share in total landings declined to between 15 and 20%, but total harvests by the EC actually increased. Ghanaian landings were low in the 1970s and 1980s but increased substantially in the early 1990s in both absolute and percentage terms (ICCAT 2007d).

Because by-catch fleets capture so much bigeye and usually take the fish before they've even had a chance to reproduce, reducing incidental harvests is a critical element in a solid management regime (ICCAT 1971–1994: 1981, 101–102). As mildly vulnerable countries, the EC (or its members press to 1997) and Ghana are expected to use primary blocking strategies whenever proposed bigeye regulations could impinge

Table 3.1
Overview of Vulnerability Response Predictions for Bigeye Tuna

Category	Countries	Predictions
Highly vulnerable	Canada, United States, and Portugal (pre-1997)	Always propose strong management measures; evince increasing but limited willingness to pay the costs of management
Gradually vulnerable	Japan (low-flex 1990)	Blocking or countermeasures prior to 1990, quickly switching to strong management after 1990. Increasing willingness to pay for management also in this period
Moderately vulnerable	Brazil, Morocco, South Africa, etc.	Blocking or countermeasures on any proposals that limit development of their fleets; side payments or concessions for cooperation
Mildly vulnerable	China, Taiwan, and the Philippines	Blocking or countermeasures on all strong management unless there are substantial side payments
	By-catch: EC and Ghana	Blocking or countermeasures on any proposals that reduce catches of targeted stocks

Notes: A list ending in "etc." indicates that countries have been omitted from this summary for ease of reference. See table B.1 in appendix B for a full list.

on the ability of their fleets to freely harvest their target stocks (see table 3.1). While the commission may run roughshod over a small developing country like Ghana, the EC is a major heavyweight in this arena and its influence is wide-ranging.[3]

As developing countries that have distant-water fleets targeting bigeye, Taiwan and China are also located in the mildly vulnerable position in the matrix. In 2005, Taiwan brought in about 20% of the Atlantic bigeye harvest. China was responsible for around 10% (ICCAT 2007d). Although there are pockets of affluence in both of these countries, cheap labor is available, along with significant government subsidies for the development of national fleets. In addition, both countries have benefited significantly from transfers of capital, owing to economic downturn and government regulations on Japanese fleets (ICCAT 1995–2007a: 2001, 206–208). Because of these factors, the Chinese and Taiwanese fleets are highly competitive, even though the latter should technically be placed in the gradually vulnerable category for recent years owing to high GDP growth. They are expected to prefer a late, weak response to biological depletion when restrictions on longlines are under consideration. Both countries can wield the threat of defection, but Taiwan is much less powerful in the ICCAT context because geopolitical factors prevent it from joining the commission and therefore it has no ability to block consensus.[4]

To date there are thirty-three countries in the moderately vulnerable category for bigeye tuna. Only three of the most vocal were included in figure 3.2, but a full list is available in appendix table B.1. The following expectations apply to all countries in the category, not just those listed in figure 3.2, and it should be noted that the vulnerability response framework was not used to predict which countries would state their positions for the record, only what they would say when they did so. The problems associated with the lack of a complete data set on national policy positions are discussed further in the conclusion to this chapter. For now, assume that silence indicates acquiescence to the ultimate decision of the commission on any particular issue.

The majority of countries in the moderately vulnerable category have taken only a small percentage of the annual bigeye harvest.[5] However, most would like to develop their fleets targeting adult bigeye to generate hard currency and increase domestic food production. Vulnerability response predicts that these countries will directly or indirectly block management measures that curtail their ability to develop their fleets, if they can. Individually, each of these states is susceptible to pressures from the rest of the commission, especially from industrialized countries with control over development assistance. Together, moderately vulnerable countries may be able to use their majority status as leverage within the commission, obtaining concessions and even side payments for their cooperation.

Japan is the only country in the gradually vulnerable category for bigeye tuna. With high costs of labor and other inputs, Japan has not been able to maintain its dominance over the production of this stock in spite of the flexibility imparted by its distant-water fleets. In 2005, Japanese fleets captured just under 20% of the total bigeye harvest in the Atlantic. That figure is down from a recent peak of about 50% in 1989, owing both to reduced Japanese landings and increased harvests by fleets from other countries (ICCAT 2007d). Because Atlantic bigeye is itself a secondary alternative to other stocks of bigeye and bluefin tuna for the

Japanese fleets, Japan is expected to prefer strong management quite early in this case. World production of bigeye by Japanese fleets flattened out in the late 1980s and has been in decline since 1990, so the country is certainly low-flex after 1990, having exhausted the cheapest alternative sources of revenue for its distant-water fleets (FAO 2007b).

A powerful force within the commission, Japan has multiple avenues by which it can build consensus on strong management measures. Most important of these is its role as the largest consumer of sushi and sashimi-quality bigeye in the world. It is the Japanese market that pays the highest prices for longline-caught bigeye, and closure of this market to a national fleet can be devastating.[6]

Finally, the United States and Canada occupy the highly vulnerable section of figure 3.2 because both countries have high domestic costs of production in combination with coastal fleets that have few cheap alternative sources of revenue.[7] Although the United States captures only about 1% of longlined bigeye in the Atlantic, that small amount is quite important to its domestic fleets. U.S. longliners started targeting bigeye seasonally in the northwest Atlantic once the price of the fish began to rise in the 1980s. Those catches became even more important in the 1990s as prices of alternative stocks such as swordfish dropped, causing U.S. longline revenues to decline as well.[8] During that same period, ICCAT adopted new regulations that limited access to both western bluefin tuna and North Atlantic swordfish for U.S. fishermen.[9] Canada catches an even smaller percentage of Atlantic bigeye, but the same political and economic forces have negatively affected its fleets (ICCAT 2007d).[10]

Having already tasted the bitterness of economic decline in these two alternative fisheries, U.S. and Canadian policy makers should be doubly wary when approaching bigeye regulations. As the most vulnerable, the United States and/or Canada are expected to be first to express concern for Atlantic bigeye. In addition, they should push for the most stringent regulatory actions throughout negotiations on bigeye management at ICCAT. However, their formidable power in most international circles is curtailed here because they harvest so little of this stock.[11] In addition, because bigeye tuna remains a small alternative source of revenue for a relatively minor industry, these countries would be unwilling to make substantial links outside of the international fisheries arena (Weber 2002, 200). They are curtailed by both international norms and domestic budget constraints.

3.2   Conflicts over Costs

Over the first two decades of ICCAT history, bigeye tuna was considered underexploited in the Atlantic. This status quickly changed with the economic and technological transformations of the fishery that were mentioned in the introduction to this chapter. As fishing effort increased, scientific assessments of the bigeye stock by ICCAT's Subcommittee on Research and Statistics moved incrementally from slightly underexploited in 1990 to severely overfished in 1998.[12] Conflicts over the allocation of the costs of management were the major impediment to preventing biological depletion in this fishery. Specifically, there were three arenas of contention over bigeye management measures:

· Protection of adults versus juveniles
· Historical versus coastal and developing status as criteria for allocation of quota
· Restriction of developing-country distant-water fleets

These obstacles mirror the national incentives of more versus less vulnerable states. Economically vulnerable members like the United States, Canada, and eventually Japan benefit from the elimination of open access, but only under certain terms. None of these countries is altruistic.

As would be expected from such a highly vulnerable state, in 1992 the United States was the first to suggest that restrictions on bigeye landings might be necessary, citing the SCRS assessment that recent landings were above maximum sustainable yield (ICCAT 1971–1994: 1993, 93). It is interesting that this occurred before the SCRS even recommended that catches should be limited. Instead, scientific advice favored full implementation of the 3.2-kg size limit for bigeye tuna, which had been adopted in the 1970s to eliminate confusion with a similar regulation on yellowfin tuna.[13] Now, studies showed that reducing fishing mortality on small bigeye could increase maximum sustainable yield by allowing more juveniles to reach spawning age. In other words, smaller harvests of young fish would allow a larger take of adult bigeye (ICCAT 1971–1994: 1992, 107).

As it had been throughout the history of discussion on bigeye size limits, mildly vulnerable Ghana was vociferous in its objections to the size limit because implementation was impossible without reducing Ghanaian harvests of small tropical tunas in the Gulf of Guinea (ICCAT 1971–1994: 1993, 93).[14] Most other countries were also unwilling to take action, although Spain (EC after 1997) pointed out that Ghana's position was completely contrary to scientific advice. This disagreement between fishing countries in the same vulnerability category is not expected based on the framework, but it should be noted that Spain and France, as well as Ghana, have completely failed to abide by the size limit.[15]

No new measures were adopted that year and so competition continued to escalate. By 1994, Japan was concerned enough to begin pushing for three measures: (1) research into the effects of fish aggregating devices, which are used by surface fleets, (2) reductions in Taiwanese catches, and (3) the extension of management measures to noncontracting parties (ICCAT 1971–1994: 1993, 93; 1995–2007a: 1995, 169).[16] Such attempts to place the burden of management costs on other shoulders are typical of early countermeasures by low-flex, gradually vulnerable states and are predicted by the satisficing assumptions of the vulnerability response model. Of course, less vulnerable states will not simply acquiesce to the demands of more vulnerable states. Hence the vigorous rebuttal of Japanese demands by Spain, whose fleets were rapidly adopting FAD technology, and Taiwan (ICCAT 1995–2007a: 1995, 169).[17] Noncontracting parties have little voice at the commission, but they continued to harvest irrespective of ICCAT regulations.

By 1995 scientific assessments of Atlantic bigeye showed that the stock biomass was at 90–92% of the level that would support MSY. With reported landings well above that benchmark, conflict over management measures intensified, but the dividing lines remained the same (ICCAT 1995–2007b: 1996, 18).[18] Japan proposed restriction of purse seine and baitboat landings as well as time-area closures on FADs. With their large purse seine fleets, Spain and France (EC) countered that longlines take the majority of the catch of bigeye tuna and should therefore make the largest cuts. As is expected of a highly vulnerable state, the United States supported both proposals, even though reductions of longline harvests would negatively affect their domestic fleets. Caught on the sidelines, Taiwan was pressed by all sides to reduce its longline effort, which had been increasing recently owing to shifts from the Indian and Pacific Oceans (ICCAT 1995–2007a: 1996, 148–150). In the end, consensus was reached on a nonbinding resolution (proposed by Spain) that urged countries to reduce their catches below MSY and set up observation programs to study the effects of FADs and catches of undersized fish (ICCAT 2007a, resolution 95-8, hereafter res.).

Only a year later, SCRS stock assessments showed that bigeye was at 70–120% of the level that would support MSY, but little else had changed (ICCAT 1995–2007b: 1997, 23).[19] Reported landings were down slightly in 1995, but the SCRS advice remained in favor of a reduction in catch to below MSY (60,000–70,000 tons) and protection of juvenile fish (<3.2 kg; ICCAT 1995–2007b: 1997, 23). Discussions again centered on who should bear the costs of restrictions—longlines or surface fleets. There was a slight movement on the part of low-flex Japan in that it seriously proposed reducing landings from all gear types, including longlines. However, Japan was not yet willing to make sacrifices unless its efforts were matched or exceeded by regulations on surface fisheries (ICCAT 1995–2007a: 1997, 127–131). Therefore, ICCAT remained in a practical impasse. A binding recommendation was adopted, but it only extended the data collection programs initiated the year before (ICCAT 2007c, recommendation 96-1, hereafter rec.).

By 1997, continued high catches of both adults and juvenile bigeye tuna further reduced the biomass of the stock to 60–80% of B_{MSY}.[20] Recognizing the uncertainty in their conclusions, the SCRS recommended that the commission reduce catches to not more than 85,000 tons for 1998. They further insisted that continued high catches of undersized fish would severely harm future abundance of the stock (ICCAT 1995–2007b: 1998, 30). In line with its previous positions, the United States proposed a 20% reduction in all landings of bigeye tuna, which would take reported harvests down to about 85,000 tons, but conflicts among other members of the commission again prevented a serious management response (ICCAT 1995–2007a: 1998, 152). However, quite a few other important changes occurred at the 1997 meeting of the commission. Although it maintained calls for reducing juvenile catches, Japan finally began pressing for limits on longline effort irrespective of actions taken on surface fisheries. Concomitantly, the main debate shifted away from the old dispute between surface and longline fleets to a conflict between historical and developing fishing countries.

With longline regulations looming, Brazil began to speak out against restrictions on the capacity of developing countries. China also entered the discussion with similar objections to proposed vessel limits. As an initial step toward excluding or limiting the effort of new entrants, Japan proposed the creation of a "white list" of vessels that were properly registered and controlled by ICCAT member states or cooperating noncontracting parties. In order to gain the cooperation of these less vulnerable states, concessions were made to exempt most developing countries (ICCAT 1997–2007a: 1998, 151–152). Moderate concessions were also made to Taiwan in return for its cooperation. Although ICCAT still adopted a nonbinding resolution that limited Taiwan's 1998 catches of bigeye tuna in the Atlantic to 16,500 tons, behind-the-scenes negotiations added 4,500 tons to Japan's original proposal of a 12,000-ton quota as per the 1995 resolution on reducing effort. (ICCAT 2007a, res. 97-15).[21] These were the first steps toward placation of moderately and mildly vulnerable countries by gradually vulnerable Japan.

No new stock assessment was conducted for bigeye tuna in 1998, but the SCRS reiterated its earlier advice to limit catches and decrease fishing mortality on juveniles (ICCAT 1995–2007b: 1999, 31). The commission was able to build on its previous initiatives. For the next year, contracting parties and cooperating noncontracting parties[22] were instructed to reduce or limit the number of commercial fishing vessels targeting bigeye that were greater than 24 meters in length to the level of the average number of such boats in 1991 and 1992 (ICCAT 2007a, rec. 98-3). Much as in 1997, owing to vehement objections from Brazil and other moderately vulnerable states, the 1998 recommendation exempted most developing countries by creating an exception for those countries that landed less than 2,000 tons on average over the previous 5 years. Also, Taiwan's quota of 16,500 tons was extended for the period (ICCAT 1995–2007a: 1999, 139).[23] The operating principle of this recommendation was that by limiting the number of vessels permitted to catch bigeye tuna, effort would also be limited and catches would decrease to the earlier levels.

In addition, a nonbinding resolution was adopted that asked the SCRS to develop rebuilding scenarios for the bigeye stock, with a special focus on the size composition of the catch (ICCAT 2007a, res. 98-16). Proposed by the United States with support from Canada, this resolution was not heartily welcomed by others, but was not strongly objected to either. Less vulnerable states, especially the EC and Japan, expressed the hope that the capacity limits, combined with a time-area closure on FADs, would be sufficient to rebuild the biomass (ICCAT 1995–2007a: 1999, 140). This latter management measure was proposed by the EC for reasons that will be discussed more in chapter 5. The recommendation established a closed season for fish aggregating devices in the Gulf of Guinea from November 1, 1999 to January 31, 2000, purportedly to protect juvenile tropical tunas in this well-known spawning area (ICCAT 2007a, rec. 98-1).

As it turned out, the 1998 regulations were not as effective as less vulnerable countries had hoped when they pushed it through as a countermeasure to catch limits. In 1999, landings of Atlantic bigeye tuna were just over 120,000 tons, the highest since the historical peak in 1994.[24] The SCRS also warned that the situation was close to recruitment overfishing, which is in itself a precursor to the collapse of a stock (ICCAT 2007a, rec. 98-1).[25] In spite of these dire warnings, little was accomplished regarding bigeye tuna in 1999. The United States did present a proposal to gradually reduce the total allowable catch to 80,000 tons in 3 years while allowing trade restrictive measures on countries found to be out of compliance with bigeye regulations. This was the first truly strong management proposal for bigeye tuna and was to be expected from a highly vulnerable country. However, there was a pervasive "wait-and-see" attitude among other members. It stemmed partly from the newness of the regulations already in place and partly from the wider conflict between historically active and developing coastal fishing states (ICCAT 1995–2007a: 2000, 167–169).[26]

Using the regulation of bigeye tuna and other stocks as leverage, the moderately vulnerable states had finally opened an official dialogue on their concerns through the new Working Group on Allocation Criteria in 1999. They were unwilling to agree on further catch or effort restrictions until the outcome of that working group was known (ICCAT 1995–2007a: 2000, 167–169).[27] Falling under the hostage or shakedown strategy in figure 2.3, this tactic was not predicted by the framework, although it does not conflict with the primary policy position expected from moderately vulnerable countries. They most certainly were protecting their ability to develop fleets targeting bigeye. Nonetheless, it should be noted here that the cross-issue linkages pursued by moderately vulnerable countries were not expected because of the stock-by-stock application of the framework as well as the complexities of international negotiations as described in section 2.4. This issue is discussed further in chapter 7 because the use of this tactic in the conflict over allocation criteria was even more outstanding in the case of southern swordfish.

By 2000, the exceptionally high landings from 1998 and 1999 were reported to the commission, making it clear that the recommendations

already in place were not effective. There was no new scientific assessment that year, but the SCRS did point out that recent high catches had
probably depressed the biomass of bigeye in the Atlantic even further. In
response to this advice, low-flex Japan and the highly vulnerable United
States presented a joint proposal to limit landings of bigeye to 80,000
tons as per SCRS advice. Also highly vulnerable, Canada supported the
proposal, but the mildly vulnerable EC was against it, citing the multispecies nature of their fishery and a preference for enforcement of measures already in place. Again, the breakdown between countries fishing
with different gear types came to the fore. Those contracting parties in
favor of the lower total allowable catch targeted the more valuable adult
bigeye with longlines, while those against it were engaged in surface
fisheries that targeted mainly yellowfin and skipjack. In the end, the less
vulnerable party won out. Taking into consideration the EC's concerns,
Japan put forward a second proposal for a binding recommendation that
again called on contracting and cooperating parties to limit their catches
to the average 1991 and 1992 level (ICCAT 1995–2007a: 2000, 191).

North-south issues cropped up as well. Although no agreement had
been reached on allocation criteria, developing coastal countries were
able to negotiate an exemption from the recommendation on catch limits. Specifically, contracting and cooperating parties that had caught less
than 2,100 tons of bigeye in 1999 were not required to limit their catches
in 2001. As in the past, Taiwan was instructed to keep its catches at
16,500 tons with a maximum of 125 vessels, but specific limits were
also established for China (4,000 tons and 30 vessels) and the Philippines
(5 vessels). Once more, Japan led the charge against these mildly vulnerable countries, alleging that the growth in China's fleet was due to the
movement of formerly unregistered vessels that had been pushed out of
the Taiwanese fleet. China did not deny the charge, but held that its
actions had been lawful and compliant with ICCAT recommendations.
In spite of its demand for a quota of 6,000 tons, China was allocated
only 4,000 tons. Although they chose not to block the consensus, the
mildly vulnerable Chinese did warn that they might have to formally object to the recommendation (ICCAT 2007a, rec. 00-1).[28]

At the turn of the millennia, ICCAT had made some progress on management measures for bigeye tuna, but the effectiveness of these regulations was undermined by conflicts between more and less vulnerable
fishing states. However, as biological depletion became more severe,
increases in governmental concern could be identified on the parts of

highly vulnerable states like the United States and Canada and gradually vulnerable Japan. As governmental concern grew among these countries, they became more willing to accommodate the demands of the moderately vulnerable countries and mildly vulnerable China and Taiwan. Although countries with longline fleets continued to pressure the hardly vulnerable EC and Ghana to reduce their landings of small bigeye, they no longer predicated regulation of adult fish on protection of juveniles. The next section discusses changes that reduced the importance of these conflicts and improved the effectiveness of the management of longlines. Regulation of surface fisheries is dealt with in chapters 4 and 5.

3.3 Overcoming Obstacles

As figure 3.3 shows, reported landings of bigeye tuna in the Atlantic declined from 2000 onward. By 2002, harvests had dropped to around 73,000 tons, 26,000 tons below the total allowable catch, and landings in the not elsewhere included category had all but disappeared (ICCAT 1995–2007b: 2004, 36–37). Also, in its 2004 assessment, the SCRS

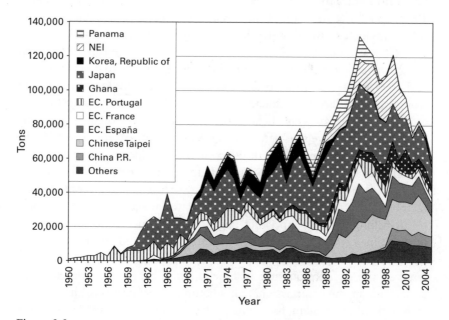

Figure 3.3
Atlantic landings of bigeye tuna by country. Source: ICCAT 2007d.

reported that the stock biomass had rebuilt to between 85 and 107% of the level needed to support maximum sustainable yield (ICCAT 1995–2007b: 2005).[29] It is interesting that the specific limits on bigeye tuna production did not change much from 1998 to 2003. Instead, changes in fishing practices and therefore in stock biomass were brought about by the implementation of monitoring and enforcement measures. Highly and gradually vulnerable contracting parties also chose to work bilaterally with developing states to control entry into the fishery. Adoption and implementation of strong and well-enforced bigeye regulations hinged on concessions from more vulnerable states as growing depletion worsened problems for the domestic fisheries of the United States, Canada, and especially Japan.

While the measures adopted at ICCAT's 1997 meeting did not reduce landings or rebuild biomass, there was a definite shift in the dialogue on effort limitations. Specifically, topics like overcapacity and flags of convenience came up for the first time in the bigeye context. Japan was especially adamant that capacity was at the heart of the overfishing problem and that movement to flags of convenience would have to be prevented if limits on contracting parties were to be effective (ICCAT 1995–2007a: 1998, 151). The roots of the Japanese concern can be seen clearly in figure 3.3, which shows reported landings of Atlantic bigeye tuna by country (ICCAT 2007d). While harvests of bigeye increased markedly from 1989 onward, the Japanese share in production fluctuated until 1994 and then went into a steep decline. Increases in landings by longlines from Taiwan, Panama, China, and the not elsewhere included category crowded historical fleets such as the Japanese and Koreans out of the market.[30] High levels of catch in the NEI category were especially disconcerting to some members of the commission, since these reflected harvests by fishers who were not associated with any particular flag state.[31]

With such large catches by noncontracting parties, many ICCAT members saw the inherent benefits in ensuring that regulations applied to all fishing entities, especially flag of convenience states like Panama (at the time) and NEI vessels. Similar monitoring and enforcement measures had initially been developed by ICCAT to deal with problems related to the overexploitation of bluefin tuna, by far the priciest of the species under the commission's jurisdiction. Over the years, the commission refined its system for dealing with monitoring and enforcement issues, including the establishment of the Permanent Working Group for the Improvement of ICCAT Statistics and Conservation Measures

(PWG) in 1992 and the ICCAT Conservation and Management Measures Compliance Committee in 1995 (ICCAT 2007a, res. 92-2, oth. 95-15). Basically, the PWG collects information and decides on trade measures to punish noncompliance by noncontracting parties, and the compliance committee serves the same purpose when dealing with infractions by contracting parties to the commission.

The first trade measures for bigeye tuna were undertaken in accordance with the 1998 Resolution by ICCAT Concerning the Unreported and Unregulated Catches of Tunas by Large-scale Longline Vessels in the Convention Area (IUU resolution).[32] This resolution set up a system by which longline vessels longer than 24 meters that fish in the convention area in contravention of ICCAT management measures could be identified, along with their flag states. Moreover, any country found to be a haven for illegal, unregulated, and unreported vessels could be instructed to alter their domestic management system to come into compliance with ICCAT regulations pertaining to large-scale longlines. If a state so identified failed to make significant improvements within a year, further action, including nondiscriminatory trade measures, could be taken by the commission on the recommendation of either the PWG or the compliance committee (ICCAT 2007a, res. 98-18). Like the "white list" of longline vessels that was started in 1997, the 1998 IUU resolution was designed to curtail harvests by fleets in the mildly vulnerable category and exempted small-scale fishing boats in deference to demands from moderately vulnerable countries (ICCAT 1994–2007a: 1998, 151–152).

In 1999, ICCAT sent letters of identification under the IUU resolution to eight noncontracting parties: Belize, Cambodia, Honduras, Kenya, the Philippines, Sierra Leone, Singapore, and St. Vincent and the Grenadines, notifying them of IUU activities undertaken by vessels flying their flags. The next year, ICCAT agreed to instruct all contracting parties and cooperating noncontracting parties to prohibit imports of bigeye tuna from Belize, Cambodia, and St. Vincent and the Grenadines. Honduras was given an extra year to complete the modifications of its management policies, while no actions were taken against the Philippines or Sierra Leone (ICCAT 2007a, rec. 00-15).[33]

Similar action was taken by the compliance committee against a single contracting party: Equatorial Guinea (ICCAT 2007a, rec. 00-16). It is interesting that this country had not sent a delegation to either the 1999 meeting of the commission, when it was identified, or the 2000 meeting, when sanctions were imposed (ICCAT 1995–2007a: 2000; 2001).

Although each noncontracting party was afforded a chance to explain itself to the PWG, without either the ability to vote or truly significant capacity to undermine ICCAT management measures, there was little that the individual states could do other than strive to comply with the demands of the commission. However, if Equatorial Guinea had been at the table, it would have had the opportunity to block the sanctions levied against it.

Also in 2000, a supplemental resolution was passed that urged and supported cooperation between Japan and China and Taiwan to reduce IUU fishing on bigeye tunas (ICCAT 2007a, res. 00-2). As a gradually vulnerable fishing country with few alternatives remaining, Japan spearheaded several of the moves to enforce ICCAT catch limits. An added incentive has been the fact that a large portion of the IUU fleet is composed of former Japanese vessels that moved on to Taiwan or other countries once Japan began cutting its production and reducing its domestic tuna operations. Indeed, by pushing for stricter recommendations, as well as supplying trade data and lists of vessels they identified as IUU, the Japanese delegation was the major motivating force behind most of the actions taken to control IUU activities (ICCAT 1995–2007a: 2000, 117). Because China and Taiwan have the ability to undermine bigeye management measures, Japan and the rest of the commission have had to engage these mildly vulnerable countries with positive as well as negative incentives to discourage IUU fishing.[34]

Japan has consistently put public pressure on Taiwan and China to reduce their effort in the Atlantic and other oceans, but it has also worked bilaterally with these countries to develop practical means of obtaining that end. For instance, in 2001 Japan and Taiwan announced a joint effort to scrap sixty-two Japanese-built, large-scale longliners that were identified as IUU vessels. They also agreed to work together on the reregistration of sixty-seven other IUU vessels in the Taiwanese fleet by 2005. Also in 2001, Japan announced that it would work with China to stem the flow of secondhand IUU vessels that had flooded the Chinese fleet after they were pushed out of Taiwan (ICCAT 1995–2007a: 2002, 322–323). In return for their cooperation, the Chinese and Taiwanese would receive a portion of the Japanese bigeye quota once IUU elements had successfully been removed from their fleets. The first of such side payments occurred in 2003, when ICCAT adopted a resolution that temporarily transferred 1,250 tons of Japanese quota to China and the same amount to Taiwan (ICCAT 2007a, res. 03-02).

Along with the sanctions and side payments that were meant to influence fishers through their flag states, ICCAT established a statistical document program (SDP) for bigeye in 2002 (ICCAT 2007a, rec. 00-22, 01-21). Modeled after a similar program set up for bluefin, the bigeye SDP was designed to create a paper trail; documents would be issued for each fish by the flag state of the harvesting vessel and move with it through every point of trade. ICCAT contracting parties were instructed to require that these documents be produced whenever bigeye was imported into their markets. Considering that the major markets for bigeye tuna all exist within ICCAT member countries, such trade measures are quite punitive. Without an authorized statistical document, no longline-caught bigeye tuna can be legally sold in the international marketplace (ICCAT 2007b, rec. 92-1). Of course, illegal sales of bigeye tuna do continue, since the high price for the species creates incentives for such risky behavior as smuggling and *fish laundering*. Coined by the Japanese themselves, this latter term refers to the transshipment of fish through ICCAT member states in order to obtain statistical documents that falsely attribute the catch to a legal source, much like money laundering.

In the past 3 years, ICCAT has continued to focus steadily on identifying sources of IUU catches of bigeye tuna and eliminating them. Sanctions have been levied on several other noncontracting parties, including Bolivia, Sierra Leone, and Georgia.[35] Further measures have also been taken to refine the statistical document program for bigeye tuna, and Japan continues to work with Taiwan, China, and other countries to scrap vessels and break ties with IUU vessel owners. The results of the commission's efforts are obvious in the decline of reported landings since 1999 and recent improvements in estimates of stock biomass for Atlantic bigeye (ICCAT 1995–2007b: 2007, 24; see also figures 3.2 and 3.4).

Less transparent are the costs that contracting parties have paid in order to successfully enforce management measures. Aside from bureaucratic costs associated with maintenance of vessel lists and statistical document programs, members can also be negatively affected by increased scrutiny of their own fleets' fishing activities. With the widespread acceptance of multilateral punitive mechanisms, the risk that even strong contracting parties like the EC, Japan, and the United States could face trade measures for failure to comply with ICCAT regulations looms closer than ever before.[36] This helps to explain why the adoption and implementation of such measures was postponed until the bigeye stock was severely depleted and more vulnerable states had lost substantial market share.

3.4   Summary

The brief but rich history of ICCAT management of bigeye tuna generally substantiates the vulnerability response framework presented in chapter 2. This can be seen clearly by comparing the countries in each vulnerability category (see figure 3.2 or table B.1), with the evidence in the cases (see table C.1 in appendix C for an overview). When countries are grouped by the nature of the policy positions they held, rather than their vulnerability, by and large their positions tended to match up with vulnerability expectations, although some tactics—such as the larger movement for recognition of coastal states' rights—were not expected. Moreover, there was a clearly increasing trend in the level of governmental concern expressed by highly vulnerable (Canada and the United States) and low-flex, gradually vulnerable (Japan) states in terms of their willingness to shoulder the costs of regulation. As expected, both moderately vulnerable (Brazil, Morocco, South Africa, etc.) and mildly vulnerable (China, Taiwan, and the Philippines) countries engaged in various blocking maneuvers until they received concessions and side payments from more vulnerable countries.

   Nonetheless, there are certain holes in the picture created by the framework. One has already been mentioned: cross-issue linkages pursued by moderately vulnerable states. Also, when comparing the two tables, one can see that there are many countries harvesting bigeye tuna in the Atlantic that were either unable or unwilling to express their positions on the record. Many of these countries, like Norway and Iceland or the Congo, Ivory Coast, and Sao Tome and Principe catch much less than 100 tons of this stock annually and so may not be interested at all. Alternatively, they may be free riding diplomatically, allowing those with either greater concern or more substantial assets to fight their battles. Regardless of the reason, we cannot know for certain what this silence means. It is hoped that some of the gaps will be filled by other cases in which stocks are more important to these seemingly quiet countries.

   In regard to aggregation, it should be noted that the success of recent monitoring and enforcement mechanisms was facilitated by the high percentage of landings by noncontracting parties. With precedents already in place, it was relatively easy for the commission to exclude outsiders.

Continued sustainable management might be more difficult, especially if prices for bigeye rebound.[37] Furthermore, such path-dependent, or historically driven factors are a good example of the complexities that thwart attempts at aggregation. Nevertheless, the commission moved through five recognizable phases in the bigeye tuna case:

• **Inactivity,** in which neither the SCRS nor the commission expresses any concern about the stock

• **Concern,** in which the SCRS and highly vulnerable countries express concern and initiate the search for alternatives

• **Conflict,** in which most countries express concern, but none are willing to pay for strong management. Highly and gradually vulnerable countries take stronger positions than moderately and mildly vulnerable countries.

• **Accord,** in which highly and gradually vulnerable countries are finally willing to make the side payments, concessions, threats, and punishments that are necessary to attain strong management

• **Postrebuilding,** in which discord again begins to be seen with the rebound of the stock and reduction of economic competition from nonmember fleets

This pattern matches well with the hypothetical representation of adaptive governance in figure 1.1. It will be interesting to see if similar dynamics emerge from the other cases.

4

Yellowfin Tuna

The fishery for yellowfin tuna is similar to bigeye in that it is divided between longline fleets that target adults of the species and surface fleets that catch younger yellowfin in combination with other small tunas. There has been less competition over Atlantic yellowfin because it is a highly productive stock—much larger than bigeye tuna—and it is also lower in price. Therefore this stock can support more fishers than are drawn in by current market conditions. This can be seen in the relatively flat trend in landings that is evident in figure 4.1 (see the introduction to part I for a more detailed comparison). However, yellowfin is still a very important stock in terms of volume caught and overall value. Also, a much larger component of the yellowfin harvest is taken by surface fleets than is the case for bigeye. There are some purse seine vessels that target free-floating schools of medium-sized yellowfin, but the problem of juvenile by-catch associated with fish aggregating devices remains.[1] Biologically and economically, yellowfin tuna inhabits an economic and political space between high-priced, low-volume bigeye and low-priced, high-volume skipjack.

As figure 4.1 shows, reported landings of yellowfin in the Atlantic have been quite high since the early 1980s, but have generally stayed within the most recent range of estimates for MSY. Scientific assessments of yellowfin tuna also suggest that the stock has been hovering around full exploitation for several decades. The SCRS reported that yellowfin was slightly depleted in the early 1990s, but has since returned to levels that would support MSY (ICCAT 1991–1994: 1993, 138; 1995–2007b: 2004, 28). No ICCAT management measures can be linked to this rebuilding, which is not surprising, given the vulnerability response framework. At low levels of depletion, no states are expected to be willing to pay for strong management measures.

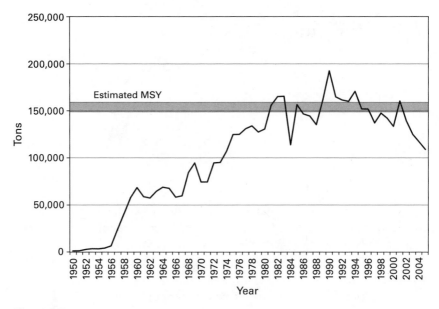

Figure 4.1
Reported landings and most recent estimate of MSY for Atlantic yellowfin.
Source: ICCAT 2007d.

Analysis of the yellowfin case must be divided into two periods. Most of ICCAT's management activity for this stock occurred prior to 1976, at a time when the Atlantic yellowfin stock was thought to be much smaller and more geographically limited than is now known. This created an early economic crunch in the fishery that lasted until offshore exploration led to the discovery of new fishing grounds. Therefore, in the pre-1976 period, competition was quite heavy and vulnerable states could be expected to evince moderate to high levels of governmental concern. After 1976, competition was substantially eased by the expansion of fishing effort and therefore governmental concern should be "reset" to the lower levels associated with an underexploited resource. Concern will build up again as the new profits or scarcity rent is dissipated, but as long as demand remains fairly stable, competition over yellowfin is not likely to reach the same levels as experienced in the bigeye case. Scientists now believe that yellowfin tuna has a flattened yield-per-effort curve, which, combined with lower prices, results in a sustainable long-run equilibrium (ICCAT 1995–2007a: 2001, 190).

		Competitiveness	
		Low	High
Flexibility	Low	Highly Vulnerable None	Moderately Vulnerable Brazil, Ghana, Morocco, etc.
	High	Gradually Vulnerable Japan (low-flex 1962) USA and Canada (low-flex mid-1970s) France and Spain (high-flex)	Mildly Vulnerable Korea and USSR

Figure 4.2
Vulnerability response matrix for yellowfin tuna (1970–1976). A list ending in "etc." indicates that countries have been omitted from this summary for ease of reference. See table B.2 in appendix B for a full list.

For comparison, the next section gives the vulnerability response predictions for each period. The pre-1976 predictions are tested in section 4.2, followed by evidence on the post-1976 political response in section 4.3. The findings from each period are summarized in section 4.4. A comparison between the two periods should be particularly interesting because, as will be explained later, several countries either shift from one vulnerability category to another, or reach the low-flex phase if they are gradually vulnerable.

4.1 Vulnerability Response Predictions Pre- and Post-1976

Figure 4.2 provides an overview of the vulnerability response matrix for yellowfin tuna prior to the expansion of the fishery in 1976 and table 4.1 lists expected responses. A full inventory of countries in each category for the years from 1970 to 1976 can be found in table B.2 in appendix B, and the following predictions apply to all countries listed there, even though many never expressed specific policy positions on the official record. Note that there are no highly vulnerable countries in this period. At the time, Atlantic yellowfin was mainly targeted by distant-water vessels from Europe, North America, and Japan, as well as coastal fleets from the equatorial regions (ICCAT 2007d). Even so, gradually vulnerable Japan, one of the biggest consumers of longline-caught yellowfin, was

Table 4.1
Overview of Vulnerability Response Predictions for Yellowfin Tuna (1970–1976)

Category	Countries	Predictions
Highly vulnerable	None	None
Gradually vulnerable	Japan (low-flex after 1962)	Propose strong management with increasing willingness to pay
	United States and Canada (low-flex after mid-1970s)	Express concern, but low willingness to accept strong management
	France and Spain	Blocking or countermeasures to strong management
Moderately vulnerable	Brazil, Ghana, Morocco, etc.	Blocking or countermeasure proposals that would limit development of their fleets; side payments or concessions for cooperation
Mildly vulnerable	Korea and USSR	Blocking or countermeasures to strong management; large side payments or concessions for cooperation

Notes: A list ending in "etc." indicates that countries have been omitted from this summary for ease of reference. See table B.2 in appendix B for a full list.

already in the low-flex phase in the Atlantic; at least it seemed that way at the time. World catches of yellowfin tuna by Japanese fleets had peaked in 1962 and steadily declined until the mid-1970s (FAO 2007b). Because of this, the Japanese delegation is expected to be highly dissatisfied with the status quo. This will lead them to favor strong management during this period, with increasing willingness to pay for it.

Also gradually vulnerable, U.S. and Canadian harvests of yellowfin were peaking world-wide when ICCAT began its deliberations in the early 1970s, and had started to decline by the middle of the decade. Always quite small, the Canadian fleet eventually disappeared, or at least changed flags, but the larger U.S. fleet gradually moved to the Pacific in the late 1970s and early 1980s. For the 1970–1976 period, however, these countries are expected to be ambivalent regarding yellowfin. They may express some preference for science-based management, but are not likely to demonstrate any willingness to pay for measures. In contrast, France and Spain—whose global harvests were still growing at the

		Competitiveness	
		Low	High
Flexibility	Low	Highly Vulnerable USA (Post-1986)	Moderately Vulnerable Brazil, Ghana, Morocco, Venezuela, etc.
	High	Gradually Vulnerable Japan (low-flex 1980) EC (France and Spain pre-1997; low-flex 1990)	Mildly Vulnerable China, Korea, Taiwan, etc.

Figure 4.3
Vulnerability response matrix for yellowfin tuna (1977–2006). A list ending in "etc." indicates that countries have been omitted from this summary for ease of reference. See table B.3 in appendix B for a full list.

time—are expected to actively resist strong management through either blocking or countermeasures (FAO 2007b). The same can be said of moderately and mildly vulnerable countries like Brazil, Ghana, and South Korea, all of which will work to maintain their access to the stock.

The post-1976 vulnerability classifications for yellowfin tuna (figure 4.3) are more similar to the bigeye matrix shown in figure 3.2. By this time, the dichotomy between longline and surface fleets is quite pronounced. U.S. longliners began targeting yellowfin off the southern Atlantic coast and in the Gulf of Mexico around 1986, after U.S. distant-water purse seines had permanently exited the fishery. Table 4.2 shows the expected responses for 1977–2006. It is difficult to pin down a specific transition year, but one can expect the U.S. position to reflect gradually vulnerable distant-water interests until the early 1980s and highly vulnerable coastal interests after 1986 (ICCAT 2007d). In this second phase, the United States should propose strong management measures and evince an increasing willingness to pay as the stock declines. However, if the stock does not decline, then by assumption competition is also stable and, while somewhat dissatisfied, the United States would not be expected to make increasing side payments or concessions to attain strong management.

Although the expansion of the fishery in 1976 helped the gradually vulnerable Japanese fleets to rebound, they were again in a low-flex phase by 1980, and will exhibit behavior that is similar to that of the

Table 4.2
Overview of Vulnerability Response Predictions for Yellowfin Tuna (1977–2006)

Category	Countries	Predictions
Highly vulnerable	United States (post-1986)	Propose strong management measures; evince increasing willingness to pay with declines in stock
Gradually vulnerable	Japan (low-flex after 1980)	Propose strong management measures; evince high and increasing willingness to pay
	EC (France and Spain; low-flex after 1990)	Pre-flex, blocking or countermeasures; low-flex propose strong management measures; low but increasing willingness to pay
Moderately vulnerable	Brazil, Ghana, Venezuela, etc.	Blocking or countermeasure proposals that would limit development of their fleets; side payments or concessions for cooperation
Mildly vulnerable	China, Korea, Taiwan, etc.	Blocking or countermeasures to strong management; large side payments or concessions for cooperation

Notes: A list ending in "etc." indicates that countries have been omitted from this summary for ease of reference. See table B.3 in appendix B for a full list.

highly vulnerable United States. Also in the gradually vulnerable category, French and Spanish fleets did not hit their low-flex phase until around 1990, when their global harvests of yellowfin flattened considerably. Therefore they are expected to use blocking or countermeasures between 1976 and 1990, then switch to a position that favors stronger management. As long as the stock is declining, these countries (or the EC, which replaced them at the negotiating table after 1997) should be more and more willing to make threats, side payments, or concessions to achieve that goal.

Moderately and mildly vulnerable countries are still expected to block or counter management measures that threaten their domestic interests in the postexpansion period. Countries like Brazil, Ghana, and Venezuela will use blocking or countermeasures if a proposed regulation would curtail their ability to develop fleets targeting Atlantic yellowfin. They may also work to prevent entry by distant-water fleets from gradually or mildly vulnerable countries. The latter, such as South Korea and China, will attempt to block limits on their fishing effort targeting yellowfin tuna unless they are faced with substantial threats or given side payments. Unable to join the commission and therefore lacking this blocking power, Taiwan will still speak out if its harvests are threatened. Table B.3 in appendix B provides a full list of moderately and mildly vulnerable countries for this period, and all are expected to evince behaviors similar to those described here.

4.2   Pre-1976 Size Limits

Of the three tropical tunas, yellowfin was the most important in the early years of the commission. In fact, it has the dubious distinction of being the first stock to be regulated by ICCAT. As early as 1970, the SCRS pointed out potential growth overfishing of the yellowfin stock in the Atlantic. The standing committee believed it likely that too many juvenile fish were being taken before they had a chance to replace themselves through reproduction. A year later, the SCRS felt confident enough to make two regulatory recommendations to the commission: increase the size at first capture and reduce overall fishing mortality. Unfortunately, it could not be more specific at that time and so no measures were adopted (ICCAT 1971–1994: 1972, 75).

At the next ICCAT meeting in 1971, the SCRS informed the commission that the optimum size at first capture for yellowfin tuna ranged between 10 and 25 kg (ICCAT 1971–1994: 1972, 92, 97).[2] Gradually vulnerable and running out of alternatives, Canada expressed concern about the stock but did not make any proposals.[3] Then, already low-flex Japan suggested that a minimum size limit should be adopted as per SCRS advice. Brazil, whose fleet is also mainly longliners, supported the need for regulation of surface fleets. In this initial discussion, most of the members with surface fleets targeting small to medium-sized yellowfin, including France, Morocco, and Spain, made statements regarding the necessity of quick adoption of regulatory measures, but did not agree to the size limit or suggest any other ideas, effectively blocking the adoption of any regulations that year (ICCAT 1971–1994: 1972, 40–42).

On the final day of the meeting, during the plenary session, Brazil, France, Korea, Morocco, Portugal, South Africa, and Spain made a joint proposal that would authorized the ICCAT council, a subset of the commission that originally met every other year, to establish a minimum size limit of between 3.2 and 10 kg for yellowfin.[4] This proposal came with the caveat that contracting parties would be able to set a certain reasonable tolerance level, or percentage of catch to be exempted from the new rule (ICCAT 1971–1994: 1972, 27).[5] Japan, Canada, and the United States raised procedural questions but were easily satisfied and the proposal was adopted. Three points are of interest here. First, this proposal was made by a coalition of countries with different levels of vulnerability. Second, it authorized a range of size limits that was well below the 10–25-kg limit mentioned by the SCRS. Third, it included a tolerance, which would give surface fleets greater flexibility in implementing the new regulation. Clearly, concessions were made by low-flex Japan and others in order to reach agreement on this rather tentative measure.

When the council met in Madrid in 1972, it was indeed supplied with more information on yellowfin tuna than had previously been available. By running several simulations of different size limits at landing, levels of fishing effort, and actual mortality of small fish, the SCRS found that a lower limit of 3.2 kg provided less potential benefit but also less potential risk of unnecessary economic losses than a higher level of 8.9 kg. While pointing out that a minimum size would only work if small fish were not discarded, they also expressed some optimism that the requirement for a minimum size at landing could change fishing practices and increase avoidance of small fish (ICCAT 1971–1994: 1973, 77).[6]

In its review of this evidence, Panel 1, the subcommittee in charge of tropical tunas, decided to recommend the lower minimum size of 3.2 kg to the council, along with a 15% tolerance level. This would mean that up to 15% of the number of fish caught could be under the 3.2-kg minimum size limit (ICCAT 1971–1994: 1973, 51; 2007a, rec. 72-1). France proposed this regulation and the United States seconded it. There was more discussion on the 15% tolerance, but specific national positions were not recorded. Any objections were overcome, and the council accepted this recommendation. They also went so far as to instruct the secretariat to inform the press of the accomplishment (ICCAT 2007a, rec. 72-1). This lower, more flexible size limit is a good example of successful secondary tactics, specifically the use of countermeasures to weaken regulations and make them less onerous for less vulnerable countries.

Countries with surface fleets may also have agreed to a size limit with no intention of enforcing it. The size limit was adopted as a binding recommendation, the strongest mechanism available at the time, but it still relied only on national rather than international monitoring and enforcement. As such, this mechanism fell well short of the trade-based measures that were adopted in the bigeye case. It is particularly telling that the yellowfin size limit, which was adopted in 1972, was never fully implemented. Year after year the SCRS has reported that undersized fish constitute a much larger proportion of the yellowfin landings than the 15% tolerance specified in the recommendation. By 1979, the SCRS began suggesting that the commission begin looking into other measures to protect juvenile yellowfin, but no such actions were taken until the late 1990s (ICCAT 1971–1994: 1980, 118). In addition, misidentification of undersized yellowfin as other species remains a serious problem to this day. In 1978, ICCAT adopted the same size limit for bigeye tuna, partly to reduce misreporting of yellowfin, but that regulation has proved equally useless in protecting either species.

In parallel with their advice on instituting a minimum size limit at landing, the SCRS also recommended that the commission limit fishing mortality on yellowfin tuna. In 1972 they suggested that the yellowfin catch should be reduced to 75,000 tons, but amended that recommendation to 90,000 tons in 1973. As expected, low-flex Japan put forth proposals to implement this SCRS advice from 1972 to 1974, but the commission could not reach any agreement (ICCAT 1971–1994: 1973, 29, 51; 1974, 36–37; 1975, 45). Access to the stocks was at the heart of the problem. Developing countries like the Ivory Coast, Senegal, and Brazil wished to expand their utilization of many highly migratory stocks and based on their coastal status, believed they had a right to do so. The representative of the UN Food and Agriculture Organization also expressed a desire that developing countries be afforded more equitable participation in the fisheries (ICCAT 1971–1994: 1975, 57). On the other hand, historically dominant fishing countries like France, Spain, the United States, and others were not willing to give up any of their share of the catch to allow such expansion under an effort limitation scheme.

Very worried by 1974, the Japanese offered to increase the total allowable catch they had set out in their 1972 proposal from 70,000 to 90,000 tons in order to allow fleet expansion developing countries, but no consensus was reached on the subject (ICCAT 1971–1994: 1975, 45). While it was not yet willing to give up some of its own claims, low-flex Japan had started trying to reach agreement on catch limits by making concessions to moderately vulnerable countries. This attempt failed and by 1975 reported landings of yellowfin tuna were almost 125,000 tons, about 30% higher than the catch limit suggested by the SCRS (ICCAT 2007d). From 1976 through 1983, reported landings of Atlantic yellowfin increased by almost 100,000 tons without eliciting further response from the commission. Driven by competition, fleets had shifted away from shore, discovering that yellowfin could be found throughout the tropical Atlantic. With this expansion, competitive pressures also eased temporarily and fishing states were satisfied again—at least for a while.

4.3   Post-1976 Management (or Lack Thereof)

From the mid-1970s onward, dispersion of fishing fleets and technological innovations allowed fishers to expand their harvests further than early models had predicted.[7] However, by the 1990s, scientists found that the yellowfin fishery for the entire Atlantic was fully exploited and in 1993 the SCRS advised that the eastern portion of the stock was at only 65% of the level of biomass that would support MSY (ICCAT 1971–1994: 1994, 176).[8] From the vulnerability response perspective, it is not surprising that the now highly vulnerable United States was the first to propose that ICCAT limit landings of yellowfin in 1992 (ICCAT 1971–1994: 1993, 79). No actions were taken until 1993, when recently low-flex France and Spain agreed to a binding U.S. proposal to limit effective fishing effort targeting yellowfin to 1992 levels for all fishing countries, whether or not they were members of the commission (ICCAT 2007a, rec. 93-4). Concerns regarding high catches in the not elsewhere included class, which fits into the mildly vulnerable category economically, were cited as the rationale for this binding recommendation (ICCAT 1971–1994: 1994, 84).

Since 1993, little has been said about yellowfin tuna at meetings of the commission. Unlike the stringent mechanisms used to enforce regulations on bigeye and several other stocks, no further actions were taken to implement the 1993 recommendation on yellowfin.[9] A lack of scientific evidence was often cited as the reason for ICCAT's inability to reach a consensus on new measures. Purportedly, such concerns prevented the Commission from acting on scientific advice to limit the total catch to 135,000 tons, which is well below the almost 152,000 tons landed in 1992 (ICCAT 1995–2007b: 1999, 19–20).[10] The SCRS remains concerned about the effective fishing effort targeting yellowfin, but the commission has not yet taken further measures to ensure compliance with the 1993 recommendation. From 1996 onward, almost all discussions focused on new measures for reducing juvenile catches of bigeye tuna, not yellowfin, as will be shown in the next chapter.

Why this sudden drop in attention to yellowfin tuna? There are three reasons. First, while it has expressed concern about the stock, the SCRS has generally assessed the biomass of Atlantic yellowfin to be relatively stable. It has not declined as drastically as bigeye tuna, and given the assumptions stated in chapter 2, this suggests that competition has not gotten much stronger in this case. Second and relatedly, the SCRS also reported that the fishing capacity of fleets targeting tropical tunas had gone down somewhat, but that efficiency had increased substantially since 1990 (3–5% per year; ICCAT 1995–2007b: 1999, 19–20).[11] Thus fishing fleets have become more efficient, reducing costs and at least temporarily relieving the pressures of competition. Finally, economic and technical changes resulted in a shift of effort away from yellowfin in the early 1990s.

Specifically, there were transfers of nominal fishing effort toward other tropical tuna species. On the one hand, as the value of bigeye tuna increased in the late 1980s, longlines that had previously targeted yellowfin switched over to the more dispersed, deeper-feeding adult bigeye (ICCAT 1971–1994: 1994, 141). On the other hand, the introduction of fish aggregating devices changed the composition of the schools that surface fleets targeted, increasing their catches of skipjack and juvenile bigeye relative to yellowfin. As figure 4.4 illustrates, the proportion of yellowfin in the total catch of tropical tunas by purse seines in the Atlantic went down by about 10–15% in the 1990s. In the same period, the skipjack and bigeye components of the stock increased proportionally. Considering that purse seines caught an average of 65% of all yellowfin tuna in the Atlantic from 1970 to 2002, this change in the composition of catches had a big effect on landings of this stock (ICCAT 2007d).

Catches of yellowfin tuna have remained close to SCRS estimates of MSY since 1995. This does not mean that they will necessarily stay so low, as shown by the high landings reported for 2001. That year, fishers harvested almost 159,000 tons, which was 11,000 tons over the most recent estimate of MSY (ICCAT 1995–2007b: 2004, 28). In 2002, landings returned to a level below MSY, but the capacity for over-exploitation of the stock continues to be cause for concern about the future of the species in the Atlantic. However, the dialogue among ICCAT

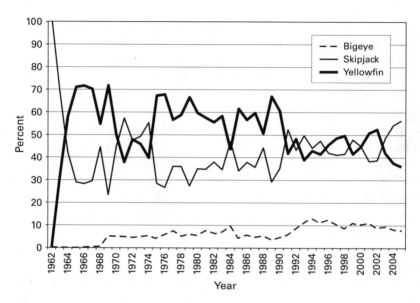

Figure 4.4
Percentage of each species in purse seine landings of tropical tunas. Source:
ICCAT 2007d.

members regarding yellowfin tuna remains sparse. As long as the fishery
hovers around maximum sustainable yield, there is just not enough governmental concern to take precautionary actions or even to enforce previous recommendations. This case reinforces the assumptions about the
temporal aspects of the vulnerability response framework. ICCAT only
took action when biological depletion and competition were high in the
early 1990s. Once the influences of rising bigeye prices and the introduction of FADs relieved those pressures, little more was done or said on the
matter of yellowfin management. If those exogenous parameters ever re-
vert to the earlier state, then economic competition may again provoke a
political response.

4.4   Summary

While it may not seem as exciting as the bigeye case, the long history
of yellowfin tuna management has provided important evidence on the
variations in policy positions that can be predicted by the vulnerability
response framework. Always gradually vulnerable, Japan's initial low-

flex phase was interrupted by the discovery of new fishing grounds, and its policy positions altered concomitantly. Indeed, the entire commission became quiescent regarding yellowfin once this discovery was made. In the interim, the U.S. distant-water fleet permanently moved to the Pacific Ocean and was replaced by coastal longlines, shifting this country from the gradually to the highly vulnerable category. As predicted, when open access once again generated heavy competition in the late 1980s, the United States proposed strong management rather than the weak countermeasures it had favored in the earlier period. Similarly, Canada showed mild concern as its distant-water fleet began to lose flexibility in the early 1970s, but none at all after this fleet abandoned the yellowfin fishery.

Although they did not change categories, France and Spain also exhibited an expected transformation in their policy positions. Reaching their low-flex phase around 1990, they too went from blocking and countering in the pre-1976 period of high competition to espousal of moderately strong management measures in 1993. About this time, bioeconomic dynamics shifted, relieving the pressure on these more vulnerable fleets. Again, dissatisfaction with the status quo was dealt with exogenously, and countries stopped engaging in yellowfin management. This is particularly interesting because with harvests hovering at relatively low levels, the commission's purported goal of management at MSY seems to be within reach, but no one is striving for it. Unfortunately (for the analyst, not the fish), there is no way of knowing whether or not escalating dissatisfaction with management would have led to even stronger measures, at least until competition over yellowfin increases again.

The yellowfin case contains other mysteries as well. For one thing, the exit of U.S. and Canadian purse seine fleets is not directly explained by the framework. Even though fish seemed plentiful after 1976, these fleets disappeared from the Atlantic. There is no evidence in the ICCAT record to explain the move, or why Japanese, French, and Spanish fleets expanded from one ocean to another while the U.S. fleet made its move more permanent. Perhaps U.S. and Canadian captains just liked southern California better than New England, but it is more likely that Atlantic fishers were caught up in the vertical integration of the North American tuna fleet, which basically means that large, consolidated processors were buying up individually owned boats. Since all of the biggest canneries in the region were located on the West Coast of the United States, most of the vessels ended up there, too (Joseph 1983, 129). So the mystery can be explained, but not by using the vulnerability response framework.

In a way, the fishery-wide reduction in landings of Atlantic yellowfin that occurred in the mid-1990s was also mysterious. Because stock declines were halted, policy positions based on the framework held true. This can be seen in the rather lackluster, low-level conflict that has continued since 1993 (see table C.2 in appendix C for a summary of national policy positions for this case). Countries had gone as far as they would go, given the current conditions, and without additional pressures from escalating competition, they would go no farther. However, an explanation of the stagnation in the yellowfin fishery itself had to be drawn from outside sources and was post hoc. Both of these "mysteries" highlight the importance of bioeconomic factors in shaping international fisheries management and the need to consider such parameters when using the vulnerability response framework.

5

Skipjack Tuna

Skipjack is the only one of the three tropical tunas that is not targeted separately from the others. It is caught mainly by surface gears, such as purse seines or baitboats, and sold almost exclusively to canneries for processing. The main value of skipjack is not in the per-unit price, but in the great volume that can be extracted at relatively low cost. A major shift in skipjack production was initiated around 1990 by the adoption of fish aggregating devices, which were described in the introduction to part I. Clearly visible in figure 5.1, this technological revolution allowed landings of skipjack to rise rapidly from just over 114,000 tons in 1989 to more than 200,000 tons in 1991. Since then, reported landings of skipjack have declined, fluctuating around 150,000 tons from 1992 to 2001 (ICCAT 2007d).[1]

From the single-stock perspective used by ICCAT, this level of skipjack production can probably be maintained in the long run.[2] The SCRS has not been able to complete a full assessment, but it did suggest that levels of harvest above 175,000 tons are unsustainable. It has also noted several times that dead discards of skipjack increased when fishers started using FADs, so actual fishing mortality has been consistently higher than reported landings. Even so, scientists are fairly complacent regarding the health of the stock (ICCAT 1971–1994: 1993, 145; 1995–2007b: 1998, 37). If this were actually a single-species fishery, the vulnerability response analysis for skipjack would be quite simple; since the stock has not been even moderately overfished, no response would be expected from any country. Indeed, there have been no expressions of concern or proposals to directly manage Atlantic skipjack to date. However, because this is a mixed fishery, a cross-over response should be included in the analysis.

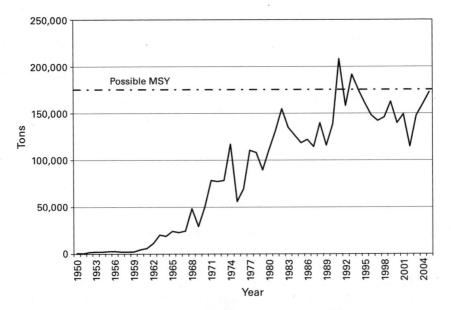

Figure 5.1
Reported and most recent estimate of MSY for Atlantic skipjack tuna. Source:
ICCAT 2007d; 1995–2007b: 1998, 38.

Adopting a mixed-fishery perspective has important implications for
the classification of countries, but will do little to alter the predictions
drawn from the vulnerability response framework. Specifically, all countries targeting any of the major stocks that are captured in the mixed
skipjack fishery will be identified in the classification exercise. This
includes countries with longline fleets that target adult yellowfin and
bigeye, as well as surface fleets that target all small tropical tunas. Otherwise, the predictions made in section 5.1 will not change. Highly and
low-flex, gradually vulnerable countries will still push for scientifically
based, well-enforced management, while mildly, moderately, and pre-
flex, gradually vulnerable countries will still use blocking or countermeasure tactics to prevent such changes. What is different is that the
analysis will track competition in multiple fisheries, and heavy competition over adult bigeye and yellowfin is expected to generate international
pressures for the regulation of the mixed fishery, which should in turn be
blocked or countered by countries that target skipjack.

The evidence presented may also seem somewhat unusual, largely because the stated positions of many countries do not even mention skip-

jack tuna. In fact, section 5.2 covers the discussion of management measures for bigeye tuna, which were adopted to prevent misreporting of juvenile yellowfin tuna in the late 1970s. What does this have to do with
skipjack? Both of these by-catch problems occurred in mixed fisheries
that primarily targeted skipjack tuna, and the proposed solutions would
negatively affect that fishery. Section 5.3 covers a later period in which
the negotiations are even more intense because the introduction of
FADs increased by-catches of juvenile bigeye and yellowfin at a time
when more vulnerable countries were under greater competitive pressures. In both sections there is a repetition of the pattern observed in the
descussions on yellowfin size limits recounted in the previous chapter;
moderately and gradually vulnerable countries block strong measures
by using weaker countermeasures. However, several kinks in this multistock approach to vulnerability response are also identified.

5.1 Vulnerability Response Predictions in the Mixed Skipjack Fishery

In order to simplify the analysis, the vulnerability response predictions
are divided into two periods, one from 1970 to 1989, when most surface
fleets were targeting yellowfin but catching skipjack incidentally (figure
5.2), and the other from 1990 to 2006, when FADs generated a shift

		Competitiveness	
		Low	High
Flexibility	Low	Highly Vulnerable **USA and Canada (post-1986), Portugal**	Moderately Vulnerable *Brazil*, Ghana, Morocco, **South Africa**, etc.
	High	Gradually Vulnerable *Japan (low-flex 1970-76 and 1980 (yellowfin))* USA and Canada (pre-1986; low-flex early 1970s **France and Spain (high-flex)**	Mildly Vulnerable *Korea and USSR*

Figure 5.2
Vulnerability response matrix for the mixed skipjack fishery (1970–1989). A list
ending in "etc." indicates that countries have been omitted from this summary
for ease of reference. Bold type, longlining countries; lightface, surface fleets;
italics, both types. See table B.4 in appendix B for a full list.

		Competitiveness	
		Low	High
Flexibility	Low	Highly Vulnerable **USA and Canada,** **Portugal (pre-1997)**	Moderately Vulnerable *Brazil*, Ghana, Morocco, **South Africa**, etc.
	High	Gradually Vulnerable **Japan (low-flex 1980** **(yellowfin) and 1990 (bigeye))** EC (France and Spain pre-1997; low-flex 1992)	Mildly Vulnerable **China, Korea, the** **Philippines, and Russia**

Figure 5.3
Vulnerability response matrix for the mixed skipjack fishery (1990–2006). A list ending in "etc." indicates that countries have been omitted from this summary for ease of reference. Bold type, countries targeting primarily adult bigeye and yellowfin; italics, both adults targeted using longlines and small tropical tunas using surface gear. See table B.5 in appendix B for a full list.

toward targeting skipjack rather than yellowfin (figure 5.3; ICCAT 1971–1994: 1992, 105). As recounted in chapter 4, two major shifts occurred in the initial period. First, the yellowfin fishery was fairly competitive until 1976, when new fishing grounds were discovered. Second, U.S. and Canadian distant-water purse seine fleets permanently exited the Atlantic in the early 1980s and were replaced in 1986 by coastal longliners targeting adult bigeye and yellowfin tunas.

These shifts are captured in figure 5.2, which presents an overview of the vulnerability response matrix for 1970 to 1989.[3] It includes countries that harvest mixed tropical tunas and those that may be indirectly affected by by-catch of juveniles. During this period, most of the surface (baitboat and purse seine) fleets were targeting small to medium-sized yellowfin and treating skipjack as an incidental though still useful part of the catch. Only Japanese and Ghanaian fleets in the Gulf of Guinea targeted skipjack specifically. Because the cost of strong measures—particularly conforming to the scientific advice on reducing catches of juvenile yellowfin and bigeye tunas—are distributed differently, countries may form coalitions based on gear type as well as vulnerability. Specifically, longlining countries (those in bold in the figure) may gang up on those with surface fleets (lightface type) in order to expand the productivity of their own fisheries. Countries with both types of fleets (in italics) will then be forced to choose sides.[4]

If this occurs as a political response to growing competition, then it may still fit into the rubric of vulnerability response. The logic is the same as that presented in chapter 2. By reducing fishing mortality on small yellowfin and bigeye, the rate of spawning and therefore the overall availability of adults should rise, (temporarily) decreasing competitive pressures for the more vulnerable fleets that target the adults. Furthermore, because longline fleets capture only large fish, they will not be negatively affected by regulations to protect small tunas, and such measures will appear to be "cheap" in political terms. With large concentrations of small fish in their harvests, surface fleets like those using purse seines and sometimes baitboats will be heavily affected by those same regulations but will not benefit. Satisfied by the status quo and threatened with high costs of regulations, these countries would resist protections for juveniles, just as any less vulnerable country would block or propose countermeasures for other curtailments of open access (see table 5.1).

However, if countries with longline fleets are only responding to competitive pressures, then they should not push for strong measures to reduce juvenile mortality unless there is evidence of such competition in the fisheries targeting adult yellowfin and bigeye. Given the assumptions of the vulnerability response framework, this means that targeted stocks must be in decline and the alternatives that impart flexibility to gradually vulnerable countries must be exhausted. The latter condition was met for the United States and Canada in the 1970s and Japan in 1980, but the primary requirement—stock decline—is not observed after 1976. Therefore no actions are expected from either highly vulnerable countries like Portugal nor low-flex, gradually vulnerable countries like Japan after that year. In fact, the shift of U.S. and Canadian fleets, which moved these countries from gradually to highly vulnerable categories around 1986, should make no difference in their behavior until bigeye becomes overfished in the early 1990s.

If any country challenges these expectations by proposing substantive management measures, pre-flex, gradually vulnerable France and Spain are expected to block or countermeasure any attempts at management in this period. Similarly, moderately vulnerable countries will strive to protect their access to all three stocks, as will mildly vulnerable countries. A few countries are in a more awkward position because they

Table 5.1
Overview of Vulnerability Response Predictions for the Mixed Skipjack Fishery (1970–1989)

Category	Countries	Predictions
Highly vulnerable	**United States and Canada (post-1986), Portugal**	Targeted stocks not overfished, no actions expected
Gradually vulnerable	*Japan (low-flex after 1970–76 and 1980, yellowfin)*	Targeted stocks not overfished, no actions expected
	United States and Canada (pre-1986; low-flex after early 1970s)	Targeted stocks not overfished, no actions expected
	France and Spain (pre-flex)	Block or countermeasure any substantive proposals
Moderately vulnerable	*Brazil*, Ghana, Morocco, **South Africa**, etc.	Block or countermeasure proposals that would limit development of their fleets; side payments or concessions required for cooperation
Mildly vulnerable	*Korea*, USSR	Block or countermeasure strong management; large side payments, threats, or concessions for cooperation

Notes: Countries in bold primarily target adult bigeye and yellowfin; countries in italics target both adults using longlines and small tropical tunas using surface gears. A list ending in "etc." indicates that countries have been omitted from this summary for ease of reference. See table B.4 in appendix B for a full list.

have fleets targeting both adults and juveniles. Most notable among these is Japan. While historically dominated by longlines, there was a large Japanese-owned fleet of baitboats that targeted skipjack in the Gulf of Guinea from 1962 to 1984. In the mid-1970s, this fleet, which was based in Tema, Ghana, produced more than 50% of Japan's Atlantic tuna landings by volume, but the longline catch was still more valuable, owing to higher prices for their catches. Countries like Brazil, South Korea, and the USSR also had both longline and surface fleets at the time and so might go either way in regard to management measures for the protection of juveniles (ICCAT 2007d).

The second period in the mixed skipjack case should be much more exciting than the first. As covered in chapter 3, the fishery targeting adult bigeye became overexploited in the early 1990s, so highly and low-flex, gradually vulnerable countries in this fishery will be pushing for strong management, including measures to reduce by-catch of juvenile bigeye in the surface fishery. Around the same time, the introduction of FADs increased the volume of undersized bigeye caught by purse seines and baitboats, making the problem of by-catch more acute. The dividing lines between countries with fleets targeting adults and those with fleets targeting small tunas are more clearly drawn in this period as well. Having given up its Tema fleet in the 1980s, Japan is firmly on the longline side, along with Russia, whose baitboat and purse seine fleets stopped targeting Atlantic tunas after the end of the Soviet Union (ICCAT 2007d).

This divide can be seen clearly in figure 5.3, which provides an overview of the vulnerability response matrix for the period from 1990 to 2006. It also shows that France and Spain, or the EC after 1997, entered into the low-flex phase of vulnerability in the early 1990s.[5] This was derived from the fact that a "mixed" version of the proxy described in section 2.5—their global landings of skipjack, bigeye, and yellowfin— flattened out around 1992. It is also important to note that France and Spain were the first to use FADs and were the largest producers of small tropical tunas in the Atlantic. Because the technology is so simple, FADs proliferated quickly, dissipating some of the initial advantage they provided. Still, neither yellowfin nor skipjack have been heavily depleted, so these countries are not expected to favor strong management (see table 5.2). Indeed, they are likely to block or countermeasure any policies proposed by more vulnerable countries with fleets targeting large bigeye and yellowfin.

The role of mildly and moderately vulnerable countries that target adult tunas is less straightforward. The second largest harvester of small tropical tunas in the Atlantic, moderately vulnerable Ghana will certainly oppose measures that would restrict those harvests. On the other hand, vulnerability response predicts that countries like South Africa, Morocco, and China should have little interest in measures to protect juveniles because they remain competitive even when the stock is declining. Nevertheless, there could be strategic benefits to siding with more vulnerable states on such measures, not least of which would be the possibility of increased leverage on quota sharing for bigeye (see chapter 3). In fact, the cases will show that such cross-linkages are prevalent in this mixed-fishery context, so much so that the vulnerability response predictions are proven to be incorrect at times.

Table 5.2
Overview of Vulnerability Response Predictions for the Mixed Skipjack Fishery (1990–2006)

Category	Countries	Predictions
Highly vulnerable	**United States and Canada, Portugal (pre-1997)**	Propose strong management measures; evince increasing willingness to pay
Gradually vulnerable	**Japan (low-flex after 1980) (yellowfin) and 1990 (bigeye)** EC (France and Spain pre-1997; low-flex after 1992)	Propose strong management measures; evince high and increasing willingness to pay Pre-flex, blocking or countermeasures; low-flex targeted stocks not depleted; no actions expected except to block or countermeasure any externally imposed policies
Moderately vulnerable	*Brazil*, Ghana, Morocco, **South Africa**, etc.	Block or countermeasure proposals that would limit development of their fleets; side payments or concessions for cooperation
Mildly vulnerable	**China, Korea, the Philippines, and Russia**	Block or countermeasures to strong management; large side payments or concessions for cooperation

Notes: Countries in bold primarily target adult bigeye and yellowfin; countries in italics target both adults using longlines and small tropical tunas using surface gears. A list ending in "etc." indicates that countries have been omitted from this summary for ease of reference. See table B.5 in appendix B for a full list.

5.2   Pre-1990 Bigeye Size Limits

It was difficult to decide where to put the section on bigeye size limits. One would think that they should go in the bigeye case study, but these regulations were not adopted just for the protection of bigeye tuna. By the mid-1970s, it was clear that many fleets had begun reporting undersized yellowfin as bigeye to circumvent the 1972 size limit on yellowfin tuna (see chapter 4). Much of the impetus for the bigeye size limit was to curtail such misreporting. So why not include this section in the case on yellowfin tuna? For one thing, the bigeye size limit has a much larger impact on the mixed surface fishery than the surface fishery target-

ing schools of yellowfin alone. In addition, the dynamics of these negotiations presage later management of the FAD fishery for mixed tunas.
For all these reasons, this section seems to fit into this case more than either of the others.

The misreporting of undersized yellowfin as bigeye tuna was first
raised in the 1974 meeting of panel 4 in their discussion of the bigeye
stock assessment (ICCAT 1971–1994: 1975, 85). Two years later it
came up again in the SCRS assessment of yellowfin and in discussions
in panel 1 (ICCAT 1971–1994: 1977, 75). In panel 4, which was responsible for bigeye until 1997, France floated the idea of a size limit on
bigeye equal to the one adopted for yellowfin in order to remove the incentive to misreport. Japan also expressed concern about the impact of
catches of small bigeye on landings of adults, but did not propose any
measures (p. 61). The SCRS was instructed to look into the effects of
such a regulation and in 1977 reported that it would benefit the bigeye
fishery as a whole, although it might also limit the total catch of skipjack
(ICCAT 1971–1994: 1978, 146). Nonetheless, several contracting parties held out against a size limit on bigeye, including the United States,
Japan, and Korea, so the decision was postponed another year (pp. 42–
43).

After 2 years, much debate, and several votes, the commission adopted
the 3.2-kg size limit for bigeye tuna (ICCAT 2007a, rec. 79-1). The
SCRS had created a special Working Group on Bigeye Size Regulations
in 1978, which confirmed its earlier conclusions about the usefulness of
such a measure. The working group felt that a matching size limit on
bigeye would not only help to counter the misreporting problem with
yellowfin but would also be good for the bigeye stock, which had come
under increasing pressure from both purse seines and longlines during
the decade (ICCAT 1971–1994: 1979, 147). That year, a joint meeting
of Panels 1 and 4 was held to tackle the issue. With eight votes for and
four against, a proposal for the 3.2-kg size limit with a 15% tolerance
was sent to the full commission for approval (see table 5.3 for a list of
votes). Since it had not obtained a simple majority, procedural questions
were raised and the recommendation was sent out for a vote by mail.
The measure was finally adopted in 1979 after another vote in which all
contracting parties but one were either in favor or abstained.

The evidence on vulnerability response in this period is not very clear.
We might expect that major purse-seining countries like France and
Spain might propose a size limit as a countermeasure to more stringent

Table 5.3
Record of Votes on 1978 Size Limit for Bigeye Tuna

For	Against	Abstain
Brazil	Ghana	Canada
Cuba	Japan	South Africa
France	Korea	United States
Ivory Coast	USSR	
Morocco		
Portugal		
Senegal		
Spain		

Source: ICCAT 1971–1994; 1979, 68.

regulations, but proactive proposition of countermeasures is not pre-dicted by the framework. Looking at the data more closely, an interest-ing observation can be made. Not all surface fleets would be equally affected by the bigeye size limit. The majority of bigeye less than 3.2 kg are caught in the Gulf of Guinea, a small area when compared with the geographic dispersion of European fleets (ICCAT 1971–1994: 1982, 121). In fact, by passing this lower size limit early on, European purse seiners could forestall the imposition of a higher, possibly more appro-priate limit, much as in the yellowfin case. So this move may indeed have been a tactic to reduce competition, but its timing was not predicted by the framework as operationalized.

Recognizing their dependence on fishing in the Gulf of Guinea, the be-havior of Japan, South Korea, and Ghana is understandable.[6] Harvests by their fleets would be deeply curtailed by the bigeye size limit. It is not surprising that when the size limit came up for extension in 1979, Ghana again chose to vote against the measure and declared its intention to raise a formal objection (ICCAT 1971–1994: 1980, 50). On the other hand, Japan chose to abstain on that vote, as did the USSR. The reasons for this change are not clear, although the USSR had low by-catches of bigeye, so its 1978 position is more mysterious. What is clear is that Jap-anese vessel owners had decided to divest themselves of the Tema fleet. After 1978, harvests by this fleet declined rapidly, disappearing by 1984 (ICCAT 2007d).

Outside of this Gulf of Guinea dichotomy, the behavior of ICCAT members makes little sense in a vulnerability response context. Russia's blocking of the measure in 1978 may have been due to misunderstanding the impacts of the measure, but its delegation also may have been responding to diplomatic overtures or any number of other influences. South Africa was in the same position, but its delegation chose to abstain rather than vote against the measure. Similarly, abstentions by the United States and Canada in 1978 could be explained by their ambivalence regarding the as-yet underexploited bigeye stock or worries regarding the effect of the size limit on their purse seine fleets.

The positions of South Korea and Japan are particularly interesting. Both claimed to oppose the measure because they were not convinced of the effectiveness of a 3.2-kg size limit for the slow-growing bigeye (ICCAT 1971–1994: 1979, 67). Furthermore, these two countries stated that they wanted a higher benchmark and better enforcement, which would make their position one in favor of strong management (ICCAT 1971–1994: 1979, 144). Yet, even if we accept that these countries were more concerned with their (admittedly much larger) longline fleets than their baitboats in the Gulf of Guinea, the framework does not predict the timing of this policy position. As with France and Spain, Japan was jumping the gun. Bigeye was not even close to being overexploited at this time, and after 1976 the commission also realized that the same was true for yellowfin. Therefore no countries were expected to favor strong management at the time when the bigeye size limit was adopted. Moreover, firmly in the mildly vulnerable category at the time, South Korea was not expected to want any management, let alone strong measures. Undisclosed side payments could explain the Korean position, but the timing issue remains.[7]

It is quite clear that the vulnerability response framework was trumped by some other force in this period. Too many countries expressed unexpected policy positions. Nevertheless, looking specifically at this mismatch in timing, it is possible that several of the proxies used to gauge the level of competition in the fishery were inaccurate. Specifically, Japanese longline fleets may indeed have been in poor economic straits and —in spite of the fact that their global harvests of tropical tunas had not peaked—Spain and France may have been closer to their low-flex phase than indicated by that proxy.[8] Landings data show that all three of these countries were losing ground to developing countries in this period, and ICCAT records mention that Spanish and French fleets had already moved back and forth from the Pacific and Indian Oceans several times.[9] Therefore they may have been less flexible and more beleaguered than the state of the stock suggests. Theoretically, it is possible that these fleets were already suffering, particularly because the low prices from increasingly integrated canneries and high costs of distant-water fleets would result in low net revenues.

In addition to these economic considerations, the framework also missed an important change in global institutions related to the oceans —the proliferation of claims to 200-mile exclusive economic zones that occurred in the mid-1970s. When this transpired, countries with distant-water fleets suddenly had to negotiate for access to fishing areas that had once been open to all (Joseph 1983, 131–133). Gradually vulnerable fleets like those of Japan, France, and Spain were temporarily impeded by the new regime, and so these countries may have been forced to engage in international management of tropical tunas earlier than they otherwise would have. As yet, the causes of the observed deviations from vulnerability response in this period are still speculative, but these institutional shifts, a failure of proxies for the level of competition, and the strategic benefits of the proposed actions are all good candidates.

5.3   Post-1990 Fish Aggregating Devices

Like the yellowfin size limit, the bigeye size limit was never effective. Ghana continued to make statements against the measure for several years and then fell silent as its continued overharvests of small fish went unnoticed. The commission was quiet on the matter of the mixed tropical tuna fishery until 1991. As described earlier, FADs came into use in the Atlantic in 1990, drastically altering the composition of purse seine and baitboat landings. The first discussion of this was limited to technical questions from developing countries (ICCAT 1971–1994: 1992, 52). Things heated up a bit in talks on bigeye in 1992 when Ghana argued against the size limits once again, proposing the prohibition of FADs as a better regulatory option. The now highly vulnerable United States agreed with Ghana, but Spain, which had recently started using FADs, said this claim had no scientific foundation.

Similar but expanded discussions occurred from 1994 to 1997. As expected from longline countries, low-flex, gradually vulnerable Japan began to take on a leadership role, along with the highly vulnerable United States and Canada. In 1995, the Japanese delegation introduced a proposal that would mandate new conservation measures on purse seines to reduce their harvests of undersized fish, including a limit on the use of FADs. It would also require specific answers from the SCRS regarding the impact of FADs on bigeye tuna and reiterated the need for compliance with the 1979 size limit for that stock. A major purse seine country, Spain countered with its own proposal for a nonbinding resolution that asked ICCAT members to reduce the total catch of bigeye below MSY and authorize more scientific research on the effect of FADs. Also home to a large purse seine fleet, France supported Spain. Taiwan and Portugal, both of which were targeting adult bigeye with longlines, supported Japan. The highly vulnerable United States supported both proposals, but the Spanish won the day (ICCAT 1995–2007a: 1996, 148–150).

Japan did not give up. In 1996 it again pushed for strict implementation of size limits on yellowfin and bigeye, along with limits on fishing and consideration of time-area closures on FADs. France and Spain (EC), countries that had introduced the technology in the Atlantic, still wanted to postpone action until better scientific advice was available (ICCAT 1995–2007a: 1997, 108–109). No real management measures were adopted, but the commission agreed to a countermeasure proposed by Spain that required members to institute national observer programs for their tropical tuna fisheries, with 25% coverage of vessels fishing off FADs and 5% coverage on all other vessels. This information was to be used by the SCRS to evaluate alternative methods to avoid catching small bigeye and yellowfin (ICCAT 2007a, rec. 96-1).

ICCAT itself did not take further measures on FADs in 1997, but France and Spain chose to implement a voluntary time-area closure on the use of fish aggregating devices by their purse seine fleets in the Gulf of Guinea from November through January of 1998. In its statement on the measures at the 1998 meeting of ICCAT, the EC[10] pointed out that the decision was based on the best data possible and that it would be enforced by 100% observer coverage. It also noted that by complying with the closure, French and Spanish boat owners would forgo about 17,500 tons of tropical tunas, representing gross revenues of about US $19 million (ICCAT 1995–2007a: 1999, 137). Much as in the case of bigeye tuna size limits, these two gradually vulnerable countries chose to lead the initiative on time-area closures rather than follow. However, this time, with their fleets firmly in the low-flex phase and considerable pressure for strong management from more vulnerable countries (in the bigeye fishery), the timing of this countermeasure fits well with vulnerability response expectations.

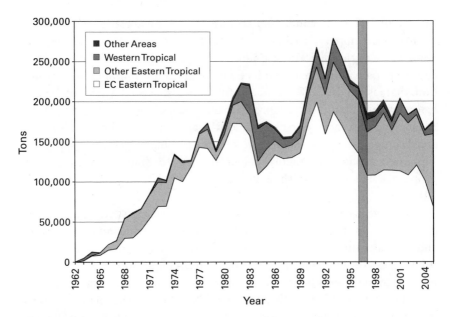

Figure 5.4
Reported landings of Atlantic tropical tunas by purse seines. Source: ICCAT 2007d.

In 1998, the SCRS found that the voluntary time-area closure had led to a reduction in landings of undersized tunas in the area. Although the major impact was on catches of skipjack, the SCRS estimated that the yield per recruit could increase by as much as 10% for yellowfin and 13% for bigeye, owing to lower mortality on small fish (ICCAT 1995–2007a: 1999, 137). As figure 5.4 shows, there was a precipitous decline in purse seine landings by France and Spain during the initial period of the time-area closure. It is interesting that this downturn was a continuation of a trend that had begun in 1993 as biological depletion and increasing competition from other fleets undermined the European market share. Also, losses by all EC fleets, including purse seines and baitboats, from 1996 to 1997 were around 30,000 tons, which was almost twice the losses France and Spain attributed to their closures in the Gulf of Guinea (ICCAT 2007d).

Given the apparent success of their voluntary moratorium, at the 1998 meeting of the commission the European Community proposed a similar but mandatory time-area closure on all purse seine fleets using FADs in the Gulf of Guinea. It also expressed hope that the commission would decide to limit longline effort targeting bigeye. While many other states welcomed the proposal, some believed that this was an insufficient response to the problem of high juvenile mortality on tropical tunas. Japan was one of the first countries to express its reservations, but Ghana was the most adamant contracting party, demanding a full 36-month closure of the FAD fishery in order to collect data on fishing without FADs in the Gulf of Guinea. Incidentally, the Ghanaian fleet was composed mainly of baitboats that did not use FAD technology at the time and were limited to near-shore waters in the gulf. The observer from Mexico—a longline country—supported the Ghanaian perspective, but in the end the EC proposal was adopted (ICCAT 1995–2007a: 1999, 140).[11]

The next year, the SCRS could report more fully on the effects of both the voluntary and mandatory moratoria on FADs in the Gulf of Guinea. Landings of undersized bigeye were down from an average of 70% to an average of 55% of the total catch of the species (ICCAT 1995–2007b: 2000, 27). On the other hand, a larger percentage of undersized yellowfin were being caught, up from about 50% to just over 66% of landings. Fewer small yellowfin were taken during the time-area closure, but higher effort throughout the rest of the year caused the annual landings of undersized yellowfin to increase (ICCAT 1995–2007b: 2000, 17). In spite of these negative repercussions on yellowfin, the commission chose to extend the moratorium indefinitely and to apply it to baitboats as well as purse seines. Furthermore, the 1999 tropical tunas recommendation required that noncontracting parties observe the time-area closure in order to deal with growing landings by flag-of-convenience states like Panama and the NEI fleets (ICCAT 1995–2007a: 2000, 167; 2007a, rec. 99-1).

There are several ways in which the gradually vulnerable EC benefited from its seemingly altruistic leadership on management measures for surface fisheries targeting small tropical tunas. First, the time-area closures were much less costly than a full implementation of the bigeye and yellowfin size limits would have been. Also, these measures gave the EC something to point to whenever countries with longline fleets accused surface fleets of not doing their part for sustainable management of bigeye and yellowfin. Third, in line with the underlying logic of the vulnerability response framework, the time-area closures on the Gulf of Guinea might have allowed the EC to gain back some market share by having a disproportionate effect on their biggest rival. Whereas Ghanaian fleets are confined to the Gulf of Guinea, EC fleets are active all over the tropical Atlantic.[12] The 1999 extension of the closure legally excluded the second largest producer of small tropical tunas in the Atlantic from utilizing this highly effective fishing technology for 3 months of the year. Finally, the 1999 measure also helped curb nonmember production in the area.[13]

There was one important flaw in the logic of the time-area closure. Although it did circumvent objections from powerful moderately vulnerable countries like Brazil and Venezuela, enforcing the closure on Ghanaian vessels was more of a challenge. By defecting and beginning to use FADs themselves, the Ghanaian fleet could fill in the gap left by European forbearance, substantially increasing their own catches. By 2002, noncompliance was so blatant that the European Community began to put heavy pressure on Ghana and other countries with fleets fishing in the Gulf of Guinea in contravention of the moratorium.[14] Furthermore, the EC also brought up the fact that vessels of 23.6 meters, just below the 24-meter exemption level, had been proliferating in recent years, undermining the effectiveness of the moratorium (ICCAT 1995–2007a: 2004, 179).

This helps to explain why the EC shifted its position in 2004, proposing to reduce the duration of the closure to 1 month and applying the measure to all surface vessels, even those fishing without FADs (ICCAT 2007a, rec. 04-1). It also sheds light on recent EC attempts to remove the size limit for bigeye tuna that France and Spain eagerly proposed in the late 1970s (ICCAT 1995–2007b: 2005, 162; 2006, 192–194). Ghana never complied with either regulation, so benefits to the EC from reduced competition were never realized. Now that the commission is developing stronger monitoring and enforcement mechanisms, the EC faces the prospect of punitive measures for its own noncompliance. This and increasing pressures from Japan, the United States, and Canada provide strong incentives to get rid of the size limit, preferably replacing it with a less costly alternative.

While extremely interesting, the maneuvers of the EC in regard to juvenile tropical tunas are not specifically predicted by the vulnerability response framework. Certainly, countermeasures were one of the tactics that countries with surface fleets were expected to use to divert diplomatic pressure from more vulnerable countries in the bigeye fishery. However, the nature of the countermeasures instituted by the EC goes well beyond the expectations of the framework. The time-area closure on the Gulf of Guinea was thinking outside the box on a grand scale that could not have been predicted without a much broader knowledge of the geopolitical implications of the regulation.[15]

Similarly, the reactions and responses of other countries were close to the vulnerability response predictions, but not quite right. Highly and low-flex, gradually vulnerable countries (Canada, Japan, and the United States) wanted more and better protection for juveniles, but were forced to acquiesce. This fits with the framework, but the behavior of moderately vulnerable countries in particular diverges from the general expectation that countries in each category will form coalitions to protect their common interests. Only Ghana, the moderately vulnerable country that would be most negatively affected by the closure, spoke out against it. Other moderately vulnerable countries supported the measure. It did not threaten their ability to develop their fleets—Ghana already had one of the largest fleets targeting tropical tunas in the Atlantic—and so there was no common ground. A more detailed set of vulnerability categories might help to tease out such differences among moderately vulnerable fleets, but it would also complicate the approach.

5.4   Summary

The case of the mixed skipjack fishery has proven to be very useful, not because the predictions were particularly precise, but because it enabled the identification of inaccuracies that pointed the analysis in new directions. Not all inconsistencies could be explained, especially in the negotiations over the bigeye size limit in the late 1970s. Nevertheless, that portion of the case was particularly constructive. It showed that the proxies for competitiveness and flexibility used throughout this text may not always be adequate. The theory should be developed further so that adjustments can be made based on different economic scenarios, such as high quantity–low price production versus low quantity–high price production. At the same time, the scope of analysis needs to be expanded to account for shifts in metanorms, such as the extension of coastal jurisdiction that occurred throughout the 1970s. This global transformation had major impacts on distant-water fleets and could be expected to generate substantial turbulence in political responses.[16]

Both periods in this case also showed that tactical moves can also cause policy positions to deviate from the predictions of the framework. Management options that are inexpensive for one group but costly for another seem to trigger earlier interventions than would otherwise be expected. The evidence on bigeye size limits is not conclusive because of confounding by the factors described earlier, but the disproportionate impacts of the regulation probably provided impetus for its espousal and subsequent adoption. This penchant for proposals that force others to pay the costs of management is more clearly demonstrated in the second period. European Community maneuvers to establish a time-area closure in the Gulf of Guinea fit into the countermeasure tactics predicted by the vulnerability response framework, but the secondary effect of the closure—substantial reductions in the fishing effort legally exerted by the EC's biggest competition in the Atlantic—was unexpected.

As noted in chapter 2, these tactical interactions cannot be predicted without much greater input of information on situational factors. Here, the most notable strategic element was the geospatial distribution of fleets relative to a particular biological hot spot where small fish were more prevalent. The SCRS and other scientific committees often include such information in their evaluations of policy options, so it would be possible to incorporate such data into the original formulation of policy predictions. Other information on strategic factors, such as the scheduling of negotiations on particular species, might also be included if the framework is operationalized more formally through computational modeling techniques. These would enable the exploration of thought experiments or counterfactuals, as well as the generation of more accurate historical expectations.[17]

For those of us who do not count Java or C++ among our language skills, the simple vulnerability response framework remains useful. In the first period of this case, it generated the right questions, and in the second period the predictions ranged from fairly accurate to near misses. Highly and low-flex, gradually vulnerable countries in the bigeye fishery pushed for strong measures, which included protections for juveniles by the surface fishery. Faced with regulations that would be costly, less vulnerable countries with surface fleets blocked these attempts by proposing the time-area closure as a countermeasure. Again, the choice of countermeasure, and the heavy impact it would have had on the Ghanaian fleet if it had implemented the closure, could not be predicted. Nevertheless, the framework helped to make sense of national policy positions in a complex, multispecies fishery.

Even more important is the aggregate pattern that emerges in this case.[18] Management of skipjack resembles that of yellowfin much more closely than bigeye. The bigeye case marches smoothly from inactivity to concern to conflict to cooperation and then its aftermath. In contrast, the yellowfin and bigeye cases flounder between conflict and inactivity, with a little concern in between. Management measures are adopted, but they turn out to be ineffective at multiple levels. Neither size limits nor time-area closures brought incidental harvests of juvenile yellowfin or bigeye down to the levels recommended by the SCRS or mandated in the measures themselves.[19] Nor was conflict among ICCAT members actually alleviated by these half-measures. As soon as depletion became evident, either directly in the yellowfin fishery or indirectly in the mixed skipjack fishery, conflict reemerged.

Billfishes

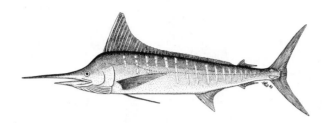

White marlin
(Tetrapturus albidus)

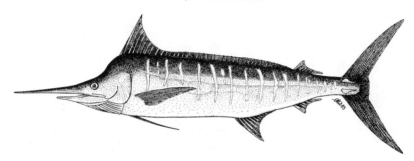

Blue marlin
(Makaira nigricans)

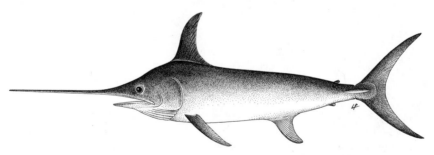

Swordfish
(Xiphias gladius)

Source: United Nations Food and Agriculture Organization

II

Billfishes

Few people are acquainted with the generic term "billfish," but members of the billfish family are iconic in many cultures around the world. Perhaps the most well-known reference to a billfish in English-speaking culture is Hemingway's description of the battle between man and marlin in his famous work, *The Old Man and the Sea*. The three cases in this section will cover vulnerability response for two stocks of Atlantic swordfish (*Xiphias gladius*) as well as two other billfish species, blue marlin (*Makaira nigricans*) and white marlin (*Tetrapturus albidus*).[1] Like bigeye management, the northern swordfish case illustrates how vulnerability response can lead to delayed but strong management. On the other hand, the southern swordfish case shows how exogenous factors can make an early response seem stronger than it actually is. Finally, the marlins case shows how vulnerability response changes with the introduction of noncommercial interests.

Reported landings for Atlantic swordfish, blue marlin, and white marlin are displayed in figure II.1. Swordfish is the largest component in the catch by far, reaching a maximum of more than 50,000 tons in the late 1980s. Landings of swordfish have been consistently much larger than landings of blue marlin and white marlin combined. In fact, since U.S. and Canadian bans on the sale of swordfish ended in 1977, reported landings quickly began to rise, reaching a peak of more than 50,000 tons in 1988.[2] Landings of marlins were highest in the 1960s, peaking at around 8,000 tons for blue marlin and 5,000 tons for white marlin. Recent landings of these species have fluctuated around 3,000 and 1,000 tons, respectively.

Swordfish is the only commercially targeted species of billfish in the Atlantic, and it is one of the most economically important fishes managed by ICCAT. Mainly targeted by longlines, it is usually sold as fillets

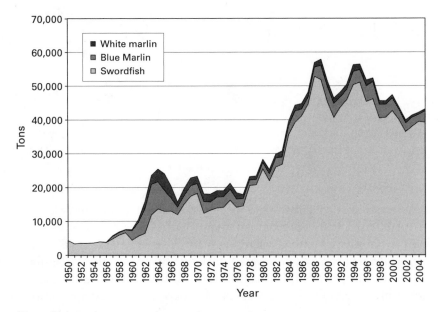

Figure II.1
Reported landings of Atlantic billfishes managed by ICCAT. Source: ICCAT 2007d.

or steaks in affluent countries for high prices (see figures II.2 and II.3). Incidental catches of juvenile swordfish have been a problem in the fishery since 1990, and the species is a common by-catch in other longline fisheries, especially those targeting bigeye tuna. Other billfish, particularly blue marlin and white marlin, have almost no commercial value but are considered highly desirable by recreational fishers. Marlins have received some attention from the commission because they are caught incidentally by longliners targeting swordfish, bigeye tuna, and other HMS stocks.[3] Otherwise known as by-catch, these chance landings of marlins can have significant impacts on the interplay of vulnerability response for these fisheries.

As figure II.2 shows, international prices for marlins have been fluctuating around US $2,000 per metric ton for most of the past decade.[4] Much lower than swordfish prices, the per-unit value of marlins is still on a par with commercially important highly migratory species such as skipjack and yellowfin tunas (FAO 2007c). The difference between these two kinds of species is that the tunas are extremely abundant, schooling fishes that can be caught cheaply and in very large quantities, whereas

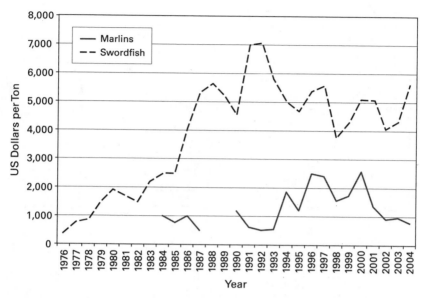

Figure II.2
Real per-unit value of world billfish landings. Source: FAO 2007c.

marlins are relatively rare and expensive to catch (ICCAT 1995–2007b: 2004).[5] Tuna fishers can make up for the low prices of the stocks they target by producing huge harvests at a low per-unit cost. Anyone wishing to target marlin would pay much more for every unit landed and receive about the same price for their output. Therefore, although marlin can be sold internationally, it is not profitable to target them specifically in the Atlantic.[6]

The landings of swordfish reported in figure II.1 come from three different management areas, which are thought to reflect the existence of three distinct swordfish stocks (see figure II.4). Separated at latitude 5° N, the Atlantic is divided into the northern management area and southern management area. The northern stock is thought to have an MSY of around 14,000 tons and the best estimate for the southern stock is approximately 17,000 tons. Little is known about the third stock, which is located in the Mediterranean, but the SCRS believes that current catch levels are sustainable in the short run (ICCAT 1995–2007b: 2006, 86, 93; 2007, 86).[7] There is a small amount of mixing between these management areas. For instance, some swordfish from the northern stock may move into the southern or Mediterranean zones, contributing to

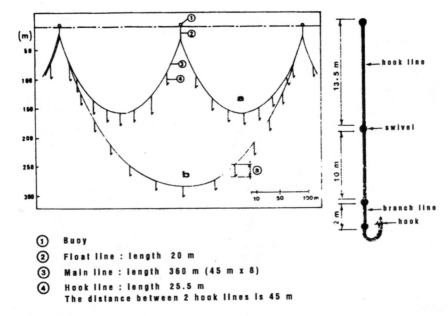

Figure II.3
Diagram of longline gear used to target (a) swordfish and (b) bigeye tuna. Long-lines are made up of thousands of baited hooks (4) that hang from a main line (3), which is in turn suspended from the float line (2) and attached to buoys (1) that keep the whole thing from being dragged to the bottom. Different species are targeted at different depths; swordfish are found closer to the surface than bigeye tuna, so fishers targeting the latter send their gear deeper by increasing the length of the mainline (and number of hooks) between the two buoys. Because the gear is passive or nonselective, some swordfish are caught on lines targeting bigeye. The reverse also occurs, but is less frequent. Source: United Nations Food and Agriculture Organization.

the spawning populations there. Movement in the opposite direction also occurs, but the commission has decided that there is sufficient biological separation to warrant independent management.

Atlantic stocks of blue marlin and white marlin are even smaller than those of Atlantic swordfish. Although there is evidence that marlins should also be divided between southern and northern management areas, assessments are carried out as if each species is a single stock in the Atlantic. Given current patterns of fishing effort, the most recent assessments place the approximate MSY for blue marlin at between 1,000 and 2,400 tons and the MSY for white marlin somewhere between

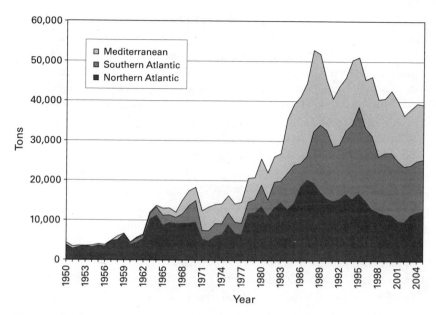

Figure II.4
Reported landings of Atlantic swordfish stocks. Source: ICCAT 2007d.

600 and 1,320 tons (ICCAT 1995–2007b: 2007, 70). Like most highly migratory species, blue marlin are also found in the Indian and Pacific Oceans, but white marlin exists only in the Atlantic. Therefore, if the Atlantic stock collapses, the species will be in danger of extinction.

It is also important to note that fishing mortality on marlins could easily be higher than that shown in figure I.1. By-catch is often discarded back into the ocean, either because of a government prohibition on landings or to make room for a more valuable species. Unless there is an observer on board, there is considerable incentive for fishers to exclude these discards from catch statistics. This is just one of the issues that make by-catch management more difficult than the regulation of targeted stocks. Chapter 5 provided an example of such potential pitfalls, but the chapters in this part will delve much more deeply into the components of by-catch management—both cross-fishery by-catch like the small tunas and noncommercial by-catch like marlins.

First, chapter 6 shows how vulnerability response predictions were fairly accurate for the northern stock of Atlantic swordfish, even though direct competition over the resource was geographically limited. This generated strong management, including the same types of catch limits and enforcement mechanisms adopted for bigeye tuna, along with measures to reduce by-catch of swordfish in the bigeye fishery. Next, the southern swordfish case is used to show how increasing direct competition can lead to relatively early management. Like the yellowfin tuna case in chapter 4, management of southern swordfish was not strong at first, but is now aligned with scientific advice because of upward revisions of stock assessments rather than changes in governmental concern.

Finally, chapter 8 looks at the impact of noncommercial interests in the marlins case. Atlantic blue marlin and white marlin are covered together because they are managed together, not just by the same panel, but in the same resolutions and recommendations. The observed management of by-catch like marlins violates the commercial interest assumption of the vulnerability response framework, so a modification to include noncommercial interests is indicated. That said, it is interesting to note that the measures adopted for marlins are neither sufficient to rebuild these stocks nor well enforced and therefore the ultimate outcome still falls in line with the overall vulnerability response expectations.

6

Northern Swordfish

Northern swordfish was one of the first stocks to be commercially exploited on a large scale in the Atlantic. Industrialization of the fishery began in the late 1800s, was briefly interrupted by the two world wars, but then picked up rapidly as fishers appropriated the latest technologies. After another temporary reduction in fishing effort in the 1970s—owing to fear of mercury poisoning from swordfish in the United States and Canada—production quickly rebounded (Johnston 1965, 72). The fishery reached a historical high in the late 1980s and then declined because of stock depletion and shifts of effort to alternative sources of revenue. International prices for swordfish peaked in the early 1990s and have since declined, owing to the increasing availability of substitutes.[1] However, northern swordfish remains a commercially and culturally important stock in Europe and North America.

The SCRS has determined that maximum sustainable yield for this stock is around 14,000 tons. As figure 6.1 shows, landings of northern swordfish were above the lower boundary of MSY estimates from 1978 to 1997 and were exceptionally high in the late 1980s. By 1996, the SCRS estimated that the biomass of northern Atlantic swordfish was down to 58% of the level that would support MSY (ICCAT 1995–2007b: 1997, 66).[2] A combination of lower prices and strong international regulations led to a steep reduction of landings from 1999 onward. In 2006, the SCRS estimated that the biomass of northern Atlantic swordfish had rebuilt to approximately 99% of that which would support MSY (ICCAT 1995–2007b: 2007, 86).[3] This concurrence of strong ICCAT management followed by stock rebuilding closely resembles the pattern observed in the bigeye case (chapter 3), but there are some important distinctions between the two.

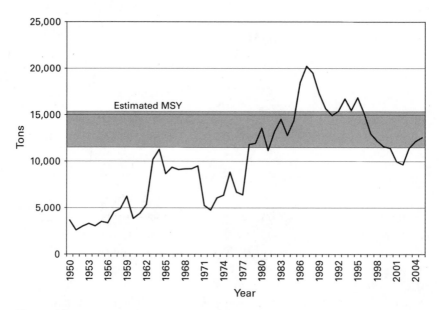

Figure 6.1
Reported landings relative to most recent estimate of MSY for northern Atlantic swordfish. Sources: ICCAT 2007d; 1995–2007b: 2007, 86.

Like the bigeye case, northern swordfish has a fairly continuous management history. Since the formation of ICCAT, there has not been a sudden increase in the availability of the stock as in the yellowfin case or the proliferation of radical new technologies as in the mixed skipjack fishery. This makes the prediction of policy positions in section 6.1 relatively simple because there is no need to derive different expectations for multiple periods. Nevertheless, the evidence in the case has been divided into two sections in order to highlight a critical breaking point in the negotiations. Section 6.2 covers the initial discussions regarding northern swordfish. It is full of disagreements and conflicts among countries. Eventually negotiations reach a turning point and the commission is able to adopt strong management in the form of a comprehensive rebuilding plan, as recounted in section 6.3.

6.1 Vulnerability Response Predictions

Situated between the two continents, the northern swordfish fishery has been dominated by European and North American fishers for centuries.[4]

		Competitiveness	
		Low	High
Flexibility	Low	<u>Highly Vulnerable</u> Canada and USA Portugal and France (pre-1997)	<u>Moderately Vulnerable</u> Brazil, Morocco, Trinidad and Tobago, etc.
	High	<u>Gradually Vulnerable</u> EC (Spain pre-1997; low-flex 1995)	<u>Mildly Vulnerable</u> By-catch: Japan, Korea, China, etc.

Figure 6.2
Vulnerability response matrix for northern swordfish. A list ending in "etc." indicates that countries have been omitted from this summary for ease of reference. See table B.6 in appendix B for a full list.

Most harvests of northern swordfish are still landed by Canada, the United States, and Spain. Landings by other countries have remained relatively stable except for those of Japan, which virtually disappeared in 1999, and small increases by Taiwan and China in the late 1980s to early 1990s. Still, direct competition has escalated with the slow decline of the stock. With fewer fish available and effective fishing effort at around twice the level that would produce maximum sustainable yield, the struggle to stay solvent in the northern Atlantic swordfish fishery became more and more difficult under open access (ICCAT 1995–2007b: 1997, 66). Moreover, international competition has also increased as production of swordfish in other oceans has risen steeply over the past three decades (FAO 2007b).

Of the fleets targeting the stock, only that of the EC features both high costs of production and high flexibility, placing it in the gradually vulnerable category in figure 6.2. With their large-scale, distant-water longliners, EC member countries, especially Spain, have been able to expand their swordfish fleets in spite of high labor costs and stock-specific biological depletion that might otherwise have resulted in a serious loss of market share.[5] Therefore the EC, or Spain prior to 1997, can be expected to forestall management measures that would reduce its landings of northern Atlantic swordfish until alternative stocks have also been seriously diminished. The low-flex period for this gradually vulnerable fleet starts around 1995, when their global production of swordfish hit its first major peak.[6] From that year on, the EC (Spain) is expected to increasingly work for strong management measures (see table 6.1).

The other big producers that directly target northern Atlantic swordfish are the United States and Canada. These countries have low flexibility because their longline fleets cannot operate more than 200 miles from port. Although fishing is not the most lucrative career in developed countries like the United States and Canada, operating costs are still high compared with most of the rest of the world. Given this combination of high costs and few alternatives, the United States and Canada are highly vulnerable to both biological depletion and outside competition. Portugal and France also fall into this category, but their interests were subsumed under Spain's when the EC replaced its individual members at the ICCAT negotiating table starting in 1997.[7] As highly vulnerable countries, these four can be expected to push for early, strong regulation of northern Atlantic swordfish. This stock is the staple of U.S. and

Table 6.1
Overview of Vulnerability Response Predictions for Northern Swordfish

Category	Countries	Predictions
Highly vulnerable	Canada and United States, Portugal and France (pre-1997)	Always propose strong management measures; evince increasing willingness to pay the costs of management with stock decline
Gradually vulnerable	EC (Spain pre-1997; low-flex after 1995)	Blocking or countermeasures prior to 1988, quickly switching to strong management after. Increasing willingness to pay for management also in this period
Moderately vulnerable	Brazil, Morocco, Trinidad and Tobago, etc.	Blocking or countermeasures on any proposals that limit development of their fleets; side payments or concessions for cooperation
Mildly vulnerable	By-catch: Japan, Korea, China, etc.	Blocking or countermeasures on any proposals that reduce catches of targeted stocks

A list ending in "etc." indicates that countries have been omitted from this summary for ease of reference. See table B.6 in appendix B for a full list.

Canadian longline fisheries, so they are expected to show higher levels of concern than in the bigeye case. Furthermore, the United States has more power in this case than in any of the tropical tuna fisheries because it lands a large percentage of the total harvest.

Japan, the fourth largest producer of northern Atlantic swordfish, is located in the mildly vulnerable position in figure 6.2, along with Taiwan and China. Swordfish are a by-catch for fleets from these countries that target bigeye tuna (ICCAT 1995–2007b: 2004, 101).[8] Since they do not directly target northern swordfish, these countries are not economically vulnerable to either depletion of the stock or increasing competition in this area. Without such vulnerability, the model predicts that the Japanese will resist any ICCAT regulations on northern swordfish that would negatively impinge on their bigeye harvest. While Japan does not catch large amounts of northern swordfish compared with the United States or the EC, it is a powerful country with multiple linkages in other fisheries (Bergin and Haward 1996, 1). More vulnerable countries will have to make significant concessions to Japan to gain its cooperation on northern Atlantic swordfish.

Finally, there are some developing countries that have interests in the management of northern Atlantic swordfish, including Brazil, Morocco, and Trinidad and Tobago.[9] Fewer moderately vulnerable countries are able to harvest northern swordfish than southern swordfish or any of the tropical tunas. Nonetheless, this set of countries has a common preference for maintaining the availability of highly migratory species for developing coastal countries.[10] As in the cases from part I, moderately vulnerable countries can be expected to resist management on northern swordfish until concessions are made that recognize their rights of access. However, their behavior in this fishery differs because of the magnitude of concern. Fewer developing countries have less to gain on northern swordfish than on bigeye tuna; this is expected to weaken their resolve, facilitating the use of side payments to satisfy individual countries and obtain consensus.

6.2   Disagreement over Distribution

Scientists in ICCAT's Subcommittee on Research and Statistics began expressing concern about Atlantic swordfish in 1979 (ICCAT 1971–1994: 1980, 150). Responding to this advice, highly vulnerable Canada, the United States, and Portugal began to push for better data collection and analysis (ICCAT 1971–1994: 1980, 77–78). Their efforts culminated in two scientific workshops on swordfish in 1987 and 1988. These confirmed that the northern stock was at or above full exploitation (ICCAT 1971–1994: 1989, 141). The following year, the United States proposed that the commission limit effort targeting northern swordfish to current levels. In this it was strongly supported by Canada, but other countries, especially the gradually vulnerable Spain (EC) and mildly vulnerable Japan were against taking such a step when the science was still uncertain (ICCAT 1971–1994: 1990, 78, 89–90).

The commission remained relatively quiescent throughout the 1980s. The United States and Canada did frequently express concern, but there was no worsening of news from the SCRS until 1989. It is interesting that highly vulnerable countries took domestic action to manage their fishers during this time. Canada put its own restrictions on effort and size at landing within its exclusive economic zone (EEZ) as early as 1980. By 1989, the United States was developing a domestic management regime to reduce catches in its EEZ (ICCAT 1971–1994: 1981, 74; NMFS 1989, 5). It is likely that these national measures increased the incentives for these highly vulnerable countries to ensure that other fleets would also be required to reduce their harvests of northern Atlantic swordfish (DeSombre 2005).

That same year, the SCRS stated that current fishing effort could not be maintained in the long run and recommended that the commission should at least prevent any further increases. The United States proposed just such a measure, and was again supported by Canada. South Korea, Japan, and Spain all opposed the measure. They cited lack of scientific information as their main rationale. In 1990, the SCRS was more certain of its results. The scientific committee advised that rebuilding the stock to optimal levels would require a greater than 50% reduction in current catches. As an intermediary measure, the commission was encouraged to reduce fishing mortality to below 1988 levels and establish measures to protect juvenile swordfish.

In the face of continuing contention over catch reductions, in 1990 ICCAT members adopted a size limit for all swordfish, as per a proposal by Canada. However, they were unable to take action on a U.S. proposal to cut catches of northern swordfish by 30% from 1986–1989 levels. Together, these measures would approximate the scientific advice, but the U.S. proposal was opposed by less vulnerable states (ICCAT 1971–1994: 1991, 86–87). Instead, the commission chose to limit catches of all

Atlantic swordfish to 1988 levels, a year of peak production in the northern fishery (see figure 6.1). Countries whose fleets harvested the northern stock as a by-catch to other fisheries were given a 10% allowance by total weight for incidental catches of swordfish. It was believed that this would keep their landings at current levels (ICCAT 2007a, rec. 90-2).

The 1990 recommendation was adopted by consensus, but Spain and Morocco both abstained. Gradually vulnerable Spain maintained that size limits were sufficient protection for the stock, and moderately vulnerable Morocco expressed the first concerns over the rights of developing coastal states in this context (ICCAT 1971–1994: 1991, 35). It is interesting that a large portion of the Spanish fleet started moving south in 1991, temporarily reducing harvests in the northern Atlantic (ICCAT 1971–1994: 1991, 214–217). In spite of this, reported landings in 1993 showed that effort was still increasing in the north and that the total catch that year was actually greater than the replacement yield for the stock. The SCRS also reported that total fishing mortality was likely to be higher than records showed, owing to unreported dead discards of small fish. This is a common result of management measures, such as the size limit that had been adopted in 1990 (ICCAT 1971–1994: 1994, 217).

By 1992, the SCRS found that the biomass of northern swordfish was between 84 and 95% of that which supports MSY (ICCAT 1971–1994: 1993, 172). In response, the highly vulnerable United States proposed a measure that would ask most countries to reduce their catches by 10% and would limit by-catches to 5% of the targeted harvest. Mildly vulnerable Japan, a major by-catch country, opposed the measure. Next, the United States and Spain proposed a measure that would require countries with small harvests of northern swordfish to reduce their catches to 1991 levels, including by-catch fleets. It also required that all live swordfish by-catch be released, rather than kept and sold, as was the common practice. Not surprisingly, Japan, Canada, and other countries with relatively low harvests rejected the measure (ICCAT 1971–1994: 1993, 100–101).

In 1994, new estimates put the biomass of swordfish in the northern Atlantic at 68% of that which would support MSY, and fishing effort was at approximately 180% of the maximum sustainable level (ICCAT 1995–2007b: 1995, 170). This represented a rapid and significant decline in the availability of the stock. At the same time, because of increasing outside competition, the value of the species had dropped from a high of almost US $8,000 per ton in 1992 to just over US $5,000 per ton in 1994.[11] Combined, these trends put serious pressures on many of the fishers targeting swordfish in the northern Atlantic. As would be expected, the hardest hit were highly vulnerable fishers in the United States and Canada. They faced relatively high costs of production, were unable to shift their effort to more abundant southern stocks, and were more strictly regulated than their counterparts elsewhere. In fact, the value of U.S. swordfish landings was cut in half over the period, falling from a peak of almost US $40 billion in 1988 to just over US $15 billion in 1994 (NMFS 2007).

Although international competition hit coastal fleets much harder than those that could move to more abundant waters, falling prices and declining availability were making the fishery less profitable for all. By 1994, most of the contracting parties that targeted swordfish in the northern Atlantic realized that serious action would have to be taken to ensure future access to the stock. As had happened before, countries lined up in support of several different countermeasures, seeking to reduce overall catches while minimizing the regulated cuts to their domestic fisheries. This time around, it was a case of major versus minor fishing states. Canada, Portugal, and Japan led an effort to place the heaviest burden of catch reduction on the fleets that had historically been responsible for the vast majority of catches in the area: those harbored by the United States and Spain.[12] In response, these two countries countered that catch reductions should be spread equally across all users of the resource. All five of these contracting parties could agree that entry or escalation of effort by fleets whose catches had been very small in the past should be prohibited until the stock was in better condition.

When the 1994 negotiations were finalized, everyone got what they wanted in terms of quota allocation, but the resulting total allowable catch was considerably higher than scientists had recommended. At the time, replacement yield was estimated to be about 13,800 tons, so ICCAT would have to limit catches to at least that level to prevent further decline in the biomass of the stock (ICCAT 1971–1994: 1994, 217). The recommendation that was finally adopted by the commission gave the four main direct producers in the area—Canada, Portugal, Spain, and the United States—national quotas that would add up to 13,200 tons in 1995 and 11,800 tons in 1996.

If those four had been the only countries exploiting the resource, then this would be sufficient. However, moderately vulnerable fishing fleets could increase landings by at least 1,600 tons and remain in compliance with the recommendation. This accommodation was made after Brazil, Uruguay, and Venezuela expressed their concerns about limits on developing coastal states. In addition, Japan was given a by-catch allowance of 8% of its total bigeye landings that would further contribute to the fishing mortality of northern Atlantic swordfish. At a minimum, landings would be 7% over replacement yield in the first year of the plan and less than 3% below in the second year (ICCAT 2007a, rec. 94-14).[13] Apparently governmental concern was not yet high enough to result in strong management.

Biomass and effort indicators estimated in 1995 showed that the biological situation had gotten slightly worse for northern swordfish. That year, the SCRS made it clear that the size limit adopted in 1990 had not been implemented and would not have prevented the overexploitation of the stock even if it had been enforced (ICCAT 1995–2007b: 1996, 69). Highly vulnerable Canada proposed the TAC that the SCRS recommended for rebuilding the stock, but this was opposed by the United States and Spain, among others. Instead, they proposed that a few other tasks should be accomplished to lay the groundwork for a rebuilding plan for northern swordfish.

First, they passed a resolution that instructed the SCRS to develop a recovery program for the stock (ICCAT 2007a, res. 95-9).[14] Also, in preparation for future negotiations the commission adopted a binding recommendation to allocate the percentage shares that would be applied to TACs from 1997 onward. The major fishing countries all received specific portions of future total allowable catches based on an agreement that was worked out in closed-door meetings (see table 6.2). All other

Table 6.2
1995 Division of Northern Atlantic Swordfish Catches

Country	Share of TAC (%)
Canada	10.00
Japan	6.25
Portugal	7.50
Spain	41.25
United States	29.00
Others	6.00

Source: ICCAT 2007a, rec. 95-11. TAC = total allowable catch.

countries wishing to harvest swordfish in the northern Atlantic would have to share 6% of whatever catch limit might be established. Although a few moderately vulnerable countries protested their small quota allocation, they were not yet unified and would not block consensus in the face of powerful members like the United States and Spain (ICCAT 1995–2007a: 1996, 150–154).[15]

Because the 1994 effort limits were insufficient and unenforced, the biomass of northern swordfish continued to decline over the next 2 years.[16] By 1996, the stock was at 58% of the level that would produce maximum sustainable yield, while fishing effort had risen to more than twice the intensity that would result in MSY (ICCAT 1995–2007b: 1997, 66). Although the SCRS was able to reach these conclusions, it could not develop the rebuilding scenario options that the commission had requested the year before. Instead, it informed members that the replacement yield for the stock had declined to 11,360 tons and that total catch would have to be limited to around 10,000 tons to ensure that the stock would return to MSY levels. Because of uncertainty in the analysis, the SCRS also noted that there was a slight chance that catches as high as 12,000 tons would serve to rebuild the stock (ICCAT 1995–2007b: 1997, 68).

Having already adopted sharing arrangements, the major countries with fleets targeting northern swordfish had only to agree on the total allowable catch in 1996. Three separate proposals were made for the stock. First, Canada proposed setting the TAC at 10,000 tons for the next 3 years, 1997, 1998, and 1999. While agreeing that action needed to be taken quickly, Spain felt that SCRS advice was overly pessimistic and proposed that the TAC be set at 14,000 tons for the next 2 years. This was unexpected because Spain reached the "low-flex" phase of vulnerability in 1995, so the framework's prediction would be for strong management. In between these two viewpoints, the United States proposed that the TAC be set at replacement yield, a second deviation from the framework's predictions for a highly vulnerable country (ICCAT 1995–2007a: 1997, 128). After private consultations and a special redrafting session, these contracting parties presented a joint proposal that would set the 1997 TAC at replacement yield and then gradually reduce it by increments of 300 tons for each of the next 2 years, as shown in table 6.3 (ICCAT 2007a, rec. 96-7).[17]

One other effort limitation for northern swordfish was adopted during the 3-year period of the 1996 scheme. In 1997, the major fishing states

Table 6.3
1996 Three-Year Plan for Northern Atlantic Swordfish

Year	TAC (tons)
1997	11,300
1998	11,000
1999	10,700

Source: ICCAT 2007a, rec. 96-7. TAC = total allowable catch.

noted that fleets from the "others" category had taken more than twice their 6% share of the TAC in 1996. This caused concern because it meant that in order to comply with the 1996 regulation, the "others" would need to drastically cut their effort levels in 1997. To ensure that this would happen, Canada drafted a proposal that would require all countries fishing from the others category to reduce their catches of northern Atlantic swordfish by 45% from 1996 levels for the next 2 years (ICCAT 1995–2007a: 1998, 168). Also, any fishing country that had landed less than 100 tons in 1996 was prohibited from increasing its harvests over 1996 levels. Bermuda, represented as an overseas territory of the United Kingdom, expressed strong reservations about the proposal and was granted its own quota of 28 tons for 1997 (ICCAT 2007a, rec. 97-6).[18]

The effectiveness of the 1996 recommendation on total allowable catches was somewhat mixed. Reported landings exceeded the TAC by about 11% for each of the 3 years of the program. Both major and minor fishing states contributed to these overages, and dead discards of small fish continued as well (ICCAT 1995–2007b: 1999, 94; 2000, 88; 2001, 88). On the other hand, by 1999, estimates of the biomass of northern swordfish had improved slightly—from 58 to 65% of the level that would support MSY. Fishing effort was down as well, but it was still 34% higher than the level that scientists estimated would produce maximum sustainable yield (ICCAT 1995–2007b: 2000, 87). ICCAT regulations could be only partly credited for this reduction since some longliners had independently chosen to move out of the northern Atlantic, while others began targeting different species, such as tunas and sharks (ICCAT 1995–2007b: 1999, 92). Still, this was a preliminary step toward strong management and the first indication that highly vulnerable states were finally willing to make sacrifices to win the cooperation of their less vulnerable counterparts.

6.3   Reaching a Rebuilding Plan

As the 1996 3-year plan on northern swordfish drew to a close in 1999, the SCRS informed the commission that recent low levels of fishing mortality would need to be maintained over a longer period of time to rebuild the stock to levels that would support MSY. Scientists estimated that an annual TAC of 10,700 tons would rebuild northern swordfish in about 15 years. They also warned that even a 10% overage on that TAC might undermine the rebuilding process. This time, competing proposals were introduced by the United States, the EC, and Japan. Seeking to restore the stock more quickly, the highly vulnerable United States proposed to set the TAC at 10,000 tons per year for 10 years. The EC preferred a more flexible approach, accepting a TAC at 10,700 tons, but only for 3 years, which fits nicely into the low-flex predictions for this fishing entity. Facing losses in its bigeye catches that were due to restrictions on swordfish by-catch, mildly vulnerable Japan proposed that the TAC be set at replacement yield, 11,700 tons (ICCAT 1995–2007a: 2000, 187–190).

As in the 1996 agreement, a compromise was reached through side negotiations and a joint proposal was put to panel 4. Major fishing countries agreed to establish a 10-year rebuilding plan, but specific TACs were set for only the first 3 years of the program. Again, a gradual reduction was factored into the scheme, with total allowable catches set as shown in table 6.4. A portion of the TAC for each year was set aside as a dead discards allowance. It was from this allotment that reductions were taken. The allowance was divided between the United States (80%) and Canada (20%), the only two countries that actually reported dead discards to the commission. Since discards counted directly against those

Table 6.4
1999 Rebuilding Plan for Northern Atlantic Swordfish

Year	TAC (tons)	Dead discards allowance (tons)
2000	10,600	400
2001	10,500	300
2002	10,400	200

Notes: TAC = total allowable catch; dead discards are fish that are caught, killed, and then discarded back into the ocean.
Source: ICCAT 2007a, rec. 99-2.

countries' quotas, they were effectively the only countries whose catches were set to decrease after the year 2000 (ICCAT 2007a, rec. 99-2).[19] These highly vulnerable states had chosen to give up some of their national quotas to bridge the gap between their own policy positions and the proposals of less vulnerable states for much higher TACs.

Japan's consent to the 1999 rebuilding plan for northern swordfish was obtained through a quota swap with the EC. Bigeye tuna, Japan's targeted species, had moved north in recent years, increasing their by-catch of swordfish in the northern Atlantic. In 1996, Japanese landings of northern swordfish jumped by about 450 tons to 1,494 tons and remained rather high until the year 2000 (ICCAT 1995–2007b: 2004, 96). Under the 1994 recommendation, Japan was granted a by-catch clause and could land up to 8% of the weight of its total catches in swordfish, so this increase was not a big problem for it, linked as it was to increased effort on bigeye in the area (ICCAT 2007a, rec. 94-14). However, under the 1995 and 1996 recommendations on catch distributions, Japan was allotted a specific portion of TAC, which amounted to around 700 tons annually for 1997–1999 (ICCAT 2007a, rec. 96-7).[20] In each of these years, Japanese landings exceeded their national quota by 400–600 tons (ICCAT 1995–2007b: 2004, 96, SWO-table 1).

This overage was a serious problem for the Japanese, who regard themselves as leaders in international fisheries management and were loath to lose face over it. Reputation is a practical issue at ICCAT. Non-compliance by Japan on swordfish could be used as a shield by countries that did not wish to comply with regulations on stocks that are targeted by Japanese fleets, like bigeye tuna.[21] In addition, at the behest of highly vulnerable countries, ICCAT had set up international compliance enforcement mechanisms for northern swordfish in 1996. Like the trade-based enforcement adopted for bigeye tuna, these measures carried the threat of sanctions if Japan could not find some way to deal with its overages (ICCAT 2007a, rec. 96-14). Foreseeing these difficulties, the mildly vulnerable Japanese negotiated some extra breathing room for themselves. In the 1996 catch limit recommendation, Japan was granted 5 years in which to adjust its catches. Most countries were only given 1 year to correct any overages (ICCAT 2007a, rec. 96-7).

Nevertheless, by 1999, Japanese overages added up to about 1,600 tons, more than 2 years' worth of its proposed quota under the new rebuilding plan (ICCAT 1995–2007b: 2004, 96, SWO-table 1; 2007a, rec. 96-7, 99-2). Even with a second 5-year grace period, there was no way that Japan could correct such a large excess catch on its own. To assist Japan, and convince it to agree to the 1999 rebuilding plan, the EC arranged for an "emergency relief" transfer of its own quota for the northern stock. In return, Japan agreed not to block consensus on the rebuilding plan and also transferred some of its quota for southern Atlantic swordfish back to the EC (ICCAT 1995–2007a: 2000, 177).[22] To prevent such large overages in the future, Japan instituted a new policy in 2000 that required all longline vessels in its Atlantic fleet to discard every swordfish, dead or alive.[23] This brought their total catches well under their quota allotment of 636 tons for 2001 and 2002.[24] With the added help of transfers from the United States in those years and north–south swaps thereafter, Japan has managed to come into compliance with regulations on northern swordfish without negatively affecting its landings of bigeye tuna.

When it came time to negotiate the total allowable catch for the next 3 years of the plan in 2002, ICCAT contracting parties were encouraged by some positive signs from the fishery. Owing in part to the effort restrictions adopted by ICCAT—along with independent shifts of the longline fleet away from northern Atlantic swordfish and relatively high recruitment around the turn of the millennium—the biomass of the stock had rebounded to 94% of that which would produce maximum sustainable yield. Furthermore, fishing effort was down to 75% of the MSY level (ICCAT 1995–2007b: 2003, 94). These optimistic results came with the caveat that overall catches had been underestimated in recent years as a result of illegal, unregulated, and unreported fishing, as well as underreported dead discards of the fish in both commercial and by-catch categories (ICCAT 1995–2007b: 2002, 93; 2003, 96). More information had become available on IUU fishing from monitoring measures included in the 1995 Swordfish Action Plan and the creation of a statistical document program for swordfish in 2001.

Because of these improvements in stock biomass, in 2002 the SCRS revised its estimate of a suitable total allowable catch upward to 14,000 tons. It advised that if annual catches were sustained at this level from 2003 to 2009, the northern Atlantic swordfish stock had a 50% chance of rebuilding to the level that would support MSY in 10 years. However, it also noted that a lower TAC would rebuild the stock more quickly and with more certainty (ICCAT 1995–2007b: 2003, 96–97). Some contracting parties were eager to take advantage of the gains that resulted from their restraint in previous years. Others, especially the highly vulnerable United States and Canada, were somewhat skeptical and pushed to keep the TAC at a lower level for a few more years to ensure that the rebuild was as robust as possible. After some discussion, the EC presented a proposal to set the TAC at 14,000 tons annually for 2003, 2004, and 2005 (ICCAT 2007a, rec. 02-2).[25] In addition, Japan was permitted to count up to 400 units of overage in the north against double that amount of quota in the south (rec. 00-3).[26]

The issue of allocation came up again as well. Even though the total allowable catch had increased significantly, small fishing states in the others category were receiving less from this recommendation than they had in 1999. The agreement differed from the previous sharing arrangement because the others category was divided into specific allocations for minor fishing states (ICCAT 2007a, rec. 02-2).[27] Mexico, Venezuela, and other coastal countries that had joined together as the amorphous Group of 18 in 1998 vociferously expressed their dissatisfaction with the portions they were allotted (ICCAT 1995–2007a: 2003, 233–234).[28] Having recently experienced severe contention over allocation of other stocks like southern swordfish and bigeye tuna, more vulnerable fishing states were well aware of the inaction that such discord could precipitate. In order to advance discussions on the matter, a small working group was formed to bring together the concerned parties. Finally, a compromise was reached in which the quota for those in the others category was increased from 835 to 1,185 tons. The dissenters did not get all that they wanted, but more vulnerable states did give up small portions of their quotas to appease these moderately vulnerable countries (ICCAT 1995–2007a: 2003, 233–234).

With a new 3-year plan in place, there was little discussion on northern swordfish from 2003 through 2005. The commission chose to postpone the next scientific assessment and the negotiations of new measures until 2006 (ICCAT 2007a, rec. 03-3, 04-2). By then, little had changed in the fishery. The SCRS was happy with the current regulations and the state of the stock, so it recommended staying the course. The chair of panel 4, who happened to be the head delegate from Japan, proposed a measure that would do just that, with the addition of some extra breathing room by extending the period of adjustment from 1 to 2 years. That would mean that all contracting parties would have 2 years in which to reduce their harvests to make up for an overage or increase their harvests to recoup any underage (ICCAT 1995–2007a: 2007, 170; author's files).

However, two other issues arose in the 2006 discussions. One was the large underharvest by the U.S. fleet in the preceding years. Owing in part to a shift in the geographic location of the stock as well as other factors, U.S. fishers had not used up all of their quota under the 2002 rebuilding plan. In fact, they had underages of more than 1,000 tons per year for each year of the plan. Even so, the United States was unwilling to permanently transfer any of its quota to other countries, probably based on the expectation that its fishery would return to higher levels of production once the stock shifted back to U.S. waters (author's files).

The second issue in 2006 consisted of demands from moderately vulnerable members and new entrants, most of which were also developing coastal states. Countries like Morocco and Mexico wanted larger quota allocations, and new members like Belize, Senegal, and the Philippines wanted their own piece of the pie. The commission accommodated these demands by adding some of the U.S. underages to the TAC of 14,000 tons per year that was set for 2007 and 2008. It also reduced the Taiwanese quota by about 40 tons (ICCAT 2007a, rec. 06-02). Table 6.5 shows which countries gained from this maneuver; all fit into either the mildly or moderately vulnerable categories.

As long as the United States continues to catch much less than it has been allocated, the 2006 compromise will keep harvests near the MSY level of 14,000 tons. On the other hand, if the U.S. fleet makes a comeback, harvests in 2007 and 2008 will be up to 1,345 tons above MSY. Hypothetically, this will not reduce the stock since the fish that the United States didn't catch in the 2003–2006 period are still out in the Atlantic. However, when the time comes to renegotiate national quotas in 2008, the commission will face considerable discord without the extra cushion of U.S. underages. Now that northern swordfish is back up to MSY levels, highly and gradually vulnerable members of the commission are much less willing to give up the access rights they worked so hard to establish.

6.4 Summary

At first glance, the northern swordfish case seems quite straightforward, particularly when compared with the winding narratives in the yellowfin and mixed skipjack cases. For the most part, the vulnerability response predictions held true.[29] The highly vulnerable United States and Canada were leaders, almost always proposing stronger management measures.

Table 6.5

Quota Allocations from the 2003 (applied 2004–2006) and 2006 (applied 2007 and 2008) Management Plans for Northern Swordfish

Contracting Parties	2006	2007	2008
European Community	6,718	6,718	6,718
United States	3,907	3,907	3,907
Canada	1,348	1,348	1,348
Japan	842	842	842
Other Contracting Parties			
Morocco	335	850	850
Mexico	110	200	200
Brazil	50	50	50
Barbados	25	45	45
Venezuela	85	85	85
Trinidad and Tobago	125	125	125
UK (Overseas Territories)	35	35	35
France (St. Pierre and Miquelon)	35	40	40
China	75	75	75
Senegal		400	400
Korea		50	50
Belize		130	130
Philippines		25	25
Ivory Coast		50	50
St. Vincent and the Grenadines		75	75
Vanuatu		25	25
Others			
Taiwan	310	270	270
Total allowable catch	14,000	15,345	15,345
U.S. Underages		1,345	1,345
Adjusted total expected catch		14,000	14,000

Notes: Shaded column = past allocation; unshaded columns = proposed allocation; numbers in bold indicate an increase in quota; numbers in italics indicate a decrease in quota. "Underages" refers to quota not harvested in previous year(s).
Sources: ICCAT 2007a, rec. 03-03, 06-02.

They also evinced increasing willingness to pay by giving up some of their own quotas to reach agreements in 1994 and after. Similarly, the EC blocked or countered strong measures until after 1995, when it was in the low-flex phase of vulnerability. Moreover, in 1999 and beyond, the EC also engaged in quota swaps to ensure that strong measures were adopted. In contrast, moderately vulnerable countries were given concessions and additional quota allocations when they raised concerns about coastal states' rights. Japan was able to leverage its position as a mildly vulnerable by-catch country to gain major dispensations from the United States and the EC.

Two minor deviations from these expectations stand out in the case. Both occurred in the mid-1990s. The first was the U.S. reluctance to accept the lower, rebuilding catch limit recommended by the SCRS in 1995 and 1996. Highly vulnerable, the United States was expected to propose "strong" measures, which would mean going with the lower number. The second was the proposal of an even higher catch limit by the EC, which had just reached the low-flex phase of vulnerability and should also prefer measures that lined up with scientific advice. For the EC, it is possible that the proxy for determining the low-flex phase was off a bit, especially because it was so close to the transition point (1995). A possible explanation of the U.S. position can be found in the inception of a swordfish fishery off the coast of Florida around the same time. While this move does not fall into the definition of flexibility used in the predictions, it does suggest that the U.S. fleet may have been less vulnerable than the bulky proxy of distant-water capacity indicated. In both cases, a more nuanced proxy might have improved predictions, although it would also have complicated an already complex analysis.

On close inspection, a few other problems with the vulnerability response framework can be identified. Both have to do with confounding variables and both have been observed in previous cases. One is the element of external competition over northern swordfish. As presented in chapter 2, the framework only uses stock abundance as a proxy for competitiveness. However, the economic conditions noted in section 6.2 amplified direct competition over northern swordfish and may have heightened political response. The same can be said of the other cases. A broader conceptualization of competitiveness could make this element of the framework more accurate.

A second concern is the behavior of Japan. The Japanese did obtain side payments for their cooperation, but it's not clear how much their status at ICCAT and other cross-issue interactions might have amplified their willingness to comply with by-catch reduction strategies. Consider the Ghanaian response to the Gulf of Guinea closure described in chapter 5. The country simply chose not to comply with this by-catch measure. As a powerful member of the commission, Japan could have done the same, but it chose to negotiate. This is an extremely important aspect of adaptive management that is not really captured in the vulnerability response framework. Like other tactical elements, this one would be exceptionally difficult to encompass without much more intensive use of information. One would need to know, not just the reputational values of Japan, but also those of Canada, the United States, the EC, and all 40+ other members of ICCAT, as well as their relationships with each other and the timing of management for all stocks within the commission's jurisdiction.

In spite of these deficiencies, an important pattern emerged from the northern swordfish case. It mirrors the bigeye tuna case in that the same five periods were observed, in the same order and in the same relation to scientific advice. In both cases, little discussion was recorded until the stock first became depleted (inactivity). This period was followed by expressions of concern around the time that the SCRS said the stock was at full exploitation and outright conflict as the stock continued to decline. However, when moderate depletion was observed, highly and low-flex, gradually vulnerable countries finally started negotiating hard for strong management. In this period of accord, rebuilding was observed although it cannot be completely attributed to ICCAT management. With that rebuilding came increased conflict as less vulnerable countries increased their demands, while more vulnerable countries stubbornly resisted changes. This certainly is not a complete pattern of adaptive governance, but its repetition provides substantial food for thought.

7

Southern Swordfish

The timeline for management of southern swordfish is much shorter than for northern swordfish, but just as tumultuous. However, unlike all of the other cases, it appears that ICCAT members reached agreement on strong measures for southern swordfish before the stock became even moderately overexploited. At first, this seems to violate one of the assumptions of the vulnerability response framework—that states will satisfice rather than optimize, leading to a delayed response in management. However, a closer look reveals that it was changes in scientific advice that created the illusion of response in this case. That said, there is evidence which suggests that the delayed response on northern swordfish preceded a slightly more proactive response for southern swordfish. There can be several explanations of such path dependence or historical determinism within a vulnerability response context. The southern swordfish case provides an opportunity to examine learning and other temporal elements of adaptive governance.

Intense commercial fishing of the southern stock of Atlantic swordfish did not start until the late 1980s, about the same time that the commission began serious discussions regarding management measures for the depleted northern stock. This change in fishing pressure can be seen clearly in figure 7.1, which shows reported landings of southern swordfish in the Atlantic. By 1990, harvests were well above the earliest estimates of MSY, which varied around 13,500 tons. After the 1995 peak in production, the SCRS found that southern swordfish was at about 99% of B_{MSY} and that fishing mortality was about 124% of the level that would produce MSY (ICCAT 1995–2007b: 1997, 66). However, there was considerable uncertainty in the SCRS analysis. This is depicted in figure 7.1 by the exceptionally wide range placed on estimates of MSY from 1996 to 2001. Conflicting data on catch per unit effort (CPUE)

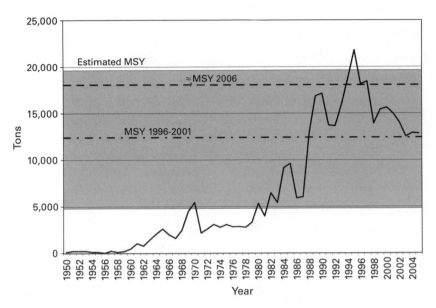

Figure 7.1
Reported landings of southern Atlantic swordfish relative to MSY. Sources:
ICCAT 2007d; 1995–2007b: 1997, 66; 2007, 86.

from target and by-catch fisheries led the SCRS to abandon these calcu-
lations in 2002. Although this CPUE divergence continues, assessments
in 2006 suggested that the MSY for southern swordfish is actually
around 17,000 tons and the stock itself is quite healthy.

Although there was such a large shift in the perception of stock abundance between 2001 and 2006, the vulnerability response predictions
recounted in section 7.1 are made without any temporal break. This is
because changes in scientific advice on southern swordfish did not reflect
an expansion of the fishery, but simply better data and methods. In the
analysis of the evidence (sections 7.2–7.4), divergences from those predictions are considered in light of the failure of scientific advice as a
proxy for competition. As in other single-period cases, this evidence is
split into several sections to highlight turning points in the negotiations.
Each section covers a different period of conflict. In section 7.2, countries
were so adamant regarding their claims on the resource that no agreement could be achieved. Section 7.3 shows how the commission was
later able to reach an agreement on access rights, but only because of an
upward revision of SCRS advice. This pattern is repeated in a more

		Competitiveness	
		Low	High
Flexibility	Low	<u>Highly Vulnerable</u> USA	<u>Moderately Vulnerable</u> Brazil, Namibia, South Africa, Uruguay, etc.
	High	<u>Gradually Vulnerable</u> EC (Spain pre-1997; low-flex 1995)	<u>Mildly Vulnerable</u> By-catch: Japan, Korea, China, etc.

Figure 7.2
Vulnerability response matrix for southern swordfish. A list ending in "etc." indicates that countries have been omitted from this summary for ease of reference. See table B.7 in appendix B for a full list.

drawn-out set of negotiations in section 7.4, and the evidence from all three of these periods is summarized in section 7.5.

7.1 Vulnerability Response Predictions

Owing to geographic location, the stock of southern Atlantic swordfish is more open to exploitation by developing coastal states than its northern counterpart (ICCAT 1971–1994: 1994, 217). Therefore there are many moderately vulnerable fleets engaged in the fishery and they are expected to show much greater concern about the exploitation of this stock. The vulnerability response matrix in figure 7.2 lists some of the most active countries in the moderately vulnerable category, but a more complete list is available in appendix B, table B.7, and this expectation applies to them all. A comparison of the predictions for each case will show that the basic expectation for moderately vulnerable countries does not change (table 7.1). They will block or countermeasure any proposals that impinge on the potential development of their fleets. Like the bigeye case, the high number of moderately vulnerable fleets with coastal zones adjacent to this stock should amplify the power of national responses relative to the northern swordfish case.

In contrast, there is only one highly vulnerable country in this fishery. A portion of the U.S. fleet has been targeting swordfish off the coast of Florida since 1996. Some of its harvests are taken just below the boundary between the southern and northern stocks (ICCAT 2007d). Because

Table 7.1
Overview of Vulnerability Response Predictions for Southern Swordfish

Category	Countries	Predictions
Highly vulnerable	United States	Always propose strong management measures; evince increasing but limited willingness to pay the costs of management
Gradually vulnerable	EC (Spain pre-1997; low-flex after 1995)	Blocking or countermeasures prior to 1995, quickly switching to strong management after 1995. Increasing willingness to pay for management also in this period
Moderately vulnerable	Brazil, Namibia, South Africa, Uruguay, etc.	Blocking or countermeasures on any proposals that limit development of their fleets; side payments or concessions for cooperation
Mildly vulnerable	By-catch: China, Japan, Taiwan, etc.	Blocking or countermeasures on all strong management unless substantial side payments

Notes: A list ending in "etc." indicates that countries have been omitted from this summary for ease of reference. See table B.7 in appendix B for a full list.

of its economic position, the United States is expected to espouse strong management of southern swordfish, particularly measures that coincide with scientific advice and are well enforced. Furthermore, its willingness to pay for such measures will increase with depletion of the stock. However, because U.S. landings of southern swordfish are a low percentage of the total Atlantic swordfish harvests, its willingness to pay may not be as high as that observed for the northern stock.

Distant-water Spanish longlines began targeting southern swordfish in 1988, placing Spain (or the EC post-1997) in the gradually vulnerable category. Because most of the Spanish fleet is distant water, the growth of its southern landings was sudden and drastic. From 0 tons in 1987 and previous years, the Spanish captured more than 4,000 tons of southern swordfish in 1988 and more than 7,000 tons in 1989. After that, harvests of the southern stock leveled off. Global harvests of swordfish by Spanish fleets peaked in the mid-1990s, so it is officially considered to be low-flex in 1995.[1] Therefore, Spain is expected to block or counter strong management prior to 1995, but increasingly favor it after that year. It is important to note that while the EC occupies the same category for both stocks of Atlantic swordfish, its flexibility was more limited at the beginning of discussions regarding the southern stock (1990) than it had been when the commission first considered measures for the north (1979).

Aside from the EC, most distant-water fleets that harvest southern swordfish do so indirectly as by-catch in fisheries targeting bigeye or yellowfin tuna. Historically, Japan was the largest producer of swordfish by-catch in the southern Atlantic, but Taiwan and China have both been increasing their harvests of this stock in recent years. Because their landings of southern swordfish are only incidental, all three of these countries fit into the mildly vulnerable category. Therefore they are expected to resist any measures that would require them to reduce harvests of their targeted stock to protect the by-catch stock (southern swordfish). It is likely that side payments will be required to obtain their acceptance of measures aimed at reducing by-catch.

7.2 Complete Conflict over Allocation

Until 1988, very little mention was made regarding the southern stock of Atlantic swordfish by either ICCAT's scientific committee (the SCRS) or the commission itself. At the time, analysis was limited to a breakdown of reported landings by country and the observation that older fish (6 years and over) were down by 60% in 1986 while younger fish were more prevalent (ICCAT 1971–1994: 1989, 139, 141). The SCRS documented the growth of Spanish landings from the southern fleet, but expressed no uneasiness regarding the state of the stock until 1991 (ICCAT 1971–1994: 1992, 133). In preceding years, the main concern of commission members, as well as scientists, was that large amounts of swordfish were being taken just south of the boundary between the two stocks (ICCAT 1971–1994: 1991, 187; 1993, 101). Highly vulnerable in the north, Canada was the first contracting party to decry this practice (ICCAT 1971–1994: 1992, 60).[2]

Largely because of the possibility that harvests just south of the completely porous boundary were actually fish from the northern stock, the commission adopted a binding recommendation that applied to all Atlantic swordfish in 1990. As recounted in chapter 6, this measure set a 25-kg size limit with a 15% tolerance by number. It also required contracting parties to reduce catches to 1988 levels, with exceptions for small fleets and a 10% allowance for by-catch fleets (ICCAT 2007a, rec. 90-2). As figure 7.1 shows, landings were reduced to near 1988 levels in 1991 and 1992, but rose again steeply thereafter. During these few years, SCRS apprehension regarding southern swordfish became more pronounced. It pointed out that the fish being captured were getting smaller—an indication that larger fish were still declining—and that while landings were increasing, the catch per unit of fishing effort was going down (ICCAT 1971–1994: 1993, 179; 1994, 215).

With diplomatic battles raging over the management of northern swordfish, few countries expressed direct interest in the southern stock during this period. In 1994 Portugal and Canada, with the support of France, all of which were highly vulnerable in the north, introduced a provision for freezing effort targeting the southern stock (ICCAT 1995–2007a: 1995, 184). This led to a flurry of statements from Uruguay, Brazil, and Venezuela. These moderately vulnerable countries recognized the need to prevent further shifts of effort from the northern to the southern stock, but also argued that developing coastal states should not be included in such a provision (ICCAT 1995–2007a: 1995, 172). A revised version of the proposal reflected these concerns by allowing countries whose catches were less than 250 tons to increase their harvests up to that benchmark for 1995 and 1996 (ICCAT 1995–2007a: 1995, 190).

Rather than staying around 1993–1994 levels (16,000–19,000 tons) as per the 1994 recommendation, reported landings of southern swordfish hit an all-time high of over 21,000 tons in 1995. Furthermore, the SCRS stated that 1992 was a better reference point for effort restrictions in order to reduce harvests to about 13,600 tons (ICCAT 1995–2007b: 1996, 70). At the 1995 meeting of the commission, Canada proposed measures in line with SCRS advice for both stocks of Atlantic swordfish. This time its proposal was rejected because of objections regarding the allocation of quotas for the northern stock (mainly from the United States and Spain, see chapter 6; ICCAT 1995–2007a: 1996, 150–151, 164). Again, intense discussions regarding northern swordfish, which was estimated to be at 67% of B_{MSY}, eclipsed concerns about the less heavily exploited southern stock (ICCAT 1995–2007b: 1996, 69).

Two factors contributed to a much different dynamic at the 1996 meeting of the commission. First, contracting parties had reached accord on northern swordfish. Quota distributions had been settled in 1995 and a 3-year management plan was adopted in 1996 (ICCAT 2007a, rec. 96-7). This freed contracting parties to focus on the southern stock. At the same time, the 1996 assessment of southern swordfish showed that the stock was down to 99% of B_{MSY} and was being fished at 124% of F_{MSY}.[3] This was the first time the SCRS was able to estimate these parameters for southern swordfish or to give advice on a specific total allowable catch. The depletion was not very heavy, but the exceptionally rapid decline of the stock certainly worried some members of the commission.

With this new information, both Canada and the now low-flex Spain proposed regulations that would set the TAC for southern swordfish at 13,000 tons, the level recommended by the SCRS (ICCAT 1995–2007a: 1997, 128, 138). Canada reiterated that its proposal was based on the belief that the two Atlantic swordfish stocks were not completely separate and that overfishing in the south could affect the rebuilding plan for the north.[4] For its part, Spain expressed interest in settling both the TAC and a quota-sharing arrangement for the southern stock. Japan, a mildly vulnerable by-catch country, agreed and pointed out that Spain and Uruguay should reduce their catches since they were the ones who had contributed most to the recent increases in fishing mortality. This precipitated defensive statements by both parties. In the end, gradually vulnerable Spain and moderately vulnerable countries like Brazil and Uruguay reached a stalemate over allocation. In spite of pressures from the highly vulnerable United States and (in the north) Canada, moderately vulnerable countries blocked consensus on new measures, and the old 1994 recommendation was renewed for the next year (ICCAT 1995–2007a: 1997, 129–130, 138–139).[5]

Another outcome of the 1996 annual meeting was an intersessional meeting of interested parties to set quota allotments for southern swordfish prior to the determination of a new TAC in 1997 (ICCAT 1995–2007a: 1997, 130). At the meeting in Joao Pessoa, Brazil, coastal developing countries, including Brazil, Venezuela, Argentina, and Uruguay, insisted on a more general discussion of allocation criteria, particularly the importance of developing and coastal status as opposed to historical catches in determining quota distributions. These claims were countered by several countries with historical fishing interests in the Atlantic, including Japan, Portugal, Spain, and the United States.[6] These countries claimed that there was no precedent for using coastal status as a criterion for quota allocation and that coastal considerations were inappropriate for a highly migratory species such as swordfish. They further argued that fishing communities in developed countries were also

Table 7.2
Distribution of Shares from 1997 Intersessional Meeting (applied 1998–2000)

Country	Share of TAC (%)
Brazil	16.00
Japan	25.75
Spain	40.00
Uruguay	4.75
Other CPs	5.50
NCPs	8.00

Notes: CP = contracting party; NCP = noncontracting party.
Source: ICCAT 2007a, rec. 97-07.

dependent on these fisheries, so economic need was not a sufficient distinguishing characteristic (ICCAT 1995–2007a: 1998, 181–188).

7.3   Negotiation of Access Rights: Round 1

It would take 4 more years of discussion, both at ICCAT meetings and in additional intersessional meetings, for contracting parties to reach agreement on general allocation criteria.[7] However, in 1997 they were able to decide on a sharing arrangement for southern swordfish (see table 7.2). Unfortunately, there is no official record of the shares proposed in 1996 to compare with those determined at the intersessional. One important change in the context of negotiations *is* documented in ICCAT's annual reports: even though no new assessment was carried out, the TAC recommended by the SCRS increased by about 1,400 tons from the 1996 level.[8] The contracting parties agreed to the shares in table 7.2 based on a TAC of 14,620 tons instead of 13,000 tons (ICCAT 1995–2007a: 1998, 188).

As difficult as the 1997 intersessional meeting was, the agreed-upon measures still had to be approved by the entire commission at its annual meeting that same year. Several parties that had not been in Joao Pessoa raised concerns about the management plan. On the one hand, Canada questioned the magnitude of the agreed TAC. Its delegate pressed the SCRS on the matter, pointing out that since harvests remained high in 1996, the replacement yield for southern swordfish would certainly be much less than 14,620 tons (ICCAT 1995–2007a: 1998, 169). The Canadian proposal of a TAC at 13,000 tons was ignored by the rest of the commission. Similarly, Chinese and Taiwanese protests regarding the shares that were set for them in absentia precipitated no changes. Both of these countries were only observers at the time (ICCAT 1995–2007a: 1998, 92, 170, 215–216).[9] In fact, most other concerns were pushed aside, including U.S. statements regarding assignment of the "other contracting parties" quota against which its harvests would be counted (ICCAT 1995–2007a: 1998, 169–170). Over these various objections, most of which came from countries that had little power within the southern swordfish context, the 1997 intersessional agreement was adopted for the 3-year period from 1998 to 2000 (ICCAT 2007a, rec. 97-7).

Also in 1997, the commission adopted a U.S. proposal to extend the compliance measures that had been adopted for northern swordfish to cover the southern stock (ICCAT 2007a, rec. 97-8). This recommendation was drafted to enhance compliance by contracting parties to the commission. It basically posited that any overages would be counted against the next year's quota unless catches went over quota for 2 years in a row, in which case the reduction would be at least 125% of the overharvest, and trade-restrictive measures (sanctions) would be considered (ICCAT 2007a, rec. 96-14). There was little discussion of this proposal in the compliance committee, but during the plenary session of the commission, Brazil protested vociferously against the use of trade measures to ensure compliance with ICCAT regulations. It believed that this method was unfair because it punished coastal developing countries, which were exporters of southern swordfish, but not the industrialized countries that imported the fish. With support from the United States, the EC, Japan, and Canada, the measure was adopted over Brazil's protests (ICCAT 1995–2007a: 1997, 38, 142).

After the commission meeting was over, Brazil lodged an official objection to the 1997 measure on compliance in the southern swordfish fishery. It was soon joined by South Africa and Uruguay, both of which moderately vulnerable countries agreed with the Brazilian stance on the inequity of sanctions as a compliance mechanism. By lodging their objections, these countries exempted themselves from the recommendation; it would not apply to them (ICCAT 1995–2007a: 1999, 6).

This dissatisfaction also translated into new proposals at the 1998 meeting of the commission. Brazil and Uruguay were concerned that their developing fleets would be unduly limited by their quota allocation and wished to renegotiate the distributions for 1999 and 2000. South

Africa also stated that the allocation of quota for "other contracting parties" was too small. Its delegation submitted a proposal that would increase the share for that category to 10% while reducing the share assigned to "other noncontracting parties" to 3.5%.[10] Before the observer from Taiwan (the major recipient of a quota in the other noncontracting parties category) could protest against this proposal, the chair of the committee responsible for swordfish and other billfishes cut short the discussion. He pointed out that the 1997 sharing arrangement was adopted for 3 years and would not be up for renegotiation until 2000 (ICCAT 1995–2007a: 1999, 159–160).

In 1999 the SCRS carried out a second full assessment of southern swordfish. The results were more positive than they had been in the past, with biomass at 110% of B_{MSY} and fishing mortality estimated at around 84% of F_{MSY} (ICCAT 1995–2007a: 2000, 87–88). The low estimate for fishing mortality was largely due to reduced landings in 1998, which the SCRS attributed to the management measures that had been adopted in 1997 (ICCAT 1995–2007a: 2000, 86). Although estimates of replacement yield (14,800 tons) were again higher than MSY (13,600 tons), the SCRS advised the commission that harvests above MSY had a greater than 50% chance of reducing the stock biomass below the level that would support maximum sustainable yield. Furthermore, it pointed out that the current TAC of 14,620 tons was above the amount that would keep the southern stock at sustainable levels. A new TAC of about 13,500 tons was recommended (ICCAT 1995–2007b: 2000, 88).

The commission's response to this advice was mixed. On the one hand, the gradually vulnerable EC and mildly vulnerable Japan supported a proposal that would keep the current sharing–TAC arrangement in spite of the changes in scientific advice. On the other hand, the highly vulnerable United States and (in the north) Canada, along with moderately vulnerable Brazil, supported a proposal to reduce the TAC to 13,600 tons for the year 2000. As in the previous year, Brazil, South Africa, and Uruguay expressed a desire to renegotiate the sharing arrangements for southern swordfish, but the committee agreed to take no new actions until 2000 (ICCAT 1995–2007a: 2000, 175). Discussions were relatively short, probably because most delegates were focused on negotiating new management measures for the northern stock, which was doing better but remained moderately overexploited (ICCAT 1995–2007b: 2000, 86). South Africa did make a long statement on its dissatisfaction with the division of southern swordfish, demanding that it be given a share at the expense of distant-water fleets (ICCAT 1995–2007b: 2000, 185).

7.4 Negotiation of Access Rights: Rounds 2–4

When it was finally time to renegotiate southern swordfish recommendations at the 2000 meeting of the commission, developing coastal countries were ready. Although the SCRS still recommended a TAC of about 13,500 tons, the EC proposed to keep the 14,620-ton TAC, along with the 1997 sharing arrangements pending finalization of the general ICCAT allocation criteria, which were still under discussion. South Africa countered with a proposal that would keep the TAC but distributed it differently, with a larger quota allocated to developing coastal states. Namibia and many other moderately vulnerable countries supported this redistribution, but consensus could not be reached on either side. Eventually, a proposal from the chair was adopted. It set the TAC at 14,620 tons and charged members with setting their own precautionary catch limits to reach that catch level (ICCAT 1995–2007a: 2001, 202–203, 232–233).

It is interesting that Japan, which is mildly vulnerable in this context, was also dissatisfied with the outcome. This delegation even went so far as to offer 1,700 tons of its own quota to coastal countries in order to get a sharing arrangement for southern swordfish (ICCAT 1995–2007a: 2001, 241). Given that their total quota was about 3,700 tons, this might seem to be a disproportionate sacrifice on the part of the Japanese (ICCAT 2007a, rec. 97-7). However, because of exogenous shifts in the distributions of bigeye tuna (Japan's target species), Japanese landings of southern swordfish had been reduced to well below 2,000 tons from 1997 onward (ICCAT 2007d). Even so, an explanation of this behavior requires a wider version of the vulnerability response framework that would encompass Japan's broader interests as a gradually vulnerable country in other fisheries, much as in the northern swordfish case. That is, Japan had incentives to (1) ensure that historical catch levels remain the central norm of allocation throughout the commission and (2) prevent disruption of ICCAT management by conflicts between coastal and distant-water countries.

Sharing arrangements were the main focus of most ICCAT members in 2000, but there were a few parties who voiced concern about the state of the stock. Highly vulnerable in the northern and southern fisheries, the

United States stated preferences for a TAC that was closer to SCRS advice, as did Canada. The latter again tabled a proposal that would set the total allowable catch at 13,650 tons. No other parties expressed support for this reduced TAC, or any interest at all in altering management to better comply with scientific advice. Both the United States and Canada expressed considerable disappointment when the higher TAC was adopted. They were also supported by the Ocean Wildlife Campaign, an environmental nongovernmental organization, but their complaints went unheeded amidst the conflict over allocation (ICCAT 1995–2007a: 2001, 62–63, 203–204, 234–235).

After four intersessional meetings of the Working Group on Allocation Criteria, which had been established in 1998, at the behest of several moderately vulnerable countries, ICCAT members were finally able to reach agreement on a general list of criteria for the distribution of quota shares in 2001. Unfortunately, this accomplishment did not make negotiations on the allocation of southern swordfish any easier. In fact, the discussions were much the same as they had been at the 2000 meeting. Japan worked to get consensus on sharing arrangements but could not bridge the gaps between the demands of coastal and distant-water countries. The result of these negotiations was the adoption of a regulation that was identical to that of the previous year. The United States and Canada again complained about this outcome, particularly because the sum of the individually determined quotas for 2000 was about 50% greater than the TAC (ICCAT 1995–2007a: 2002, 314–316, 331, 333–335).

When left to themselves, many countries set their own quotas above their actual capacity to harvest southern swordfish. This is evinced by the relatively low overharvests for 2000 and 2001, which were only about 1,000 tons higher than the TAC, rather than 7,000 tons (ICCAT 2007d). In the meantime, SCRS advice had changed again. No new assessments were preformed, but divergences between catch per unit effort for fleets targeting swordfish (i.e., the EC and Brazil) and those that captured swordfish as by-catch in bigeye fisheries (i.e., Japan and Taiwan) led the SCRS to doubt the outcome of their 1999 assessment.[11] Lack of data and late reporting of national landings magnified this problem over the next few years. Owing to the uncertainties created by these trends, the SCRS altered its advice in 2002, recommending that the total catch be kept around current levels (14,000–15,000 tons), rather than reduced to 13,500 tons (ICCAT 1995–2007b: 2003, 95–97).

Table 7.3

Comparison of Quota Allocations and TAC (tons) from the 1997 (applied 1998–2000) and 2002 (applied 2003–2006) Management Plans for Southern Swordfish

Country	2000	2003	...	2006
Brazil	2,339.2	4,086	↑	4,365
Japan	3,764.6	1,500	—	1,500
EC (Spain)	5,845	5,950	↓	5,780
Uruguay	694.5	850	—	850
CPs using others quota under 1997 plan				
South Africa		890	↑	1,140
Namibia		890	↑	1,140
United States		100	↑	120
Ivory Coast		100	—	100
China		315	—	315
UK (Overseas Territories)		25	—	25
Total other CPs	804.1	2,320	↑	2,840
Taiwan (NCPs)	1,169.6	925	↓	720
Total allowable catch	14,620	15,631	↑	16,055

Notes: CP = contracting party; NCP = noncontracting party.
Sources: ICCAT 2007a, rec. 97-07, 02-03.

For a second time, agreement on southern swordfish allocation was facilitated by a positive revision of scientific advice. At the 2002 meeting of the commission, the EC and Japan proposed a 3-year plan for the management of southern swordfish from 2003–2005 that was acceptable to most parties. In fact, there was so little disagreement over sharing arrangements in the plan that a Japanese proposal to extend the arrangements through 2006 was easily accepted. Table 7.3 compares the national quota allotments and TAC from the 2002 southern swordfish management plan with those designated in the final year of the 1997 plan (2000). Note that Japan and Taiwan took the biggest hits in the new arrangements, while developing coastal countries like Brazil, South Africa, and Namibia gained much from the agreement. Expected to share the 804 tons of "others" quota in the earlier plan—along with the United States, Ivory Coast, China, and the UK Overseas Territories—South Africa and Namibia were each granted 890 tons of quota for 2003. This increased gradually to 1,140 tons in 2006. Brazil, previously allowed to capture about 2,340 tons of southern swordfish, received a quota of 4,086 tons in 2003, which rose to 4,365 tons for 2006. EC quotas started higher than the 1997 levels in 2003, but declined to slightly below that benchmark by 2006 (ICCAT 2007a, rec. 97-7, 02-3).

Although Japan's quota was cut by more than half, a clause was included that would allow that level to be renegotiated if Japanese by-catch of southern swordfish increased to over 1,500 tons during the period (ICCAT 1995–2007a: 2003, 234–235). There was a second reason that Japan accepted this quota reduction. Owing to problems in the northern Atlantic, Japan instituted a new policy in 2000 that required all longline vessels in its fleet to discard every swordfish, dead or alive. This substantially reduced their reported landings of southern swordfish without affecting their harvests of the targeted species, bigeye tuna.[12] Even so, Japan strategically held on to much of its quota, using it as leverage to negotiate side payments for the cooperation of both moderately and mildly vulnerable countries. Again, this behavior falls outside of the purview of basic vulnerability response and could not be predicted unless a wider net were cast.

Almost every contracting party was satisfied with this proposal. Only two countries expressed any objections to either version of the 2002 management plan; Canada and the United States were both concerned with the fact that the TAC was above SCRS recommendations for 2003 and increased by more than 1,000 tons by 2006. This can be clearly seen in the last row of table 7.3, which sums the quota shares for each year. Other countries, particularly Japan, Brazil, and the EC, stated that the high TAC was of little concern because actual catches would undoubtedly fall below this level. The United States and Canada were again supported by the observer from the Ocean Wildlife Campaign, but were unable to alter the positions of other delegates and unwilling to block consensus on the measure (ICCAT 1995–2007a: 2003, 234–235). The 2002 recommendation was adopted with the sharing arrangements and TACs as described in table 7.3.

As it turned out, reported landings were well below the total allowable catch for 2003, 2004, and 2005. Referring again to figure 7.1, catches during these years seem to have stabilized just below 13,000 tons after a bumpy decline from the historical maximum in 1995. The SCRS attributes this trend both to ICCAT regulations and to shifts of fishing effort to other oceans or other stocks of fish. Several important fleets, including those from the EC and Brazil, had modified their operations to opportunistically target tunas and sharks when swordfish prices were low (ICCAT 1995–2007b: 2006, 106–107).

Subsequent discussions about southern swordfish have been fairly un-eventful.[13] The most recent scientific assessment of the stock was more optimistic than any previous SCRS report. It was also more uncertain than any since 1997. The MSY is currently thought to be around 17,000 tons, but no other benchmarks could be estimated because of the continued divergence between catch per unit effort data from fleets that target swordfish and those that harvest it incidentally as by-catch (ICCAT 1995–2007b: 2007, 85). As per a proposal from the chair of panel 4, the TAC was set at 17,000 tons per year from 2007 to 2009. Shares were similar to the 2002 agreement. As table 7.4 shows, quotas for a few developing countries increased, while those for distant-water countries, particularly Japan and Taiwan, were reduced. Also, eight new

Table 7.4
A Comparison of Quota Allocations and TAC (tons) from the 2002 (applied 2003–2006) and 2006 (applied 2007–2009) Management Plans for Southern Swordfish

Country	2006	2007	...	2009
Brazil	4,365	4,365	—	4,365
Japan	1,500	1,315	↓	1,080
EC	5,780	5,780	—	5,780
Uruguay	850	1,500	—	1,500
South Africa	1,140	1,200	—	1,200
Namibia	1,140	1,400	—	1,400
United States	120	100	—	100
Ivory Coast	100	150	—	150
China	315	315	—	315
UK (Overseas Territories)	25	25	—	25
Taiwan	720	550	—	550
Angola		100	—	100
Ghana		100	—	100
Sao Tome and Principe		100	—	100
Senegal		300	↑	500
Philippines		50	—	50
Korea		50	—	50
Belize		150	—	150
Vanuatu		20	—	20
Total allowable catch	16,055	17,000	—	1,700

Note: TAC = total allowable catch.
Sources: ICCAT 2007a, rec. 02-03, 06-02.

countries were added to the list. Vanuatu and the observer from Taiwan both complained about the size of their quotas, but no changes were made and the proposal was adopted.

7.5 Summary

Much as in the mixed skipjack case, there are several major deviations between the vulnerability response predictions and observed policy positions on southern swordfish. The only consistent coalition in the case occurred among moderately vulnerable countries like Brazil, Uruguay, Venezuela, South Africa, and Namibia. Individually, these countries are fairly weak, but together they negotiated effectively for room to develop their fleets within this fishery. At first these countries received only small concessions, but eventually they were able to get significant transfers of quota from more vulnerable contracting parties like the United States and the EC. Unexpectedly, mildly vulnerable Japan also contributed some of its by-catch quota to finally obtain sharing arrangements in 2002.

This discrepancy can be linked to several factors, not least of which is Japan's vested interest in maintaining a particular set of measures—a TAC with quota sharing and international enforcement mechanisms— throughout the entire ICCAT regime. As shown in chapter 3 and chapters 9–10, these measures are extremely important to Japan in its attempts to protect both bigeye and bluefin tuna. Furthermore, having already made the sacrifice of forgoing sales of swordfish by-catch as part of agreements on northern swordfish, Japan had little more left to lose by 2002. Discarding all swordfish would reduce their by-catch substantially in the south as well as the north, without reducing harvests of their target species. Other mildly vulnerable by-catch countries did not have it so easy. Since at was unable to sit at the negotiating table, Taiwan's allowance of southern swordfish was reduced substantially, as was the overall share for nonmembers.

Geospatial considerations also played a confounding role, particularly in the persistent Canadian proposals to reduce harvests of southern swordfish, even though Canada is not even active in this fishery. As stated frequently by their delegates, the Canadians were concerned that large catches just south of the boundary between the stocks included fish from the north and were therefore contributing to the decline of that stock. Highly vulnerable in the northern swordfish fishery, Canada could afford to press for measures in the south that might improve matters in the north. As noted in chapter 5, the vulnerability response framework does not predict such cross-stock maneuvers. The evidence from this case simply confirms the necessity of including geospatial parameters in the operation of the framework.

Another, much more fundamental problem that arises in the southern swordfish case is the fact that countries engaged in management without much evidence of direct competition in the fishery. International competition was certainly escalating throughout most of the negotiations (see section 6.4), but the race for southern swordfish seemed to run out of steam with the geographic and economic transfer of fishing effort in the mid-1990s. Problems in the north probably intensified the U.S. response in this period, as might the global limits on Spanish fleets. Again, the proxy used for flexibility seemed to fail in this case. Looking at the data more closely, it is likely that Spain may not have reached the low-flex phase of its vulnerability until around 2002, when its harvests in the Indian and Pacific Oceans generated a secondary peak in its global landings (FAO 2007b).

In spite of all these rationalizations, there is one other explanation that appeals to me. It is quite likely that path dependence affected the management of southern swordfish. Certainly, there is an interesting lag between the actions taken for northern swordfish and those adopted for the less depleted southern stock. Quota-sharing arrangements and scientific TACs were first adopted for northern swordfish in 1995 and 1996, with the same occurring for southern swordfish in 1997 (ICCAT 2007a, rec. 97-7). Enforcement measures such as the 1995 Swordfish Action Plan and the 2001 Swordfish Statistical Document Program were adopted concomitantly for all stocks of Atlantic swordfish (rec. 95-13, 01-22).

More important than institutional precedent, the dogged demands of moderately vulnerable countries could have been generated by learning rather than by competitive pressures. They had lost out in negotiations over bigeye tuna and its higher-priced counterpart, bluefin tuna (see chapters 9–10), so this time they were prepared. The tremendous influx of Spanish vessels in 1988 and 1989 could not have been ignored, either. Between this patent potential for crowding out by distant-water fleets and their previous experience with the exclusionary tactics of more vulnerable countries, this choice to engage in negotiations in the absence of economic competition becomes clear. More vulnerable countries may be responding to international competition, but moderately vulnerable countries could be looking at past losses to plan future successes.

It will require considerable effort to incorporate learning into the vulnerability response framework, but it will be a fascinating project. For now, it is important to note that the pattern of the southern swordfish case is one of prolonged conflict. Compared with the northern swordfish and bigeye tuna cases, strong management for southern swordfish happened almost accidentally, linked as it is to highly uncertain changes in scientific advice. In order to accommodate all demands for quota, almost all of the TACs negotiated for southern swordfish were higher than those recommended by the SCRS, even though those recommendations kept increasing, along with the uncertainty surrounding them. The rollercoaster negotiations recounted here suggest that conflict has not stopped; it has simply paused. Any downturns in this fishery, particularly the return of fleets targeting other stocks or operating in farther seas, will probably send southern swordfish into decline and return the commission to the bitter conflict of the 1990s.

8

Blue Marlin and White Marlin

Since the commission has undertaken regulation of blue marlin and white marlin simultaneously, these two stocks are discussed together. Compared with swordfish, the role of marlins in commercial fisheries in the Atlantic is minuscule. Combined, these two species represent less than 1% of the biomass managed by ICCAT (ICCAT 1971–1994: 1989, 69). With very little commercial value, marlins have not received much attention from contracting parties to the commission. However, stocks of marlins have certainly been affected by commercial fishing operations and ICCAT regulations. As by-catch species, these populations have been severely depleted as a result of incidental fishing mortality by longlines targeting swordfish, bigeye tuna, and other commercially valuable stocks. In addition, marlins are prime game fishes, and are often targeted by recreational fishers. Although ICCAT has virtually ignored the plight of marlins over most of its history, some actions have been taken recently to halt the depletion of Atlantic stocks of these species.

Figure 8.1 shows reported landings of blue marlin and white marlin in the Atlantic, along with the most recent estimates of maximum sustainable yield, as calculated by the SCRS. There is a large margin of error in the estimates for blue marlin, but it is still evident that the stock has been overexploited for much of the time series. In 2000, the SCRS calculated that the biomass of blue marlin was about 40% of what would be needed to keep harvests at maximum sustainable yield and that fishing mortality was four times the MSY level (ICCAT 1995–2007b: 2004, 77).[1] White marlin was more severely overfished, with estimates of abundance ranging from 12 to 22% of the biomass that would support MSY, and fishing mortality at between five and eight times the maximum sustainable level. It is clear that marlin stocks have faced a deep biological

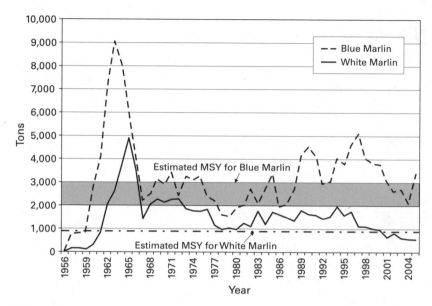

Figure 8.1
Reported landings of Atlantic blue marlin and white marlin relative to MSY.
Sources: ICCAT 2007d; ICCAT 1995–2007b: 2001, 66; ICCAT 1995–2007b:
2003, 77.

crisis, even though they are not commercially targeted (ICCAT 1995–
2007b: 2004, 85).[2]

Because marlins are a minor by-catch in larger fisheries, archetypal
commercial fishing interests will not experience serious losses as these
species are depleted. Therefore, much as in the mixed skipjack case, analysis using the unaltered framework is incredibly straightforward. As
explained in section 8.1, no national fleets target the stock; therefore no
countries are vulnerable and no proposals or actions are expected from
any of ICCAT's contracting parties. However, the evidence of the case,
which is presented in section 8.2, shows that this prediction does not
hold true for all ICCAT member countries. Further investigation reveals
that this divergence can be attributed to the activities of noncommercial
interests in the more concerned countries. In order to evaluate the impact
of this violation of the commercial-interests only assumption on patterns of adaptive governance, section 8.3 presents a detailed comparison between the measures adopted for commercially valuable species like

		Competitiveness	
		Low	High
Flexibility	Low	<u>Highly Vulnerable</u> none	<u>Moderately Vulnerable</u> none
	High	<u>Gradually Vulnerable</u> none	<u>Mildly Vulnerable</u> By-catch: Brazil, Canada, China, EC, Japan, Korea, South Africa, USA, etc.

Figure 8.2
Vulnerability response matrix for blue marlin and white marlin. A list ending in "etc." indicates that countries have been omitted from this summary for ease of reference. See table B.8 in appendix B for a full list.

northern swordfish and bigeye tuna and those adopted to protect by-catch species like blue and white marlin.

8.1 Vulnerability Response Predictions with Noncommercial Interests

Atlantic marlins are not directly targeted by the commercial fishing industry. Therefore, when only commercial interests are included in the decision function as per the assumptions stated in chapter 2, all countries with harvests of blue marlin or white marlin fall into the mildly vulnerable category as by-catch countries (see figure 8.2). This means that they are expected to block or counter attempts at management only if harvests of their targeted species are threatened. Substantial threats or large side payments will be required to obtain their cooperation on such measures, as was observed for Japanese by-catch in the northern swordfish case. However, without highly or low-flex, gradually vulnerable countries to propose measures, there should be no need for such tactics, so no proposals are predicted, no matter what happens to stocks like Atlantic blue marlin and white marlin (see table 8.1).

Given these predictions, the evidence section of the case should be short, but it isn't. The behavior of one country in particular stands out; the United States frequently presses for measures to protect marlins, even though these fishes are a by-catch for its commercial longline fleets. This

Table 8.1
Overview of Vulnerability Response Predictions for Blue Marlin and White Marlin

Category	Countries	Predictions
Highly vulnerable	None	Not applicable
Gradually vulnerable	None	Not applicable
Moderately vulnerable	None	Not applicable
Mildly vulnerable	By-catch: Brazil, Canada, China, EC, Japan, Korea, South Africa, United States, etc.	Blocking or countermeasures on management that might reduced targeted harvests unless there are substantial threats or side payments

Notes: A list ending in "etc." indicates that countries have been omitted from this summary for ease of reference. See table B.8 in appendix B for a full list.

is explained in greater depth later, but for now it should be noted that examination of the ICCAT reported landings record shows that the United States reports fairly substantial landings of Atlantic marlins by sportfishers. These catches are much smaller than their commercial harvests of other species, such as bigeye, swordfish, and yellowfin tuna, but they are still much higher than recreational marlin harvests reported by other countries.[3] This suggests that the United States may be more susceptible to recreational interests than other fishing countries and therefore more likely to deviate from the vulnerability response predictions.

8.2   Partial Management Response

As figure 8.1 shows, incidental landings of blue and white marlins in the Atlantic have remained well above estimates of maximum sustainable yield throughout ICCAT's history. In contravention of vulnerability response expectations, the United States has consistently expressed apprehension about the status of marlin stocks and pushed for better management of the species.[4] First voicing concern in 1975, the United States subsequently asserted that catches of billfish were too high in 1977 and announced its intention to introduce regulations on the species 2 years later (ICCAT 1971–1994: 1976, 69; 1978, 69; 1980, 77–78). Although the United States did institute domestic legislation to reduce its own landings of Atlantic marlins by 20% in 1981, its intentions to propose measures at ICCAT meetings were forestalled by lack of scientific data and internal dissension among commercial fishers, conservationists, and recreational fishers (ICCAT 1971–1994: 1982, 81). It was not until 1985 that the United States again spoke out on marlins, asking the SCRS to prepare plans for a billfish research program to be instituted the next year (ICCAT 1971–1994: 1986, 73).

In 1986, the SCRS submitted its proposal for an Enhanced Research for Billfish Program (ERBP). The United States supported this program, along with Cuba, but other members raised major concerns regarding funding.[5] In order to get the research program approved, the United States proposed that ICCAT allot only US $10,000 for the first year of the ERBP. The rest of the program's budget, US $25,000, would be raised from private sources in the United States (ICCAT 1971–1994: 1987, 126). Although ICCAT's contribution to the ERBP was only about 1.7% of its annual budget and was minuscule relative to the amounts expended for research on bluefin, skipjack, and yellowfin tunas, a few contracting parties still expressed reservations about funding the program (ICCAT 1971–1994: 1987, 51, 127). However, the ERBP was approved, with its budget, and began its activities in 1987.

After its first year of operations, all of the funding for the program was provided by private sources (ICCAT 1971–1994: 1989, 69). By 1994, the ERBP was attracting as much as US $68,000 a year from nongovernmental organizations (ICCAT 1971–1994: 1994, 114–115). Most of the money came from groups of recreational fishers in the United States who were dismayed at the decline in their catch per unit effort from 1980 to 1987 (ICCAT 1971–1994: 1988, 151).[6] Other countries with recreational fisheries targeting marlins contributed to the ERBP as well, including Venezuela, whose sportfishers were also observing fewer billfish on their lines (ICCAT 1971–1994: 1989, 69; 1991, 177). This evidence suggests that the unexpected interest in Atlantic marlins can be linked to the influence of recreational fishing interests.

Progress on the ERBP was slow at first, mainly because there was so much that needed to be done to improve databases and analytical techniques. Solid results were not available until 1992, when the SCRS asserted with certainty that both blue marlin and white marlin were overfished (stock biomass was below the level that would support MSY), and that overfishing (fishing effort was above the level that would produce MSY) was still occurring for the species in the Atlantic (ICCAT

1971–1994: 1993, 164–165). It also advised the commission to decrease harvesting of both species, saying that live release of incidental marlin catches could reduce fishing mortality by as much as 37% (p. 168). Two years later, the scientific prognosis had gotten worse, as the biomass of the stocks had declined further and indirect effort was increasing fishing mortality on marlins (ICCAT 1995–2007a: 1995, 172).

As SCRS advice became more solid, discussions regarding billfish at ICCAT meetings became more substantial. In 1992, the United States put forth a proposal that would require all contracting parties to release whatever billfish they caught, dead or alive. Other countries also spoke out. Japan expressed its concern, offering to cooperate but insisting that recreational fishers should share the burden of catch limits with commercial fishers. It also rankled at the idea of discarding dead marlins, believing it to be a wasteful practice. Spain announced that it had started research into billfish by-catch in 1990 and was currently studying the issue. Thus a dialogue began, but no actions were taken that year. Similar discussions were held in 1993 and 1994. No consensus could be reached and ICCAT continued to do nothing because of the blocking tactics of countries that were dominated by commercial fishing interests (ICCAT 1971–1994: 1993, 94–95).

By 1995, the SCRS was able to estimate that—in *1990*—the biomass of blue marlin had been 42% of that which supports MSY (B_{MSY}). White marlin was even more adversely affected, with 1990 biomass being 25% of the level that would enable maximum sustainable yield (ICCAT 1995–2007b: 1996, 51–53).[7] These numbers were very disturbing to the United States, which claimed that its recreational fisheries for billfish were worth more than US $15 billion. In response to serious biological depletion, the United States proposed a 12-year scientific program that would require longlines to release all live billfish caught (other than swordfish) and tag them if possible (ICCAT 1995–2007a: 1996, 166). Japan again raised concerns about the equitability of such a program, insisting that longlines not be singled out and that recreational fishers should also have to reduce their catches. During this discussion, the United States pointed out that recreational fishers already release about 80% of the billfish they catch. Other countries, such as South Korea and Spain, suggested that live release should be voluntary and that rewards should be provided for tagging (ICCAT 1995–2007a: 1996, 155). Eventually, a watered-down, nonbinding resolution was adopted that established a 5-year scientific program during which contracting parties were encouraged to promote the live release and tagging of billfish by both commercial and recreational fishers (ICCAT 2007a, res. 95-12).

The next year, more current estimates of biological parameters were available, putting the biomass of blue marlin at 24% of B_{MSY} and the biomass of white marlin at 22.6% of B_{MSY} (ICCAT 1995–2007b: 1997, 51, 58). Also, a workshop on billfish held in the United States had found that the use of monofilament, rather than steel lines, in fishing gear could reduce by-catch mortality of species like marlin. Building on this information, the United States proposed a recommendation to promote a change from steel to monofilament lines and to expand research on the results of the switch (ICCAT 1995–2007a: 1997, 88). Again, there was resistance to making such a transition mandatory, especially from countries like Brazil and Spain, who questioned the impact that monofilaments would have on billfish mortality and landings of targeted species. Other countries were concerned about the costs of the changeover (ICCAT 1995–2007a: 1997, 129–130). After some discussion, ICCAT adopted another nonbinding resolution that urged contracting parties to promote the use of monofilament lines, but left out much of the research included in the original U.S. proposal (ICCAT 2007a, res. 96-9).

Although no new assessments were carried out for marlins in 1997, the United States put forth a new proposal that would prohibit all landings of blue marlin and white marlin except for tournament fish (ICCAT 1995–2007a: 1998, 172). Such a drastic measure was unacceptable to most members of the commission. A second proposal was developed in informal meetings between the United States, Japan, Canada, and other interested parties. Rather than a complete moratorium, the joint proposal required a 25% reduction in landings of blue and white marlins from 1996 levels by the end of 1999 (ICCAT 2007a, rec. 97-9). U.S. perseverance had finally brought about the first binding recommendation adopted for any noncommercial by-catch species under ICCAT's jurisdiction. This was only achieved after major concessions, such as the modification of the original U.S. proposal that lowered the mandated reduction in marlin landings from 100 to 25%.[8] It is also interesting to note that this big push by the United States came the year after the passage of domestic legislation that could reduce U.S. longline effort and effectiveness in order to protect Atlantic marlins (Webster 2006).[9]

As revolutionary as the 1997 recommendation was, its immediate effect was to undermine reporting of marlin landings in the Atlantic. In 1998, 34% of the states that had previously provided data on landings of blue marlin reported nothing on the species, and 12% stopped report-ing data on white marlin (ICCAT 1995–2007b: 1999, 69, 76). Even so, the United States proposed to keep landings of blue marlin and white marlin at 1998 levels for 1999. Initially, the recommendation also in-cluded instructions for SCRS to develop a recovery plan for the two mar-lin stocks (ICCAT 1995–2007a: 1999, 161). Opposition from Japan and the EC forced the United States to remove that portion of the proposi-tion, postponing the next assessment of the stocks until 2000 (ICCAT 1995–2007a: 1999, 73; 2007a, rec. 98-10). It is important to note that both Japan and the EC faced much bigger commercial losses from regu-lation of marlins than the United States did. Their longline operations, targeting bigeye tuna and swordfish, respectively, were much greater in volume and value than U.S. fisheries for the species (ICCAT 2007d). This gave them considerable power within the fisheries and ensured that commercial fishing interests could overwhelm any noncommercial inter-ests at the domestic level.[10]

For several years, nonreporting prevented assessment of either stock as well as an evaluation of the effectiveness of the 1997 regulation. Little was said about billfish during the 1999 meeting of the commission, but discussions resumed with new scientific analysis in 2000. Although the 2000 assessment was somewhat more optimistic for blue marlin, indica-tions were much worse for white marlin than they had been in 1996. The 2000 biomass of blue marlin was estimated to be 40% of that which would support MSY. On the other hand, fishing mortality for the species was estimated at four times the maximum sustainable level in 1999 (ICCAT 1995–2007b: 2001, 66). For white marlin, the 2000 biomass was only 15% of that which would support MSY, but fishing mortality was at seven times the level that would produce MSY (p. 73). The fact that the biological situation for marlins had deteriorated so much indi-cated that earlier resolutions and recommendations had been ineffective.

The 2000 SCRS report instigated a protracted discussion about the fundamental scientific basis for the stock assessments of blue marlin and white marlin. Japan presented its own interpretations of the data, which showed that the biomass of marlins was much healthier than the official scientific report. In response, the United States defended the original analysis on a point-by-point basis. The U.S. delegation also pointed out that representatives of Japan had been present at SCRS meetings and had approved the scientific report (ICCAT 1995–2007a: 2001, 230–231). In addition, the United States brought up the possibility that international nongovernmental organizations would attempt to have white marlin listed for protection under the Convention for International Trade in Endangered Species if ICCAT did not take serious actions soon (pp. 241–242).[11]

Convinced that a complete rebuilding program was necessary to reverse negative trends in the abundance of blue marlin and white marlin, the United States presented a detailed proposal designed to further decrease fishing mortality for the species. After much discussion, mainly involving the usefulness of requiring marlin to be discarded if brought in dead, amounts of marlins that could be retained by fishers, and appropriate size limits for the species, a long-term plan was finally adapted. Specifically, the commission agreed that for the next 2 years, all countries fishing in the Atlantic Ocean would be required to reduce their landings of blue marlin and white marlin to 50 and 33% of 1999 levels, respectively.

Also included in the recommendation were regulations aimed at reducing the mortality of marlins in recreational fisheries. The United States agreed to limit its recreational landings of Atlantic marlins to a total of 250 fish, all of which would be taken in duly monitored tournaments. All other countries were required to establish size limits for both species in their recreational fisheries. The scheme was scheduled for review after a new assessment and development of rebuilding plans in 2002 (ICCAT 2007a, rec. 00-13).[12] Since the United States shouldered much of the burden, countries like Japan, Spain, and Canada, all of which had expressed concern about the equal implementation of marlin measures, were mollified. Between these concessions on recreational fishing and various other maneuvers, the U.S. proposal was adopted.

By the end of the 1990s, the U.S. position on marlins represented the influence of conservation as well as recreational interests. In addition to reported landings from recreational fisheries, evidence of noncommercial activities within the U.S. policy process can be found in their presence in the U.S. delegation and at meetings of the national advisory committee that formulates U.S. ICCAT policy (U.S. Congress 1975, chap. 16A, sec. 971a, para. a2B). Recreational interests had long been active on both levels, and their importance is indicated by the fact that of the three U.S. commissioners to ICCAT, one is always a representative of recreational fishers (chap. 16A, sec. 971b, para. a1). Only a few other countries, such as Venezuela and Cuba, have ever had representatives of noncommercial interest groups on their delegations.[13] Although there are some groups, like Greenpeace Europe, that are active in other ICCAT member countries, they have little direct influence on policy making and are not represented on national delegations (Lequesne 2004, 40). Without pressure from such interests, these countries behaved as expected, blocking and undermining U.S. proposals.

Mainly owing to staunch opposition from countries with pure commercial interests, the management of Atlantic marlins does not fall into the "strong" category as described in chapter 2. Reported landings of both species have declined, but nonreporting and misclassification have increased, obscuring actual fishing mortality on the species. This has amplified the uncertainty of stock assessments. In their next assessment of these stocks for the 2006 meeting of the commission, the SCRS was unable to generate estimates of biomass or fishing mortality relative to MSY. It informed the commission that recent abundance (2001–2004) was slightly increasing for white marlin and possibly stabilized for blue marlin. Given the data available, the SCRS cautiously stated that continued effort at recent levels would result in the rebuilding of both stocks. However, it also pointed out that current data were unverified and there was considerable incentive for fishers to underreport marlin mortality, simply discarding them back into the Atlantic without recording the catch. Thus, the 2006 assessment could be based on biased information (ICCAT 1995–2007b: 2007, 70).

8.3   Special Monitoring and Enforcement Issues

In order to explore the aggregate differences among management of bycatches with different types of commercial value, this section reviews the measures that were adopted to manage commercially targeted stocks and the protections that were adopted for the Atlantic marlins. The most obvious difference observed in the marlins case is that measures were delayed much longer relative to the level of overexploitation. Regulation of northern swordfish and bigeye tuna began at moderate rather than high levels of depletion, and the measures that the commission put in place for these commercially targeted stocks were more in line with scientific advice than those adopted for marlins. Of equal relevance are the international monitoring and enforcement mechanisms that were designed to ensure compliance with regulations for commercially valuable stocks; equivalent measures were not adopted to enforce the marlin measures. Details on this divergence are provided in the following paragraphs.

In 1995, a year after ICCAT adopted its first catch limits for northern swordfish, the commission passed a resolution initiating a compliance regime known as the Atlantic Swordfish Action Plan. Similar to a plan adopted previously for bluefin tuna (see chapter 9), this plan briefly provided for review of compliance by contracting parties, then went on to discuss methods of ensuring that noncontracting parties also abide by ICCAT regulations. The commission was directed to identify noncontracting parties who were fishing for Atlantic swordfish in a manner that undermined ICCAT conservation measures. To do this, ICCAT would have to compile reported landings data, trade statistics, and other information relevant to the impact of noncontracting parties on swordfish stocks. Reviewing these data annually, the commission, through its subsidiary body, the Permanent Working Group for the Improvement of ICCAT Statistics and Conservation Measures, would take nondiscriminatory trade measures against noncontracting parties identified as being noncompliant (ICCAT 2007a, res. 95-13).

When ICCAT adopted its second set of catch limits for northern Atlantic swordfish in 1996, the commission also amended the swordfish action plan to make sure that contracting parties would have incentives to adhere to their quota allocations. Under the auspices of the compliance committee, which had been established in 1995, contracting parties to the commission were required to report their landings of northern swordfish, explain any overharvest, and describe domestic measures they had taken to prevent future overages. More important, any contracting party that landed more than its share of the TAC in 1 year would have the amount of that overharvest subtracted from the next year's quota. If a contracting party were to go over its quota 2 years in a row, ICCAT could reduce its catch limits to a minimum of 125% of the overage, with the option to enact trade measures on the offending country (ICCAT 2007a, rec. 96-14).[14]

The first trade-restrictive measures against noncontracting parties under the 1995 Swordfish Action Plan were taken in 1999. Contracting parties were instructed to ban imports of Atlantic swordfish and any of its products from Belize and Honduras. In 1998, these countries had been identified as providers of flags of convenience for fleets targeting Atlantic swordfish in contravention of ICCAT regulations, and a letter had been sent to each of them explaining the nature of their infraction and the results of continued noncompliance (ICCAT 2007a, rec. 99-8). The initial response of these parties was deemed insufficient and so sanctions were imposed. Both countries have taken measures to curb the non-compliant activities of their fleets. ICCAT maintained sanctions on these countries until they could prove that they no longer harbored illegal, unregulated, or unreported vessels.[15]

ICCAT also uses a statistical document program (SDP) to monitor and enforce regulations limiting catches of Atlantic swordfish. Originally developed to track the valuable Atlantic bluefin tuna, ICCAT applied SDPs to swordfish and bigeye tuna in 2001. The purpose of the SDP is to facilitate trade measures related to Atlantic swordfish by creating a paper trail that traces landings from point of capture to point of final sale. Issued and validated by a vessel's flag state, a statistical document verifies that the Atlantic swordfish being exported was caught in compliance with all ICCAT regulations for the stocks. At the other end of the trade, importers for contracting parties to ICCAT are instructed to require a statistical document for all Atlantic swordfish entering their markets. Both exporter and importer should then report all data collected under the SDP to the ICCAT secretariat. This information is used to cross-check reported landings and other catch statistics (ICCAT 2007a, rec. 01-22).

Although some data on landings of marlins are provided to both the compliance committee and PWG, ICCAT has not adopted any recommendations to effectively monitor or enforce regulations for these types of by-catch internationally. In fact, most of the methods that ICCAT has developed to ensure compliance with its management measures would not really work for marlins. One important problem is that fishers have the option to discard incidental catches rather than altering their fishing practices to avoid them. Statistical document programs could be used to track and limit trade in by-catch, but that would just be a shadow of the true rate of extraction. Only with very well-structured monitoring programs that include onboard observers can actual fishing mortality on by-catch be documented.

In fact, the commission has recognized and acted on this need when dealing with other by-catch issues. It has adopted several measures requiring observer coverage to ensure compliance with time-area closures and minimum size limits for bigeye and yellowfin tuna in the mixed tropical tuna fishery (ICCAT 2007a, res. 95-8, rec. 96-1). These measures have yet to be effective, but at least there are estimates of undersized fish and the amount of discards for important fleets. Similarly, ICCAT required that Japan have at least 5% observer coverage in its bigeye fleet to monitor discards of northern swordfish after Japan's prohibition on landings of this stock (ICCAT 2007a, rec. 00-3). No similar mandates have been adopted for Atlantic marlins, even though the SCRS recommended that ICCAT members initiate an observer program for these stocks in 2000 (ICCAT 1995–2007b: 2001, 65).

If total catches, including dead discards, could be accurately estimated, it would be possible for ICCAT to use many of the same measures to enforce regulations on by-catch of marlins or small swordfish in the Atlantic. This has actually taken place for a commercially valuable species. In 1999 and 2002, the United States and Canada were granted dead discard allowances for incidental catches of juvenile swordfish, with the stipulation that any overages of discards were counted against their landings quotas (ICCAT 2007a, rec. 99-2, 02-2).[16] If there had been sufficient governmental concern, a similar system might be used to enforce regulations on by-catch of noncommercial species. Incidental catches of marlins could be counted against contracting parties' landings quotas for bigeye or swordfish, making their capture more costly to fishers and fishing countries. This system could also be used to enforce by-catch regulations on noncontracting parties, but it is unlikely that such steps would be taken.

The SCRS has also recommended time-area closures to protect marlins when they congregate to spawn (ICCAT 1995–2007b: 2006, 65). Except for some key closures that the United States established within its own exclusive economic zone, the commission has been unwilling to use this important tool in reducing by-catch of Atlantic marlins. In contrast, large time-area closures have been adopted to protect juvenile tropical tunas and juvenile bluefin tunas. More important, the commission has established a reporting and punishment system for vessels found targeting bluefin tuna in contravention of this closure (see chapter 10). Similar closures in the U.S. EEZ cannot be enforced in this way, but it is unlikely that any larger, international closures will be adopted as long as ICCAT management is dominated by commercial interests.

In order to apply any of these international enforcement mechanisms to by-catch species, the commission would have to be willing and able to impose sanctions on targeted stocks as punitive measures for excessive incidental catches of marlins. As yet there is insufficient governmental concern for marlins, and ICCAT is not likely to adopt such costly enforcement mechanisms. The vast majority of countries that harvest marlins incidentally face minimal domestic repercussions from the biological depletion of these stocks, but they would encounter political backlash if landings of targeted species had to be reduced to limit marlin by-catch. Therefore, while a politically strong state that is highly susceptible to noncommercial interests, like the United States, might persuade the commission to adopt weak management measures for marlins, substantial monitoring and enforcement mechanisms will not be acceptable to most members.

8.4 Summary

The case of Atlantic blue marlin and white marlin shows how noncommercial interests can alter the behaviors predicted by the vulnerability response framework through countervailing domestic pressures. Susceptible to recreational fishing interests and conservation organizations, the United States deviated from the vulnerability response expectations by pushing for relatively strong management of Atlantic marlins. It is interesting that the United States did not propose any measures that would explicitly curtail targeted commercial harvests in order to protect by-catch species. Instead, it proposed that all marlins should be discarded, dead or alive. This would allow commercial fishers to operate normally, but discourage high-grading, in which fishers keep lower-value fish as a hedge in case they are unable to fill their holds with the higher-value targeted species.[17]

Even though harvests of their targeted stocks were not threatened, most other members of the commission balked at a complete prohibition on landings. This specific position was not predicted by the framework, either. Since a prohibition on landings of marlins would not reduce targeted harvests, mildly vulnerable by-catch countries were not expected to waste effort blocking it. Nonetheless, many ICCAT contracting parties resisted the U.S. proposals and used countermeasures to weaken them.[18] Explanations for this deviation could be either institutional or tactical. Resistance could reflect the meta norm of conservation for use—use being food and jobs, not fun or existence—that pervades international fisheries management. Alternatively, it could simply be that commission members were leveraging their cooperation on marlin management in order to pressure the United States in other arenas.

Whatever the rationale for the reluctance described here, it is clear that incorporating noncommercial interests into the framework will raise many new questions. Indeed, the U.S. positions in the marlins case could lead one to wonder if its behavior in other cases is also generated by noncommercial interests. While it is completely possible that the U.S. response on other stocks was magnified by noncommercial interests, there are a few factors that support the argument for vulnerability response. The first is that commercial interests have a much larger representation on U.S. delegations than noncommercial ones and also are represented by one of the U.S. commissioners to ICCAT.[19] Second, even in defending marlins, the United States did not propose measures that would force commercial fishers to reduce their harvests of targeted stocks.[20] Third and relatedly, the U.S. has not evinced the high willingness to pay for protection of tunas and tuna-like species—including marlins—that it has shown in other forums where conservation interests were paramount, such as the protection of dolphins and sea turtles.[21] Finally, the United States has not shown a consistent position in favor of protection in allocation disputes in the other cases.

One other note on observed policy positions corroborates the framework further. Canada is a highly vulnerable country in almost every case, and generally pushes for strong management. In fact, it evinced forceful leadership in the southern swordfish case even though it doesn't directly participate in that fishery. So, one might think that the Canadian position might be influenced by conservation more than by commercial fishing interests. However, in the case of Atlantic marlins, Canada is neither highly vulnerable nor does it take a position favoring strong management. Instead, Canada expressed positions much closer to those of Japan, the EC, and other countries that favored commercial interests. Given that southern swordfish was never thought to be more than fully exploited and that blue marlin and white marlin are severely depleted, it would seem that a country with conservation or other noncommercial interests would work harder for protection of the latter.

The pattern of management for this case is also interesting. It starts with inactivity, as most other cases do, but quickly transitions into a very long period of concern. This reflects the difficulty of collecting data on by-catch species, as well as a lack of incentive for investment in research on noncommercial stocks. Like the other cases, concern transitions into conflict when the United States proposes management and then moves into accord. As yet, the measures adopted by the commission do not meet the strong criteria used for other cases, nor has substantial rebuilding been reported by the SCRS (see section 8.3). Perhaps in the absence of a powerful international movement to protect Atlantic marlins, there is a glass ceiling on management; one that is set by commercial fishing interests.

Bluefin Tuna

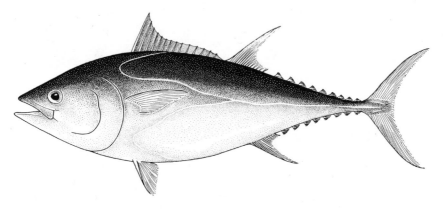

Atlantic Bluefin tuna
(Thunnus thynnus thynnus)

Source: United Nations Food and Agriculture Organization

III

Bluefin Tuna

While yellowfin was the first species to be managed by ICCAT, bluefin tuna (*Thunnus thynnus thynnus*) has been the focus of regulation more than any other species in the commission's jurisdiction. As figure III.1 shows, fifty-four regulations have been adopted specifically for management of Atlantic bluefin tuna, almost twice as many as for any other species. In addition, many of the administrative measures in the general, miscellaneous, and terms-of-reference categories were also adopted to deal with bluefin in particular. Perhaps more important, the commission pioneered the use of statistical document programs, positive and negative vessel lists, and trade-restrictive measures to curtail illegal, unregulated, and unreported harvests of bluefin.

In spite of all the commission's efforts, both the larger eastern stock and the much smaller western stock of Atlantic bluefin have been severely overfished for many years (see figure III.2). One of the highest-priced fishes in the world, Atlantic bluefin tuna is targeted by a wide range of fishers from many different countries. Large bluefin are usually sold to Japanese brokers for between US $10,000 and $20,000 per ton, although historically prices have been as high as US $23,000 per ton (NMFS 2007). These fish usually weigh between 350 and 560 kg, so just one fish can be worth between US $3,000 and $11,500 depending on size, quality, and the state of the market (FAO 2007a). Smaller bluefin are also sold locally in coastal countries. Prices are not as high as for sushi-quality fish destined for Japan, but are still better than for many other species (Oceanic Development et al. 2005).

Because of its exceptional commercial value, ICCAT negotiations on bluefin tuna have been extremely contentious over the years. This generated a considerable amount of dialogue—more than for any of the previous cases. Other complicating factors include the decision to establish a

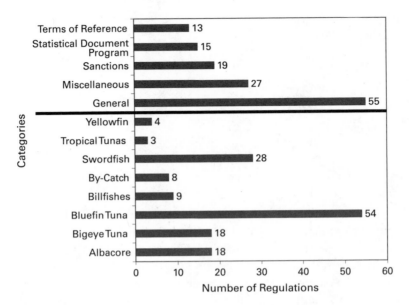

Figure III.1
Resolutions and recommendations adopted by ICCAT from 1969 to 2006.
Source: ICCAT 2007a.

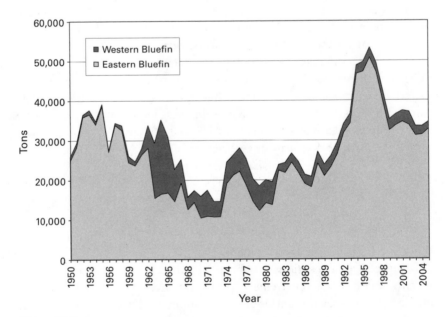

Figure III.2
Reported landings of Atlantic bluefin tuna by stock. Source: ICCAT 2007d.

two-stock management system and the development of bluefin ranching techniques in the Mediterranean. The prevalence of mixing between the eastern and western stocks of Atlantic bluefin results in a heightened interaction between the two cases. A similar situation was observed in the southern and northern swordfish cases, but conflict between countries targeting different stocks is much more acute for bluefin tuna. Potential mixing also adds to uncertainty regarding scientific advice, particularly for the smaller western stock (ICCAT 1995–2007b: 2007, 52).

Bluefin ranching, or *farming* as it is sometimes called, began in the Mediterranean in 1997. Using this technique, fishers can fatten bluefin caught in the wild, keeping them in pens until they reach an optimal size and/or the market is most favorable. Like fish aggregating devices in the mixed tropical tuna case, this development creates a bifurcation in both bluefin cases. Farming substantially reduces the cost per unit of production, altering the economics of direct competition over the eastern stock and indirect competition in the international marketplace. It also exacerbates conflict over mixing because fishers in the west are geographically unable to take advantage of ranching technologies.[1]

Chapter 9 shows how the early enclosure of western Atlantic bluefin has undermined management by reducing direct competition for the stock and thereby limiting governmental concern. Geographic serendipity and a lack of substitutes for the extremely high-priced bluefin are credited as the main causes of divergence from the vulnerability response predictions. In particular, these elements generated the demand for preemptive exclusion on the part of coastal fishing countries in this rather small fishery. Chapter 10 will show how the buildup of governmental concern regarding eastern bluefin receded with the proliferation of ranches in the Mediterranean. Much like the yellowfin case, new farming technologies eased competitive pressures in the fishery, lessening political response. This, combined with the higher levels of flexibility in the east, will then be linked to the current heavily depleted status of the stock.

9

Western Bluefin Tuna

Western Atlantic bluefin is an exceptional fishery in many ways. High-priced like the eastern stock but with a much smaller biomass, western bluefin has received more attention than any other stock in the commission's jurisdiction. In fact, the total allowable catch plus national quota distribution system that is ICCAT's most common management tool evolved in the 1980s as a response to declining populations and harvests of western bluefin. The international monitoring and enforcement mechanisms that were used to such good effect on northern swordfish and bigeye tuna were also pioneered to deal with illegal, unregulated, and unreported harvests of Atlantic bluefin in the 1990s. Moreover, the total allowable catch levels set by the commission have been lower for this stock than for any other.

Given all this, one would think that this case should be ICCAT's greatest success story. However, western bluefin continues to be severely depleted. Owing to the huge spike in landings of western bluefin in the 1960s (see figure 9.1), scientists were already concerned about the fishery by the time the commission began its deliberations in 1970. ICCAT restricted effort and size at first capture as early as 1974, but the western stock continued to decline. In 1981, the SCRS found that western bluefin was severely overexploited (ICCAT 1971–1994: 1973, 85; 1982, 131). Management measures were adopted and harvests were limited from 1982 to date, but significant rebuilding has not been observed. In its most recent assessment, the SCRS found that the spawning stock biomass for western bluefin was around 41% of the level that would support maximum sustainable yield.[1] Only two other stocks that are managed by the commission have been reduced to lower levels, and both of those are by-catch species (see chapter 8).

Like the yellowfin and mixed skipjack cases, the western bluefin case must be divided into two different periods because of changes in

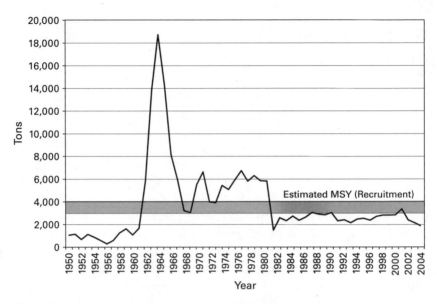

Figure 9.1
Reported landings of western Atlantic bluefin tuna relative to MSY. Source: ICCAT 2007d.

the nature of the fishery. Details on this transformation and its expected impact on national policy positions at ICCAT are laid out in section 9.1. Evidence on response prior to 1979 is presented in section 9.2. It shows that much as with Atlantic marlins, the United States played an unexpected role, owing to the influence of recreational fishers. Section 9.3 then covers the negotiations from 1980 to 1990, when the United States and Canada teamed up against Japan to curb the influx of vessels from its distant-water fleet. Finally, section 9.4 recounts the political response to increasing competition from IUU fleets and from bluefin farms in the eastern Atlantic. It also describes an important intervention by international conservation interests that catalyzed stronger management for western bluefin tuna.

9.1   Vulnerability Response Predictions

By the time the commission began its work in 1969, most of the alternative sources of bluefin tuna, i.e. Pacific and southern bluefin tuna, were already heavily exploited, with little room for expansion. This was due to high demand for bluefin in Japan (ICCAT 1971–1994: 1971, 85–86, 117–118). Until the late 1970s, however, Atlantic bluefin tuna was mainly captured incidentally in swordfish or tropical tuna fisheries. A few countries like Cuba, Morocco, and Panama would sometimes capture bluefin, and some traditional trap fisheries operated in Canada, Spain, and Italy. Otherwise, only the Japanese targeted bluefin in the Atlantic. With the appropriation of air freight technologies around 1979, fishers quickly started targeting bluefin directly to ship it to Japanese sushi markets. There were also management changes around that time. In 1980, the commission established two separate management zones for bluefin tuna, one in the east and the other in the west. Because of these fundamental changes, the western bluefin tuna case is divided into two periods; the first ranges from 1970 to 1978 and the second covers the years from 1979 to 2006.

Like northern swordfish, western bluefin is geographically isolated. Three countries have been able to dominate the fishery from the 1950s onward. After World War II, Japan quickly rebuilt its tuna fleets with postwar technologies, creating one of the first distant-water fleets of the era. They began targeting bluefin in the Pacific, then the Indian Ocean, and finally in the Atlantic. Japanese fleets were responsible for the sudden increase in landings of western Atlantic bluefin in the 1960s that is shown in figure 9.1.[2] They even developed processing facilities in the United States and the Bahamas to facilitate this distant-water enterprise (Christy and Scott 1965, 120–121). Owing to the growth of a purse seine fleet that harvested bluefin and skipjack tunas, U.S. landings of the former were also exceptionally high in the 1960s, although the prices that U.S. fishers received were quite low (around US $0.05–0.10 per pound or $125–270 per metric ton). Canadian harvests at the time were largely by-catch in their fisheries targeting swordfish, although some coastal communities used traps to seasonally harvest the species (ICCAT 1971–1994: 1971, 85–86, 117–118).

The vulnerability response matrix shown in figure 9.2 reflects these commercial interests but also includes countries with harvests in the east because the Atlantic was a single management zone at the time. A note on the eastern and western predictions: there was no indication during this period that the eastern stock of bluefin was overexploited, but the SCRS reported multiple signs of overfishing for the western stock. Therefore the only highly vulnerable country, Portugal, is not expected to express much concern regarding bluefin. Other eastern countries, which are

		Competitiveness	
		Low	High
Flexibility	Low	<u>Highly Vulnerable</u> Portugal	<u>Moderately Vulnerable</u> **Brazil, Mexico, Panama, Cuba,** Tunisia, Libya, etc.
	High	<u>Gradually Vulnerable</u> *Japan (low-flex 1962)*	<u>Mildly Vulnerable</u> By-catch: **Canada and USA,** Spain, France, Italy, etc.

Figure 9.2
Vulnerability response matrix for bluefin tuna (1970–1978). Countries shown in bold type harvest eastern stock; countries in italics harvest both stocks; all others harvest western stock. A list ending in "etc." indicates that countries have been omitted from this summary for ease of reference. See table B.9 in appendix B for a full list.

indicated in plain font in the matrix, are likewise expected to be rather apathetic about the stock as long as their targeted harvests are not threatened.

Already low-flex by 1970, gradually vulnerable Japan targets both stocks and is expected to propose strong management measures that are relatively well enforced. In this part of the historical context, this refers to binding rather than nonbinding resolutions. Although their landings of this stock are quite small, moderately vulnerable countries will still use blocking or countermeasures to protect their rights to develop their fishing fleets. Likewise, since bluefin is a by-catch for U.S., Canadian, French, Spanish, and several other fleets, these countries are expected to work to prevent the adoption of any measures that would force them to reduce harvests of their targeted stocks (see table 9.1).

After 1980, the two stocks were split into separate management categories, so the second set of vulnerability predictions only includes countries with fleets harvesting western bluefin (see table 9.2). Coastal fleets bordering the western Atlantic did not gain access to the lucrative Japanese market until the 1970s, when the establishment of exclusive economic zones forced the Japanese to cut back their distant-water fleets. North American fishers altered their strategies to target larger bluefin, and new air freight technologies were adopted to fly the fish from the United States and Canada to Tokyo. This inaugurated the second period in the

Table 9.1

Overview of Vulnerability Response Categorization and Prediction for Bluefin Tuna (1970–1978)

Category	Countries	Predictions
Highly vulnerable	Portugal	Propose strong management, with increasing willingness to pay if *eastern* stock is depleted
Gradually vulnerable	*Japan (low-flex after 1962)*	Propose strong management, with increasing willingness to pay
Moderately vulnerable	**Brazil, Mexico, Panama, Cuba,** Tunisia, Libya, etc.	Blocking or countermeasures on any proposals that limit development of their fleets; side payments or concessions for cooperation
Mildly vulnerable	By-catch: **Canada and United States,** Spain, France, Italy, etc.	Blocking or countermeasures on any proposals that reduce catches of targeted stocks

Notes: Countries in bold harvest eastern stock; countries in italics target both stocks; all others harvest western stock; A list ending in "etc." indicates that countries have been omitted from this summary for ease of reference. See table B.9 in appendix B for a full list.

management of western bluefin tuna. A few additional fleets entered after 1979, but the biggest difference is that the United States and Canada move to the highly vulnerable category, as shown in figure 9.3. As such, they are expected to prefer strong management and evince increasing willingness to pay as the stock is depleted. As in previous cases, no response is predicted until the SCRS signals that the stock is overfished.

Other countries in the fishery are expected to maintain the same policy positions as in the previous period. However, there are two other major changes that occurred after 1979. First, in the late 1980s, IUU fleets began targeting western bluefin. With exceptionally low operating costs and high flexibility, these fleets fit into the mildly vulnerable category economically. These fishers are not represented by a particular country, so there is no potential for political response, unless noncompliance can be considered as such. However, the incursion of IUU fleets increases direct competition over the stock and may therefore magnify political response by more vulnerable countries. Similarly, the introduction of farming technologies in the eastern and southern bluefin fisheries heightened international competition throughout the 1990s by allowing fleets in

Table 9.2
Overview of Vulnerability Response Predictions for Western Bluefin Tuna (1979–2006)

Category	Countries	Predictions
Highly vulnerable	Canada and United States	Always propose strong management measures, evince increasing but limited willingness to pay the costs of management .
Gradually vulnerable	Japan (low-flex after 1962)	Propose or accept strong management, with increasing willingness to pay for management also in this period
Moderately vulnerable	Brazil, Mexico, Panama, etc.	Blocking or countermeasures on any proposals that limit development of their fleets; side payments or concessions for cooperation
Mildly vulnerable	Korea and NEI[a]	Blocking or countermeasures on all strong management unless there are substantial side payments

Notes: A list ending in "etc." indicates that countries have been omitted from this summary for ease of reference. See table B.10 in appendix B for a full list.
[a] Economic position only. Not contracting parties to ICCAT, therefore no political response is predicted.

		Competitiveness	
		Low	High
Flexibility	Low	Highly Vulnerable Canada and USA	Moderately Vulnerable Brazil, Mexico, Panama, etc.
	High	Gradually Vulnerable Japan (low-flex 1962)	Mildly Vulnerable Korea and NEI

Figure 9.3
Vulnerability response matrix for western bluefin tuna (1979–2006). Prediction for NEI is economic position only. Since they are not contracting parties to ICCAT, no political response is predicted. A list ending in "etc." indicates that countries have been omitted from this summary for ease of reference. See table B.10 in appendix B for a full list.

those areas to sell larger fish, increasing the quantity supplied and driving down prices (FAO 2007b, 2007c). A recession in Japan added to this impact, putting further economic pressure on the fleets targeting western bluefin (Bestor 2000).

9.2   The Recreational Interests Exception (Pre-1979)

When the commission commenced its activities in 1970, scientists knew little about Atlantic bluefin. It was thought that there might be two stocks, one in the east and one in the west, but the SCRS also recognized that there was some mixing between them and could not be certain that they were truly separate (ICCAT 1971–1994: 1971, 69, 117–118). By 1971, the SCRS began recommending a limit on the size at first capture for bluefin and by 1974 it also recommended a temporary reduction in harvests of large fish to maintain the spawning stock (ICCAT 1971–1994: 1972, 95–97; 1975, 76–82). Contrary to expectations, the mildly vulnerable United States and Canada worked to push through both minimum size and effort limits (ICCAT 1971–1994: 1975, 28, 33, 47, 50–53).[3] These measures fell short of SCRS advice and were not fully enforced, but were still much stronger than would be expected from the framework.

Given the historically high landings by recreational fishers in the United States and Canada, it is likely that these noncommercial interests were responsible for the 1974 regulations, much as in the marlins case presented in chapter 8 (ICCAT 1971–1994: 1980, 131).[4] Canada was also home to a small trap fishery that served a domestic market for bluefin tuna. This may have contributed to its behavior as well.[5] Contemporary evidence is available regarding the intervention of recreational fishers in the United States. Prior to the ICCAT meeting in 1974, U.S. recreational fishers proposed western bluefin as a "threatened species" under the Endangered Species Act of 1973. Successful listing would result in the reduction of human activities seen to be harmful to the stock within U.S. jurisdiction. According to an account from recreational fishers, this caused the United States to work with Canada to develop a bilateral management plan for their coastal waters (*SFI Bulletin* 1974, 2).[6] It would not be surprising if this cooperation extended to similarly reducing Japanese harvests through ICCAT.

A similar pattern continued as long as the price of North American landings remained low.[7] Although the SCRS reported small positive indications regarding the health of the stock in 1977, the United States and Canada began recommending measures that would separate the two stocks and prohibit shifts in effort from the east to the west. In 1978 they went further, proposing that catches be limited to the average of landings from 1970 to 1974 and the size limit increased to 28 kg (ICCAT 1971–1994: 1978, 63–65, 72; 1979, 60–61; 1980, 71).[8] This would reduce overall landings by about 300 tons, but would have a disproportionate impact on the Japanese, whose harvests had grown from 1975 to 1980, while U.S. and Canadian landings declined (see figure 9.1). The Japanese themselves must have noticed this, because they expressed a preference for a 1975–1978 reference period (ICCAT 1971–1994: 1979, 60–61). It is interesting that because the Japanese harvested larger fish, they would be competing directly with recreational fishers for one of their most coveted trophy species.

This was the first political attempt by coastal countries to exclude others from the fishery targeting western bluefin. It occurred at a time when scientific concern was relatively low—the SCRS did recommend finding alternative means of reducing fishing pressure on small fish, but was generally satisfied with other aspects of the stock (ICCAT 1971–1994: 1979, 128).[9] Again, this level of interest is not predicted by the vulnerability response framework because bluefin was still a by-catch for U.S. and Canadian commercial fleets. Much as in the southern swordfish case, the evidence suggests that this was a tactical move by coastal countries to limit access by distant-water fleets. Noncommercial interests also played a larger role than predicted by vulnerability response, which explains the higher than expected political will to limit the growth of Japanese landings.

Most of the other positions expressed in this period were more in line with the vulnerability response expectations. Brazil spoke up for the rights of coastal countries, although it did not block consensus or object to the bluefin measures. On the eastern side, Morocco spoke out against effort limits based on its need for flexibility as a by-catch country. Other countries, like France, Spain, and Italy, accepted the relatively toothless measures proposed in 1974, but resisted attempts to reduce bluefin landings in 1977 and beyond (ICCAT 1971–1994: 1975, 33).[10] For its part, low-flex Japan expressed grave concern about the stock and willingly accepted the 1974 minimum size limit. However, the Japanese were not yet willing to give up their access to adult bluefin, as evinced by their statements against the 1978 proposal to limit effort. In fact, their suggestion for a different reference period is a classic example of countermeasure tactics, although in the end neither proposal on effort restrictions was adopted by the commission.

9.3   Initial Exclusionary Measures (1980–1990)

From 1979 on, conflicts between recreational and commercial interests grew within the United States and Canada as commercial fleets began targeting adult bluefin. This made reducing catch levels more difficult, but increased incentives to shift the costs of management to other countries. At the international level, U.S. and Canadian proposals on two-stock management were blocked by an informal coalition consisting of Japan, Korea, and countries that were gradually and moderately vulnerable in the fishery for eastern bluefin (ICCAT 1971–1994: 1978, 63–65, 72; 1979, 60–61; 1980, 71).[11]

In 1980, that coalition dissolved and the two-stock management approach was adopted. This time Portugal proposed the division, with the support of Brazil and Canada. There is no direct explanation for the change in the commission's perspective on the separation of eastern and western stocks. The SCRS did not alter its position on the matter, and no statements were made by parties regarding the change (ICCAT 1971–1994: 1981, 44, 68–69, 78–79, 80).[12] However, two interesting items show up under closer scrutiny. First, the dividing line between the stocks was set at longitude 45° W, 15 degrees further west than the initial boundary proposed in 1977, reducing the size of the western management area while increasing the size of the eastern zone (ICCAT 1971–1994: 1979, 60; 1981, figure 1). Canada also sought to placate moderately vulnerable Brazil and gradually vulnerable Japan by recognizing their interest in the stock and stating that management costs should be borne evenly (ICCAT 1971–1994: 1981, 78–79). Such tactical moves are not predicted by the framework, but this underlines the importance of incorporating a geospatial element into future analyses.

Aside from accepting the two-stock management approach, no new measures were approved in 1980, but substantial changes were adopted in 1981. A new assessment showed that the western stock of Atlantic bluefin was much more severely depleted than scientists had previously believed. To prevent further declines, the SCRS recommended large reductions in fishing mortality on all fish, but particularly 1–4-year-olds (ICCAT 1971–1994: 1982, 129, 131). Supported by Canada, the United

States presented a bold proposal to reduce landings of western bluefin from almost 6,000 tons to a mere 545 tons, to be taken for scientific purposes. Countries targeting eastern bluefin were concerned that such a drastic reduction would cause a transfer of fishing effort to the east, so a clause was added to prohibit such a shift. Japan vociferously objected to the proposal and the science upon which it was based. The scientific quota was increased to 800 tons, but this did not satisfy the Japanese and the proposal was adopted by majority vote in spite of their objections (ICCAT 1971–1994: 1982, 45–46, 74–75, 84–87).[13]

National allocations of this scientific quota were not adopted in 1981, but from reported landings data it is clear that the greatest burden of the mandated catch reduction was borne by Japan. Its harvests were reduced by more than 3,000 tons to less than 300 tons. Some of the displaced Japanese effort shifted to target bigeye tuna in tropical waters, while about 16% of their longline fleet exited the Atlantic (ICCAT 1971–1994: 1984, 269). In addition, landings reported by the United States and Canada were reduced by almost half from 1981 to 1982.[14] Even so, the value of U.S. and Canadian catches went up because prices virtually doubled in that one year (NMFS 2007). However, the distribution of catch changed drastically. In the United States, purse seine harvests were severely reduced, whereas recreational and longline catches increased somewhat. Canadian purse seiners also lost out, replaced at first by trap fisheries and later by recreational fishers (ICCAT 2007d).[15]

Between increasing prices and redistribution of catches, the countries dominating western bluefin management faced considerable domestic pressure to expand production after the drastic reduction of 1981. At the 1982 meeting of the commission, the less vulnerable Japanese were particularly adamant that the science that had led to the 1981 regulations was overly pessimistic (ICCAT 1971–1994: 1983, 87–88). The SCRS scientists themselves had to admit that 1982 harvests, which were about 600 tons above the mandated 800 tons, were insufficient for assessments. Still, the SCRS recommended that the commission continue the 1981 regime for a few years to give western bluefin a chance to rebuild (ICCAT 1971–1994: 1983, 122, 126). At the insistence of Japan, and with little discussion from others, Canada presented a new proposal that was similar to the previous year's regulations except that it would set the scientific quota for 1983 at 2,660 tons, more than four times the recommended limit. It also closed the Gulf of Mexico to targeted bluefin harvests to protect spawning fish and juveniles (ICCAT 1971–1994: 1983, 79).

Sharing arrangements were adopted along with the higher scientific quota in 1983. Shares were established as per those agreed for 1982, with the addition of a minor exception to placate Brazil. Although there is no official record of the distribution of this scientific quota—which was negotiated in a trilateral consultation among the major players, not at the actual commission meeting—an analysis of reported landings suggests that the United States received about 55% of the catch, while Japan and Canada split the remainder. It is also important to note that landings for scientific purposes are processed and sold just like any other harvest.[16] So domestic fishers were still able to take advantage of skyrocketing prices for Atlantic bluefin throughout the 1980s. Moreover, fleets from the United States, Canada, and Japan were guaranteed a virtual monopoly on the western stock of the species. Distant-water fishing fleets from Taiwan or Korea were now politically excluded. Geographically excluded countries like Brazil could be accommodated because they were not likely to catch more than a few metric tons per year in their coastal zones.[17]

As long as western bluefin remained overexploited, the three major fishing countries would have to keep their landings relatively low, but they would also be able to justify the exclusion of potential competitors. These circumstances were even more advantageous for the United States and Canada, which could also use the state of the stock as leverage to curtail production by the more flexible Japanese fleet. Throughout the 1980s, these highly vulnerable countries maintained the need for stringent management measures, refuting continued Japanese insistence that the science was wrong and higher catches could be sustained. Japan consistently proposed a scientific quota of 3,850 tons but could never gain the agreement of the United States and Canada, who stuck to the 2,660-ton limit.

While U.S. and Canadian restraint is laudable in some ways, SCRS expectations regarding the quota levels of the 1980s were never very optimistic. Uncertainty was part of the problem, insofar as the scientists were unable to agree on specific estimates for benchmarks like MSY and B_{MSY}.[18] Even so, the best evaluation of the 2,660-ton scientific quota was the 1984 assessment that it might rebuild the stock in 30 years' time (ICCAT 1971–1994: 1985, 132, 135). A year later, this assessment was revised to suggest that mortality at 2,660 tons could rebuild the stock 10% over its current level, but that the biomass of large, spawning fish would continue to decline because the current mortality was too high (ICCAT 1971–1994: 1986, 124–127). For the rest of the decade, SCRS advice vacillated between assessments that predicted small amounts of rebuilding and those that estimated a flat trend in abundance (ICCAT 1971–1994: 1989, 131; 1990, 156).

Continued adherence to the 2,660-ton scientific quota in spite of the relatively lower assessments of the SCRS contrasts sharply with the risk aversion displayed by these same countries in the bigeye and northern swordfish cases, neither of which was ever as heavily overexploited as western bluefin. Temporal elements may be to blame, including the state of the science in the 1980s relative to the 1990s. Also, the experience with bluefin tuna may have been a learning opportunity for these two countries. That said, one cannot rule out the possibility that U.S. and Canadian policy preferences were less conservative because they were not vulnerable to competition from countries with lower costs of production. Evidence for this lies in the redistribution of landings after 1981, which allowed these countries to appropriate a larger percentage of the smaller catch and thereby enlarge their share in an increasingly lucrative marketplace. In addition, the rapid retrenchment to a higher scientific quota in 1982 was not recommended by the scientific community, nor was it ever thought to be a fully effective measure. However, it would give U.S. and Canadian commercial fishers room to expand production.

9.4   The Conservation Interests Exception (Post-1990)

By the mid-1980s, commercial interests were deeply entrenched in the bluefin fisheries of the United States and Canada. Recreational interests were not completely displaced, but much of their power was coopted. As long as commercial fishers were secure in their ability to appropriate revenues from the stock, these two sets of interests were at odds. Once the direct threat of IUU harvests and the indirect threat of farmed bluefin production took off in the post-1990 period, both types of fishers from these now highly vulnerable countries had substantial incentives to prefer stronger management measures. Nevertheless, the records of the period suggest that management was shaped by more than just vulnerability response augmented by recreational fishing interests.

Although it was a bit early for vulnerable countries to feel the pressure of competition from nascent IUU and farming production, 1991 was an important year in the timeline of bluefin tuna management. The SCRS undertook an extensive scientific study of the stock, utilizing several new assessment techniques as well as improved databases. Given the minimal nature of management in the 1980s, it is not surprising that the results of these studies were either mildly encouraging or deeply disturbing, depending on the perspective of the reader. Basically, the SCRS reported that the decline in small and medium-sized fish had been arrested, but that the population of adult, spawning bluefin had a 50% chance of being lower in 1993, *even if* the total catch were cut in half. In fact, it was expected that spawning fish would remain below 1992 levels until 1995 and could stay depressed even longer.[19]

Without outside pressure, ICCAT members might not have responded to this assessment any more strongly than they had to previous SCRS statements about declines in the spawning population. However, in 1991, international conservation organizations like the National Audubon Society and the World Wildlife Fund worked with Sweden in an attempt to list Atlantic bluefin tuna under the Convention for International Trade in Endangered Species of Fauna and Flora (CITES). Because such a listing would result in prohibition of trade in Atlantic bluefin, this maneuver certainly got the attention of ICCAT contracting parties. With little discussion, commission members targeting western bluefin tuna agreed to a 4-year plan that would gradually reduce allowable landings of the stock from 2,660 to 1,729 tons, as shown in table 9.3 (ICCAT 2007a, rec. 91-1).

Intervention by conservation organizations through the CITES proposal does not directly violate the commercial-interest assumption that underlies the vulnerability response framework. Granted, Sweden's role

Table 9.3
Scientific Quota Scheme from 1991 Management Plan for Western Bluefin Tuna

Period	Maximum in period (tons)	Maximum in first year (tons)	Remainder (tons)
1992 and 1993	4,788	2,660	2,128
1994 and 1995	3,990	2,261	1,729

Source: ICCAT 2007a, rec. 91-1.

in this maneuver could not be predicted by the framework, but the responses of ICCAT members would still be focused on neutralizing the exogenous threat to their domestic fishing fleets. That said, there is evidence that certain members of the commission were not completely dominated by commercial interests. Most notably, conservation organizations had first pressured the United States to recommend western bluefin for listing under CITES. Their efforts resulted in a National Marine Fisheries Service plan to propose the species for listing, but public response to the idea was strongly negative and so the U.S. government chose not to move ahead with the plan (ICCAT 1971–1994: 1992, 25).

Another major shift in 1991 was a pronounced and concerted movement by all three major fishing countries to prevent nonmembers from exploiting western bluefin tuna. At their behest, the commission took its first steps toward more effective monitoring and enforcement measures by setting up a working group to look into the technical aspects of trade documentation and the legal implications of sanctions (ICCAT 2007a, res. 91-2). Such measures had been discussed in the past, but there was never enough political will to generate action. Between the CITES threat and evidence of increasing harvests by fleets from nonmember countries, incentives to exclude these countries were much higher in the 1990s than they had been in previous decades. By 1992 the commission adopted a statistical document program for bluefin tuna so that it could track trade in the species (ICCAT 2007a, rec. 92-1). This was closely followed by the 1994 Bluefin Action Plan, which provided for multilateral trade measures and the first enforcement via sanctions, levied in 1996 against Belize, Honduras, and Panama (ICCAT 2007a, res. 94-3; rec. 96-11, 96-12).

Although trade-based monitoring and enforcement measures seemed to be quite effective at excluding nonmembers, the conservation mechanisms adopted for western bluefin were insufficient to rebuild the stock. According to the 1993 assessment, reported landings in 1992 were below the scientific quota for western bluefin but were still too high to prevent further declines in the stock. Preliminary estimates showed that the biomass of the stock was down to 8–26% of the 1975 level and was probably at 6–12% of B_{MSY}. The SCRS stated that catches would need to be reduced to 1,200 tons just to get a 50% chance of maintaining the stock at current levels (ICCAT 1971–1994: 1994, 204–205).

At the subsequent meeting of the commission, Japan, Canada, and the United States all expressed consternation regarding the continued decline

Table 9.4
1993 Quota Scheme for Western Bluefin Tuna

Year	Scientific quota (tons)	Japanese quota (tons)
1994	1,995	250
1995	1,200	150

Source: ICCAT 2007a, rec. 93-5.

of western bluefin tuna. The cuts they had made had been drastic and difficult, so they expected some return in the form of increased biomass. None of these delegations recognized that past management measures had never quite matched up with SCRS recommendations (ICCAT 1971–1994: 1994, 86–88). Even as it questioned the accuracy of the scientific advice, the United States acted on that year's findings by proposing a plan to cut the scientific monitoring quota to 800 tons by 1998, with distribution the same as in the past (pp. 103–104). Given the impact that these measures would have had on its harvests, it is not surprising that gradually vulnerable Japan was unwilling to accept such a large cut (ICCAT 1971–1994: 1994, 90).

Eventually the commission agreed to set the quota for western bluefin according to the scheme shown in table 9.4. This would result in a TAC in line with SCRS advice by 1995. It would also limit the Japanese portion to 400 tons for the 2-year period, about half of what their reported landings had been in previous years (ICCAT 2007a, rec. 93-5). This measure was coupled to another that limited take in the central Atlantic to a total of 1,300 tons for the 1994–1995 period (rec. 93-6). Technically, this region fits into the eastern management area, but because it also has implications for the western stock, it is reported here. Harvests in that location, which is just on the eastern side of the management boundary, had increased over the past decade as Japanese fishers who had been pushed away from the western stock moved east. Since the presumable overlap between the two stocks would be greatest in the center, it was felt that the Japanese should decrease their harvests to reduce landings of both stocks (ICCAT 1971–1994: 1994, 90, 92, 108).

Japan was not the only member pressured to cut back its harvests at the 1993 meeting. Highly vulnerable countries also criticized the contracting parties targeting eastern bluefin for ignoring management measures (ICCAT 1971–1994: 1994, 89). Having pushed two-stock management through in the 1970s, the United States and Canada now questioned the boundary. They suggested, as Japan had all along, that mixing between the two stocks might mean that separate management was not equal. Moreover, they asked the SCRS to investigate the possibility that overfishing in the east might have undermined the conservation measures adopted for the west. This was a significant escalation in the rhetoric that western fishing countries used against their counterparts in the east (ICCAT 1971–1994: 1994, 207).

The 1994 meeting of the commission brought a respite for fishers targeting western bluefin, but no reduction in their stance toward IUUs and eastern management. New and very uncertain scientific analysis suggested that replacement yield, the amount of harvest that would prevent further decline, was around 2,660 tons instead of 1,200 tons. The consultative body recommended a scientific quota of between 2,000 and 2,200 tons (ICCAT 1995–2007b: 1995, 159–160). This was fortuitous since none of the fleets targeting western bluefin had kept to their allotted quotas in 1994 (see figure 9.1). Japan questioned the precautionary quota levels recommended by the SCRS, but a new scientific quota of 2,200 tons was adopted with little discussion. Having paid the price the previous year, Japan was rewarded with a larger percentage of the new catch level. Nonetheless, its harvests in the central Atlantic remained limited.

While western management suddenly became less restrictive, rhetoric about the impact of east-west mixing on the western stock intensified, as did discussions on the exclusion of nonmember fleets. The mixing issue precipitated an as-yet cordial discourse, particularly between the United States, Canada, and Japan on the one hand and Spain and France on the other. All of these countries agreed that fishing by nonmembers was a serious problem that needed to be solved (ICCAT 1995–2007a: 1995, 157–163, 175–177). To do this, they adopted the 1994 Bluefin Action Plan, which established the process through which nonmember countries could be sanctioned for continued violation of ICCAT regulations. They also created a "white list" of vessels authorized to fish for bluefin tuna in the Atlantic (ICCAT 2007a, res. 94-8). Last but not least, the commission passed a measure that urged contracting parties to collect information on vessels seen fishing for bluefin tuna in contravention of ICCAT management measures. This information would be reported to the secretariat, which would pass it on to the responsible flag state (ICCAT 2007a, res. 94-9).

In 1994, a review committee was established to broach the subject of noncompliance by members as well, followed by the official establishment of the ICCAT Compliance Committee in 1995 (ICCAT 2007a, oth. 95-15). Thus the commission set up a dual-track compliance system, with members evaluated under the compliance committee and nonmembers evaluated by the Permanent Working Group for the Improvement of ICCAT Statistics and Conservation Measures, which had been created in 1992 (ICCAT 2007a, rec. 92-2). Moreover, the enforcement mechanisms applied to each group were slightly different in that members could be punished first by downward adjustment of their quota. Only overages for two consecutive years might result in trade measures (ICCAT 2007a, rec. 96-14). Hypothetically, since ICCAT generally operates through consensus, members could prevent trade-based enforcement on their domestic fleets by blocking consensus.[20]

Discussions regarding the scientific quota for western bluefin in 1995 and subsequent years were similar to those of the 1994 meeting, although conflicts between east and west were much more rancorous than they had been in the past (see chapter 10). Recriminations were exchanged between countries targeting the western and eastern stocks, with everyone heaping blame on Japan for its harvests in the central Atlantic and on IUU fleets for undermining management of both stocks. In 1996, the SCRS estimated that up to a quota of 2,500-tons had a 50% chance of rebuilding the stock to 26% of B_{MSY} in 20 years (ICCAT 1995–2007a: 1997, 112). Japan proposed that ICCAT should set the scientific quota at 2,354 tons for 1997 and 1998. The premise of this proposition was that this level would result in an overall fishing mortality of 2,500 tons after unreported catches. The United States and Canada grudgingly accepted the increase, most of which went to Japan, although both delegations expressed a strong interest in faster rebuilding levels.

Two years later, countries targeting western bluefin agreed to a total allowable catch of 2,500 tons for 1999. This was a compromise between the Japanese proposal of 3,000 tons and the Canadian proposal of 2,000 tons. As expected, the proposal from highly vulnerable Canada was much more conservative than the proposal from gradually vulnerable Japan (ICCAT 1995–2007a: 1999, 143–146, 166–168). According to one of the SCRS assessments, a fishing mortality of over 2,500 tons would be unsustainable, but a different model showed that catches above 2,000 tons could not be maintained in the long run. In an intriguing

Table 9.5
2002 SCRS Assessment Scenarios for Western Bluefin Tuna

	Optimistic model (low recruitment)	Pessimistic model (high recruitment)
TAC at 3,000 tons	83%	11%
TAC at 2,500 tons	97%	20%

Source: ICCAT 1995–2007b: 2003, 76–78.

twist, the compromise quota was incorporated in a 20-year rebuilding plan in which the annual scientific quota could be adjusted only if the SCRS determined that the new level would result in a 50% chance of rebuilding to MSY within the 20-year period. The plan also included a convoluted distribution scheme that would essentially reward Japan if ICCAT increased the quota, but penalize it if the quota needed to be reduced at some future point (ICCAT 2007a, rec. 98-7).

Having struck this bargain, the countries targeting western bluefin stuck to it for 4 years, during which time the scientific assessments became even more uncertain. In 2000, SCRS advice was split along two sets of assumptions because of competing ideas regarding the recruitment level of the stock. One perspective was much more optimistic than any of the past assessments.[21] Japan expressed a preference for the more hopeful scenario in 2000, but no changes were made until 2002, when the results of the two models diverged even further (see table 9.5; ICCAT 1995–2007b: 2003, 76–78). With most of the discussion focused on reducing eastern catches, countries targeting the western stock agreed to increase the TAC to 2,700 tons (ICCAT 2007a, rec. 02-7).

The only comments directly targeted at western management in 2002 were (1) a proposal made by the United States to move the boundary between the two stocks, resulting in a higher quota in the west, and (2) various requests for a quota from developing countries, several of whom had already been accommodated with small allocations. Eastern countries quickly shot down the first proposal, but there was considerable discussion on the second issue. In spite of substantial posturing, Mexico received a quota of 25 tons—their delegation had requested 180 tons—while Bermuda and St. Pierre and Miquelon had to remain content with the 4 tons that had been allotted to them previously (ICCAT 1995–2007a: 2003, 309–310). Neither the United States nor Canada mentioned its reasons for accepting the more optimistic model, but it is interesting to note that the quota distribution was temporarily set so that Japan gave up the bonus amount that it was allotted in the 1998 rebuilding plan (ICCAT 2007a, rec. 02-7).

ICCAT kept the western bluefin quota at 2,700 tons for 4 more years. The next scientific assessment was postponed until 2006 so that the impact of the new measures could be incorporated into the analysis. By this time, the different recruitment scenarios had been reconciled, so SCRS advice was more straightforward. It said that the current TAC was likely to result in an annual decline of about 3% in the spawning stock biomass. It further stated that reducing the total catch to about 2,100 tons would allow the spawning stock biomass to increase about 1.5% per year. Even more alarming to some was the recent failure to catch the full TAC for western bluefin. After more than a decade of overharvests, reported landings had dropped to about 2,350 tons in 2003 and declined to around 1,830 tons by 2005. The SCRS could not determine whether this reduction was due to a northward shift of the stock or to an overall decline in biomass (ICCAT 1995–2007b: 2007, 51–53).

Either way, the United States was not very happy since its fleets were the most deeply affected by the deficits. Together with Japan, the United States proposed a TAC of 2,100 tons. This was adopted after the United States agreed to a 2-year temporary quota transfer to Mexico for 2007 (75 tons) and 2008 (100 tons). These amounts were taken out of U.S. underages from previous years and so did not reduce its overall quota (ICCAT 1995–2007a: 2007, 160–161). Mexico has never reported more than 30 tons of bluefin tuna in a single year and—assuming that Mexican fleets abide by it—the 1982 closure of the Gulf of Mexico would constrain their ability to capture the species (ICCAT 2007a, rec. 82-1). Still, moderately vulnerable Mexico was able to capitalize on the deep concern of the highly vulnerable United States to collect a substantial side payment. Other moderately vulnerable countries have also negotiated for concessions or quota allocations, as predicted by the framework. In contrast, mildly vulnerable fleets, particularly those made up of IUU vessels, were only brought in line by threats and strong punitive measures.

9.5 Summary

The case of western bluefin tuna shows many of the same shortcomings that were observed in other tests of the framework. Noncommercial interests played a role in both periods, violating the assumption of "purely commercial interests" that underlies the vulnerability response framework. The 1991 CITES nomination was exceptional in that conservation organizations mobilized an international institution to pressure ICCAT members, rather than just working through domestic decision makers. Geopolitical tactics were also observed in U.S. and Canadian maneuvers to limit the expansion of Japanese effort in the late 1970s. Much as in the southern swordfish case, these coastal countries proactively pursued the political and economic benefits of curtailing access by distant-water fleets before heavy competition was evident in the fishery. On the other hand, competition might have been tougher than indicated by the proxy of scientific estimates of biological depletion because the science was so uncertain at the time. The sudden discovery that the western bluefin stock was severely depleted in 1981 suggests that previous assessments did not really reflect the seriousness of the situation.[22]

What is more disconcerting is the behavior of highly vulnerable and low-flex, gradually vulnerable countries after that first dire announcement. As expected, the highly vulnerable United States and Canada initially proposed strong management. However, their position changed within a year, meeting the much less cautious position of low-flex, gradually vulnerable Japan by 1982. Moreover, these countries continued to maintain relatively high catch levels until the CITES threat of 1991. Once that threat was removed, these members quickly returned to their previous positions.[23] By 1996, the scientific quota for western bluefin tuna was back to pre-1991 levels and stock estimates for western bluefin tuna are only marginally larger today than they were in the early 1990s (ICCAT 1971–1994: 1991, 168–172; 1995–2007b: 2006, 53).

Japan proposed most of the increases in the scientific quota through the 1990s, and its proposals usually fit the strong criterion insofar as they lined up with scientific advice.[24] As in several other cases, this advice had become much less certain over the years, but it is also important to note that the underlying goal of SCRS advice for western bluefin was not the same as for other commercially targeted stocks. Rebuilding plans for bigeye tuna and northern swordfish called for a 50% chance of rebuilding biomass to the level that would support MSY in 10 years. The best expectation from advice on western bluefin was that the stock would double its current level in 20 years. The SCRS posited that much bigger cuts would be required to get to the biomass that would support MSY in the same time frame.

Another contributing factor here was a much slower growth in willingness to pay than was observed in the other cases. With the split in scientific advice in the late 1990s, the United States and Canada expressed a preference for more cautionary levels yet acceded to the more optimistic interpretation of the science espoused by Japan. Until the most recent assessment in 2006, the catch levels that were adopted would not have been expected to reduce the stock further, but rebuilding would be much slower if the more pessimistic hypothesis turned out to be true. So, the behavior of these more vulnerable states is not an abrogation of the vulnerability response predictions per se, but their positions do suggest that there was some limit on their willingness to pay. Rebuilding could have been faster and more certain if the United States and Canada had been willing to give up some of their quotas to reduce harvests. Yet from 1994 on, highly vulnerable countries made no cuts in their harvests until the United States temporarily transferred some of its quota to Mexico in 2006 (See appendix C, table C.7 for an overview of this evidence).

All of this suggests that more vulnerable countries were just not that willing to pay to rebuild this highly valuable stock—at least not in terms of additional reductions in their domestic landings. This lack of concern seems counterintuitive, particularly when compared with the other, more successful cases. There are a few possible explanations. For Japan specifically, it may be that it truly believes the more optimistic science, but it is also possible that its interest in maintaining high bluefin prices has led to a preference for low availability. On the other hand, perhaps the price of bluefin is so high and the growth rate of the stock is so low that collapse is a more economically viable option.[25] There is also an alternative that fits with the vulnerability response framework. Bluefin tuna is an exceptional fish. It has few substitutes. In addition, western bluefin tuna is geographically isolated, and political exclusion has prevented the influx of large distant-water fleets (other than the Japanese). Therefore there is much less competition over this stock and much less incentive to engage in strong management.

In fact, all three of these countries have strong domestic controls on their bluefin fleets, reducing domestic as well as international competition. By establishing access rights early in the fishery, countries targeting western bluefin tuna succeeded in limiting access, prolonging their profitability. However, the stock remains severely depleted and the SCRS continues to recommend stringent catch limits. It is likely that biophysical factors like the slow growth of bluefin and mixing between the eastern and western stocks has contributed to this problem, but the long, incautious interpretation of highly uncertain science may also have undermined the rebuilding of western bluefin. In any case, the vulnerability response framework does not seem to apply well in fisheries where competition is limited. The resultant pattern for this case differs from the others in that accord is reached at an early stage but the stock remains severely depleted.

10

Eastern Bluefin Tuna

Much like its western counterpart, eastern Atlantic bluefin tuna has been heavily overexploited as a result of high demand and a lack of effective management intervention. However, because the eastern stock is larger and more prolific than the western stock, it has been able to sustain higher catch levels over the same period. The eastern stock is also targeted by fishers from a wider variety of countries, mostly in Europe and North Africa. Historically, these fishers served domestic markets for bluefin tuna, but began exporting large fish to Japan in the early 1980s (Sahrhage and Lundbeck 1992, 48; Oceanic Development et al. 2005). Coastal markets for bluefin have made recent innovations in trade-based monitoring and enforcement much less effective in the east than they were in the west. While they may not receive exceptionally high prices for landings sold domestically, fishers can easily cash in on illegal or undersized catches by selling them at home, where trade documents are not required.[1] Farming and transshipment also provide fishers harvesting eastern bluefin with opportunities to circumvent trade documentation schemes.

The degree of uncertainty regarding harvests of eastern bluefin has seriously undermined scientific assessment of the stock; so much so that the SCRS could not provide an estimate of MSY or B_{MSY} in 2006. Instead it used an approximation that allowed it to compensate for discrepancies between landings data and known capacity in the area. This suggested that long-run sustainable yields could be maintained at around 45,000 tons or more, but that current fishing effort was more than three times sustainable levels. Using the reported landings only, which were close to the TAC for recent years, the SCRS estimated that the 2004 spawning stock biomass of eastern bluefin was 48% of 1974–1975 levels, which would already have been reduced, owing to relatively high

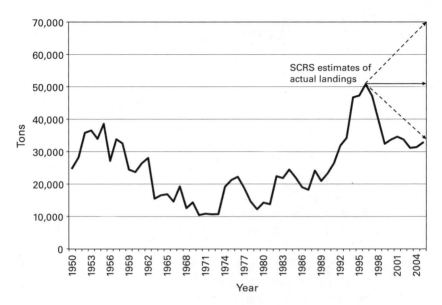

Figure 10.1
Reported landings of eastern bluefin tuna. Source: ICCAT 1995–2007b: 2007, 59, 64; BFTE, figure 1.

catches in the 1950s. It also suggested that the actual condition of the stock was probably much worse because of unreported harvests, which were estimated to be about 15,000 tons above reported landings (see figure 10.1).[2]

Because of the high importance of mixing between the eastern and western Atlantic bluefin stocks, this case is treated in much the same way as the mixed skipjack tuna case presented in chapter 5. As was seen in the southern swordfish case, countries that are vulnerable in one management area may try to influence the management of another area when mixing is suspected. Therefore countries that are vulnerable in the western bluefin case will be identified along with those targeting the eastern stock. Once the vulnerability response predictions are made for these fleets in section 10.1, the evidence is presented in sections 10.2–10.4. The first of these sections describes how political response began building in the early 1990s. Section 10.3 recounts how countries quickly shifted their positions once farming technologies were introduced—temporarily reducing competition—in the mid-1990s. Finally, section 10.4 shows how responsive behavior resumed after that technological advantage was dissipated and section 10.5 summarizes these findings.

10.1   Vulnerability Response Predictions

The eastern stock of bluefin tuna is not as isolated as the western stock, either through geography or political–economic forces. In the 1950s and 1960s, European and North African fleets harvested bluefin for sale in domestic markets, either targeting the fish opportunistically or using traditional tuna corrals.[3] In the 1960s and 1970s, overall fishing effort targeting tunas in the eastern Atlantic gradually shifted toward capture for industrialized canneries. Bluefin was incidental in these fisheries and was not directly targeted by large-scale commercial fishers until the early 1980s, when buyers began using airplanes to transport fresh bluefin to Japan, where it would bring much higher prices. That said, smaller-scale production for domestic consumption continues as an important source of income for local fleets to this day (Oceanic Development et al. 2005, 118).

Technically there should therefore be predictions for at least two periods of vulnerability response—one prior to the shift to direct targeting in 1983 and one after. However, because all of the evidence on vulnerability response for the pre-1983 period was covered in chapter 9 (these stocks were managed together until 1980), and because the eastern stock was not considered to be overexploited in that period (therefore no response is expected), the discussion here is limited to expectations for policy positions after 1983. Figure 10.2 presents the vulnerability matrix under those conditions. Note that countries targeting western bluefin are included in the figure, even though they do not directly target the eastern stock. This is because mixing between the two stocks raises the prospect that overfishing in the east could be depleting the western stock, giving western states an interest in the management of the eastern fishery.

A modification of the original vulnerability response framework, this relaxation of the assumption of separate stocks was incorporated because of the Canadian policy positions that were observed in the southern swordfish case (see chapter 7). As in the mixed skipjack case in chapter 5, this modification will only alter the range of countries identified, not the predictions of their policy preferences (see table 10.1). Thus, Canada and the United States, countries that are highly vulnerable in the western bluefin tuna fishery, are still expected to work for strong management of the eastern fishery. They will increase this pressure as the western stock declines. The motivation for this behavior is also the same as that described in chapter 5: western countries hope that stronger

		Competitiveness	
		Low	High
Flexibility	Low	Highly Vulnerable Canada, USA, and **EC** **(Spain, France** and **Portugal** pre-1997)	Moderately Vulnerable Brazil, **Morocco, Libya,** **Tunisia,** etc.
	High	Gradually Vulnerable *Japan (low-flex 1962)*	Mildly Vulnerable *China, Korea, Taiwan*

Figure 10.2
Vulnerability response matrix for eastern bluefin tuna (1978–2006). Countries in bold primarily harvest the eastern stock; countries in italics harvest both stocks; all others harvest western stock. A list ending in "etc." indicates that countries have been omitted from this summary for ease of reference. See table B.11 in appendix B for a full list.

Table 10.1
Overview of Vulnerability Response Predictions for Eastern Bluefin Tuna (1979–2006)

Category	Countries	Predictions
Highly vulnerable	Canada, United States, and **EC (Spain, France,** and **Portugal** pre-1997)	Always propose strong management measures; evince increasing willingness to pay the costs of management as *targeted* stock declines
Gradually vulnerable	*Japan (low-flex after 1962)*	Propose or accept strong management, with increasing willingness to pay for management
Moderately vulnerable	Brazil, **Morocco, Libya, Tunisia,** etc.	Blocking or countermeasures on any proposals that limit development of their fleets; side payments or concessions for cooperation
Mildly vulnerable	*China, Korea, and Taiwan*	Blocking or countermeasures on any proposals that reduce catches of targeted stocks. Side payments or threats for cooperation

Notes: Countries in bold primarily harvest the eastern stock; countries in italics harvest both stocks; all others harvest western stock. A list ending in "etc." indicates that countries have been omitted from this summary for ease of reference. See table B.11 in appendix B for a full list.

management in the east will increase the availability of fish in the west, thereby reducing competitive pressures in the western fishery.

These countries from the western case are joined in the highly vulnerable category by the European Community, or its constituent member states prior to 1997. Categorizing the EC was rather difficult in this case because it really fits somewhere between the highly and gradually vulnerable categories. Much of the EC catch comes from the Mediterranean, where coastal countries claim only 12-mile territorial seas, rather than 200-mile exclusive economic zones (Cacaud 2005). This circumstance smudges the distinction between coastal and distant-water fishing fleets. For instance, most of the European vessels that target bluefin in the Mediterranean have a shorter range than those that operate in the Atlantic, but they still harvest the fish on the high seas, in areas that would otherwise be part of someone else's EEZ. Similarly, Spanish vessels that operate in the Atlantic can go beyond the Spanish EEZ, but do not travel to the Southern Ocean or the Pacific to target other stocks of bluefin (Oceanic Development et al. 2005, chap. 3). In both cases, the flexibility of EC fleets is still much lower than that of truly distant-water vessels, such as those flagged by Japan, Korea, and Taiwan.

Therefore, in the post-1983 period, Spain, France, and Portugal fit into the highly vulnerable category for eastern bluefin. The responsiveness of Spain and France is expected to be somewhat lower than for other highly vulnerable countries because of the increased flexibility imparted by access to the Mediterranean. Nevertheless, these countries are still expected to be leaders in management of the stock. Once the European Community replaces these EU members of the commission in 1997, it will take on the position of its major fishing countries, France and Spain.

There are many countries in the moderately vulnerable category for eastern bluefin. Mostly bordering the Mediterranean, these include North African countries, such as Algeria, Morocco, Turkey, and Tunisia, as well as Croatia, which joined the commission in 1997 soon after the dissolution of the former Yugoslavia. As coastal countries with low costs of production, they are expected to express concern about the state of the stock, but their participation in any management regime will be contingent on sufficient allowances for the development of their fleets. All Mediterranean countries, both highly and moderately vulnerable, are likely to prefer exclusion of distant-water fleets to a reduction of their own catches.

Of the countries with distant-water fleets targeting eastern bluefin, only Japan is gradually vulnerable. Because its alternative sources of revenue—other stocks of bluefin tuna—have already been overfished, Japan is in the less flexible phase of its fishery by the 1980s, so it is expected to show a fair amount of concern regarding the stock. In contrast, the several mildly vulnerable countries with fleets harvesting eastern bluefin will not exhibit such concern. Taiwan, South Korea, and China will require significant side payments or threats in order to agree to reduce their by-catches of the stock. Considerable ability to monitor and enforce measures will also be necessary to curtail the operations of IUU and flag-of-convenience fleets. In addition, Norway, Iceland, and the Faroe Islands are all high-income countries whose fleets target bluefin opportunistically when the fish are in range. The rest of the time—which can be decades—their fleets target other species and therefore these countries can be extemporaneously placed in the mildly vulnerable category.

Another element that complicates the analysis of the eastern bluefin case is the explosion of farming or ranching activities around 1997. For the western stock, this was just the continuation of a trend: increasing competition for shares in the international marketplace. Implemented in the east rather than the west, farming technologies reduced the costs of production for sashimi-quality bluefin from that stock. This created a temporary boom that increased profits (or more accurately, scarcity rent) in the fishery, reducing competitive pressures on fishers who could cash in on the new technology (Oceanic Development et al. 2005, chap. 4). Mediterranean countries that otherwise would have shown increasing concern are expected to suddenly favor less restrictive measures after 1997. EC members, such as France, Spain, and Italy, will be especially reluctant to reduce farming activities because they benefit doubly from domestic cages and through foreign investment in farms in other Mediterranean countries. In addition, vessels from European fleets often supply farms in developing countries (ICCAT 1995–2007b: 2001, 54).

10.2   Prefarming Response (Pre-1997)

Until the late 1980s, scientists and decision makers alike expressed little concern about the eastern stock of Atlantic bluefin. The SCRS noted signs of overfishing for the entire Atlantic in the 1970s, but once it began running two-stock models in 1978, its evaluation of the eastern stock was fairly positive. Still, full assessments remained impossible because of lack of data through most of the 1970s and 1980s (ICCAT 1971–1994:

1987, 159). With improved data sets in 1988, the SCRS was able to estimate that the biomass of large and medium-sized eastern bluefin tuna
had been reduced by 70 to 80% from 1970 to 1986 (ICCAT 1971–
1994: 1989, 130).[4] The biomass of small fish could not be estimated,
but the scientific report said that minimum estimated landings of undersized fish were about 62% of harvests by numbers in 1986, and might be
as high as 89% in the Mediterranean for that year (ICCAT 1971–1994:
1989, 132, table 18).[5]

Prior to the 1988 assessment, the only concerns expressed by members
targeting eastern bluefin were in regard to the potential for a transfer of
effort to the east, owing to restrictive management measures for western
bluefin. These comments were largely aimed at Japan, the only distant-
water country targeting both stocks at the time. As expected, highly vulnerable countries, namely Spain, France, and Portugal, led the charge to
ensure that the Japanese fleet would not be able to increase its harvests of
eastern bluefin. It was these countries that negotiated the "no eastward
shift" clause that has been included in western management measures
since 1981 (ICCAT 1971–1994: 1982, 74–75).

In the mid-1980s, these countries became alarmed about the growing
presence of Japanese longliners in the Mediterranean. No ICCAT measures were adopted to deal with this problem because Japan enacted domestic regulations that would cap the number of its vessels in that area
and that established a time-area closure on large-scale longlines in the
Mediterranean as well. As a gradually vulnerable country whose fleets
had run out of room, it is not surprising that Japan took steps to pre-
empt multilateral measures like the severe catch restrictions that had
been adopted for western bluefin (ICCAT 1971–1994: 1985, 69–70;
1986, 66–67). On the other hand, this interaction adds to the evidence
that the coastal–distant-water dichotomy has implications that go beyond the basic vulnerability response framework that was presented in
chapter 2.

After the rather pessimistic assessment of eastern bluefin in 1988,
highly vulnerable France and Spain were the first countries to express
concern about the state of the eastern stock. They were especially
worried about the impact of recent increases in effort by member fleets,
nonmember fleets, and those flying flags of convenience. These two countries, whose own landings had exploded in the past decade, reminded
members not to fish too much and called for improved science on the
stock. In its statement to the commission, Spain particularly asked the

secretariat to remind members of their obligations under existing regulations, notably the 1974 recommendation that established the 6.4-kg minimum size and required fishing countries to maintain their effort at "recent levels."[6]

By 1991, reported landings were not much higher than they had been in 1988. This was around the time that Sweden nominated Atlantic bluefin for a CITES listing. Since the eastern stock was less overexploited than the west, the Swedes proposed it under appendix II of the CITES agreement. The consequences of such a listing would be less severe than under appendix I, because appendix II is a watch list rather than a ban on trade in the stock. Since their fleets were not as threatened, the response of countries targeting eastern bluefin was less intense than that of their western counterparts. Targeting both stocks, Japan worked feverishly to ensure that no such listing could take place, but this is to be expected from a gradually vulnerable country that had run out of viable alternatives. Morocco also joined with the United States, Canada, and Japan in their statement to CITES regarding the responsibilities of ICCAT toward bluefin tuna (ICCAT 1995–2007a: 1991, 26, 68–69).

So, while 1991 was an important turning point in the management of western bluefin tuna, it had little impact on the eastern stock. Reported landings increased substantially in subsequent years, peaking at over 50,000 tons in 1996, which was more than twice the 1991 levels of production. SCRS assessments reflect the impacts of this trend. In 1992, the state of the eastern bluefin stock was worse than it had been in 1988. Scientists estimated that the spawning stock was at about 50% of the average level from 1970 to 1972. Big fish were reduced even further, to about 30% of the biomass estimates for the early 1970s (ICCAT 1971–1994: 1993, 158–159). By 1995, these numbers had declined even further and by 1996 the SCRS informed the commission that continued catches at current levels had a 90% chance of radically reducing the population of spawning bluefin within 10 years (ICCAT 1995–2007b: 1996, 38; 1997, 42–43).

During this period, highly vulnerable countries expressed increasing levels of concern about the state of the eastern stock. At the 1992 meeting of the commission, Spain and France called for more science, particularly in regard to reducing landings of small fish in the Mediterranean. They also joined forces with Portugal, Canada, Japan, and the United States to develop the first trade documentation scheme, which applied to both stocks of Atlantic bluefin (ICCAT 1971–1994: 1993, 67–68,

82–87). This statistical document program could only track bluefin through international markets and therefore applied mainly to large fish that were shipped to Tokyo. While these were the highest-priced individuals and therefore heavily targeted, the trade document did little to track harvests of smaller fish that were usually sold domestically in Mediterranean countries.

In 1993 several measures were adopted to protect spawning fish. These included a time-area closure on large longliners in the Mediterranean and a limit on landings from the central Atlantic, just east of the division between the stocks. The former measure was proposed by Japan. It extended the time-area closure for the Japanese fleet to other large-scale longliners that targeted bluefin in the Mediterranean. Panamanian, Taiwanese, and Korean vessels had moved into the eastern management area earlier in the decade. Spain and France were not thrilled with the measure, but accepted it with the clarification that the closure would apply to nonmembers as well as members (ICCAT 1971–1994: 1994, 90–91).

As explained in chapter 9, the 1993 regulation that limited landings in the central Atlantic was part of a dispute between Japan and the coastal states targeting western bluefin. The latter felt that harvests so close to the boundary were most likely to impact the western stock and therefore they worked strenuously to get Japan to reduce its harvests in the area. Other than Japan, the only country harvesting eastern bluefin that commented on this proposed measure was Spain. Spanish representatives made sure that the catch limit was only temporary, stating that they would like to maintain the option of targeting bluefin in that area in future years (ICCAT 1971–1994: 1994, 90–92). This preference for pliable regulations is another reflection of the midrange flexibility of Spanish fleets.

Rhetoric from western countries regarding the need for better management in the east increased with improved scientific knowledge on the level of mixing between the two areas. At the 1994 meeting, the United States led with a proposal to first cap landings of eastern bluefin to 1993–1994 levels in 1995, followed by a 25% reduction from 1996 to 1998. Since it expected the harvests in those years to be around 27,000 tons, effective implementation of this measure would have resulted in landings close to the level recommended by the SCRS. The measure also included a clause that encouraged fleets to take measures to reduce catches of age 0 fish (<1.8 kg), which had been briefly mentioned by

Spain and France the previous year. Japan and Canada added their support for the measure. The two major European fishing countries were reluctant to accept the proposal because they feared that nonmembers would undermine its effectiveness. At this the United States and Japan laid out their plans for mechanisms to ensure compliance by nonmembers. The U.S. proposal was adopted, with additional language on requests for compliance from nonmembers (ICCAT 1971–1994: 1995, 58–59).[7]

At that same meeting, ICCAT adopted several new measures to ensure the effectiveness of their conservation programs, including the bluefin action plan, which covered both stocks of Atlantic bluefin tuna. This plan provided the commission with a means of enforcing regulations through trade sanctions on Atlantic bluefin imports from offending countries (ICCAT 2007a, res. 94-8, 94-9). Spain, France, and Portugal were just as eager as their counterparts in the west to ensure that nonmembers complied with ICCAT regulations. Along with Japan, these countries were particularly concerned about the potential for incursions by mildly vulnerable fleets from Taiwan and various flag-of-convenience fleets. Panama was one of the biggest providers of flags of convenience at the time. Its fleet, which was composed mostly of former Japanese vessels, began harvesting eastern bluefin in 1990, catching about 74 tons. Reported landings by Panama increased gradually until 1994, when they reached 1500 tons, more than three times the 1993 level of production (ICCAT 2007d).

After the cordial discussions of 1994—the Spanish delegate actually thanked the United States for its candor on the mixing issue—the conflicts that arose at the 1995 meeting of the commission seemed exceptionally heated. The same three points were raised over and over, with increasing stridency. Countries targeting western bluefin, particularly the highly vulnerable United States and Canada, blamed overfishing in the east for undermining rebuilding in the west. Spain and France countered by suggesting that failure in the west was a result of insufficient management rather than mixing. Parties on both sides further blamed Japan for harvesting in the central Atlantic. Japan, which had made sacrifices in the east and the west, defended its record. In fact, most members rationalized their own actions, and rights to harvest either stock, while blaming others for the current situation (ICCAT 1995–2007a: 1996, 135–143, 157–161).

This east–west acrimony was linked to the jump in landings of eastern bluefin from around 27,000 tons in 1993 to about 34,000 tons in 1994.[8] France's landings in particular were quite high, and their delegates had a hard time convincing the rest of the commission that this was not intentional overreporting in order to set a false benchmark for the landings reductions mandated the year before. In their defense, the French proposed that the 1994 recommendation should be amended to allow them to use the average of 1993 and 1994 rather than one or the other. Other members were not satisfied with this, so a measure was adopted that set specific quotas for the French fleet. Countries with smaller catches, particularly Morocco and Taiwan, also reported higher landings in 1994, but they were adamant that they would honor the 1994 recommendation as it was, taking the higher of the two reference years (ICCAT 1995–2007a: 1996, 138–141, 157–158).

The 1996 meeting of the commission was somewhat less hostile than 1995, but the mixing issue remained a central point of contention. Production of eastern bluefin had continued to increase in spite of ICCAT's 1994 reduction scheme, reaching a reported level of over 39,000 tons. The SCRS stated that catches of 25,000 tons could keep the biomass stable. Some rebuilding might even be possible at that level, but the commission would have to restrict harvests to 20,000 tons to have a 50% chance of rebuilding the stock to the level that would support MSY in 20 years. This would require countries with fleets targeting eastern bluefin to reduce their harvests by 35% from known levels for 1994 and 1995. The SCRS also restated its call for a reduction in fishing mortality on juvenile fish, as per the 1974 size limit (<6.4-kg minimum size with 15% tolerance by number) and the 1994 size limit (all necessary measures to prevent capture of fish < 1.8 kg; ICCAT 1995–2007b: 1997, 42–44).

In response to this assessment, countries targeting eastern bluefin chose to focus on noncompliance by nonmembers rather than on further reductions in their own catches. Japan led the discussion, naming a wide array of Mediterranean countries along with Taiwan as prime suspects. Spain, France, and Portugal were enthusiastic about finding ways to enforce the 1994 measures on nonmembers, settling on the need to ban imports from countries that would not comply (ICCAT 1995–2007a: 1997, 116–117). It was decided that commission members should ban imports of Atlantic bluefin from Panama, Honduras, and Belize. All of these countries had flagged vessels that were found to be fishing in the Mediterranean contrary to ICCAT management measures and had failed to correct the problem after several requests from the secretariat. None were present at the meeting (ICCAT 1995–2007a: 160–162, 165).[9]

A few other measures were adopted for eastern bluefin in 1996, mainly at the behest of Japan, the United States, and Canada. The Japanese proposed to extend the June/July time-area closure in the Mediterranean to cover all types of gear and therefore all other national fleets. Neither the French nor the Spanish were willing to go so far. Based on information from France, a second proposal was tabled that would close the Mediterranean to purse seining for bluefin in August while prohibiting the use of spotter aircraft in June. The intention of the August closure was to protect small fish, which are more often caught by purse seiners (ICCAT 1995–2007a: 1997, 115–118). It also happens to be one of the less productive months for the fishery supplying large fish to Japan, which peaks in June and July. The prohibition on spotter planes or helicopters, which are used to find schools of large bluefin, would reduce the efficiency of purse seine fleets in one of their most productive months (European Commission 2007). Although they were highly vulnerable, the French were using countermeasures to reduce the costs of management.

As the Japanese noted at the meeting, these modifications to the Mediterranean closure would have a minimal impact on the European purse seiners, which brought in the majority of bluefin harvests (ICCAT 1995–2007a: 1997, 134). The actions taken to prevent fishing mortality on age 0 bluefin were more severe, insofar as the binding recommendation adopted by the commission contained a prohibition on retaining, landing, or selling such small fish. The United States and Canada pressed this proposal, along with one that would limit catches of eastern bluefin to 25,000 tons, as per SCRS advice. No other delegation even responded to the suggested TAC, but informal discussions on protections of size 0 fish were successful. France and Spain also informed the commission that they would be developing domestic mechanisms to enforce the ban (ICCAT 1995–2007a: 1997, 117–118).

At this point, it is safe to say that the commission's overall response on eastern bluefin management was not yet as strong as that observed for other stocks in similar circumstances. The SCRS' best estimates put the spawning stock at about 19% of the level that would support MSY. The contemporary estimate for western bluefin was 13% and around

58% for northern swordfish, both of which stocks were under much stricter management by 1996 (ICCAT 1995–2007b: 1997, 42, 66). Such variation is partly owing to the fact that fish still seemed plentiful in the east, particularly in the Mediterranean. Also, high prices allowed the fishery to remain profitable at lower biomass as a percentage of B_{MSY} than the smaller western bluefin stock or the lower-priced northern swordfish. Highly vulnerable countries targeting these stocks would have been experiencing much greater costs than their counterparts targeting eastern bluefin. Moreover, the singular nature of the species would insulate these countries from international competition, and the openness of the Mediterranean would allow them greater flexibility. The next section will show how farming exacerbated this dynamic, further undermining willingness to pay for management of this important stock.

10.3 Postfarming Breakdown (1997–2000)

Although there were many changes in the commission and in the fisheries in 1997, it was a relatively quiet year for discussions on eastern Atlantic bluefin. Farming or ranching of bluefin tuna was introduced into the Mediterranean that year, but would not be brought up at ICCAT until the 2000 meeting. On the other hand, a big difference at the negotiating table was the presence of the European Community in place of several EU members: Spain, France, Portugal, and the United Kingdom. The EC would represent Italy as well, bringing in a country that had not been a member in previous years but that had major fleets targeting eastern bluefin tuna. Croatia and Tunisia, two countries that had substantially increased their harvests of eastern bluefin in recent years, also joined the commission in 1997 (ICCAT 2007b).

Owing to new data from these entrants and others, the SCRS revised its reported landings database upward by more than 15,000 tons for 1994. This would make the reference value for the 25% reduction mandated by ICCAT that year about 43,000 tons instead of the 27,000 tons that were expected at the time (ICCAT 1995–2007b: 1998, 60). Backed up by Canada and the SCRS, the United States made the point that catches would have to be reduced by more than 25% now that landings were known to be so high. These interventions were ignored in favor of discussions on protection of age 0 fish, reporting of statistics in the not elsewhere included category, and the appropriate period for the 1995 time-area closure for the Mediterranean. The U.S. proposal to ban sales of age 0 fish (<1.8 kg) was adopted without much ado, as was the EC proposal on reporting of NEI data. Croatia wanted to alter the closure on purse seines, proposing May 15–June 15 as a better period in which to protect juveniles in the Adriatic. The EC and other countries said that a dual closure would cause too many enforcement problems, so the proposal was dropped (ICCAT 1995–2007a: 1998, 56–59).

By 1998, catches of eastern bluefin were supposed to be down to about 20,000 tons, as per the reduction schedule agreed to in 1994, but instead they were up to at least 41,000 tons. The SCRS said that limiting catches to 25,000 tons might arrest the decline in the stock, but there was no longer any chance of rebuilding it without harsher measures (ICCAT 1995–2007b: 1999, 58–60). The United States and Canada again pressed countries with fleets targeting the eastern stock to reduce their harvests as per SCRS advice. They were not satisfied when the EC proposed a TAC of 33,000 tons for 1999. However, the EC, along with Morocco, Turkey, China, and Tunisia, claimed that socioeconomic factors also had to be considered, particularly in light of the uncertainty associated with the SCRS assessments. After considerable discussion, and a threat from the EC to link all other matters to getting its way on eastern bluefin, the commission adopted a TAC of 32,000 tons for 1999 and 29,500 tons for 2000, with quota-sharing arrangements (ICCAT 1995–2007a: 1999, 146–147, 170–172).

The allocation of national quotas almost held up this new measure. Elsewhere in the commission, contracting parties were already in ongoing negotiations over the definition of allocation criteria (see chapter 7). A major point of contention between developing and historically dominant countries, this issue had not yet arisen for eastern bluefin because the nature of regulations had not been so restrictive nor so well enforced in the past. Morocco was one of the first gradually vulnerable countries to speak out, joined later by Libya and Turkey. These countries demanded that allocations be decided at an intersessional meeting early in 1999, after the next meeting of the ICCAT Committee on Allocation Criteria. With considerable pressure from the EC and others, they finally agreed to settle for a footnote that said the commission would reconsider the shares for 2000 (see table 10.2) at its 1999 meeting (ICCAT 1995–2007a: 1999, 35–36, 149–150, 173).[10]

Demands from mildly vulnerable countries were also voiced in 1998, although these complaints were less vociferous than those of moderately vulnerable countries. China requested a quota of 500 tons, but agreed to

Table 10.2

Quota Allocations and TAC from the 1998 Management Plan for Eastern Bluefin Tuna (applied 1999–2000)

Country	1999 (tons)	2000 (tons)
Contracting Parties		
China	82	76
Croatia	950	876
EC	20,165	18,590
Japan	3,199	2,949
Korea	672	619
Libya	1,300	1,199
Morocco	820	756
Tunisia	2,326	2,144
NCPs (excluding Taiwan)	1,772	1,633
Taiwan	714	658
Total allowable catch	32,000	29,500

Note: NCP = noncontracting party.
Source: ICCAT 2007a, rec. 98-05.

accept its allotment because the negotiations had been so difficult. Originally Taiwan's allocation had been lumped in with all noncontracting parties, but quiet requests on their part established a specific share of that allotment (ICCAT 1995–2007a: 1999, 36, 149). As table 10.3 shows, the quotas set for mildly vulnerable countries did not require substantial catch reductions; in fact they would allow increases in most cases. Those set for moderately vulnerable countries, particularly Morocco, Libya, and Turkey, required cutbacks of more than 50%, depending on the measure of "recent" catch levels, which could be either the 1993–1994 reference period mandated by the 1994 recommendation on catch reductions, or a more inclusive reference point, such as the 1993–1997 average shown in table 10.3.[11]

For comparison, another moderately vulnerable country, Croatia, would have to reduce its harvests by about 23% from either reference point to comply with the 1998 recommendation. The table also shows that the EC (mainly Spain, France, Greece, Italy, Malta, and Portugal) would reduce their harvests by about 17% from 1993–1994 levels but about 26% if more recent landings were included in the calculation. In absolute terms, these countries would bear a large portion of the costs of management, but they would also take the lion's share of the harvest.

Table 10.3
Comparison of Quota Allocations (tons) for 1999 with Indicators of Recent Landings (tons)

Country	Quota for 1999	Average 1993–1994			Average 1993–1997		
		Landings	Absolute change	Percent change	Landings	Absolute change	Percent change
Contracting Parties							
China	82	49	34	69	75	7	9
Croatia	950	1,234	−284	−23	1,231	−281	−23
EC	20,165	24,270	−4,105	−17	27,108	−6,943	−26
Japan	3,199	2,944	255	9	3,574	−375	−10
Korea	672	688	−16	−2	662	10	2
Libya	1,300	2,453	−1,153	−47	1,203	97	8
Morocco	820	1,029	−209	−20	1,649	−829	−50
Tunisia	2,326	1,153	1,173	102	2,279	47	2
Noncontracting Parties (if Turkey is only other noncontracting party)							
Turkey	1,772	3,275	−1,503	−46	4,096	−2,324	−57
Taiwan	714	532	183	34	508	206	40

Notes: Turkey's quota was approximated by subtracting Taiwan's quota from the noncontracting parties' quota. In actuality, the reduction for this nonmember would be much greater since it is supposed to share this amount with all other noncontracting parties.

Sources: Quotas from ICCAT 2007a, rec. 98-5; landings and average landings computed from ICCAT 2007d.

Japan, on the other hand, would not have to cut back at all from 1993–1994 levels, but would face a 10% reduction over the longer period. It is interesting that this country would actually be able to land 88% more bluefin according to the 1999 distribution than it had reported in 1997.

Several other measures were adopted for eastern bluefin in 1998. In one, the ban on landing, retention, or sale of age 0 fish was extended to include any fish of 3.2 kg or less (ICCAT 2007a, rec. 98-4). This measure was proposed by the EC and adopted with little discussion. The SCRS had already pointed out that age 0 fish were still being caught; they were simply not reported anymore because of the ban. It also informed the commission yet again that the minimum size limit of 6.4 kg that had been adopted in 1974 was ineffective (ICCAT 1995–2007b: 1999, 59). In regard to protecting juveniles, Croatia once more requested that the time-area closure on purse seines be changed from August to May in the Adriatic. The EC also proposed that the purse seine closure be changed to July 16–August 15 for the rest of the Mediterranean. A combined proposal that included both closures and a prohibition of the transfer of effort from one area to the other during each period was adopted with little fanfare (ICCAT 1995–2007a: 1999, 148).

All in all, 1999 was a quiet year for eastern bluefin. In spite of their demands in 1998, Morocco, Libya, and Turkey made no new requests to change their quota allocations for 2000 at the 1999 meeting of the commission. Both Morocco and Libya had formally objected to the 1998 recommendation that set the TAC and catch allocation for eastern bluefin. By doing so, these countries exempted themselves from the regulation, setting their own national quotas for 1999 and 2000. Turkey was not a contracting party at the time and so had no such recourse. In addition, a few nonmembers made requests for quotas and statements on the rights of coastal countries; the sanctions against Panama were lifted; and new trade measures on bluefin imports were adopted for Equatorial Guinea. Otherwise, only the United States spoke up again regarding the sacrifices that had been made to conserve western bluefin and criticizing management of the eastern stock (ICCAT 1995–2007a: 2000, 182–184; 2007a, rec. 99-9, 99-10).

ICCAT's annual meeting for the year 2000 was held in Marrakech, Morocco. Eastern bluefin management was up for renegotiation, so the discussion was much livelier than it had been the year before. The SCRS reiterated its opinion that current harvests of eastern bluefin were too high and that further reductions were needed to halt the decline or possibly rebuild the stock. It also pointed out that underreported catches had increased substantially since 1999 and suggested that the reported harvest of around 31,500 tons was at least 3,000 tons below the actual harvest level. Estimates of unreported catches were made using trade documentation, but this method was not available for small fish that were destined for domestic markets. Nonreporting of size data under-mined scientific assessment of the stock and made evaluation of the effec-tiveness of size limits quite difficult (ICCAT 1995–2007b: 2001, 54–57).

As usual, highly vulnerable countries with fleets targeting the western stock responded most strongly to this advice. Evidence on mixing be-tween the two stocks and its impact on western management had been mounting in recent years, largely owing to scientific programs initiated by the United States and Canada (ICCAT 1995–2007b: 1997, 44; 1999, 54, 60; 2001, 49; 1995–2007a: 1997, 118; 1998, 158; 2001, 197; 2007a, res. 96-5, 97-16, rec. 00-8). In 2000, their calls for manage-ment of eastern bluefin with a TAC of 25,000 tons and better compli-ance with all measures, as per SCRS advice, were supported by Mexico, which was not yet a member of the commission, and the Ocean Wildlife Campaign, a conservation organization based in the United States (ICCAT 1995–2007a: 2001, 194, 212–213). The countries that actually harvested eastern bluefin—and would have to make the cuts proposed by the United States and Canada—had different ideas about the appro-priate level of catch. The EC was the most conservative among these, proposing a TAC of 29,500 tons for 2001 and 2002, along with quota shares that were similar to the previous distribution. The delegate from the EC defended this choice by pointing out that it was within the range of sustainable estimates presented by the SCRS. While this lone, highly vulnerable fishing entity (targeting the eastern, rather than the western stock) favored continuity, other members proposed TACs as high as 34,500 tons (ICCAT 1995–2007a: 2001, 195).

Unfortunately the rapporteur for the 2000 meeting of Panel 2, the sub-committee that handles bluefin within the ICCAT framework, was less detail oriented than his predecessors and the specific parties who pro-posed these higher TACs are not named in the official record. However, it is likely that gradually vulnerable countries like Morocco and Libya proposed the higher TACs to accommodate their demands for larger quotas. Much as in 1998, there was considerable discussion regarding the distribution of eastern bluefin quotas in 2000. The EC proposal set the average of 1993–1994 landings levels as the point of reference for distributing quotas and refused to raise the TAC to accommodate the demands of individual countries. Morocco and others were unhappy with that arrangement and wanted to wait until the commission reached agreement on official allocation criteria to divide up the harvests (ICCAT 1995–2007a: 2001, 195–196).

By the time agreement was reached, none of the members were pleased with the outcome. Morocco and Libya were so disappointed with the final quota distributions that they declared they would object to the proposal and set their own quotas, as shown in table 10.4. These independently determined quotas set a dangerous precedent and led to a lengthy debate. If Morocco and Libya were allowed to increase their catches well above most historical reference points, what would prevent other disgruntled members from doing the same? In the end, the EC, Japan, and the remainder of the countries harvesting eastern bluefin chose to keep the TAC of 29,500 tons and quota allocations as they were, but to remove Morocco and Libya from the list of countries with quotas. Instead, their independently set quotas were noted in a separate paragraph of the recommendation. Because of this discrepancy, the total expected catch under the 1999 management scheme was just over 32,000 tons, which disappointed the United States and Canada because legal catches would surpass the SCRS recommendation by about 7,000 tons (see table 10.4; ICCAT 1995–2007a: 2001, 62–63, 196, 215–218).

Farming activities also came up for the first time in 2000. The United States mentioned the need for more information on farming in its initial statement to the commission (ICCAT 1995–2007a: 2001, 194). Later, the EC proposed that the SCRS should be asked to provide a report on bluefin farming and its potential impacts on the bluefin statistical document program within the next year. This proposal was accepted with little comment (ICCAT 1995–2007a: 2001, 196). The SCRS response to this request was to list several new types of research activities that would be needed to fully answer the questions posed. These suggestions were approved with the SCRS report in 2001, but the issue of growing production from bluefin farms was largely eclipsed by other matters.

The 2001 meeting of the commission opened with much acclaim for the recently adopted ICCAT Criteria for the Allocation of Fishing Possibilities (ICCAT 2007a, oth. 01-25). It was this agreement—and the recognition of coastal and developing country rights that it contained—for which Morocco, Libya, and other gradually vulnerable countries had been waiting. Since the 2000 management program only applied for 1

Table 10.4
Comparison of Quota Allocations (tons) for 2001 with Indicators of Recent Landings (tons)

Country	Quota for 2001	Average 1993–1994			Average 1993–1997		
		Landings	Absolute change	Percent change	Landings	Absolute change	Percent change
Contracting Parties							
China	76	49	28	57	75	1	1
Croatia	876	1,234	–358	–29	1,231	–355	–29
EC	18,590	24,270	–5,680	–23	27,108	–8,518	–31
Japan	2,949	2,944	5	0	3,574	–625	–17
Korea	619	688	–69	–10	662	–43	–6
Tunisia	2,144	1,153	991	86	2,279	–135	–6
Noncontracting Parties (if Turkey is only other noncontracting party)							
Turkey	1,633	3,275	–1,642	–50	4,096	–2,463	–60
Taiwan	658	532	127	24	508	150	29
Subtotal	**27,545**	Total allowable catch		29,500	Remainder		1,955
Quotas Set Independently							
Libya	1,570	2,453	–883	–36	1,203	367	31
Morocco	3,028	1,029	2,000	194	1,649	1,379	84
Total	**32,143**	Total allowable catch		29,500	Remainder		**–2,643**

Sources: Quotas from ICCAT 2007a, rec. 00-9; landings and average landings computed from ICCAT 2007d.

year, they would be able to renegotiate their shares of the TAC for eastern bluefin under the auspices of the new allocation criteria. Initially, the EC tabled a joint proposal written with Morocco and Algeria, a new member to the commission. It basically rewarded member countries with coastal state status while penalizing distant-water fleets and non-members. This proposal also contained a key that established percentage shares for individual countries that would be fixed in the medium term (5 years) and would not change with the TAC. Japan backed the joint proposal, stating that distant-water countries, particularly Taiwan and Korea, had sacrificed considerably to make the proposal possible. This was unexpected from mildly vulnerable countries without some threat or side payment to compensate for opportunities forgone (ICCAT 1995–2007a: 2002, 306).

As it turns out, none of the mildly vulnerable countries targeting bluefin were truly willing to give up their shares for moderately vulnerable countries. South Korea was a member of ICCAT but had not joined Panel 2, where bluefin measures are first approved before being sent to the full commission. As observers at the panel meeting, the South Korean delegates voiced considerable discontent with the EC proposal, but they could not vote on the measure in subcommittee. Taiwan is not able to be a member of the commission at all and would likewise be unable to protect its interests without the cooperation of some contracting party like Japan. A member of Panel 2 as well as the full commission, China complained loudly about cuts to its quota in the EC proposal (ICCAT 1995–2007a: 2002, 306–307, 327–328).

Nonmembers were not pleased with the proposal either. Observers from Turkey, Iceland, and the Faroe Islands protested the lack of room for new members of ICCAT. The 5-year duration of the proposed sharing scheme would mean that there would be only a small window in which to receive a quota if they were to join the commission. Furthermore, the amount allotted for nonmembers was quite small relative to their fishing capacity. Turkey's fleets alone could catch more than twice the allotment for all nonmembers other than Taiwan. In their protests, these countries were joined by Brazil, an observer on the bluefin panel and an architect of the new allocation criteria. The Brazilian delegate said that the proposal clearly resulted from a misunderstanding of that document (ICCAT 1995–2007a: 2002, 306–307).

Brazil was referring in part to the lack of consideration for new members, but also to the astonishing change in the level of TAC that had been

Table 10.5

Comparison of Quota Allocation and TAC (tons) for 1999 (adopted in 1998), 2001 (adopted in 2000), and 2002–2005 (adopted in 2001)

Country	1999	2001	2002	2003	2004	2005
Contracting Parties						
Algeria			1,700	1,725	1,775	1,783
China	82	76	77	77	76	75
Croatia	950	876	1,000	986	1,011	1,086
EC	20,165	18,590	20,355	20,055	19,590	18,969
Japan	3,199	2,949	3,000	2,928	2,861	2,795
Korea	672	619	50	60	72	88
Libya	1,300	**1,570**	1,370	1,389	1,478	1,534
Morocco	820	**3,028**	3,030	3,052	3,029	3,064
Tunisia	2,326	2,144	2,150	2,110	2,127	2,147
Noncontracting Parties						
Taiwan	714	658	330			
Others	1,772	1,633	863	1,116	1,017	885
Total allowable catch	32,000	29,500	33,925	33,425	32,925	32,425
Total estimated catch		**(32,143)**				

Notes: Shaded columns are past allocations; unshaded columns are proposed allocations; bold text denotes individually determined quotas.
Sources: ICCAT 2007a, rec. 98-5, 00-9; author's files.

proposed by Algeria, Morocco, and the EC. Even though SCRS advice had not changed, they proposed to set the TAC for 2002 at 33,925 tons—almost 4,500 tons over the previous TAC and 18,925 tons over the SCRS' highest recommended catch level. The TAC would be gradually reduced from 2002 to 2005 but, as shown in table 10.5, would not come anywhere near the scientific recommendation. Because of this increase, coastal countries would actually receive higher quotas than they had in the past even as mildly vulnerable countries and nonmembers would be required to make substantial cutbacks.

As might be expected, the United States and Canada were up in arms over this new TAC scheme for eastern bluefin. They believed that overfishing in the east was directly affecting their ability to sustainably manage western bluefin because of the mixing between the stocks. In addition, higher production in the east would increase the global supply of sashimi-grade bluefin and could cause the price to decline further. Together, the United States and Canada blocked consensus on the recommendation in panel. After considerable debate, the chair of Panel 2, who happened to be a member of the EC's delegation, sent the proposal to the full commission with the stipulation that there was no consensus as yet (ICCAT 1995–2007a: 2002, 306–308, 327–328).

On the final day of the 2001 meeting, in the plenary session, the United States, Canada, and South Korea chose to block consensus on the management plan for eastern bluefin. For its part, the EC would discuss no other measures until the bluefin issue was settled. ICCAT does have a procedure for adoption of recommendations by majority voting, but several members were absent and they were just short of a full quorum. Since none of the delegations would back down, the meeting ended simply because they ran out of time. Without a new TAC and sharing arrangement for eastern bluefin, countries would set their own quotas for 2002. They were enjoined to honor the EC proposal unofficially. All twenty-five other resolutions and recommendations that were on the table, including bluefin sanctions on Honduras and two new research programs on bluefin mixing, were adopted later by mail vote (ICCAT 1995–2007a: 2002, 55–57, 308).

10.4   Postbreakdown Response (2002–2006)

The breakdown of the 2001 negotiations was a wake-up call of sorts. Western countries displayed their resolve but risked the entire enterprise. Much would depend on reconciliation between the countries with fleets targeting the two Atlantic bluefin stocks. Mildly good news on eastern bluefin was provided by the SCRS, although it had little impact on the tenor of the negotiations. Reported landings of the stock were only about 33,700 tons for 2002, which was somewhat less than the TAC that had been proposed for that year, but was still well above the scientifically recommended level. New data caused the SCRS to revise its assessment of the stock. Spawning stock biomass for 2000 was estimated at around 86% of the 1970 level. The highest sustainable catch level was also revised upward to 26,000 tons instead of 25,000 tons (ICCAT 1995–2007b: 2003, 80–83).

In spite of this mildly positive advice, most of the same themes regarding eastern bluefin were raised in 2002. However, the brinkmanship displayed at the previous meeting had had a sobering effect on all sides. Also, international prices for eastern Atlantic bluefin had dipped by about €7,400 per ton from 2000 to 2002 (European Commission 2007).

A cutback in supply could help to increase prices, bringing benefits to most of the members targeting eastern bluefin. Last but certainly not least, western bluefin management was also on the table that year and the United States, Canada, and Japan were contemplating rather risky increases in the TAC for that stock (see chapter 9). Thus the United States and Canada gave up some of the high ground and were susceptible to the same blocking tactics that they had used the previous year.

Even so, these two countries continued to press for management that would reduce the impact of eastern fishing on the western stock. Supported by Canada, the United States went so far as to propose that the boundary between the stocks should be shifted to the east, from longitude 45° W to 30° W (ICCAT 1995–2007a: 2003, 308, 322–324). An SCRS analysis had shown that there was considerable mixing in the central area and that extension of the western zone would result in much better assessments of the western stock (ICCAT 1995–2007b: 2003, 149). Consistent with past statements, gradually vulnerable Japan stated that its delegation still believed that Atlantic bluefin should be managed as a single stock. Neither of these proposals had any chance of acceptance, since each would result in a smaller share of Atlantic catches for countries operating in the east. The EC, Morocco, and China simply stated that changing the boundary could not be justified given the current science—which was true in a quantitative sense—and left it at that (ICCAT 1995–2007a: 2003, 308–309).

Next, the EC presented a package of three proposals on eastern bluefin. One was a combined TAC and quota-sharing scheme; the second was aimed at reducing fishing mortality on juvenile bluefin; and the third was a proposal from Japan for a cap on harvests in the central Atlantic area. None of these proposals was accepted at first, but all three were adopted after some changes (ICCAT 1995–2007a: 2003, 309–310). The TAC was set at 32,000 tons annually for 2003–2006, as originally proposed, but sharing arrangements were altered. Mainly, the EC gave up about 300 tons per year on average, which was dispersed among various moderately vulnerable countries. Beneficiaries of this included Tunisia, Morocco, Iceland, and Croatia, which received, respectively, 159, 103, 28, and 9 tons on average per year (ICCAT 2007a, rec. 02-8; author's files).[12]

As table 10.6 shows, sharing arrangements for 2003 were little different than those set for 2001, except that several new moderately vulnera-

Table 10.6

Comparison of Quota Allocations and TACs (tons) for 1999, 2001, 2002, and 2003–2006

Country	1999	2001	2002	2003	2004	2005	2006
Contracting Parties							
Algeria			1,700	1,500	1,550	1,600	1,700
China	82	76	77	74	74	74	74
Croatia	950	876	1,000	900	935	945	970
EC	20,165	18,590	20,355	18,582	18,450	18,331	18,301
Iceland				30	40	50	60
Japan	3,199	2,949	3,000	2,949	2,930	2,890	2,830
Korea	672	619	50	1,904 t ⇒ 1.5% share = 480 tons/year			
Libya	1,300	**1,570**	1,370	1,286	1,300	1,400	1,440
Morocco	820	**3,028**	3,030	3,030	3,078	3,127	3,177
Tunisia	2,326	2,144	2,150	2,503	2,543	2,583	2,625
Noncontracting Parties							
Taiwan	714	658	330	835 t ⇒ 1.5% share = 480 tons/year			
Others	1,772	1,633	863	1,146	1,100	1,000	823
Total underages for Taiwan and Korea				2,739			
TAC	32,000	29,500	33,925	32,000	32,000	32,000	32,000
TEC		(32,143)					

Notes: 1999 adopted in 1998, 2000 adopted in 1999, 2001 adopted in 2000, 2003–2006 adopted in 2002. Shaded columns are past allocations; unshaded columns are proposed allocations; bold text denotes individually determined quotas. TAC = total allowable catch; TEC = total estimated catch.
Sources: ICCAT 2007a, rec. 98-5, 00-9, 02-8; author's files.

ble countries were accommodated at the expense of mildly vulnerable countries and nonmembers. Of particular interest is the system set up to deal with South Korea and Taiwan. Both of these countries had accrued considerable underages from 1999 to 2001, largely because their fleets had shifted to target other species. Instead of designating a quota for these countries, the commission stipulated that their historically based shares of 1.5% each would be reinstated once those underages were used up. This would mean that these two mildly vulnerable countries could harvest up to 2,739 tons over and above the TAC in just 1 year or spread out over several years, depending on the vagaries of their distant-water fleets. Presumably, the reinstitution of their shares once these overages were used up would be undertaken at the expense of all other quota holders, but this is not dealt with in the recommendation (ICCAT 2007a, rec. 02-8).

Like the 2001 proposal before it, the 2002 TAC–quota regime included a stepwise reduction in shares for highly vulnerable EC countries and gradually vulnerable Japan, while quotas for moderately vulnerable countries increased. This is indicative of the moderate side payments that are expected to flow from highly and gradually vulnerable countries to moderately vulnerable countries to obtain their cooperation. Additional room was also created by reducing the quota available to nonmembers, which went from 1,772 tons in 1999 to 1,146 tons in 2003 to only 823 tons in 2006. This total amount could also be cut in half at any point if the Taiwanese quota was ever reinstated (ICCAT 2007a, rec. 02-8).

As in the past, the EC proposal caused considerable consternation among nonmembers, including Turkey, Norway, and the Faroe Islands. While the latter two countries would be easily accommodated, as Iceland had been, Turkey had historical catch levels in the thousands of metric tons (ICCAT 1995–2007a: 2003, 310, 327–328). Although Turkey joined ICCAT in 2003, its subsequent requests for larger quotas were denied until the scheduled renegotiation of the eastern TAC–quota scheme in 2006 (ICCAT 1995–2007a: 2004, 183–184, 203–205). Norway faced similar treatment when it joined the commission in 2004. Since it would not be given its own quota, Norway announced that it would take 100 tons of the others' quota for 2005 (ICCAT 1995–2007a: 2005, 167). This was an exercise in optimism, since Norway had reported a total of 5 tons of bluefin harvest since the late 1980s (ICCAT 2007d).

Along with the TAC scheme, several additional rules were proposed to change regulations on juvenile bluefin in the east. The second proposal in the EC's package instructed contracting parties to look into new ways of protecting small bluefin (<6.4 kg and <3.2 kg). It was adopted with a few amendments. Pushed by the United States and Canada, these changes focused on setting specific goals, including reducing the number of <6.4 kg fish caught in the Mediterranean by 60%. They also insisted on making this a binding recommendation rather than a nonbinding resolution. In addition, a proposal from Croatia was incorporated into the EC's TAC–quota scheme. It would repeal the closed season on purse seines for the Adriatic and replace it with the July 16–August 15 closure that applied to the entire Mediterranean (ICCAT 1995–2007a: 2003, 308–310; author's notes).[13]

The third proposal in the EC's package came from Japan. It was a resolution that would cap harvests of bluefin in the central Atlantic at their 1999/2000 level for 2003 and 2004. Apparently, gradually vulnerable Japan was concerned about new entrants into this area, which it had dominated for years. The proposal was adopted as a nonbinding resolution with the addition of text that would limit the scope of the measure to large-scale longliners. This change was introduced by the EC, which mainly harbors purse seiners, and the behavior of both countries fits neatly into the vulnerability response predictions. Gradually vulnerable Japan protected its access to valuable fishing grounds, while the highly vulnerable but still relatively flexible EC kept its options open by ensuring that its fleets have the legal right to fish the mid-Atlantic region (ICCAT 1995–2007a: 2003, 310; author's notes).[14]

Last but not least, the commission adopted a comprehensive recommendation on the monitoring and reporting of data on bluefin farming activities. Discussions on this were largely technical, dealing with the difficulties of determining the weight of live fish in purse seine nets or fattening cages. Most of these issues were raised by moderately vulnerable countries with large farming operations, such as Croatia and Morocco. Nonetheless, the proposal was accepted with only a few changes. In addition to log books on the transfer of bluefin to cages and ownership lists for farming operations, the new recommendation also mandated 10% observer coverage of vessels that capture wild bluefin for transfer to farming cages. It further required that such information be reported to the secretariat on an annual basis and disseminated to relevant parties prior to each meeting of the commission. Noncontracting parties were asked to comply as well (ICCAT 1995–2007a: 2003, 310).

Over the next 3 years, farming became a central issue in discussions on eastern bluefin. As expected, countries without the advantage of farms, particularly the United States, Canada, and Japan, were most adamant about the need for better monitoring of farming activities. However, several farming countries also acted as leaders, owing to their concern about escalating production from farms owned and operated by citizens from noncontracting parties. In 2003, the commission developed an official Declaration on Caging form, which would streamline data reporting, and started a list of authorized farming facilities. The new recommendation also mandated national sampling programs to gather information on the size and age structure of the fish fattened on farms. At the same meeting, the EC, Croatia, Malta, and Morocco all pointed out the impracticalities of having observers at caging facilities. Over protests from the United States and Canada, the paragraph on observer coverage was removed from the farming recommendation (ICCAT 1995–2007a: 2004, 183–185, 204–205).

Additions to this regime were relatively small in 2004, but in 2005 proposals from the EC and Turkey were combined to substantially improve monitoring and enforcement on bluefin farms (ICCAT 1995–2007a: 2006, 197). First, the new recommendation required that all boats and tugs that supply cages with bluefin be outfitted with satellite-based vessel monitoring systems (VMS) so that their positions could be tracked. Second, the 2005 recommendation directed contracting parties and cooperating noncontracting parties to prohibit imports from any farming facility that was not registered on the ICCAT list of farming facilities. Finally, the recommendation created a list of vessels authorized to supply bluefin to farms and enjoined countries to prevent farms from accepting bluefin from vessels that were not on that list (ICCAT 2007a, rec. 05-4).

The 2005 farming measures are indicative of an increase in the willingness to pay for eastern bluefin management, especially on the part of the highly vulnerable EC. At its 2006 meeting, the commission adopted a new 15-year management plan for eastern bluefin. This 14-page recommendation combined many of the previous measures on size limits and farming operations with new rules for recreational fishing, carryover of underages, quota transfers, chartering, transshipment, observer coverage, joint international inspections, and minimum standards for data collection and reporting. Many of these measures are aimed at reducing unreported catches domestically as well as through trade protective measures (author's files).[15]

The 2006 recovery plan also set the TAC for 2007 at 29,500 tons, with gradual reduction to 25,500 tons by 2010 (ICCAT 2007a, rec. 06-5). Even though this catch level was closer to prior SCRS advice than any of the previous TAC schemes, it was too little, much too late. Unfortunately, the 2006 assessment of eastern bluefin suggested that catches of 15,000 tons or less, combined with full protection of juvenile fish, would be necessary to stop the decline of the stock. As usual, the United States and Canada pointed out these deficiencies (ICCAT 1995–2007b: 2007,

61). They had cut the western bluefin TAC that year and continued to blame the failure of their own rebuilding plan on mismanagement in the east. In spite of sharp words, these countries could not block consensus on the proposal. There was a quorum present at the 2006 meeting, and the EC had the votes to pass the measure (ICCAT 1995–2007a: 2007, 183–184).

With the "recovery" plan adopted, there was still one more hurdle to overcome. As part of their proposal, the EC had postponed the allocation of quotas until an intersessional meeting to be held in 2007. Otherwise arguments over shares of the TAC would probably have derailed the entire discussion. Bargaining was hard at that meeting; distribution was decided by majority vote rather than consensus. For its part, the highly vulnerable EC bore the brunt of the catch reductions. Its quota was scheduled to drop by about 1,500 tons in 2007 and go down by around 500 tons per year until 2010, when it would drop by over 1,100 tons. Nonetheless, Libya and Turkey were dissatisfied with their shares and declared their intention to formally object. With their independently defined shares, which are the same as those listed in table 10.6, the total legal catch would go up by almost 3,000 tons from the 29,500 ton TAC set in 2006 (ICCAT 2007c, 2, 9).

Like many rollercoaster rides, this final phase in the management of eastern bluefin is likely to go downhill. Combined with the independent quotas, the total legal catch for 2007 will be higher than the 32,000 tons that had been maintained from 2003 to 2006. Moreover, there are no guarantees that the additional monitoring and enforcement measures that were adopted in 2006 will be effective at reducing the excessive unreported harvests of eastern bluefin. Furthermore, there are no signs that moderately vulnerable countries will be more willing to curb their production in the future. Unless the highly (but not quite as highly as all the others) vulnerable EC and gradually vulnerable Japan substantially increase their transfers to moderately vulnerable countries, it is quite possible that the eastern bluefin fishery will collapse.

10.5   Summary

The policy positions expressed in the eastern bluefin case are more in line with the vulnerability response predictions than the western bluefin case, but important deviations were still observed. While highly vulnerable countries targeting the western stock (Canada and the United States) did press for stronger management in the east, their responses were constrained by tactical considerations linked to management of the western stock. Highly vulnerable in the east, European positions followed the expected pattern more closely, demonstrating a higher willingness to pay before farming operations began in the mid-1990s, then quickly reverting to low but increasing concern. Nonetheless, the European response prior to farming was not as strong as that observed for other stocks at similar levels of depletion. This may be linked to their higher flexibility in the Mediterranean but also to the general lack of substitutes for bluefin tuna, which restricts economic competition in international markets.

Direct competition over the eastern stock was still an important driver of policy in this case. The EC made this clear in its willingness to make concessions to moderately and mildly vulnerable countries, albeit at the expense of higher catch limits. While mildly vulnerable countries did make demands for larger quotas, access by these fleets was curtailed early on, so their harvests were not as much of a threat as they had been in the tropical tuna cases. This is reflected in the small quota increases granted to mildly vulnerable countries like South Korea and Taiwan in the 1990s, and the reductions imposed on them as farming grew in the Mediterranean. On the other hand, moderately vulnerable countries did have considerable capacity to exploit the eastern bluefin stock, which only increased with the introduction of farming technologies. Initially, European countries tried to curtail these fisheries, "punishing" post-1994 increases in harvests with small quota allocations. However, as moderately vulnerable countries learned to use their power to undermine management measures, they began to receive considerable unofficial quota transfers. Formal objections raised by Morocco and Libya were perceived as a substantial threat to the effectiveness of the commission and so these countries were placated in subsequent rounds of negotiations.

Through all of this, low-flex, gradually vulnerable Japan took a more defensive position than one might expect based on the vulnerability response framework. Having agreed to unilaterally limit its fleet's harvests of eastern bluefin in the mid-1980s, Japan was not asked to give up much of its quota in the postfarming phase of management. However, it did propose a few other measures, including time-area closures on the Mediterranean and a cap on effort in the central Atlantic. The latter move was made specifically to prevent entry by distant-water fleets, but the former is a bit more nuanced. Like the EC, Japan had initiated this policy domestically first, then proposed it to the rest of the commission so as to extend the reach of the measure. Indeed, it first proposed the closure for longlines only in 1993, but pushed for an extension to all other fleets a few years later. As in the western bluefin case, Japan's reluctance to push for stronger measures in the east is not explained by the framework, but may be linked to consumer and processor interests at the domestic level or the lack of substitutes for this species.

Otherwise, noncommercial interests had less impact on the management of this stock than either the western bluefin or the marlins case. Nevertheless, we still observe a prolonged period of conflict in this case (see appendix C, table C.8). Judging by the sudden increase in cooperative catch limits that occurred in the mid-1990s, it seems that the introduction of farming technologies could have reduced aggregate as well as national concern about the stock by easing competitive pressures within the fishery. This extended the period of conflict by dampening the EC's willingness to pay while at the same time it increased demands from moderately vulnerable countries. As yet, no accord has been reached, and conflicts over access rights continue to inflate total allowable catch limits well above SCRS recommendations. At the same time, overfishing is leading scientists to recommend lower and lower limits on fishing mortality just to keep the stock from declining further. If this trend continues, ICCAT regulations may simply trail behind SCRS recommendations until the fishery collapses. Here again is evidence of path dependence in the emergence of adaptive governance.

11

Conclusion

Rapid and extensive changes are a hallmark of the modern era. Progress brings catastrophe more often than most people would like to admit. As such, our collective ability to recognize and respond to the kinds of creeping calamities that are often associated with environmental problems will necessarily affect the well-being of future generations. In this larger context, vulnerability response is a way to begin to understand the emergent characteristics of adaptive governance. It recognizes that global political will is not always sufficient to prevent the overexploitation of common-pool resources, but that the threat of losses closer to home can generate enough concern to precipitate positive change. Nonetheless, this is a precarious process and, as the cases show, international response may be too little, too late.

Because of world-wide overcapacity in the fishing industry and growing international demand for fish products, we are at a pivotal juncture in the management of highly migratory species of fish. During this crucial stage, management efforts by ICCAT and other regional fisheries management organizations have the potential to direct future multilateral regulation toward greater timeliness and effectiveness. New institutions may arise and learning may take place as states collectively come to terms with the limited nature of fisheries resources. Moreover, a better understanding of the sources of stability and change in the international fisheries sector can provide insights into broader problems of global environmental governance.

The main focus of this study has been to develop and test hypotheses regarding the relationship between increasing economic competition and political response by developing a framework based on economic vulnerability. I have used a hybrid approach that combines the economics of comparative advantage and common-pool dynamics with domestic

interest-based politics and a general set of international negotiating tactics.[1] The resultant vulnerability response framework can be used to predict how national policy positions can be expected to change as a stock
of fish becomes overexploited and international competition escalates.
These expectations were then tested by formulating predictions of national policy positions on the management of nine Atlantic HMS stocks
and comparing those expectations with records of actual proposals and
position statements made by ICCAT members. Collective outcomes—or
the management measures that were adopted by ICCAT—were also analyzed to identify resultant patterns of adaptive governance.

The evidence from the cases is reviewed in section 11.1. While many
countries exhibited policy positions that matched the vulnerability response expectations, there were also many deviations from the predictions. Most of these variations occurred when some underlying
assumption of the framework was violated. The five most important
sources of deviation were (1) the influence of noncommercial interests;
(2) tactical or geopolitical considerations that were outside the scope of
the framework; (3) proxies that failed to reflect the target data correctly;
(4) geographic, biological, and economic factors that limited the level of
competition in a fishery; and (5) path dependence in the form of learning,
precedent, and availability. Each of these failures is discussed in section
11.2.

At the end of each case, the pattern of aggregated outcomes was
identified. A comparative examination of these patterns shows that the
commission was only able to reach agreement on strong, well-enforced
management when more vulnerable countries were willing and able to
meet the political demands of less vulnerable countries while remaining
within the confines of scientific advice. This *transformative* pattern of
adaptive governance occurred in two of the cases and is discussed in section 11.3. Several variations on this pattern were observed in the other
cases. Some, like the yellowfin tuna and skipjack tuna cases covered fisheries that have not yet become heavily overexploited and so have not
reached the transformative phase. Others, like the marlins and bluefin
cases, have become mired in conflict or reached a management glass ceiling. These variations on the transformative pattern are covered in section
11.4.

In order to provide a more complete view of adaptive governance, the
vulnerability response framework needs to be refined and expanded. Additional theoretical work needs to be done to bring in noncommercial in-

terest groups, enlarge the scope of potential responses, and incorporate the national and international levels of decision making. Expansion to other regional fisheries organizations and nonfisheries issue areas could be used to test these new ideas and build a larger set of known patterns of adaptive governance. Cases for which better data are available would be particularly helpful, especially in analyzing the hypothesized interactions between biological depletion and economic competition. Section 11.5 suggests some ways to improve and generalize the vulnerability response framework. This research program could lead to the development of a theory of social adaptation that would apply more generally across different types of environmental governance.

11.1   Evidence of Vulnerability Response

In chapter 2, I proposed that countries, reified as states, are satisficing rather than optimizing, which leads to responsive rather than proactive management. Furthermore, I hypothesized that different states would respond at different times and with different levels of governmental concern, depending on the vulnerability of their domestic fleets to the economic costs of overfishing. Fleets that are more vulnerable will experience costs earlier and more deeply than their less vulnerable counterparts. This is expected to generate a political response as domestic fleets lobby for government protections, which include increasing total revenues and setting national quota shares through cooperative international management.

The most important indicators of economic vulnerability were identified as the relative size of a fleet's average production costs (competitiveness) and the opportunity cost of shifting effort to alternative sources of revenue (flexibility). Proxies for these indicators were specified, respectively, as the production power parity per capita gross domestic product and distant-water fishing capacity, indicated by reported landings that are noncontiguous to national coastlines. To test the validity of the framework and explore its implications, these measures were used to classify countries with fleets targeting nine different stocks of highly migratory species in the Atlantic. Predictions were then drawn from the framework and compared with recorded national policy positions in management negotiations at ICCAT meetings.

For the most part, the cases validated the model as it was presented in chapter 2. While there were many exceptions, ICCAT records showed that the actual policy positions of many countries were in line with the vulnerability response expectations. When they participated in one of these commercial fisheries, highly vulnerable fishing countries were always the first to propose management measures and consistently pushed for regulations that were fully in accord with scientific advice. For instance, in the early 1980s, highly vulnerable countries like Canada and the United States were the first to express concern about the biological situation for northern Atlantic swordfish and invested heavily in scientific research on the stock throughout the decade (ICCAT 1971–1994: 1984, 80). Once estimates of biological parameters were available, these two countries were also the first to propose effort limits. Starting in 1989, U.S. and Canadian delegates put forth recommendations to either freeze or actually reduce catches of northern Atlantic swordfish as per recommendations from ICCAT's Subcommittee on Research and Statistics (ICCAT 1971–1994: 1990, 78).

In contrast, gradually vulnerable countries generally opposed early intervention, often citing uncertainty in the scientific advice and the political and economic costs of regulation as the reasons for their positions. This was certainly the perspective of the European Community and Japan for all of the stocks other than eastern bluefin.[2] Furthermore, these gradually vulnerable countries (or fishing entities in the EC case)—whose fleets are relatively expensive to operate but who are able to cushion the effects of a decline in a single fishery by exploiting alternative stocks—frequently switched to stronger policy positions once their flexibility declined because of the global expansion of fishing effort. This low-flex phase was indicated by a peak or plateau in global landings of that species by a particular fleet. For instance, the EC became more amenable to effort limits on northern Atlantic swordfish after its global harvests of swordfish peaked in 1995, and Japan made a similar transition after its world landings of bigeye peaked in 1990.

Countries whose fleets were moderately vulnerable because of more efficient cost functions did not show such increasing governmental concern and were able to gain some concessions from their more anxious counterparts. Note the exceptions made for small fishing states in almost every effort or catch limitation passed by the commission in the past decade. Indeed, even though most of the countries in this category are relatively small and wield little power separately, united as the Group of 18, they were able to postpone the institution of a quota system to regulate catches of bigeye tuna until their demands for recognition of developing coastal countries' rights were met in the commission's adoption of new allocation criteria in 2001 (ICCAT 1995–2007a: 1999, 139). Quota concessions were also made to several moderately vulnerable countries in the swordfish and bluefin cases.

Finally, the least vulnerable countries—either because they were highly competitive and mobile or because their only interest in the stock was as a by-catch to another fishery—tended to be the most reluctant and were able to obtain the largest side payments for their cooperation on management measures. Most notable among these were the concessions and quota transfers made by Japan to China and Taiwan for their co-operation in reducing landings of bigeye tuna in the Atlantic (ICCAT 1995–2007a: 2004, 198–199). As both a high-cost producer and major consumer of bigeye, Japan found itself vulnerable to the decreasing availability of stocks throughout all of the oceans and has therefore made side payments to countries whose fleets extract high quantities of bigeye at lower costs. In contrast, Japan refused to limit its own landings of bigeye in order to reduce by-catches of northern Atlantic swordfish. Instead, Japan agreed to ban landings of swordfish, but only after more vulnerable countries/fishing entities such as the United States and the EC provided them with concessions and quota transfers (ICCAT 1995–2007a: 2000, 177).

11.2 Exceptions to Vulnerability Response

While much of the national behavior that was reported in the cases conformed to the vulnerability response expectations, there were many exceptions as well. These fit into five different categories, each of which is related to a different underlying assumption of the framework or its application. First, there were several instances in which noncommercial interests were able to affect national policy preferences, either at the domestic or the international level. This violates the assumption that commercial interests are always paramount. Second, certain policy preferences were not predicted because context-specific geopolitical or geospatial elements were not included in the analysis. Third, in a few cases proxies failed to accurately reflect underlying parameters, owing to scientific uncertainty or exogenous forces. Fourth, in the marlins case and both bluefin cases, bioeconomic and geographic factors limited competition, reducing the demand for political response in spite of the depletion of the stock. And finally, there was evidence of path-dependent divergence in the cases, in that the timing of certain events may have affected subsequent responses in ways that are not predicted by the framework.

The impact of noncommercial interests was most visible in the marlins case (chapter 8) and that of western bluefin tuna (chapter 9). In the former, recreational and conservation interests clearly pushed the United States toward a more protective stance on Atlantic marlins. By persuading such a powerful country, noncommercial interests were able to effect changes in the management of these by-catch species. Nonetheless, ICCAT's regulation of blue marlin and white marlin is much less rigorous than its management of commercially valuable by-catch like juvenile bigeye or swordfish. Similarly, recreational interests were able to affect the early management of western bluefin through the United States, but were quickly overruled by commercial interests once prices for the species began to rise. More recently, the international threat to list western bluefin tuna under the Convention for International Trade in Endangered Species generated temporary cutbacks in harvests of the stock, but these were not sustained for more than a few years.

As it happens, the country that seems most susceptible to noncommercial interests, the United States, also was a highly vulnerable country in most of the cases. Therefore, noncommercial interests are a potential confounding variable. One piece of evidence for vulnerability response is that the United States was reluctant to accept strong management measures in the first period of the yellowfin tuna case, when its fleet fit into the pre-flex phase of the gradually vulnerable category. Also, in the conflict phase of the cases, the highly vulnerable United States still engaged in countermeasures designed to pass the costs of management on to others. One could assert that this reflects commercial much more than noncommercial interests. On the other hand, the United States was a leader in the marlins case even though it was mildly vulnerable as a by-catch country, like all other ICCAT members. Contemporary documentation shows that this position was a result of political maneuvers by noncommercial interests.

Additional evidence on the interaction between the commercially based predictions of vulnerability response and the actions of noncommercial interests can be drawn from comparisons between the United States and Canada. The latter is highly vulnerable in most cases, too, but its response on marlins was muted, especially when compared with its interventions on commercially valuable stocks. It is also remarkable that the United States and Canada both began as leaders on western bluefin management, proposing limits in accordance with scientific advice, but quickly altered their positions once the species became more valuable in the late 1970s. They both acceded to management measures that were risky at best, even though the United States is somewhat susceptible to noncommercial interests.

This evidence suggests that noncommercial interests should be incorporated into the vulnerability response model, but that commercial interests remain the primary drivers of national policy in the international fisheries context. The cases also show a high degree of satisficing on the part of noncommercial interests, insofar as their most adamant and successful lobbying occurred when a stock or species was severely depleted. Partly this is because the members of an interest group tend to make greater contributions and take stronger political action as the threat of collapse or loss of recreational amenity increases with the decline of a stock. Also, in highly and gradually vulnerable countries, commercial opposition to international management will be much lower when the stock is depleted. As was observed in both the marlins and the western bluefin tuna cases, there can be a convergence of domestic interests, as per DeSombre's (1995) baptists and bootleggers assertion.[3]

Another set of exceptions in the cases was related to the scope of expectations for national policy preferences. Three obvious examples stand out. The first is the time-area closure of the Gulf of Guinea, which was described in chapter 5. In this case, the EC seemed to be pushing for the closure to protect juvenile bigeye, which was unexpected because these fish are by-catch for EC fleets. Closer inspection showed that the measure would have sharply curtailed the harvests of Ghana, the EC's biggest rival in the Atlantic skipjack tuna fishery. Thus the move fit the spirit of the framework, but was unexpected because geospatial elements were not included in the preliminary prediction phase. More generally, mixing of stocks or species invalidated some single-stock predictions, particularly interventions by Canada in the southern swordfish case. A temporary solution to this type of problem was developed in chapters 5 and 9, but more systematic methods for dealing with mixed fisheries should be developed.

On the other hand, the movement by the Group of 18 for greater recognition of the rights of coastal and developing countries was not predicted because of the focus on specific stocks as opposed to the larger regime. As part of a broader strategy, this coalition of developing coastal countries, which now has more than eighteen members, blocked or otherwise undermined distribution agreements for several stocks, including southern swordfish and bigeye tuna. By doing so, they were able to start a dialogue on access rights that culminated in the 2001 Criteria for the Allocation of Fishing Possibilities (ICCAT 2007a, oth. 01-25). Again, this move was close to the vulnerability response expectations for moderately vulnerable countries, but it was not predicted for the cases because the scope of the strategy extended beyond a single stock, or even mixed fishery interactions.

At the same time, the southern swordfish and western bluefin tuna cases both showed that coastal countries may tactically choose to try to limit access by distant-water fishing fleets earlier than predicted by the vulnerability response framework. A critical determinant of this behavior may be the availability of information on the influx of such fleets and institutional mechanisms for pursuing such limitations. These elements overlap with the path dependence of response, which is discussed later, in that the timing of moves by distant-water fleets is key. In both the southern swordfish and western bluefin cases, distant-water fleets rapidly increased their landings after ICCAT had been established. In contrast, distant-water fisheries targeting tropical tunas had entered the Atlantic in the 1950s and 1960s, before many of the commission members were even independent countries. Gradual influx in a period when information was much less available and institutions had not been established could not trigger such a strong reaction. Thus both temporal and broader geopolitical factors would have to be incorporated into the framework to account for this behavior.

The third type of exception occurred when proxies diverged or were diverted from their target parameter. As discussed in chapter 2, competition usually escalates in the wake of overexploitation under open access. These relationships seemed valid in most of the cases, but not all. Sometimes technological advances would generate sudden shifts in the level of competition relative to stock depletion. The introduction of fish aggregating devices reduced competition in the yellowfin fishery but amplified competition in the bigeye fishery. Having encountered this problem early in the study, I was careful to include hypotheses about the impacts of technologies on competition in other cases, but the implications of this issue could certainly be explored further.

At other times, the relationship between biological depletion and economic competition was obscured by changes in scientific assessments.

The southern swordfish case is an excellent example of this problem. Initial responses to scientific signs of depletion conformed to vulnerability response expectations. Conflict among countries with different levels of vulnerability resulted in insufficient management measures. However, as time went by, scientifically recommended catch levels were revised upward, not downward, as is usually the case under excess effort. A similar dynamic was observed in the bluefin cases, but was much more detrimental to those stocks.

In fact, benchmarks like maximum sustainable yield and replacement yield varied in most of the cases, often becoming more optimistic after the implementation of management measures. Because there are usually scientific rationales for changes in stock assessments, such as new data, new estimation techniques, or changes in the fishery, it is difficult for this author, as a social scientist and an observer, to criticize the seeming unreliability of SCRS advice. Nonetheless, the reliance on ICCAT science as an indicator of both the biological welfare of the stocks and the economic health of the fishery is one of the weakest points in the analysis. Uncertainty and politicization call into question the strength of measures adopted in successful cases and the weakness of regulations for stocks that remain depleted.

A fourth but related concern is cases in which competition is limited by bioeconomic or geographic factors. The eastern and western bluefin cases are good examples. Even though bluefin is one of the highest-priced fishes in the world, both Atlantic stocks are severely depleted. Furthermore, more vulnerable countries, such as low-flex, gradually vulnerable Japan and the highly vulnerable United States, Canada, and EC, did not respond as strongly to the depletion of these stocks as the framework would have predicted. Uncertainty is one explanation, but so too is the singular nature of the species, which minimizes competition from substitutes. Shutting out moderately vulnerable countries in the west and mildly vulnerable countries in both areas reduced direct competition as well.

This brings us back to the last and most evocative set of deviations from the vulnerability response framework. Path dependence was already mentioned in regard to the impact that the timing of entry by distant-water fleets can have on the policy positions of coastal countries. Other historical influences were also observed in the cases. The earliest was the establishment of EEZs in the mid-1970s, which affected Japanese competitiveness at the time (a proxy violation), but also laid the groundwork for the demands of the Group of 18. Similarly, moderately vulnerable countries seemed to learn from experience, particularly in the southern swordfish and eastern bluefin cases. Having been denied sufficient amounts of quota in earlier regulations, these countries banded together to protect their access rights in cases where quotas had not yet been set. Precedent also played a role in the bigeye tuna and southern swordfish cases because the monitoring and enforcement mechanisms that had been developed for bluefin tuna were easily adopted for these other stocks. These variations will be discussed more as the aggregate implications of the analysis are considered in the next section.

All of these exceptions to the vulnerability response framework are important, and section 11.5 describes some possible fixes. For now, though, consider the tradeoffs of inclusiveness. Even in its simplest form, the framework was difficult to operationalize because of the sheer number of countries involved and the lack of data on everything from the economics of their domestic fleets to their internal decision processes. Certain complications, such as multistock interactions and technological innovations, could be incorporated fairly readily, but dealing with the larger temporal and geopolitical context will require the collection and systematic analysis of even greater amounts of information. In addition, causal pathways become more convoluted with the inclusion of new explanatory variables. As it is now, the vulnerability response framework minimizes data requirements but also allows the analyst to identify areas where deeper inspection is necessary.

11.3   Transformative Pattern of Aggregate Response

There are different ways of evaluating international governance. Authors like Oran Young (2002) focus on institutional design, seeking to identify rules and norms that generate effective governance. Others like Haas, Keohane, and Levy (1995) look at the strategic nature of international relations, attempting to show how international institutions emerge from strategic national interests. Both of these schools are complemented by works from authors like DeSombre (2005), who seek to expose the domestic sources of national policy preferences. The vulnerability response framework presented in chapter 2 was designed as a first step toward bridging the gap between these approaches. This section provides a second step by comparing the patterns of collective behavior that were observed in the cases. Linkages between the vulnerability response dynamic and changes in collective action are reported, along with exogenous factors and path-dependent elements.

Some important patterns of aggregate response were revealed in the cases. This is not an exhaustive list of all potential patterns, but it is a starting point for future work. As national policy positions changed with the depletion of a stock—largely in accordance with vulnerability response expectations—aggregate concern also shifted, altering cooperative management. Because of this, different periods of aggregate response can be correlated with different levels of stock depletion as long as the underlying assumptions of the framework hold. These include a period of inactivity, a period of concern, a period of conflict, a period of accord, and a period of reversion. Figure 11.1 shows the observed relationship between each of these periods and (1) the aggregate level of governmental concern, (2) the level of overexploitation of the stock, and (3) the strength of ICCAT management measures.

Except for yellowfin and bluefin tuna, all of the cases started out in a period of inactivity, when there was no evidence of overexploitation

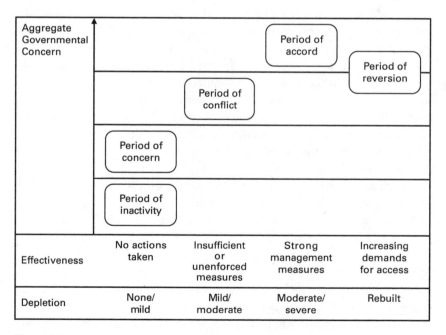

Figure 11.1
Transformative pattern of aggregate response observed in the cases.

and no management actions were even under discussion.[4] As scientists started reporting signs of stock depletion, highly vulnerable countries would begin expressing concern about the stock; hence the period of concern that follows the period of inactivity. Because other countries do not yet feel the need for management, no direct actions would be taken during this period, either.[5] With the continued decline of the stock, the commission tended to move into a period of conflict in which most countries recognized the need for action, but none were willing to make the necessary sacrifices. Any management measures adopted in this period were either insufficient, in that they fell short of scientific advice, or were not enforced, either at the domestic or international levels. Countermeasures such as size limits and vague instructions to countries to limit catches or effort to "recent levels" fall into this category.

Many of the cases ended in one of these "early" periods, either because overexploitation had not yet set in or because negotiations became mired in a period of conflict owing to factors that will be discussed later. However, the northern swordfish case and the bigeye tuna case evinced two subsequent periods. In each, conflict was followed by accord as highly and low-flex, gradually vulnerable countries took responsibility for attaining cooperative management. After further declines in the stock, these countries took on most of the costs of management, making the necessary concessions and side payments to their less vulnerable counterparts in order to achieve agreement on strong management. This usually included the introduction of international enforcement mechanisms. Reduction of the flexibility of gradually vulnerable countries through the depletion of alternative fisheries was also a critical determinant of the switch from conflict to accord.

Once stock rebuilding was achieved, the political will to maintain management started to erode, and the commission moved into a period of reversion. While the evidence on postrebuilding behavior is incomplete, increasing demands from developing countries and new entrants, as well as a shift to less precautionary interpretations of scientific advice, suggest that conflict may again undermine management as the availability of fish—and revenues—increases. So far, accord has not broken for either of the rebuilt stocks, but increasing tension presages a return to the period of conflict. It is possible that future management will vacillate in a dynamic equilibrium of depletion, response, and rebuilding. Although we will have to wait for history to reveal the rest of the pattern, this movement from the period of inactivity to the period of reversion as per figure 11.1 will be labeled the *transformative pattern* of aggregate response.

Collective management occurred as it did in these cases because the most powerful countries were bearing the brunt of the costs of exploitation. If less powerful countries had been the more vulnerable, then the outcome would be quite different; the commission might not even exist at all. As described in chapter 2, the position of industrialized countries in the highly and gradually vulnerable categories is not a coincidence. Because the early capital requirements for harvesting highly migratory species were high, only fishers in industrialized countries could afford to enter the marketplace. This provided them with a historical foothold in the fisheries and allowed them to build large fleets. It also gave them something to lose as competition increased under open access. Most other tuna management bodies face similar circumstances, but adaptive governance in nonfisheries issue areas might take alternative paths, owing to different combinations of power and vulnerability.

In fact, the distribution of power among the different vulnerability categories was a key determinant of this pattern of aggregate response. During the period of conflict, mildly and moderately vulnerable fishing countries were making inroads into these fisheries, while highly and gradually vulnerable countries were losing market share. This dynamic would not have been possible without the dispersion of fishing technology and increased access to international markets associated with a globalized economy (Lawson 1984, 21). One blatant instance of competition exacerbated by global interconnectedness was the rapid appropriation of fish aggregating devices on the part of Ghana and other less vulnerable countries only a few years after they were first utilized in the Atlantic by France and Spain (ICCAT 1995–2007b: 1997, 22). Another example would be the explosive price increases for bigeye and bluefin tuna, which would not have benefited Atlantic fisheries if they did not have access to the Japanese sushi market.[6]

In addition, all but one of the cases showed that strong management has occurred at ICCAT only after gradually vulnerable distant-water countries began to feel the pinch of increasing competition along with their highly vulnerable counterparts. Distant-water fishing countries with high costs of production like those of the EC and Japan are running out of cheap alternatives as HMS stocks have been depleted globally. With fewer and fewer fresh stocks to exploit, these countries are quickly losing the advantage that distant-water capabilities imparted to them in the past. Facing recession in its fisheries, Japan has moved to reduce its capacity and redirect its industry into processing and other alternative modes of production (Bergin and Haward 1996, 108–109). In contrast, because their survival strategies included expansion and subsidization of their fishing operations, fleets from several EC member countries continue to be overcapitalized. Also, Japan appears to have undertaken a global approach to fisheries management, whereas the EC may be engaging in pulse management, which, like pulse fishing, capitalizes on their ability to move from one stock to another to avoid economic catastrophe.[7]

If global stocks continue to decline in spite of international management efforts, gradually vulnerable fishers may be forced to either leave the industry or migrate to countries where production costs are lower, much as fishers from the United States and Canada have done. Japanese fishers have already started such moves, and EC fishers may follow. The repercussions of these types of alternatives, as opposed to the distant-water fishing option that was a major determinant of vulnerability in the cases, are far reaching. Essentially, these fishers would be choosing exit over voice, to use Hirschman's (1970) famous terminology. Even though there would still be economic costs involved in such a transition, the exit of large portions of a domestic fleet could substantially reduce its political importance.

Furthermore, when regulations are unsuccessful, either in terms of rebuilding a stock or protecting vulnerable fleets, highly and gradually vulnerable countries could be pushed out of a fishery entirely, leaving those in the mildly and moderately vulnerable categories to take their place. While the equity of such an occurrence is debatable, the implications under the vulnerability response framework undeniably point toward a prolonged period of overexploitation and a lower likelihood that sustainability will be achieved. That said, such a shift could provide grounds for the establishment of an internationally traded quota system as the pressure to base allocation on historical catch levels dissipates. Quota transfers and swaps on a piecemeal basis were observed in the cases here, so some mechanisms for exchange already exist.

This similarity between the patterns of response in these two cases is particularly interesting because of the variance in the timing of the periods. Table 11.1 lists the duration of each period for each of the cases in this book. Compare the two cases that exhibited the basic cycle of aggregate response—bigeye tuna and northern swordfish. The timing and du-

Table 11.1
Timing of Aggregate Response, Evidence from Cases

Pattern	Case	Periods				
		Inactivity	Concern	Conflict	Accord	Reversion
Transformative	Bigeye tuna	1969–1991[a]	1992–1994	1995–1999	2000–2002	2003–2006
	Northern swordfish	1969–1978	1979–1988	1989–1998	1999–2001	2002–2006
Incidental	Skipjack tuna	1969–2006				
Positively interrupted	Yellowfin tuna		1970–1976			
		1977–1990	1991–1992	1993–2006		
Negatively interrupted	Eastern bluefin tuna	1969–1982	1983–1987	1988–1996		
				1997–2006		
Pseudo-successful	Southern swordfish	1969–1988	1989–1993	1994–2006		
Premature exclusion	Western bluefin		1970–1973		1974–2006	
Glass ceiling	Blue and white marlins	1969–1972	1973–1991	1992–1999	2000–2006	
	Mixed tropical tunas		1974–1976	1977–1984		
		1985–1991		1992–2006		

[a] ICCAT adopted a size limit for bigeye tuna in 1979 to prevent misreporting of undersized yellowfin tuna.

ration of each period varies widely for the two stocks. There are several reasons for this. First, industrialized fishing fleets began targeting northern swordfish much earlier than bigeye tuna, largely because demand for the latter was quite low until the 1980s. Second, early growth in production of northern swordfish required the investment of new capital and the building of new boats, whereas the later rush to target bigeye occurred after the overcapitalization of other fisheries. Once prices started to rise, there were fewer barriers to entry into the bigeye fishery than there had been at the outset for the northern swordfish fishery. Third, while gradually vulnerable fleets started harvesting swordfish in the northern Atlantic and then spread out from there, Atlantic bigeye was one of the last stocks of this species to be targeted. Therefore, gradually vulnerable countries ran out of viable alternatives much earlier in the latter case.

Other factors had similar impacts on both cases. For instance, the period of conflict was extended because of powerful countries that fell into the mildly vulnerable category owing to by-catch harvests by their fleets. In the northern swordfish case, Japanese fishers were catching significant amounts of swordfish while targeting bigeye tuna. Alternatively, EC fleets harvested large numbers of juvenile bigeye tuna in their fishery targeting skipjack and other small tropical tunas. Unwilling to reduce its harvests of the targeted stock, Japan received quota swaps for northern swordfish. Effective measures to reduce landings of undersized bigeye have yet to be adopted. Instead, countries targeting adults have settled for lower harvests. Even so, the EC was allowed to go ahead with its plan to establish time-area closures in the Gulf of Guinea, in spite of the skepticism of countries targeting adult bigeye.

Finally, institutional precedent also facilitated the switch to accord in both cases. The sharing and exclusion mechanisms that were adopted for these species had been pioneered previously for western and eastern bluefin tuna. Establishing such a system was not easy. By adopting quota-based management, countries agreed to forgo the opportunity to appropriate shares of the harvest through economic competition. Less vulnerable countries required considerable convincing—largely through exceptions for small fleets or quota transfers—in order to accept such a measure. However, once established for one or two stocks, these methods would be easily transferred to others, such as northern swordfish and bigeye tuna. In fact, these measures have also been adopted in other regional fisheries management bodies, including the Inter-American

Tropical Tuna Commission, the Indian Ocean Tuna Commission, and the Commission for the Conservation of Southern Bluefin Tuna (CCSBT).

11.4   Variations on the Transformative Pattern of Aggregate Response

With a few exceptions, similar international and bioeconomic factors were also found in the cases that exhibit different, less successful, patterns. Yet, there were also key distinctions that pushed aggregate response away from the strong management that is associated with the northern swordfish and bigeye tuna cases. By comparing aggregate responses in these disparate examples, it is possible to identify the causes of such variations in management, contributing to the understanding of adaptive governance as described in chapter 1. Pertinent distinguishing factors range from differences in the mix of countries targeting a stock to exogenous interruptions in the economics of overexploitation to pushes and nudges from noncommercial interests.

As table 11.1 shows, none of the other cases covering commercially targeted stocks reached a period of accord. Some have yet to be substantially overexploited. Skipjack, the major component in the mixed tropical tunas fishery, is so abundant and so low priced that open-access production has not yet reduced the stock below full exploitation. No ICCAT members have proposed any measures to ensure that effort remains at full exploitation or even expressed any concern for the future of the stock. It has remained in the inactive period for the entire history of the commission.[8] Nonetheless, skipjack production has been affected by measures that were adopted to protect juvenile bigeye and yellowfin tunas. This by-catch interaction places the management of the entire fishery for small tropical tunas in the glass ceiling category, which is discussed further on.

Slightly less abundant and higher priced, yellowfin tuna was thought to be moderately exploited prior to the geographic expansion of fishing effort in 1976 and has since been mildly overexploited. Very early in the history of the commission, aggregate response pre-1976 moved quickly from concern to conflict. This pattern was repeated in the early 1990s when the entire Atlantic stock was thought to be mildly overexploited. This time the reprieve was economic, in that increasing demand for bigeye tuna and the introduction of FADs caused fishing effort to shift away from yellowfin. Thus the endogenous process of overexploitation that drives vulnerability response has been interrupted twice in the yellowfin fishery, each time easing competitive pressures while also delaying further depletion of the stock.

Not all interruptions have been so benign. The proliferation of farming technologies in the Mediterranean had a drastic impact on the size of the eastern bluefin stock as well as the pattern of aggregate concern. Prior to the use of cages to fatten bluefin, the collective response seemed to be transitioning from a period of conflict to a period of concern. That is, more vulnerable countries were starting to make concessions, even though they were not yet willing to ensure strong management. Bluefin farming temporarily reduced economic competition by providing a more efficient mode of production. Without competitive pressures, aggregate concern at ICCAT fell, earlier gains were erased, and management response returned to the period of conflict. Unchecked development of farming technology increased harvests substantially and led to severe depletion, which may soon result in the collapse of the fishery.

The distinction between the *positively interrupted cycle* recorded in the yellowfin tuna case and the *negatively interrupted cycle* found in the eastern bluefin case is illustrated in figure 11.2. Aggregate management for yellowfin starts in a period of concern, moves into conflict, but is "reset" by the discovery of new fishing grounds, returning the commission to a period of inactivity. However, because open access continues, this change is temporary and so the cycle starts again, only to be interrupted a second time. In contrast, the eastern bluefin case moved through inactivity, concern, and conflict, but the transition to accord was cut off by technological change. Aggregate concern was reduced and conflict was prolonged, leading to severe depletion of the stock.

Like eastern bluefin, the southern swordfish and the western bluefin cases also remain in periods of conflict, even though current regulations meet or come close to the criteria for strong management. Western bluefin is a case of premature exclusion—access rights and enforcement mechanisms were developed before moderately or mildly vulnerable countries had a chance to enter the fishery. This was precipitated by the isolated location of the stock, the lack of viable substitutes, and several strong nudges from noncommercial interest groups at both domestic and international levels. It might seem that negotiating strong management for this fishery would be easier without the objections of less vulnerable countries, but the absence of either direct or indirect competition undermined the buildup of aggregate concern.

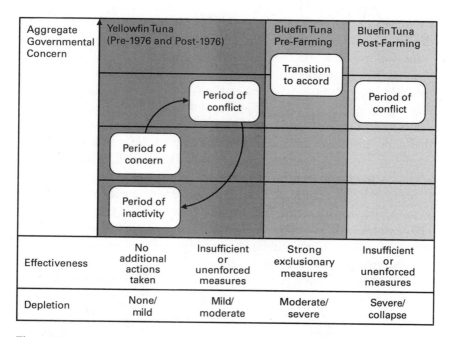

Figure 11.2
Interrupted patterns of aggregate response.

Without the driver of economic competition from less vulnerable states, countries targeting western bluefin were not able to maintain regulations that completely conformed to scientific advice. Even a big shove from conservation interests—in the form of the nomination of western bluefin for the Convention on the International Trade in Endangered Species prohibition list—was not sufficient to permanently generate accord among ICCAT members. It did provide extra impetus for the development of trade-based monitoring and enforcement mechanisms, which were then taken up in the swordfish and bigeye fisheries. However, the main target of trade-based measures, IUU fishing, was a major concern before the CITES threat.

In addition, the issue of mixing between the eastern and western stocks, which is a variant of commercial by-catch, increased competitive pressures on western fleets but also acted as a scapegoat. Instead of compensating for mixing, as in the bigeye case, countries with fleets targeting the western stock adopted risky measures while pushing for better management in the east. It's quite amazing that the aggregate response pattern of *premature exclusion* holds in spite of this and other factors that could easily have resulted in a transition to stronger management.

In contrast, management of southern swordfish seems much more positive. ICCAT regulations are enforced via international trade-based mechanisms, and the TAC now conforms to scientific advice. Nevertheless, recent measures fit the definition of "strong management" only because of an upward revision of the assessment for that stock. Prior to that shift, there was no indication that any of the members targeting southern swordfish were willing to make the sacrifices necessary to achieve strong management. Even now, with a much larger TAC than in previous years, several moderately vulnerable countries are dissatisfied with sharing arrangements but have not been mollified by highly vulnerable countries. Clearly, there is no accord on southern swordfish; aggregate demands for access still outweigh aggregate concern for the stock.

These two patterns are contrasted in figure 11.3. Both cases are stuck in conflict, but for the western bluefin case, premature exclusion leads to a very different outcome. Countries targeting the stock work out sharing arrangements but fail to curtail their harvests sufficiently. Overexploitation may be delayed, as exemplified by the drawn-out decline of this stock, but eventually severe depletion or collapse can be expected. If competition from eastern bluefin farms continues, aggregate concern might increase, shifting the case into a period of accord. However, this may not occur until the mixing issue is settled so that the countries targeting western bluefin can focus on their own management problems.

The pattern of *pseudo-success* in the southern swordfish case is shown by an extension of the period of conflict. An optimistic analyst could hope that the current apparently strong measures will prevent over-exploitation of the stock. After all, capacity in this fishery is still less than the scientifically recommended—and commission mandated—catch level. However, it is more likely that agreement will break down as capacity grows and moderately vulnerable countries demand greater access, much as was observed in the eastern bluefin case. With the absence of large, highly vulnerable fleets and early exclusion of mildly vulnerable fleets, the transition to a period of accord will be quite difficult; countries with highly vulnerable fleets exhibit substantial concern while mildly vulnerable fleets create concern through the threat of expanded competition.

Like northern swordfish and bigeye tuna, the case of Atlantic blue marlin and white marlin has reached a period of accord. Even though the measures adopted for these species are not likely to rebuild the stocks

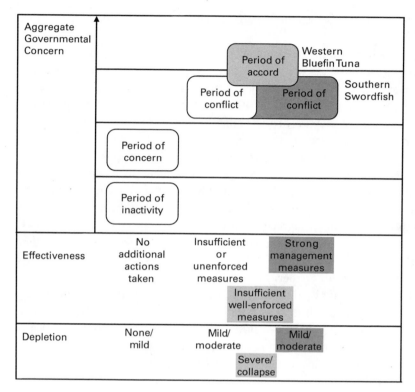

Figure 11.3
Premature patterns of aggregate response.

to MSY, most parties seem content with the current arrangements. However, the reasons for this early agreement are very different for these by-catch species, which are not targeted by commercial fleets in the Atlantic. In the marlins case, the problem is both a lack of competition and the minor influence of noncommercial interests relative to commercial interests. They are not as widespread or well resourced as their commercial counterparts, who would have to pay the costs of marlin protections.

In addition, the responsive nature of noncommercial interests ensures that they will expend enough effort to obtain measures only when a stock is severely overexploited. The combined result is a *glass ceiling*; aggregate concern will go so far, but no farther. This is very different than the dynamic observed in the dolphin–tuna controversy that plagued the Inter-American Tropical Tuna Commission for many years. There, conservation groups focused on protection of dolphins at all costs and had the political strength to alter management for the long term (DeSombre 1999).

Commercial by-catch of juvenile bigeye and yellowfin in the fishery targeting skipjack also seemed to reach a glass ceiling. In this case, the EC was willing to forgo some skipjack harvests to protect juvenile bigeye, but only when it would allow them to reduce competition by setting a time-area closure of the Gulf of Guinea. Yet this policy has not been effective; by-catch of undersized bigeye is still quite high and Ghana has not complied with the closure. Thus, conflict over by-catch in the skipjack fishery continues. Only the development of a cheap by-catch avoidance mechanism has the potential to dislodge this equilibrium. The same can be said of commercial by-catch problems in the other cases. For instance, the Japanese agreed to discard incidental harvests of northern swordfish, but would not alter their fishing practices to protect that stock. Again, mildly vulnerable by-catch countries will allow regulations to go so far, but no farther.

One last potentially distorting factor must be considered, although its impact on the patterns discussed here is difficult to discern. There is some evidence in the cases that decision makers and interest groups can learn from encounters with heavy competition. The experience of highly vulnerable countries shows that when fishers themselves are convinced of the importance of sustainable management, decision makers find it much easier to push for an early, strong response to biological depletion (DeSombre 1995; Webster 2006). The same issues of scope and scale in HMS fisheries that make scientific analysis difficult also inhibit fishers' perceptions of biological depletion and recession in its early stages. However, once fishers have experienced the costly adjustment and rebuilding process for one stock of fish, they may be more willing to compromise on management of other stocks.[9] For example, the U.S. longline fleet was hit hard by the rebuilding plan for bluefin tuna in the early 1990s. Forced to give up all exploitation of the highly valuable bluefin, these fishers became even more concerned about the status of their main target species, northern swordfish, as did U.S. representatives at ICCAT.[10] Moreover, the 1996 adoption of the Sustainable Fisheries Act suggests that a broader movement toward science over vested interests may be occurring in the United States, although the act and its implementation remain contested issues (Weber 2002, chap. 10).

Returning to the larger picture, it would seem that this type of learning is not highly transferable. That is, less vulnerable states are not necessarily made more cautious by the example set for them when their more vulnerable counterparts pay the economic costs associated with the depletion of a stock.[11] More important, the changes caused by learning are not unidirectional. This is because it is not limited to states that desire early, strong responses. Experience with vulnerability response for one stock of fish may cause a member of ICCAT to be more circumspect in regard to other stocks, but that caution can include machinations aimed at inhibiting early action rather than preventing additional depletion. Contracting parties with more competitive fleets can increase their benefits, both in terms of market share and side payments from more vulnerable states, if they postpone action on stocks whose biomass has fallen below MSY (Barkin and Shambaugh 1999b, 16). Moderately or mildly vulnerable fishing states that have been pressured into acquiescence in the past may learn better ways to maximize those benefits when dealing with other stocks of fish.[12]

Much more information is needed to incorporate this important factor into a consolidated model of vulnerability response. Furthermore, Haas and Haas (1995, 261) point out that for organizational learning to occur in multilateral settings, a coalition of hegemonic member states must be committed to advocating the measures prescribed by a consolidated epistemic community. That coalition certainly does not yet exist at ICCAT, and given the predicted propensities of gradually vulnerable states regarding flexibility in management of various stocks, it may never occur in any generalized way. Furthermore, given the level of disputation within the commission's scientific committee, one could also question the existence of a cohesive epistemic community within this issue area.[13]

11.5   Making Progress with Vulnerability Response

Like progress, the concept of vulnerability as a driving force in world affairs is not new. Its application in political philosophy can be traced as far back as Thucydides' argument regarding the necessity of war, in which he asserts that the Lacedaemonians waged war on Athens because they felt vulnerable to their neighbor's growing power (Alker 1996, 23). This type of military vulnerability has long dominated the discourse in international relations, but economic or environmental vulnerabilities have recently been recognized as well (Keohane and Nye 2001, intro. to 3rd ed.). The vulnerability response framework presented and tested here shows how global environmental governance can evolve based on the bioeconomic vulnerabilities of fishing countries. However, there is still much that needs to be done to refine the framework and extend it to other issue areas.

Perhaps the greatest contribution and the worst pitfall of the vulnerability response approach is its disciplinary scope. By bringing together biological, economic, organizational, political, and international theories, the framework revealed new roles for old actors and led to the identification of important patterns in the evolution of international fisheries management. Without such a framework, one could easily become entangled in the complexities of interactions among fish, fishers, and fishing countries, not to mention all of the important elements that were highlighted by deviations from the vulnerability response expectations. Moreover, if any one piece had been left out of the framework, explanatory power would have been lost. Portions of the cases might be explained with a less inclusive analysis, but not the dynamic coevolution of the entire system. Nevertheless, it is impossible for one person to fully grasp the subtleties of each of these perspectives, so the framework is also oversimplified in several ways.

Limiting domestic preferences to match commercial fishing interests was sufficient in many cases, but in others, noncommercial interests influenced the decision process as well, either through direct lobbying or through the manipulation of institutional interplay. At the other end of the spectrum, limiting the assessment of success to the adoption of regulations that conformed to scientific advice and included international enforcement mechanisms provided only a minimal measure of effectiveness. While it is true that estimates of fishing effort and stock biomass both moved in the right direction after the implementation of strong management, considerable uncertainty in scientific assessments tends to undermine the credibility of that coincidence. Furthermore, the plethora of alternative explanations for changes in stock size brings up questions of causality, even if one accepts the precept of scientific accuracy.[14]

The remaining causal questions run in two directions. First, there is the possibility that ICCAT management was not responsible for rebuilding even though there is a lagged correlation between implementation, reported catch reductions, and increased biomass. Second, there is the concern that overexploitation, as represented by reduced biomass, is not a very accurate proxy for economic competition. In both instances, expansion of the analysis to other issue areas in which data on physical and economic factors are more abundant and relationships between the two are well fleshed out would be helpful. Unfortunately, few such examples exist in the global arena, but scaling down to smaller regimes (geographically and in the number of members) could provide the necessary cases. Certain elements of the framework would need to be reevaluated for application elsewhere. Competitiveness and flexibility might not always be the best indicators of vulnerability. Indeed, economic vulnerability is not always the paramount concern of vested interests. This is explained further in a few paragraphs.

Some critics would probably go even further than the objections mentioned here, rejecting the notion of an evaluation based on single-stock, maximum sustainable yield criteria. Certainly, there are biological arguments for the use of more inclusive ecosystem management. Given the complexities of ocean life, the removal of a large portion of a single stock can be detrimental to the entire system (Worm et al. 2006a,b). Legal and institutional arguments for alternative management approaches have also been posited in recent years, focusing on ideas like marine protected areas and spaced-based management (Crowder et al. 2006; Young et al. 2007). While such concerns are not dealt with explicitly in the framework, evidence from the cases suggests that the implementation of such measures will be difficult in the highly migratory species arena. Many countries have a vested interest in the current system that will be difficult to dislodge. Furthermore, issues of fairness must be considered, as shown by the strategic manipulation of biological and geographical opportunity in the mixed tropical tunas case.

That said, it would be quite useful to extend the model to include a wider variety of management options. In their search for satisfactory policy choices, national decision makers have proven to be highly innovative, even within the constraints of international bargaining. While the complexity of global environmental issues precludes true prediction— that is, fortune telling without recourse to historical context—thought experiments based on vulnerability response can be used to explore multiple scenarios of institutional evolution. Complemented by case analysis, this work can expose the practical difficulties of achieving specific management goals as well as the prevalent direction of adaptation. Different assumptions regarding bioeconomic forces, interest group influence, international power structures, and institutional precedent can be used to broaden the set of possibilities and incorporate greater complexities into the exercise.[15]

The other regional fisheries management organizations could serve as useful cases in pursuit of a more nuanced framework. Most international regimes that deal with tunas and tunalike species have evolved economic and institutional systems that parallel those described here, so extension of the framework to these arenas should not be too difficult. The historical–developing and coastal–distant-water dichotomies are similar in all of the oceans and were generated by the same economic forces.[16] Likewise, most of the tuna RFMOs operate on the basis of consensus rather than voting, utilize MSY as a de facto goal, and have access to various escape clauses, such as the objection procedure. Struggles over access rights and allocation criteria, prevalent illegal, unreported, and unregulated fleets, and increasing competition are also common to all of these bodies.

Because of these similarities, analogous policy positions and patterns would be expected to emerge in other tuna RFMOs. Nevertheless, there are differences among these regimes that should serve as useful sources of comparison. For instance, the IATTC and CCSBT have independent scientific bodies instead of the collaborative group system used by ICCAT. Peterson (1995) hypothesized that independent science is more persuasive in international fisheries management, so either of these bodies would be a good test of a new and improved version of the framework. The IATTC has also been greatly affected by noncommercial interests working for the protection of dolphins. Unlike the recreation and conservation organizations that were active in the Atlantic, these groups were able to mobilize the public, particularly in the United States, so this would be a good case in which to explore vulnerability response with both commercial and noncommercial interest groups.

Some of the most interesting variations among RFMOs are in the mix of countries that participate in each commission. The United States was highly vulnerable in most of the cases presented here, but would be gradually vulnerable in the Pacific. On the other hand, the United States is not even a member of the Indian Ocean Tuna Commission. Instead, Australia and New Zealand fill the highly vulnerable position there. Japan, France, and Spain are ubiquitous and gradually vulnerable in all of the RFMOs except for the CCSBT, which was long dominated by Japan, Australia, and New Zealand until South Korea and Taiwan joined recently. Along with China, Indonesia, and the Philippines, these countries are also mildly vulnerable members of the other RFMOs. Moderately vulnerable countries have been more assertive in the IATTC and have much more power in the new Western and Central Pacific Fisheries Commission (WCPFC) because Pacific island states control so much of that area. It will be interesting to see how vulnerability response and adaptive governance play out in these different contexts.[17]

Development of a general approach—one that extends beyond international fisheries—will require a more flexible conceptualization of vulnerability. Even in these cases, additional sources of vulnerability were observed. Recreational fishers, conservation organizations, and even Japanese consumers were posited sources of national vulnerability. In addition, Sprinz and Vaahtoranta (1994) have already explored the idea of vulnerability based on the public health concerns associated with transboundary pollution. Other environmental problems carry similar dangers, which may be experienced differently by different people. For instance, Zahran et al. (2006) connect experienced costs of climate change, such as temperature fluctuations, sea level rise, and increasing natural hazards, with trends in political activities regarding climate change. This is just one set of vulnerabilities that could be triggered by global warming. Economic vulnerabilities associated with rising costs of fossil fuels, nutritional vulnerabilities generated by changes in rainfall, and even existence vulnerabilities triggered by concern over impacts on charismatic megafauna or wilderness areas may also engender political responses (Ando 1999).

All of these different reactions will interact in diverse ways, making the type of theoretical approach used here even more difficult. Yet the lessons we have to learn may be worth the extra effort. For instance, from the vulnerability response perspective, there are both optimistic and pessimistic possibilities for the future of HMS fisheries in the Atlantic. On the one hand, ICCAT seems to have rebuilt several stocks under its jurisdiction and created important institutions for monitoring and enforcing its management measures. The commission has been especially successful in excluding nonmembers from exploiting its stocks and in eliminating illegal, unregulated, and unreported fishing. In addition, learning and domestic change have taken place in highly vulnerable fishing countries, appreciably increasing their sensitivity to competition and actually altering the way they value HMS stocks in the Atlantic. Even gradually vulnerable fishing countries have begun to feel the pinch of resource scarcity under competition and have supported rebuilding plans for bigeye tuna and northern swordfish. All of these things are indicative of more timely and effective management of HMS stocks in the future.

On the other hand, conflict over allocation and escalating demands for access to HMS stocks threaten the viability of continued cooperation at ICCAT. Increasing market demand, combined with the facile movement of fishing capital in pursuit of lower costs of production, has brought an influx of new members to the commission. Most of these recent additions are in the moderate to mildly vulnerable categories and they are all jockeying for access to ICCAT stocks. In spite of attempts to address conflicts over access rights through recommendations such as the allocation criteria adopted in 2001, sharing arrangements are an increasingly bulky impediment to improving the vulnerability response pattern at ICCAT. The pressures created by increasing membership and declining stocks could eventually lead to a much more authoritative system of management if contracting parties can make the transition to a vote-based system of decision making. However, those same forces could also tear the commission apart if the policy impact of fleet declines in more vulnerable countries does not keep pace with the ambitions of less vulnerable countries.

Because of this tension, each stock that is depleted represents both a threat and an opportunity for HMS management at ICCAT. Understanding the forces behind the responsive behaviors of fishers and other interest groups, fishing countries, and the commission itself is the key to unlocking that potential. Vulnerability response is a nascent approach, but it has illuminated both the microlevel decision making and the macrolevel patterns that emerge in this complex system. It also provides a foundation for multidisciplinary research that has proven to be particularly difficult in this issue area. Additional refinement and testing of the framework developed here can shed even more light on the human–environment interface and the evolution of environmental governance. As occupants of a planet, we face similar precarious opportunities in other arenas. The identification of additional driving forces that are associated with the ambiguous benefits of progress, and the vulnerabilities they trigger, will help us to analyze our resilience in a changing world.

Appendix A
Group of 18

The Group of 18 is a nebulous term, largely used by moderately vulnerable countries like Brazil and South Africa to describe a coalition of coastal states. Most are self-identified as "developing," but they have been joined by a few Scandinavian countries that target ICCAT stocks opportunistically. It is interesting that although I have heard the group invoked many times in the six annual meetings that I have attended, there is no mention in the official record except very early on, in 2000, when there were only sixteen members. Table A.1 provides the best list of possible members of the group that can be drawn from ICCAT records.

Table A.1
Possible Members of the Group of 18

Initial proposal for Working Group on Allocation Criteria	Group of 16 (as per 2000 reference by Brazil)	18 Countries with similar preferences at third meeting of the Working Group on Allocation Criteria
Contracting Parties		
Angola	Brazil	Algeria
Brazil	Libya	Angola
Ivory Coast	Morocco	Brazil
Libya	Namibia	Gabon
Morocco	Panama	Ivory Coast
Sao Tome and Principe	South Africa	Libya
South Africa	Uruguay	Morocco
Uruguay	Venezuela	Namibia
Venezuela		South Africa
		Trinidad and Tobago
		Tunisia
		Uruguay
Noncontracting Parties (at the time)		
Guatemala	Belize	Argentina
Mexico	Colombia	Faroe Islands*
Namibia	Faroe Islands*	Iceland*
Panama	Guatemala	Mexico
	Iceland*	Norway*
	Mexico	St. Vincent and the Grenadines
	Namibia	
	Norway*	
	Turkey	

Notes: * Technically fall into highly vulnerable category, but only harvest opportunistically; target other species.
Sources: ICCAT (1995–2007: 1999, 92; 1995–2007: 2001, 80, 85; in re ICCAT 1995–2007: 2000, 110; 1995–2007: 2002, 121).

Appendix B

Comprehensive Vulnerability Classifications

In the text, only selected countries were listed in the vulnerability response matrices and prediction summaries for each case. However, a full list of countries harvesting each stock in each year of every case was compiled and used in the analysis. Here, aggregate lists of countries in each vulnerability category are provided for the various major periods in the cases. The year of membership in ICCAT (year) is provided to let the reader know when a country became active in management of the stock at hand. Some countries with fleets that harvest a stock during the case period may not have joined until a later date and so the years in this column do not always match the years covered by the table. Dominant gear type is provided for countries whose fleets harvest a large proportion of the stock (>100 tons) on average over the period as well (gear). This provides information on the potential for strategic positions related to dominant gear types and also informs readers about the most active countries in a fishery. While it is not always the case, usually countries that harvest large amounts of a particular stock tend to be more active in the management process. This is yet another possible revision of the vulnerability response framework, an additional expectation that the level of involvement with management will usually reflect the level of harvests of a particular stock. Readers who would like to examine the original data used in determining these vulnerability classifications can go to http://mitpress.mit.edu/adaptive_governance to download the author's files.

Table B.1
Vulnerability Classification of Countries Harvesting Bigeye Tuna

Highly vulnerable			Gradually vulnerable			Moderately vulnerable			Mildly vulnerable		
Country	Year	Gear	Country	Year	Gear	Country	Year	Gear	Country	Year	Gear
Contracting Parties											
Canada	1968	LL	Japan	1967	LL	Angola	1976	B/L	China P.R.	1996	LL
United States	1967	LL				Barbados	2000		Korea, Republic of	1970	LL
Portugal (pre-1997)	1969	BB				Brazil	1969	LL	Philippines	2004	LL
						Cape Verde	1979		Russian Federation	1977	
						Equatorial Guinea*	1987		*By-catch*		
						Fr. Overseas	1968		EC (France and Spain)	1997	B/P
						Gabon	1977			(1968/9)	
						Guatemala	2004	PS	Ghana	1968	B/P
						Ivory Coast	1972		*Opportunistic*		
						Libya	1995	LL	Iceland	2002	
						Mexico	2002		Norway	2004	
						Morocco	1969	PS			
						Namibia	1999	B/L			
						Panama	1998	L/P			
						S. Tome and Principe	1983				
						Senegal	2004	BB			
						South Africa	1967	B/L			
						St. Vincent and Grenadines*	2006	LL			
						Trinidad and Tobago	1999				
						UK Overseas Terr.	1995				
						Uruguay	1983	LL			
						Vanuatu	2002	LL			
						Venezuela	1983	B/L/P			

	Gear
Cooperating Noncontracting Parties	
Chinese Taipei (Taiwan)	LL
NEI/IUU	P/L
Cambodia*	
Netherlands Antilles	PS
Seychelles	
Opportunistic	
Faroe Islands	
Noncontracting Parties	
Argentina	
Benin	
Congo	
Cuba	L/P
Dominica	
Grenada	
Liberia	
Sierra Leone*	
St. Lucia	
Togo	

Notes: Aggregate list for years from 1970 to 2006. Year is year of membership in ICCAT. Gear types reported only for entities with average annual reported catch > 100 tons. BB or B = baitboat, LL or L = longline, PS or P = purse seine. By-catch refers to fleets that target some other species but harvest bigeye incidentally. Opportunistic refers to fleets that can only target bigeye infrequently, often going for years without any bigeye harvest at all.
* Formerly subject to sanctions for IUU activities.
Sources: ICCAT 2007d, 2007b.

Table B.2
Vulnerability Classification of Countries Harvesting Yellowfin Tuna (1970–1976)

Highly vulnerable			Gradually vulnerable			Moderately vulnerable			Mildly vulnerable		
Country	Year	Gear	Country	Year	Gear	Country	Year	Gear	Country	Year	Gear
Contracting Parties											
			Canada	1968	PS	Angola	1976	BB	Korea, Republic of	1970	LL
			France	1968	B/P	Barbados	2000	LL	Panama	1998	LL
			Norway[b]	2004	PS	Brazil	1969	BB	USSR	1977	B/L
			Spain	1969	PS	Cape Verde	1979	B/P	*By-catch*		
			United States	1967	PS	Ghana	1968	PS	Portugal[a]	1969	
			Japan	1967	LL	Morocco	1969				
						S. Tome and Principe	1983				
						South Africa	1967				
						UK Overseas Terr.	1995				
						Venezuela	1983	B/L			
Cooperating Noncontracting Parties											
									Chinese Taipei (Taiwan)		LL
Noncontracting Parties											
						Argentina			Cuba		L/P
						Grenada			NEI/IUU		P/L
						St. Lucia			Netherlands Antilles		PS

Notes: Aggregate list for years from 1970 to 1976. Year is year of membership in ICCAT. Gear types only reported for entities with average annual reported catch > 100 tons. BB or B = baitboat, LL or L = longline, PS or P = purse seine. By-catch refers to fleets that target some other species but harvest yellowfin incidentally. [a] Less than 5 tons/year in 1975 and 76 from baitboat fishery targeting bigeye (ICCAT 1971–1994: 1976, 206). [b] Only 1 year of reported landings.
Sources: ICCAT, 2007d, 2007b.

Table B.3
Vulnerability Classification of Countries Harvesting Yellowfin Tuna (1977–2006)

Highly vulnerable			Gradually vulnerable			Moderately vulnerable			Mildly vulnerable		
Country	Year	Gear	Country	Year	Gear	Country	Year	Gear	Country	Year	Gear
Contracting Parties											
United States (post-1986)	1967	LL	Japan	1967	LL	Angola	1976	B/L	China P.R.	1996	LL
Portugal (pre-1997)	1969	B/L	EC (France and Spain)	1997	B/P	Barbados	2000		Korea, Republic of	1970	LL
				(1968/9)		Brazil	1969	B/L	Philippines	2004	LL
						Cape Verde	1979		USSR (pre-1990)[b]	1977	PS
						Equatorial Guinea	1987		*Opportunistic*		
						Gabon	1977	Oth.	Norway[a]	2004	PS
						Ghana	1968	B/P	*By-catch*		
						Guatemala	2004	PS	Canada (post-1986)	1968	
						Ivory Coast	1972	Oth.			
						Libya	1995				
						Mexico	2002	LL			
						Morocco	1969	L/O			
						Namibia	1999	B/L			
						Panama	1998	L/P			
						S. Tome and Principe	1983	Oth.			
						Senegal	2004	BB			
						South Africa	1967	B/L			
						Trinidad and Tobago	1999	LL			
						UK Overseas Terr.	1995				
						Uruguay	1983	LL			
						Vanuatu	2002	LL			
						Venezuela	1983	B/L			

Table B.3
(continued)

	Highly vulnerable			Gradually vulnerable			Moderately vulnerable			Mildly vulnerable	
Country	Year	Gear	Country	Year	Gear	Country	Year	Gear	Country	Year	Gear
Cooperating Noncontracting Parties											
									Chinese Taipei (Taiwan)		LL
Noncontracting Parties											
						Argentina			NEI/IUU		P/L
						Benin			Cambodia		
						Cayman Islands[a]		PS	Netherlands Antilles		PS
						Congo			Seychelles		
						Cuba		LL	*Opportunistic*		
						Dominica			Faroe Islands[a]		
						Dominican Republic		Oth.	Georgia[a]		
						Gambia			Ukraine[a]		
						Grenada					
						Jamaica					
						Liberia					
						St. Vincent					
						Sta. Lucia					
						Ukraine					

Notes: Aggregate list for years from 1977 to 2006; year is year of membership at ICCAT; gear types only reported for entities with average annual reported catch > 100 tons. BB or B = baitboat, LL or L = longline, PS or P = purse seine, Oth. or O = other surface gears. Opportunistic refers to fleets that can target yellowfin only infrequently, often going for years without any yellowfin harvest at all.

[a] Less than 5 years in which landings were reported. [b] The Russian Federation did not report any landings from 1990 to 2004.

Source: ICCAT 2007a, 2007b.

Table B.4
Vulnerability Classification of Countries Harvesting Mixed Skipjack (1970–1989)

Highly vulnerable			Gradually vulnerable			Moderately vulnerable			Mildly vulnerable		
Country	Year	Gear	Country	Year	Gear	Country	Year	Gear	Country	Year	Gear
Contracting Parties											
Portugal *Post-1986*	**1969**	**BB**	France	1968	B/P	**Angola**	**1976**	**B/L**	**Korea, Republic of**	**1970**	**LL**
			Spain	1969	PS	Barbados	2000		*Panama*	*1998*	*B/L/P*
Canada	**1968**	**LL**	**Japan**	**1967**	**LL**	*Brazil*	*1969*	*B/L*	*USSR*	*1977*	*B/L/P*
United States	**1967**	**LL**	*Pre-1986*			Cape Verde	1979	BB			
			Canada	1968	PS	Ghana	1968	B/P	*Opportunistic*		
			United States	1967	PS	Morocco	1969	PS	Norway[a]	2004	PS
						S. Tome and Principe	1983				
						South Africa	**1967**	**B/L**			
						UK Overseas Terr.	1995				
						Uruguay	**1983**	**LL**			
						Venezuela	*1983*	*B/L/P*			
Cooperating Noncontracting Parties											
									Chinese Taipei (Taiwan)		LL
Noncontracting Parties											
						Argentina			**NEI/IUU**		LL
						Cuba		**B/P**	Cayman Islands		PS
						Grenada			Netherlands Antilles		PS
						St. Lucia					

Notes: Aggregate list for years from 1970 to 1989. Countries in boldface target both adult bigeye and small tunas; countries in italics target small tunas only. Year is year of membership in ICCAT. Gear types reported only for entities with average annual reported catch > 100 tons. BB or B = baitboat, LL or L = longline, PS or P = purse seine. Opportunistic refers to fleets that can target tropical tunas only infrequently, often going for years without any tropical tuna harvest at all. [a] Only 2 years of reported landings.
Sources: ICCAT 2007d, 2007b.

Table B.5
Vulnerability Classification of Countries Harvesting Mixed Skipjack (1990–2006)

Highly vulnerable			Gradually vulnerable			Moderately vulnerable			Mildly vulnerable		
Country	Year	Gear	Country	Year	Gear	Country	Year	Gear	Country	Year	Gear
Contracting Parties											
Canada	1968	LL	Japan	1967	LL	Algeria[a]	2001		China P.R.	1996	LL
United States	1967	LL	EC (France and Spain)	1997 (1968/9)	B/P	Angola	1976	BB	Korea, Republic of	1970	LL
Portugal (pre-97)	1969	B/L				Barbados	2000		*Panama*	*1998*	*L/P*
						Brazil	*1969*	*B/L*	Philippines	2004	LL
						Cape Verde	1979	BB	Russian Federation[b]	1977	PS
						Equatorial Guinea[a]	1987				
						Gabon	1977	Oth.			
						Ghana	1968	B/P			
						Guatemala	2004	PS			
						Ivory Coast	1972	Oth.			
						Libya	1995	LL			
						Mexico	2002	LL			
						Morocco	1969	O/P			
						Namibia	1999	B/L			
						S. Tome and Principe	1983	Oth.			
						Senegal	2004	BB			
						South Africa	1967	B/L			
						St. Vincent and Grenadines	2006	LL			
						Trinidad and Tobago	1999	LL			
						UK Overseas Terr.	1995	BB			
						Uruguay	1983	LL			
						Vanuatu[a]	2002	LL			
						Venezuela	1983	B/L			

Cooperating Noncontracting Parties

Chinese Taipei (Taiwan)	LL	
NEI/IUU	B/L/P	
Cambodia		
Netherlands Antilles	PS	
Romania	Oth.	
Seychelles[a]		

Noncontracting Parties

Argentina	Oth.	
Benin		
Colombia	PS	
Congo		
Cuba	BB	
Dominica		
Dominican Republic	Oth.	
Grenada	L/O	
Jamaica[a]		
St. Vincent		
St. Lucia		

Notes: Aggregate list for years from 1990 to 2006. Countries in boldface target adult bigeye and small tunas; countries in italics target both adult bigeye and small tunas; all others target small tunas only. Year is year of membership in ICCAT. Gear types reported only for entities with average annual reported catch > 100 tons. BB or B = baitboat, LL or L = longline, PS or P = purse seine, Oth. or O = other surface gear. Opportunistic refers to fleets that can target tropical tunas only infrequently, often going for years without any tropical tuna harvest at all. [a] Less than 5 years in which landings were reported. [b] The USSR reported both purse seine and longline landings in 1990.
Sources: ICCAT 2007d, 2007c.

Table B.6
Vulnerability Classification of Countries Harvesting Northern Swordfish

Highly vulnerable			Gradually vulnerable			Moderately vulnerable			Mildly vulnerable		
Country	Year	Gear	Country	Year	Gear	Country	Year	Gear	Country	Year	Gear
Contracting Parties											
Canada	1968	LL	EC (Spain)	1997 (1969)	LL	Barbados	2000		USSR	1977	
United States	1967	LL				Brazil	1969	LL	*By-catch*		
Portugal (pre-1997)	1969	LL				Mexico	2002		China P.R.	1996	
France (pre-1997)	1968					Morocco	1969	LL	Japan	1967	LL
						Panama	1998		Korea, Republic of	1970	LL
						Senegal	2004		Philippines	2004	
						St. Vincent and Grenadines	2006		*Opportunistic*		
						Trinidad and Tobago	1999	LL	Iceland	2002	
						UK Overseas Terr.	1995		Norway	2004	LL
						Vanuatu	2002				
						Venezuela	1983				
Cooperating Noncontracting Parties											
									By-catch		
									Chinese Taipei (Taiwan)		LL

Noncontracting Parties

	LL	NEI/IUU	LL
Cuba		By-catch	
Dominica		Seychelles	
Grenada		Opportunistic	
Liberia		Faroe Islands	
Sierra Leone*			
St. Lucia			

Notes: Aggregate list for years from 1970 to 2006. Year is year of membership in ICCAT. Gear types reported only for entities with average annual reported catch > 100 tons. LL = longline. By-catch refers to fleets that target some other species but harvest swordfish incidentally. Opportunistic refers to fleets that can target swordfish only infrequently, often going for years without any swordfish harvest at all.

* Formerly subject to sanctions for IUU activities.

Sources: ICCAT 2007d, 2007b.

Table B.7
Vulnerability Classification of Countries Harvesting Southern Swordfish

Highly vulnerable			Gradually vulnerable			Moderately vulnerable			Mildly vulnerable		
Country	Year	Gear	Country	Year	Gear	Country	Year	Gear	Country	Year	Gear
Contracting Parties											
United States	1967	LL	EC (Spain pre-1997)	1997 (1969)	LL	Angola	1976	LL	*By-catch*		
						Brazil	1969	LL	China P.R.	1996	LL
						Equatorial Guinea	1987		Korea, Republic of	1970	LL
						Gabon	1977		Japan	1967	LL
						Ghana	1968	Oth.	Philippines	2004	LL
						Honduras*	2001				
						Ivory Coast	1972				
						Namibia	1999	LL			
						Panama	1998				
						S. Tome and Principe	1983				
						South Africa	1967	LL			
						UK Overseas Terr.	1995				
						Uruguay	1983	LL			
						Vanuatu	2002	LL			
Cooperating Noncontracting Parties											
									By-catch		
									Chinese Taipei (Taiwan)		LL

Noncontracting Parties

		Oth.	*By-catch* NEJ/IUU	P/L
Argentina			Cambodia	
Belize*			Seychelles	
Benin				
Cuba				
Liberia				
Nigeria				
Togo				

Notes: Aggregate list for years from 1970 to 2006. Year is year of membership in ICCAT. Gear types reported only for entities with average annual reported catch > 100 tons. LL or L = longline, P = purse seine, Oth. = other surface gear. By-catch refers to fleets that target some other species but harvest swordfish incidentally. Opportunistic refers to fleets that can target swordfish only infrequently, often going for years without any swordfish harvest at all.

* Formerly subject to sanctions for IUU activities.

Sources: ICCAT 2007d, 2007b.

Table B.8
Vulnerability Classification of Countries Harvesting Blue Marlin and White Marlin

Mildly vulnerable By-catch

Country	Year	Gear	Country	Year	Gear
Contracting Parties					
Barbados	2000		Panama	1998	LL
Brazil	1969	LL	Philippines	2004	
Canada	1968		Russian Federation	1977	
China P.R.	1972	Oth.	S. Tome and Principe	1983	
EC (France, Portugal,	1997		Senegal	2004	
and Spain pre-1997)	(1968,	L/O	South Africa	1967	
	1969)		St. Vincent and	2006	
Gabon	1977	Oth.	Grenadines		
Ghana	1968		Trinidad and Tobago	1999	
Honduras	2001	LL	United States	1967	LL/S
Ivory Coast	1996	LL	UK Overseas Terr.	1995	
Japan	1967	LL	Uruguay	1983	
Korea, Republic of	1970		Vanuatu	2002	
Mexico	2002		Venezuela	1983	L/O
Morocco	1969				
Cooperating Noncontracting Parties					
Chinese Taipei (Taiwan)		LL			
Noncontracting Parties					
Argentina			Grenada		
Belize			Jamaica		
Benin			Liberia		Oth.
Cambodia			NEI		L/O
Costa Rica			Netherlands Antilles		
Cuba		L/O	St. Vincent and		
Dominica			Grenadines		
Dominican Republic			St. Lucia		
			Ukraine		

Notes: Aggregate list for years from 1970 to 2006. Year is year of membership in ICCAT. Gear types reported only for entities with average annual reported catch > 100 tons. LL or L = longline, Oth. or O = other surface gear, S = sportfishing. By-catch refers to fleets that target some other species but harvest blue marlin and white marlin incidentally.
Sources: ICCAT 2007d, 2007b.

Table B.9
Vulnerability Classification of Countries Harvesting Bluefin Tuna 1970–1978

	Highly vulnerable			Gradually vulnerable			Moderately vulnerable			Mildly vulnerable		
	Country	Year	Gear	Country	Year	Gear	Country	Year	Gear	Country	Year	Gear
Contracting Parties												
	Portugal	1969	BB	*Japan*	*1967*	LL	Algeria	2001		*By-catch*		
							Brazil	**1969**	O/T	**Canada**	**1968**	**P/S/T**
							Libya	1995		France	1968	B/P
							Mexico	**2002**	Oth.	Italy	1997	P/S/T
							Tunisia	1997	T	*Korea, Republic of*	*1970*	
							Turkey	2003		Morocco	1969	P/T
										Norway	2004	PS
										Panama	**1998**	**LL**
										Spain	1969	B/T
										United States	**1967**	**P/S/T**
Cooperating Noncontracting Parties												
										By-catch		
										Chinese Taipei (Taiwan)		
Noncontracting Parties												
							Argentina					
							Cuba		LL			
							Yugoslavia		PS			

Notes: Aggregate list for years from 1970 to 1978. Countries in boldface harvest both stocks; all others target the eastern stock. Year is year of membership in ICCAT. Gear types reported only for entities with average annual reported catch > 100 tons. B = baitboat, LL or L = longline, PS or P = purse seine, Oth. or O = other surface gears, S = sportfishing, T = trap. By-catch refers to fleets that target some other species but harvest bluefin incidentally. Sources: ICCAT 2007d, 2007b.

Table B.10
Vulnerability Classification of Countries Harvesting Western Bluefin Tuna 1979–2006

	Highly vulnerable			Gradually vulnerable			Moderately vulnerable			Mildly vulnerable		
	Country	Year	Gear	Country	Year	Gear	Country	Year	Gear	Country	Year	Gear
Contracting Parties												
	Canada	1968	L/O/S	*Japan*	1967	LL	**Brazil**	1969		*Korea,*	1970	
	Portugal	1969					Mexico	2002		*Republic of*		
	United States	1967	O/P/S				**Trinidad and Tobago**	1999		*Panama**	1998	
							UK Overseas Terr.	1995				
							Uruguay	1983				
Cooperating Noncontracting Parties										*Chinese Taipei (Taiwan)*		
Noncontracting Parties							**Argentina**			NEI/IUU		LL
							Cuba					
							St. Lucia					

Notes: Aggregate list for years from 1979 to 2006. Countries in boldface harvest the western stock; countries in italics harvest both stocks; all others target the eastern stock. Year is year of membership in ICCAT. Gear types reported only for entities with average annual reported catch > 100 tons. LL or L = longline, O = other gear, P = purse seine, S = sportfishing.
* Formerly subject to sanctions for IUU activities.
Sources: ICCAT 2007d, 2007b.

Table B.11
Vulnerability Classification of Countries Harvesting Eastern Bluefin Tuna 1983–2006

Highly vulnerable			Gradually vulnerable			Moderately vulnerable			Mildly vulnerable		
Country	Year	Gear	Country	Year	Gear	Country	Year	Gear	Country	Year	Gear
Contracting Parties											
Canada	1968	O/S/T	*Japan*	1967	LL	**Algeria**	**2001**	L/P	*"By-catch"*		
EC	1997	B/P/T				Brazil	1969		*China P.R.*	*1996*	
France	1968	PS				**Cape Verde**	**1979**	PS	*Korea,*	*1970*	*L/P*
Greece	1997	L/P/S				Croatia	1997		*Republic of*[b]		
Italy	1997	L/P/S				Fr. Overseas Terr.	1968		*Panama*[a]	*1998*	*LL*
Portugal	1969	B/L				**Guinea Conakry**	**1991**	Oth.	*Opportunistic*		
Spain	1969	B/P/T				Libya	1995	L/P	Iceland	2002	
United	1967	L/P/S				Mexico	2002		Norway	2004	
States						**Morocco**	**1969**	P/S/T			
						Trinidad and Tobago	1999				
						Tunisia	**1997**	PS			
						Turkey	**2003**	PS			
						Uruguay	1983				
Cooperating Noncontracting Parties											
									"By-catch"		
									Chinese Taipei (Taiwan)		*LL*

Table B.11
(continued)

Highly vulnerable			Gradually vulnerable			Moderately vulnerable			Mildly vulnerable		
Country	Year	Gear	Country	Year	Gear	Country	Year	Gear	Country	Year	Gear
Noncontracting Parties											
Israel[c]						Argentina			*NEI/IUU*		P/L
						Cuba			*"By-catch"*		
						Serbia and			**Seychelles**		
						Montenegro					
						Sierra Leone[a]		LL	Opportunistic		
						St. Lucia			**Faroe Islands**		

Notes: Aggregate list for years from 1970 to 2006. Countries in boldface harvest the eastern stock; countries in italics harvest both stocks; all others target the western stock. Year is year of membership in ICCAT. Gear types reported only for entities with average annual reported catch > 100 tons. BB or B = baitboat, LL or L = longline, PS or P = purse seine, Oth. or O = other surface gears, S = sportfishing, T = trap. "By-catch" refers to fleets that target some other species but harvest bluefin incidentally. The term *by-catch* is in quotes because bluefin is higher priced than any other tuna species and therefore is not often discarded like other by-catches. Opportunistic refers to fleets that can target bluefin only infrequently, often going for years without any bluefin harvest at all. [a] Formerly subject to sanctions for IUU activities. [b] Korea began targeting bluefin with purse seines in 2004. [c] Israel has just started targeting bluefin commercially.
Sources: ICCAT 2007d, 2007c.

Appendix C
Summary of Evidence from the Cases

The following tables provide a summary of the evidence from the cases presented in this book. Each table is divided into several "periods" to display the pattern of aggregate response for a particular case. Periods can fall into five categories, as described in section 3.4: inactivity, concern, conflict, accord, and postrebuilding. Notice that the scientific advice is presented first, indicating the level of overexploitation of the stock(s), followed by expressed policy positions and actual management decisions. Policy positions are grouped according to similarity in expressed preferences, not vulnerability, but a comparison of the tables in appendix B and those here reveals that countries frequently coalesced around expected positions as per the vulnerability response framework.

Table C.1
Summary of the Evidence for the Bigeye Tuna Case

	Inactivity 1969–1991[a]	Concern 1992–1994	Conflict 1995–1999	Accord 2000–2002	Postrebuilding 2003–2006
SCRS Reports	No signs of overfishing	Overfishing	Stock overfished	Moderately overfished → signs of rebuilding	Stock near level that supports MSY[b]
Preferences Expressed No statements/proposals		United States—concerned, should do something	United States proposes TAC as per SCRS; Canada supports	United States proposes rebuilding TAC, Canada supports	United States, Canada, and Japan pleased with improvements; careful not to relapse
		Japan—science uncertain	Japan proposes vessel limits	Japan proposes sustainable catch limit	EC proposes higher but sustainable TAC with quota distributions (2004)
			Brazil and Venezuela—no limits on developing coastal fleets Taiwan opposes limits on its harvests EC—won't reduce skipjack or yellowfin to protect bigeye All but United States expect someone else to pay	Brazil (Group of 18)—no quotas without new allocation criteria Taiwan and China oppose limits on their harvests	Brazil, Cape Verde, Panama, South Africa, St. Pierre and Miquelon, Guatemala, Morocco, Gabon, Venezuela, Mexico, and Trinidad and Tobago—91/92 allocation unfair, need room for developing coastal states China, Philippines, and Taiwan—limits on them unfair

Actions Taken

Sanctions on bigeye from Belize, Cambodia, St. Vincent and the Grenadines, Equatorial Guinea (2000–2004), Honduras (2001–2002), Bolivia (2002-date), Sierra Leone (2002–2004), and Georgia (2003-date)	Vessel limits < scientific advice (1998)	TAC sustainable as per scientific advice (2000)	TAC sustainable but high (2004)
	Exception for coastal developing countries	Exception for coastal developing countries	Exception for coastal developing countries; limits for Panama
	Taiwan assigned specific quota (1997)	Specific limits on Taiwan, China, and the Philippines	Further side payments from Japan to Taiwan (small) and China (large)
	Sanctions adopted (1998)	Side payments from Japan to Taiwan (small) and China (big)	Improved monitoring/enforcement by Japan, United States, Canada, and EC
		New allocation criteria (2001)	
		Statistical Document Program (2001)	

Notes: TAC = total allowable catch, SCRS = Standing Committee for Research and Statistics. [a] ICCAT adopted a size limit for bigeye tuna in 1979 to prevent misreporting of undersized yellowfin tuna. [b] Rebuilding was only partly due to ICCAT management; biophysical conditions were also favorable in this period.

Table C.2
Summary of the Evidence for the Yellowfin Tuna Case

Concern 1970–1976	Inactivity 1977–1990	Concern 1991–1992*	Conflict 1993–2006
SCRS Reports			
Growth overfishing	Underfished	Full exploitation	Mildly depleted (1998)
Positions Expressed			
Japan proposes 10–25 kg size limits and TAC as per SCRS Brazil, France, Korea, Morocco, Portugal, South Africa and Spain propose 3.2-kg size limit with 15% tolerance United States, France, Spain—no TAC if reduces their harvests; Spain—time-area closure would be better Brazil, Senegal, Ivory Coast—no TAC if it limits development of their fleets	1976–1979 Discussion regarding size limit on bigeye to reduce misreporting of small yellowfin; See chapter 5 for details.	United States proposes freeze effort to 1991 levels as per SCRS (1992) Spain—some of its vessels have left Atlantic, might not need limit	United States proposes effort limit to 1992 levels (1993) United States and Japan—need to reduce harvests of juveniles Spain and France/ EC—need better method than size limits to avoid juveniles
Actions Taken			
3.2 kg size limit with 15% tolerance			Freeze effort to 1992 levels (1993)
See chapter 5 re size limits and the mixed fishery			

Notes: TAC = total allowable catch; SCRS = Standing Committee for Research and Statistics; * From 1990–1991 the SCRS did suggest that the eastern stock of yellowfin might be at full exploitation. Responses to this were largely recriminations between France and Spain about which of them was causing the problem.

Table C.3
Summary of the Evidence for the Mixed Skipjack Case

	Concern 1974–1976[a]	Conflict 1977–1984	Inactivity 1985–1991	Conflict 1992–2006
SCRS Reports				
Skipjack: underfished	underfished	underfished	underfished	uncertain with FADs
Bigeye: uncertain	full exploitation	underfished	overfishing/overfished
Yellowfin: overfished	underfished	underfished[b]	full-moderately over
bigeye/yellowfin	3.2 kg size limit good for	3.2 kg size limit good for	3.2 kg size limit good for
misreporting = problem	bigeye & yellowfin	bigeye & yellowfin	bigeye & yellowfin
Positions Expressed				
France proposes 3.2 kg size limit for bigeye (same as yellowfin)	France proposes 3.2 kg size limit for bigeye; Ivory Coast, Cuba, Spain, Senegal, Portugal, Canada, and Brazil support	(Gabon did ask about the impact of FADs in 1991)	Japan, United States, Canada, Portugal (pre-1997), Taiwan & Mexico push to reduce bigeye/yellowfin < 3.2 kg and propose limits on FADs
Japan expresses concern	USSR, Japan, Korea vote against in 1978 but not 1979		France & Spain implement time-area close on FADs in Gulf of Guinea (1997), then push for its adoption for all fleets, especially Ghana
	Ghana staunchly opposes size limit		Ghana opposes size limit & time-area closure. Does not block adoption but fails to comply

Table C.3
(continued)

Concern 1974–1976[a]	Conflict 1977–1984	Inactivity 1985–1991	Conflict 1992–2006
Actions Taken			
	3.2 kg size limit for bigeye tuna w/ 15% tolerance		Time-area closure on FADs in the Gulf of Guinea (1998) Closure expanded to all surface gears but reduced in size & temporal scope (2005, 2006)

Notes: FADs = Fish Aggregating Devices; [a] Though not included in this table, 1970–1973 can be considered as a period of conflict. See table 4.4 for details; [b] From 1990–1991 the SCRS did suggest that the eastern stock of yellowfin *might* be at full exploitation. Responses to this were largely recriminations between France and Spain about which of them was causing the problem.

Table C.4
Summary of Evidence for the Northern Swordfish Case

	Inactivity 1969–1978	Concern 1979–1988	Conflict 1989–1998	Accord 1999–2001	Postrebuilding 2002–2006
SCRS Reports	No signs of overfishing	Signs of overfishing	Stock overfished (1990)	Moderately overfished → signs of rebuilding	Stock near level that supports MSY[a]
Preferences Expressed	No statements or proposals	United States, Canada, and Portugal express concern	United States and Canada propose measures as per SCRS	United States and Canada propose rebuilding TAC for 10 years	United States and Canada propose cautious TACs
			Spain—proposes measures < SCRS advice	Spain/EC—proposes rebuilding TAC for 3 years	EC proposes higher, still sustainable TAC with quotas for "others"
			Morocco, Brazil, Uruguay, Venezuela—concerned about rights of coastal developing countries	Bermuda (1999) and St. Pierre and Miquelon and Trinidad and Tobago (2001) demand quota	Mexico, St. Pierre and Miquelon, Venezuela, Morocco, and Trinidad and Tobago demand higher quotas
			Japan and Korea—won't reduce bigeye to protect swordfish	Japan—swordfish reductions shouldn't change bigeye harvest	Japan TAC should be higher
			All expect someone else to pay		China should be exempt if <100 tons

Table C.4
(continued)

Inactivity 1969–1978	Concern 1979–1988	Conflict 1989–1998	Accord 1999–2001	Postrebuilding 2002–2006
Actions Taken				
		Size limits (1990), TAC < scientific advice for rebuilding (1994 and 1996)	TAC below replacement yield, but not lowest (1996, 1999)	TAC at replacement yield
Sanctions on swordfish from Belize (1999–2005), Honduras (1999–2001), and Sierra Leone (2002–2004)		Canada, Portugal, Spain, and United States assigned quotas; share small harvest reductions	Permanent percentage shares for Canada, Japan, Portugal, Spain, United States, and others (1995)	Small increase in quotas for Mexico, St. Pierre and Miquelon, Venezuela, Morocco, and Trinidad and Tobago
		Small fleets limit, not reduce harvests	Small quota for Bermuda (1999) and St. Pierre and Miquelon and Trinidad and Tobago (2001)	Improved monitoring and enforcement by Japan, United States, Canada, and EC
		8% by-catch allowance	Rollover of underages and overages (1998)	Continue rollover for flexibility
			Transfer of some EC (2000) and United States (2001 and 2002) quota to Japan	
			Sanctioning procedures adopted (1995)	
			Quota reduction for repeated overages (1996)	
			Statistical Document Program (2001)	

Notes: TAC = total allowable catch; SCRS = Standing Committee on Research and Statistics. [a] Rebuilding was only partly due to ICCAT management—biophysical conditions were also favorable in this period.

Table C.5
Summary of Evidence for the Southern Swordfish Case

	Inactivity 1969–1988	Concern 1989–1993	Conflict 1994–1996	1997–2001	2002–2006
SCRS Reports	No signs of overfishing	Most catch just south of boundary	Signs of overfishing → slight depletion	Slightly underexploited	Uncertain
Preferences Expressed	No statements or proposals	Canada—concern about catches just south of boundary; proposes size limit for all Atlantic Swordfish	Canada pushes to limit or reduce catches in south (as per SCRS 1995–1996)	Canada and United States—TAC too high (as per SCRS except 1997); United States proposes international enforcement (1997)	Canada and United States—TAC is too high; United States gives up some of own quota to achieve sharing
		United States—proposes cap on effort in south (1992)	France and Portugal support Canada (1994)	EC—TAC is okay, keep shares as is	Japan, EC, and Brazil—higher TAC OK because actual catches will be lower
		Uruguay expresses concern (1993)	Spain and United States focus on North in 1995, but support Canada in 1996

Brazil, Uruguay, and Venezuela—reduce distant, not coastal fleets | Brazil, South Africa, Uruguay, Namibia—TAC OK, more quota for coastal states; protest sanctions as unfair to coastal developing countries

Japan—TAC OK; will give up 1,700 tons to get sharing (1999)

China and Taiwan—want more room for by-catch | |

Table C.5
(continued)

Inactivity 1969–1988	Concern 1989–1993	Conflict 1994–1996	1997–2001	2002–2006
Actions Taken				
	Size limit and cap effort to 1988 all Atlantic; countries with small catches exempt, by-catch limit at 10% catch of target stock (1990)	Countries with catch > 250 ton limit to 93/94 levels, countries with catch < 250 ton limit to 250 tons (1994)	TAC at 14,620 tons with sharing 1998–2000 (1997; as per SCRS advice, but higher than 1996 SCRS advice) TAC at 14,620 tons without sharing 2001–2003 (2000; total individually set shares 7,000 tons > TAC; SCRS TAC = 13,500 tons)	TAC at 15,631, and up with sharing 2003–2005 (2002; SCRS TAC = 14,000–15,000 tons) TAC at 16,055 and up with sharing 2006–2009 (2005; SCRS TAC = 17,000 tons but uncertain)
Sanctions on swordfish from Belize (1999–2005), Honduras (1999–2001), and Sierra Leone (2002–2004)			Increase share of "other contracting parties" and reduce that of "other noncontracting parties" Sanctions procedures and quota reductions for repeated overages adopted (1997) Statistical Document Program (2001)	Quota transfers from United States, EC, and Japan to moderately vulnerable countries Taiwan's share also reduced to make room for moderately vulnerable countries to get more quota

Notes: TAC = total allowable catch, SCRS = Standing Committee on Research and Statistics.

Table C.6
Summary of Evidence for the Blue Marlin and White Marlin Case

	Inactivity 1970–1972	Concern 1973–1991	Conflict 1992–1999	Accord 2000–2006
SCRS Reports				
Blue: uncertain		Signs of overfishing	Overfished (1992–1994) → severely overfished	
White: uncertain		Signs of overfishing	Overfished (1992–1994) → severely overfished	
Positions Expressed				
No statements or proposals		United States—concerned about marlins; need better science; proposes research program	United States—proposes prohibition on marlin landings (1992, 1997), release of live marlins, and switch to monofilament lines (1994, 1995)	United States—proposes reduction in landings of blue marlin to 50% and white marlin to 33% of 1999 levels (2000)
		Cuba supports research	Japan—keeping dead, live discards OK; science too pessimistic; costs shared equally between recreation and commercial fishers	Japan—SCRS is too pessimistic about marlins; reduction should be from higher of 1996 or 1999 (2001)
		Brazil, Spain, and "some countries"—concern about costs of research program	Canada, Korea, France, Portugal, and Spain (EC post-1997) and Taiwan expresses position similar to Japan's	EC—proposes catch, not landings, limit to facilitate data collection (Japan, Canada, Brazil oppose)
			Brazil—need to exempt small-scale fishers	Canada supports U.S. measure

Table C.6
(continued)

	Inactivity 1970–1972	Concern 1973–1991	Conflict 1992–1999	Accord 2000–2006
Actions Taken		Enhanced Research Program for Billfish (1986; paid for largely by private sources in United States, Venezuela)	Nonbinding resolutions to encourage voluntary tag and release, promote monofilament use (1995 and 1996) Binding recommendation to reduce marlin landings by 25% from 1996 level by 1999 and keep that way for 2000 (1997 and 1998; small-scale exemption and additional restrictions on U.S. recreational fishers)	Binding recommendation to reduce landings of blue marlin to 50% and white marlin to 33% of 1999 levels (adopted in 2000 for 2001–2002; amended to 1996 or 1999 levels in 2001; renewed several times, including 2006 extension to 2010)

Notes: TAC = total allowable catch; SCRS = Standing Committee on Research and Statistics.

Table C.7
Summary of Evidence for the Western Bluefin Tuna Case

Concern	Accord			
	1970–1973	1974–1980	1981–1992	1993–2006
SCRS Reports				
Signs of overfishing	Signs of overfishing		Severely overfished (worst assessments, 1981, 1993, and 2006)	
Positions Expressed				
United States and Canada express concern	United States and Canada propose size and effort limits as per SCRS advice; also propose separate eastern and western managment		United States and Canada propose precautionary SciQ (545 tons, 1981), then increase to 2,660 tons with closure of Gulf of Mexico to protect spawning (1982)	United States and Canada propose precautionary SciQ (800 tons, 1993); grudgingly accept higher quotas as per SCRS
United States proposes size limit as per SCRS advice		Japan OK with size and effort limits; prefers different reference years (when own landings were higher)	Japan prefers higher SciQs but does not block consensus; maintains that SCRS advice is too pessimistic	Japan claims SCRS is still too pessimistic but proposes SciQ as per SCRS advice; pushes for more "optimistic" science when assesments disagree
		Brazil and Morocco[a] oppose limits on effort for small or developing fleets	Brazil, Cuba, and South Korea request exemptions	Mexico, Bermuda, and St. Pierre and Miquelon request quota allotment
		Various eastern[a] countries block east-west split until boundary is moved west	Sweden and various conservation groups[b] nominate western bluefin for CITES listing (1991; app. I)	Canada, Japan, and United States complete international monitoring and enforcement measures (1992)

Table C.7
(continued)

Concern	Accord			
1970–1973	1974–1980	1981–1992	1993–2006
		Canada, Japan, and United States lay groundwork for international monitoring and enforcement (1992)	
Actions Taken			
	Size limit and freeze on effort (1974) Split eastern and western management zones (1980; farther west than original proposal; Canada recognizes rights of Brazil and Japan)	Measures adopted as per U.S. and Canadian proposals (1981–1990; exemptions for Brazil and Cuba) 4-year recovery plan to reduce SciQ from 2,660 to 1,729 tons (1991)	Measures adopted as per Japanese proposals (1,200 tons 1993, 2,200 tons 1994, 2,500 tons) Small quotas to Mexico, Bermuda, and St. Pierre and Miquelon; U.S. transfer of quota to Mexico (2006)
	Sanctions on Belize, Honduras, and Panama (1996); Equatorial Guinea (1999); and Sierra Leone (2002)	Statistical Document Program to track international trade in bluefin tuna (1992)	Bluefin tuna action plan provides for "white list" of vessels and trade-based enforcement mechansims (1994)

Notes: SCRS = Standing Committee on Research and Statistics, SciQ = scientific quota, CITES = Convention on International Trade in Endangered Species. [a] See table 10.1 for vulnerability responses classifications of countries targeting eastern bluefin tuna. [b] Sweden does not target Atlantic bluefin. Conservation groups include the National Audubon Society and the World Wildlife Fund.

Table C.8
Summary of Evidence for the Eastern Bluefin Tuna Case 1983–2006

Concern	Conflict			
	1983–1987	1988–1996	1997–2001	2002–2006
SCRS Reports Rebuilding/full		Moderately overfished	Heavily overfished	Severely overfished
Positions Expressed France and Portugal—concerned about shifts from west to east		United States and Canada propose size and catch limits as per SCRS advice	United States and Canada push for catch limits as per SCRS advice and return to one-stock management	United States and Canada propose size and catch limits as per SCRS advice and return to one-stock management
Japan—effort in east not up, just CPUE; will take domestic measures to reduce landings		Japan, United States, and Canada propose international enforcement mechanisms Japan accepts catch limits, proposes time-area closures in Mediterranean	Japan accepts higher TACs, but not large reductions in its own harvests EC proposes TACs well above SCRS recommendations	Japan accepts higher TACs, proposes cap on catches in central Atlantic EC proposes TACs well above SCRS recommendations but decreasing over time + measures to monitor farming
		France, Portugal, and Spain—generally accept proposals as long as other fleets must reduce too; propose countermeasures on time-area closure in Mediterranean	China, Korea, Libya, Morocco, Taiwan, Tunisia, and Turkey either oppose quota reductions or demand more quota	China, the Faroe Islands, Iceland, Korea, Libya, Morocco, Taiwan, Tunisia, and Turkey either oppose quota reductions or demand higher quotas

Table C.8
(continued)

Concern	Conflict		
	1983–1987	1988–1996	1997–2001	2002–2006

Concern 1983–1987	1988–1996	1997–2001	2002–2006
	Morocco—proposes exemption for fleets with small harvests	United States, Canada, and Korea block EC proposals; negotiations break down (2001)	
	Korea and obs. from Taiwan—protest further catch reductions		
Actions Taken			
"No eastward shift" clause in western regulations	Gradual 25% reduction in catches from 1996 to 1998 (1994)	TACs as per EC proposals; extend ban on sales of small fish (<3.2 kg)	TACs as per EC proposals; some variations on time-area closure in the Mediterranean
	Time-area closure on longlines in the Mediterranean; extended to purse seines as per French counterproposal	EC agrees to reduce own harvests (1997–2000) but then increases (2001)	EC agrees to reduce own harvests, invests in monitoring and enforcement for farms
		Moderately vulnerable countries and nonmembers also curtailed	Mildly vulnerable countries and nonmembers also curtailed
	Ban on sales and landing of age 0 fish (<1.8 kg)	Morocco and Libya formally object in 2000	Cap on longlines in the central Atlantic
	Statistical Document Program (1992); bluefin tuna action plan (1994)		

Sanctions on Belize, Honduras, and Panama (1996);
Equatorial Guinea (1999); and Sierra Leone (2002)

Notes: TAC = total allowable catch, CPUE = catch per unit of effort, SCRS = Standing Committee on Research and Statistics. See table C.7 for 1970–1982.

Appendix D
Proxy Indicators for Competitiveness

Because it reflects the relative value of inputs such as labor in local markets, purchasing power parity (PPP) per capita gross domestic product (GDP) was used as a proxy for the economic competitiveness of domestic fleets. Data for most countries were obtained from the World Bank's World Development Indicators Database (World Bank 2006), which covered the years from 1975 to 2004 at the end of 2006. This does not completely cover the time period represented in the cases, but because this measure is not subject to precipitous changes, missing data were not crucial to the analysis. A few countries, notably Taiwan, were not included in the World Bank's data set and so the equivalent indicator from the International Monetary Fund's World Economic Outlook Database (IMF 2006) was substituted. Data on some other fishing entities, notably small island countries, were not available from either source and so the most recent value as reported in the Central Intelligence Agency's World Factbook (Central Intelligence Agency 2007) was used.

A dividing line of US $15,000 was selected as the most sensible break in the data and each country in each case was evaluated against this benchmark. Figure D.1 and table D.1 both provide the annual average for the period for which data were available as an overview. The full data set may be downloaded at http://mitpress.mit.edu/adaptive_governance. Most of the delineations obtained in this manner were cut and dried. However, near the dividing line, it becomes more difficult to assign competitiveness. For instance, both Portugal and Taiwan are on the cusp at times, but the former is a smaller-scale producer and thus cannot take advantage of economies of scale in either harvesting or shipping, while the latter is in the opposite position. Moreover, European fishers are subject to greater regulation and taxation than their

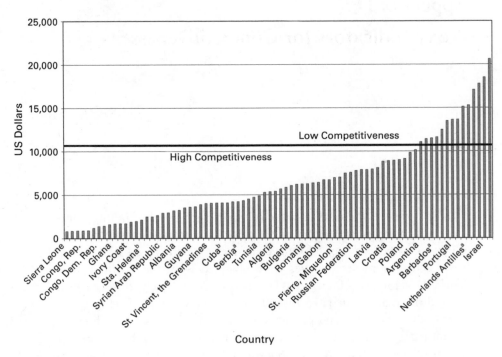

Figure D.1
Average purchasing power parity (PPP) per capita gross domestic product (GDP)
for countries harvesting species covered in the cases. Notes: Black line indicates
approximation of annual division that is not exact because average is used here.
Primary Source: World Bank 2006. Source for Serbia is International Monetary
Fund (2006) averaged over 1980–2005.

Taiwanese counterparts, further increasing costs of production. Because
of this, Portugal is considered in the "low competitiveness" category and
Taiwan is placed in the "high competitiveness" category even though
their average PPP per capita GDPs are quite close together.

The average rather than the annual value for the proxy is shown here
because it captures most of the important changes in relative competitiveness over time. However, a close examination of the annual data
shows that several countries have exhibited large changes in their relative
GDPs, which makes sense when you consider how much economic development and inflation took place between 1970 and 2006. For instance,
many of the "Asian tigers" showed strong GDP growth in the 1980s
and 1990s and are now on par with some developed countries in terms
of PPP per capita GDP. While most of these countries have managed to

Table D.1

Average Purchasing Power Parity per capita Gross Domestic Product for Countries Harvesting Species Covered in the Cases

	1970–2004 average	Competitiveness (generally)
Albania	3,261	high
Algeria	5,404	high
Angola	1,964	high
Antigua and Barbuda	7,854	high
Argentina	11,081	high
Barbados[a]	11,608	high
Belize	4,222	high
Benin	904	high
Bermuda[b]	69,900	low
Brazil	6,718	high
British Virgin Islands[b]	38,500	low
Bulgaria	6,051	high
Cambodia	1,712	high
Canada	22,539	low
Cape Verde	4,069	high
Chile	6,411	high
China	2,118	high
Colombia	5,676	high
Congo, Dem. Rep.	1,383	high
Congo, Rep.	900	high
Costa Rica	6,958	high
Croatia	8,923	high
Cuba[b]	4,100	high
Cyprus	13,642	low
Denmark	23,811	low
Dominica	4,202	high
Dominican Republic	4,718	high
Equatorial Guinea	4,094	high
Estonia	9,008	high
Faroe Islands[b]	31,000	low
France	21,313	low
Gabon	6,702	high
Gambia, The	1,699	high
Georgia	3,619	high
Germany	20,609	low
Ghana	1,692	high

Table D.1
(continued)

	1970–2004 average	Competitiveness (generally)
Greece	15,103	low
Grenada	6,242	high
Guatemala[a]	2,963	high
Guyana	3,644	high
Honduras	2,510	high
Iceland	23,569	low
Ireland	17,766	low
Israel	18,513	low
Ivory Coast	1,893	high
Italy	20,760	low
Jamaica	3,531	high
Japan	21,653	low
Korea, Republic of	10,140	high
Latvia	7,916	high
Lebanon	4,023	high
Liberia[a]	891	high
Libya[a]	8,839	high
Lithuania	8,965	high
Malta	11,413	high
Mexico	7,861	high
Morocco	3,198	high
Namibia	6,353	high
Netherlands Antilles[a]	15,265	high
Nigeria	863	high
Norway	26,285	low
Panama	5,279	high
Philippines	3,884	high
Poland	9,153	high
Portugal	13,629	low
Romania	6,247	high
Russian Federation	7,761	high
Sao Tome and Principe[a]	1,184	high
Senegal	1,427	high
Serbia[a]	4,355	high
Seychelles	12,498	high
Sierra Leone	820	high
South Africa	9,851	high

Table D.1
(continued)

	1970–2004 average	Competitiveness (generally)
Spain	17,078	low
St. Kitts and Nevis	7,464	high
St. Lucia	4,520	high
St. Pierre and Miquelon[b]	7,000	high
St. Vincent and the Grenadines	4,055	high
St. Helena[b]	2,500	high
Sweden	21,473	low
Syrian Arab Republic	2,910	high
Taiwan[a]	13,485	high
Togo	1,599	high
Trinidad and Tobago	8,089	high
Tunisia	4,879	high
Turkey	5,364	high
Turks and Caicos[b]	11,500	high
Ukraine	5,856	high
United Kingdom	21,283	low
United States	27,745	low
Uruguay	7,539	high
Vanuatu[a]	2,670	high
Venezuela, RB	6,205	high

Primary source: World Bank 2006.
[a] Source: IMF 2006; averaged over 1980–2005.
[b] Source: Central Intelligence Agency 2007; most recent year.
Notes: Units = US$; competitiveness indicates > US $13,500 (low) or <US $13,500 (high). Benchmark altered to provide closer approximation to annual categorization.

keep production costs low through heavy subsidies and imports of cheap labor, recent shifts of fishing effort away from Taiwan and South Korea toward cheaper ports in China and the Philippines have certainly made the former less competitive now than they had been in the past.

In retrospect, using a rolling benchmark, such as the average PPP per capita GDP for each year, might have captured relative competitiveness more accurately. Nevertheless, discrepancies would certainly remain as long as there are countries with high PPP per capita GDP and fishing subsidies or cheap sources of labor. While it would be difficult, collecting

Table D.2
Countries for which PPP per capita GDP Crossed the US $15,000 Benchmark during the Time Period Covered in the Cases

	Year > US $15,000
Barbados	1997
Cyprus	1989
Equatorial Guinea	1999
Ireland	1988
Korea	1995
Malta	1994
Netherlands Antilles	1991
Portugal	1989
Puerto Rico	1987
Seychelles	1992
Spain	1976
Taiwan	1993

Sources: World Bank 2006; IMF 2006.

data on factor prices at the domestic level would help to solve this problem. In the meantime, systematic incorporation of some measure such as the Gini coefficient could further improve the accuracy of the proxy. Table D.2 lists all of the countries that crossed this dividing line during the period for which data were available and the year in which they did so.

Appendix E
Proxy Indicators for Flexibility

Flexibility was measured via the proxy of distant-water fleets, which can be established through the ICCAT Landings Database (ICCAT 2007d) by comparing the area of capture with the geographic location of a particular country. Countries with landings only in areas that are contiguous to the national exclusive economic zone (200 miles from the coastline) are considered to have coastal fleets and are therefore in the low flexibility category, whereas those with landings throughout the Atlantic are placed in the high flexibility category. Because distant-water fleets can move suddenly, flexibility was gauged on an annual basis rather than on an average over the period. The number of years for which data were reported between 1970 and 2005 is also given to indicate the duration of fishing operations. When small, isolated harvests from a non-contiguous area are reported and large, long-term harvests originate from coastal regions, countries remain in the low-flexibility category.

In some cases, more detailed information was gathered from the ICCAT database and in the reports of ICCAT's scientific committee. For example, table E.1 provides a breakdown of U.S. landings of bigeye tuna by area and gear type. It clearly shows that bigeye tuna was initially harvested by U.S. purse seine fleets in the eastern Atlantic (making them distant water) but that these were eventually replaced by longlines and other surface fleets in the western Atlantic (making them coastal). Additional information from the SCRS verifies this transformation and suggests that the early harvests were by-catch in the fishery targeting yellowfin tuna. Other by-catch designations are obtained in a similar manner, either through direct identification by the SCRS, as cited in the text for the cases, or based on a more general observation by the SCRS regarding the nature of a mixed fishery. For instance, the mixed skipjack fishery is composed largely of surface fleets, so small landings of bigeye tuna by countries with only surface fleets suggest that these harvests are by-catch, while small landings of skipjack by countries with longline fleets and large bigeye or swordfish harvests indicate that skipjack is not targeted. Not all by-catch countries can be identified in this way, but the most predominant can be recognized.

Because of space constraints, the rest of the tables in this appendix contain only the average annual landings (tons) by area for each species covered in the cases. Multiple stocks of the same species will be listed together so that the distant-water nature of highly flexible fleets will be more apparent. Data on marlins will be relayed as well, even though all countries are considered to be highly flexible for these by-catch species. The full set of tables used in the compilation of this book, including breakdowns by gear as well as area, is available from http://mitpress.mit .edu/adaptive_governance. Like the previous set of proxy data, these numbers are not always perfectly reflective of flexibility; this is pointed out in the text wherever possible. Those interested in the overlap classifications from chapters 5, 7, 9, and 10 can refer to the full data sets or compare the tables provided here.

Comparing the tables in appendix B with those listed here, you may note that some have been omitted from the former. This is purely a matter of conservation of space and in no way alters the analysis in the cases. Specifically, some EC members with harvests of Atlantic tunas were not included in appendix B either because they were not actively fishing or engaging in management prior to 1997, when the EC joined ICCAT. Also, several former members of the USSR and countries in the Soviet block reported small landings of various species for a single year. Except for Russia and Croatia, these countries were never active in the commission and so were omitted from appendix B. They are included here in the interest of full disclosure and also because these tables are not meant to be an overview, but a window onto the actual data used in the analysis.

Table E.1
U.S. Landings (tons) of Atlantic Bigeye Tuna for 1970–2005 by Area and Gear

Gear	Area	1970	1971	1972	1973	1974	1975	1976	1977	1978
Longline	Gulf of Mexico									
	Northwest Atlantic									
	Northwest Central Atlantic									
	Southwest Atlantic									
	West Tropical Atlantic									
Longline total										
Other surf.	Gulf of Mexico									
	Northwest Atlantic									
	West Tropical Atlantic									
Other surf. total										
Purse seine	Northeast Atlantic	195	544	212	113	865	67	28	331	248
	Northwest Atlantic	195	544	212	113	865	67	28	331	248
	Southeast Atlantic									
Purse seine total		195	544	212	113	865	67	28	331	248
Grand total		195	544	212	113	865	67	28	331	248

Gear	Area	1979	1980	1981	1982	1983	1984	1985	1986	1987
Longline	Gulf of Mexico			0.01	6	12	10	13	12	7
	Northwest Atlantic		0.31	1	36	251	480	409	561	499
	Northwest Central Atlantic								36	70
	Southwest Atlantic									
	West Tropical Atlantic								110	205
Longline total			0.31	1.01	42	263	490	422	719	781

Table E.1
(continued)

Gear	Area	1979	1980	1981	1982	1983	1984	1985	1986	1987
Other surf.	Gulf of Mexico		0.15				0.24		0.86	4.22
	Northwest Atlantic		1	29	35	52.45	45.36	217.07	365.28	289.19
	West Tropical Atlantic									
Other surf. total			1.15	29	35	52.45	45.6	217.07	366.14	293.41
Purse seine	Northeast Atlantic		58		345					
	Northwest Atlantic	212	143	128			3			
	Southeast Atlantic	212	201	128						
Purse seine total					345		3			
Grand total		212	202.46	158.01	422	315.45	538.6	639.07	1,085.14	1,074.41

Gear	Area	1988	1989	1990	1991	1992	1993	1994	1995	1996
Longline	Gulf of Mexico	29	61	39	60	36	52	26	69	29
	Northwest Atlantic	306	334	428	618	377	600	782	660	384
	Northwest Central Atlantic	70	84	37	149	121	149	77	130	129
	Southwest Atlantic									33
	West Tropical Atlantic	305	121	55	28	30	35	58	123	138
Longline total		710	600	559	855	564	836	943	982	713
Other surf.	Gulf of Mexico	0.2	1.01	0.32	0.09	0.37	50.19	0.11		
	Northwest Atlantic	199	245.63	64.07	119.46	249.11	203.4	459.28	227	169.01
	West Tropical Atlantic									
Other surf. total		199.2	246.64	64.39	119.55	249.48	253.59	459.39	227	169.01

		1997	1998	1999	2000	2001	2002	2003	2004	2005
Purse seine	Northeast Atlantic	218								
	Northwest Atlantic									
	Southeast Atlantic									
Purse seine total		218								
Grand total		1,127.20	846.64	623.39	974.55	813.48	1,089.59	1,402.39	1,209	882.01
		1997	1998	1999	2000	2001	2002	2003	2004	2005
Longline	Gulf of Mexico	34	26	55	44.46	15.33	40.98	26.21	20.249	25.223
	Northwest Atlantic	476	544	738	333.23	506.13	329	169.25	267.041	271.88
	Northwest Central Atlantic	92	48	36	63.06	60.96	45	36.87	5.009	6.92
	Southwest Atlantic	143	29	78	77.39	68.18	91	44.55	14.39	
	West Tropical Atlantic	50	49	23	13.73	31.89	29.55	7.04	3.497	6.897
Longline total		795	696	930	531.87	682.49	535.53	283.92	310.186	310.92
Other surf.	Gulf of Mexico	0.05	0.14	2.24	0.07	0.5	0.56	0.27	6.216	0.172
	Northwest Atlantic	342.53	232.86	330.17	40.14	401.73	64.5	194.59	99.606	172.289
	West Tropical Atlantic			0.15	1.49			3.57	0.06	0.04
Other surf. total		342.58	233	332.56	41.7	402.23	65.06	198.43	105.882	172.501
Purse seine	Northeast Atlantic									
	Northwest Atlantic									
	Southeast Atlantic									
Purse seine total										
Grand total		1,137.58	929	1,262.56	573.57	1,084.72	600.59	482.35	416.068	483.421

Sources: ICCAT 2007d.

Table E.2
Average Landings of Atlantic Bigeye Tuna for 1970–2005 by Area

Flag	Area	Average	No. of years	Flexibility	Vulnerability
Contracting Parties					
Angola	Southeast Atlantic	276	2	low	mod
Barbados	North Atlantic	11	1	low	mod
	Northwest Atlantic	8	2		
	West Tropical Atlantic	19	4		
Brazil	Northwest Atlantic	415	1	low	mod
	Southwest Atlantic	983	35		
Canada	Northwest Atlantic	135	21	low	high
Cape Verde	Azores Islands area	105	2	low	mod
	Northeast Atlantic	88	35		
China, P.R.	Atlantic unclassified	374	4	high	mild
	East Tropical Atlantic	372	2		
	Northeast Atlantic	136	1		
	North Atlantic	2,854	7		
	Northwest Atlantic	700	1		
	Southeast Atlantic	102	2		
	South Atlantic	3,947	7		
	Southwest Atlantic	147	1		
EC Spain	Canary Islands area	3,851	36	by-catch	mild
	East Tropical Atlantic	5,876	36		
	Mediterranean Sea	0	2		

Country	Region				
	Northeast Atlantic	346	27		
	North Atlantic	161	7		
	Northwest Atlantic	9	11		
	Southeast Atlantic	196	11		
	South Atlantic	180	6		
EC France	Southwest Atlantic	114	9	by-catch	mild
	East Tropical Atlantic	5,936	36		
	Northeast Atlantic	98	4		
EC Ireland	Northeast Atlantic	14	3	low	high/opp
EC Poland	Northeast Atlantic	4	1	low	mod
EC Portugal	Azores Islands area	2,497	36	low	high
	Cape Verde area	3	1		
	East Tropical Atlantic	162	2		
	Madeira Islands area	1,956	36		
	Northeast Atlantic	45	16		
	Northwest Atlantic	88	2		
	Northwest Central Atlantic	24	1		
	Southeast Atlantic	281	21		
	South Atlantic	46	1		
	Southwest Atlantic	57	2		
European Community					
Equatorial Guinea	East Tropical Atlantic	4	1	by-catch	mild
Fr. St. Pierre and Miquelon	Northwest Atlantic	14	4	low	mod
Gabon	East Tropical Atlantic	86	5	low	mod
	Southeast Atlantic	121	1	low	mod

Table E.2
(continued)

Flag	Area	Average	No. of years	Flexibility	Vulnerability
Ghana	East Tropical Atlantic	6,816	5	by-catch	mild
	Southeast Atlantic	2,965	28		
Guatemala	West Tropical Atlantic	998	1	low	mod
Iceland	Northeast Atlantic	1	1	low	opp
Ivory Coast	East Tropical Atlantic	2	1	low	mod
Japan	Mediterranean Sea	1	4	high	grad
	Northeast Atlantic	5,621	8		
	North Atlantic	10,090	28		
	Northwest Atlantic	4,617	8		
	Southeast Atlantic	2,356	23		
	South Atlantic	14,861	28		
	Southwest Atlantic	520	4		
	West Tropical Atlantic	4	1		
Korea, Republic of	Northeast Atlantic	2,502	6	high	mild
	North Atlantic	1,997	22		
	Northwest Atlantic	1,826	7		
	Southeast Atlantic	1,556	18		
	South Atlantic	2,810	24		
	Southwest Atlantic	336	7		

Libya	Atlantic unclassified	593	2	low	mod
	Northeast Atlantic	452	10		
	East Tropical Atlantic	331	11		
	Northeast Atlantic	668	7		
Mexico	Gulf of Mexico	4	11	low	mod
Morocco	Atlantic unclassified	913	1	low	mod
Namibia	Southeast Atlantic	227	12	low	mod
Norway	Northeast Atlantic	60	1	low	opp
Panama	Atlantic unclassified	4,751	13	by-catch	mod
	East Tropical Atlantic	1,799	14		
	Northeast Atlantic	455	3		
	North Atlantic	1,062	11		
	Northwest Atlantic	470	4		
	Southeast Atlantic	504	11		
	South Atlantic	1,179	11		
	Southwest Atlantic	149	4		
Philippines	Northeast Atlantic	232	5	high	mild
	North Atlantic	260	1		
	Northwest Atlantic	435	7		
	Southeast Atlantic	384	7		
	South Atlantic	715	1		
	Southwest Atlantic	309	7		
Russian Federation	East Tropical Atlantic	26	6	high	mild
S. Tome and Principe	East Tropical Atlantic	5	1	low	mod
Senegal	East Tropical Atlantic	517	15	low	mod

Table E.2
(continued)

Flag	Area	Average	No. of years	Flexibility	Vulnerability
South Africa	Southeast Atlantic	170	28	low	mod
St. Vincent and Grenadines	Atlantic unclassified	574	3	low	mod
	North Atlantic	13	1		
	Northwest Atlantic	12	11		
	South Atlantic	1	1		
	West Tropical Atlantic	0	1		
Trinidad and Tobago	North Atlantic	21	2	low	mod
	Northwest Atlantic	18	11		
	West Tropical Atlantic	85	7		
United States	Gulf of Mexico	31	26	low	high
	Northeast Atlantic	345	1	(by-catch 1970–1979)	
	Northwest Atlantic	596	26		
	Northwest Central Atlantic	72	20		
	Southeast Atlantic	257	12		
	Southwest Atlantic	64	9		
	West Tropical Atlantic	71	20		
USSR	Northeast Atlantic	437	11	high	mild
	Southeast Atlantic	1,941	20		
UK Bermuda	Northwest Atlantic	0	6	low	high
UK St. Helena	Southeast Atlantic	9	24	low	mod
Uruguay	Southwest Atlantic	153	25	low	mod

Vanuatu	Northwest Atlantic	100	2	low	mod
	Southeast Atlantic	13	1		
Venezuela	Northwest Atlantic	754	33	low	mod
Cooperating Noncontracting Parties					
Chinese Taipei (Taiwan)	Northeast Atlantic	670	11	high	mild
	North Atlantic	2,744	25		
	Northwest Atlantic	874	11		
	Southeast Atlantic	2,301	11		
	South Atlantic	8,149	25		
	Southwest Atlantic	493	11		
Noncontracting Parties					
Argentina	Southwest Atlantic	63	15	low	mod
Benin	East Tropical Atlantic	15	16	low	mod
Cambodia	Southeast Atlantic	32	1	high	mild
Congo	East Tropical Atlantic	11	13	low	mod
Cuba	East Tropical Atlantic	16	6	low	mod
	North Atlantic	536	23		
	Northwest Atlantic	16	2		
	South Atlantic	696	23		
Dominica	Northwest Atlantic	3	2	low	mod
Faroe Islands	Northeast Atlantic	10	2	low	opp
Grenada	Northwest Atlantic	12	11	low	mod
Liberia	East Tropical Atlantic	57	11	low	mod
	Northeast Atlantic	69	4		

Table E.2
(continued)

Flag	Area	Average	No. of years	Flexibility	Vulnerability
NEI (ETRO)	East Tropical Atlantic	2,220	22	high	mild
NEI (Flag related)	Atlantic unclassified	7,812	20	high	mild
	East Tropical Atlantic	5	1		
	Northeast Atlantic	4	1		
NEI (UK Overseas Terr.)	Atlantic unclassified	36	1	high	mild
Netherlands Antilles	East Tropical Atlantic	2,457	10	high	mod
Seychelles	Northwest Atlantic	58	1	high	mild
	Southeast Atlantic	162	1		
Sierra Leone	Northeast Atlantic	4	2	low	mod
St. Lucia	Northwest Atlantic	1	9	low	mod
	West Tropical Atlantic	1	2		
Togo	East Tropical Atlantic	33	1	low	mod
	Southeast Atlantic	23	15		
Total		77,938	36		

Notes: Average = average of available data from 1970 to 2005, No. of years = number of years with data from 1970–2005, flexibility = "low" if areas with majority of harvest are contiguous to national EEZ and "high" otherwise. "By-catch" indicates that the species is not directly targeted by this fleet. Vulnerability = "high" if highly vulnerable, "grad" if gradually vulnerable, "mod" if moderately vulnerable, "mild" if mildly vulnerable, and "opp" if opportunistic. NEI = not elsewhere included, NEI catch is estimated in several different ways, depending on the stock, fleet, and area covered. Because some overlap may exist between different measures of NEI harvests, these entries are not additive and so are reported separately under the names used in the ICCAT database. ETRO = East Tropical Atlantic.
Sources: ICCAT 2007d.

Table E.3
Average Landings of Atlantic Yellowfin Tuna for 1970–2005 by Area

Flag	Area	Average	No. of years	Flexibility	Vulnerability
Contracting Parties					
Angola	East Tropical Atlantic	470	35	low	mod
	Southeast Atlantic	111	1		
Barbados	West Atlantic	116	3	low	mod
	West Tropical Atlantic	107	29		
Brazil	Northwest Atlantic	38	1	low	mod
	Southwest Atlantic	2,720	36		
Canada	East Tropical Atlantic	99	3	low	high
	Northwest Atlantic	96	21	(high 1970–1973)	(grad 1970–1973)
	West Tropical Atlantic	161	1		
	Azores Islands area	1	1		
Cape Verde	East Tropical Atlantic	1,694	35	low	mod
	Southeast Atlantic	80	3		
China, P.R.	Atlantic unclassified	155	4	high	mild
	East Atlantic	1,030	7		
	Northeast Atlantic	64	2		
	Northwest Atlantic	571	1		
	Southeast Atlantic	14	2		
	Southwest Atlantic	57	1		
	West Atlantic	278	7		

Table E.3
(continued)

Flag	Area	Average	No. of years	Flexibility	Vulnerability
EC Spain	Canary Islands area	1,040	36	high	grad
	East Tropical Atlantic	35,374	36		
	Northeast Atlantic	34	21		
	North Atlantic	8	1		
	Northwest Atlantic	9	8		
	Southeast Atlantic	26	17		
	South Atlantic	10	1		
	Southwest Atlantic	39	12		
	West Tropical Atlantic	1,371	11		
EC Estonia	East Tropical Atlantic	234	1	high	mild
EC France	East Tropical Atlantic	33,915	36	high	grad
	Northeast Atlantic	18	1		
	West Tropical Atlantic	1,028	5		
EC Ireland	Northeast Atlantic	3	1	low	high
EC Latvia	East Tropical Atlantic	166	14	high	mild
EC Lithuania	East Tropical Atlantic	332	1	high	mild
EC Poland	East Tropical Atlantic	20	1	high	mild
EC Portugal	Azores Islands area	38	14	high (1978–2005)	grad (1978–2005)
	Cape Verde area	5	1		
	East Tropical Atlantic	408	7	by-catch (1975–1976)	mild (1975–1976)

Country	Region				
	Madeira Islands area	24	27		grad
	Northeast Atlantic	14	22		mod
	Northwest Atlantic	94	1		mod
	Northwest Central Atlantic	0	1		mod
	Southeast Atlantic	199	17		mod
	Southwest Atlantic	29	2		mod
European Community				high	grad
Equatorial Guinea	East Tropical Atlantic	1	1	low	mod
Gabon	East Tropical Atlantic	161	13	low	mod
Ghana	East Tropical Atlantic	10,356	34	low	mod
Guatemala	West Tropical Atlantic	2,906	1	low	mod
Ivory Coast	East Tropical Atlantic	290	7	low	mod
Japan	East Atlantic	2,937	4	high	grad
	East Tropical Atlantic	4,203	32		
	West Atlantic	776	4		
	West Tropical Atlantic	2,168	32		
Korea, Republic of	East Tropical Atlantic	3,791	30	high	mild
	Northwest Atlantic	394	1		
	Southeast Atlantic	240	6		
	Southwest Atlantic	186	1		
	West Tropical Atlantic	2,397	26		
	Atlantic unclassified	73	4	low	
Libya	Northeast Atlantic	208	1		mod
Mexico	Gulf of Mexico	990	11	low	mod
	West Tropical Atlantic	474	17		

Table E.3
(continued)

Flag	Area	Average	No. of years	Flexibility	Vulnerability
Morocco	Atlantic unclassiffed	79	1	low	mod
	East Tropical Atlantic	2,365	14		
	Northeast Atlantic	129	3		
Namibia	Southeast Atlantic	82	12	low	mod
Norway	East Tropical Atlantic	344	1	low	opp
	Northeast Atlantic	1,060	5	(high 1973)	(grad 1973)
Panama	Atlantic unclassified	3,040	14	high	mild
	East Tropical Atlantic	3,212	28		
	Northwest Atlantic	1	1		
	Southwest Atlantic	4	1		
	West Tropical Atlantic	752	13		
Philippines	East Atlantic	86	1	high	mild
	Northeast Atlantic	33	5		
	Northwest Atlantic	95	7		
	Southeast Atlantic	47	7		
	Southwest Atlantic	45	7		
	West Atlantic	78	1		
Russian Federation	East Tropical Atlantic	2,606	11	high	mild
S. Tome and Principe	East Tropical Atlantic	108	24	low	mod
Senegal	East Tropical Atlantic	288	17	low	mod
South Africa	Southeast Atlantic	400	34	low	mod

Trinidad and Tobago	West Atlantic	125	1	low	mod
United States	West Tropical Atlantic	160	19	low	high
	East Tropical Atlantic	5,404	13	(high 1970–1979)	(grad 1970–1979)
	Gulf of Mexico	2,441	26		
	Northwest Atlantic	3,568	26		
	Northwest Central Atlantic	11	20		
	Southwest Atlantic	57	9		
	West Tropical Atlantic	476	31		
USSR	East Tropical Atlantic	1,759	21	high	mild
UK Bermuda	Northwest Atlantic	54	5	low	high
	West Tropical Atlantic	31	26		
UK St. Helena	Southeast Atlantic	97	33	low	mod
UK Turks and Caicos	Northwest Atlantic	0	1	low	mod
Uruguay	Southwest Atlantic	152	25	low	mod
Vanuatu	Northwest Atlantic	685	2	low	mod
	Southeast Atlantic	24	1		
Venezuela	East Tropical Atlantic	634	1	low	mod
	Northwest Atlantic	1,091	1		
	West Tropical Atlantic	10,053	36		
Cooperating Noncontracting Parties					
Chinese Taipei (Taiwan)	East Atlantic	4,276	3	high	mild
	East Tropical Atlantic	1,754	33		
	West Atlantic	1,026	3		
	West Tropical Atlantic	1,497	33		

Table E.3
(continued)

Flag	Area	Average	No. of years	Flexibility	Vulnerability
Noncontracting Parties					
Argentina	Southwest Atlantic	91	21	low	mod
Benin	East Tropical Atlantic	25	23	low	mod
Cambodia	Southeast Atlantic	7	1	high	mild
Cayman Islands	East Tropical Atlantic	721	3	high	mild
Colombia	West Tropical Atlantic	656	23	low	mod
Congo	East Tropical Atlantic	28	14	low	mod
Cuba	East Tropical Atlantic	1,832	28	high	mild
	West Atlantic	65	4		
	West Tropical Atlantic	626	29		
Dominica	Northwest Atlantic	106	3	low	mod
	West Tropical Atlantic	57	10		
Dominican Republic	West Tropical Atlantic	208	8	low	mod
Faroe Islands	Northeast Atlantic	1	1	low	opp
Gambia	East Tropical Atlantic	11	3	low	mod
Georgia	East Tropical Atlantic	19	3	high	mild
Grenada	West Tropical Atlantic	339	36	low	mod
Jamaica	West Tropical Atlantic	21	2	low	mod
NEI (ETRO)	East Tropical Atlantic	6,733	22	high	mild
NEI (flag related)	Atlantic unclassified	3,299	21	high	mild

Netherlands Antilles	East Tropical Atlantic	4,883	9	high	mild
	West Tropical Atlantic	155	31		
Seychelles	Northwest Atlantic	32	1	high	mild
	Southeast Atlantic	11	1		
Seychelles (foreign obs.)	Southeast Atlantic	6	1	high	mild
St. Vincent and Grenadines	Atlantic unclassified	1,192	3	low	mod
	East Atlantic	1	1		
	Northwest Atlantic	963	5		
	West Atlantic	871	1		
	West Tropical Atlantic	31	15		
St. Lucia	West Tropical Atlantic	87	36	low	mod
Ukraine	Northeast Atlantic	215	1	high	mild
Total		136,855	36		

Notes: Average = average of available data from 1970 to 2005; no. of years = number of years with data from 1970 to 2005; flexibility = "low" if areas with majority of harvest are contiguous to a national EEZ and "high" otherwise. "By-catch" indicates that the species is not directly targeted by this fleet. Vulnerability = "high" if highly vulnerable, "grad" if gradually vulnerable, "mod" if moderately vulnerable, "mild" if mildly vulnerable, and "opp" if opportunistic. NEI = not elsewhere included, NEI catch is estimated in several different ways, depending on the stock, fleet, and area covered. Because some overlap may exist between different measures of NEI harvests, these entries are not additive and so are reported separately under the names used in the ICCAT database. ETRO = East Tropical Atlantic.
Sources: ICCAT 2007d.

Table E.4
Average Landings of Atlantic Skipjack Tuna for 1970–2005 by Area

Flag	Area	Average	No. of years	Flexibility	Vulnerability
Contracting Parties					
Algeria	Mediterranean Sea	95	4	low	mod
Angola	East Tropical Atlantic	949	34	low	mod
	Southeast Atlantic	10	1		
Barbados	West Tropical Atlantic	21	20	low	mod
Brazil	Southwest Atlantic	16,300	32	low	mod
Canada	East Tropical Atlantic	753	4	low	high
	Northwest Atlantic	89	3	(high 1970–1973)	(grad 1970–1973)
	West Tropical Atlantic	97	2		
	Azores Islands area	10	2		
Cape Verde	East Tropical Atlantic	1,063	36	low	mod
	Southeast Atlantic	193	3		
China, P.R.	Southeast Atlantic	4	1	high	mild
EC Spain	Canary Islands area	3,122	36	high	grad
	East Tropical Atlantic	32,440	36		
	Mediterranean Sea	12	5		
	Northeast Atlantic	43	16		
	North Atlantic	7	1		
	Northwest Atlantic	0	3		
	Southeast Atlantic	4	8		
	South Atlantic	8	1		
	Southwest Atlantic	1	2		
	West Tropical Atlantic	909	11		

EC Estonia	East Tropical Atlantic	102	1	high	mild
EC France	East Tropical Atlantic	20,672	36	high	grad
	Mediterranean Sea	22	1		
	Northeast Atlantic	9	2		
	West Tropical Atlantic	293	5		
EC Germany	East Tropical Atlantic	3	1	high	mild
EC Greece	Mediterranean Sea	100	3	low	high
EC Ireland	Northeast Atlantic	14	2	low	high
EC Italy	Mediterranean Sea	21	4	low	high
EC Latvia	East Tropical Atlantic	92	1	high	mild
EC Lithuania	East Tropical Atlantic	221	1	high	mild
EC Portugal	Azores Islands area	3,197	36	low	high
	Cape Verde area	56	1		
	East Tropical Atlantic	238	7		
	Madeira Islands area	1,223	36		
	Northeast Atlantic	23	22		
	Northwest Atlantic	34	2		
	Northwest Central Atlantic	1	3		
	Southeast Atlantic	37	18		
	Southwest Atlantic	4	3		
European Community					
Gabon	East Tropical Atlantic	35	7	high	grad
	Southeast Atlantic	101	1	low	mod
Ghana	East Tropical Atlantic	20,801	33	low	mod
Guatemala	West Tropical Atlantic	6,389	1	low	mod

Table E.4
(continued)

Flag	Area	Average	No. of years	Flexibility	Vulnerability
Ivory Coast	East Tropical Atlantic	614	6	low	mod
Japan	Atlantic unclassified	1	1	high	grad
	East Tropical Atlantic	8,565	24		
	West Tropical Atlantic	662	3		
Korea, Republic of	Atlantic unclassified	90	12	high	mild
	East Tropical Atlantic	2,929	18		
	West Tropical Atlantic	14	3		
Mexico	Gulf of Mexico	27	11	low	mod
	West Tropical Atlantic	13	14		
Morocco	East Tropical Atlantic	1,623	12	low	mod
	Mediterranean Sea	7	19		
	Northeast Atlantic	876	35		
Namibia	Southeast Atlantic	3	8	low	mod
Norway	Northeast Atlantic	660	2	low	opp
Panama	Atlantic unclassified	42	1	high	mild/IUU
	East Tropical Atlantic	4,176	26		
	West Tropical Atlantic	636	3		
Russian Federation	East Tropical Atlantic	1,116	10	high	mild
S. Tome and Principe	East Tropical Atlantic	42	20	low	mod
Senegal	East Tropical Atlantic	956	17	low	mod
South Africa	Southeast Atlantic	36	30	low	mod
Trinidad and Tobago	West Tropical Atlantic	1	6	low	mod

United States	East Tropical Atlantic	8,515	13	low	high (grad 1970–1979)
	Gulf of Mexico	23	24	(high 1970–1979)	
	Northwest Atlantic	273	26		
	Southwest Atlantic	0	1		
	West Tropical Atlantic	302	28		
USSR	East Tropical Atlantic	1,880	20	high	mild
UK Bermuda	Northwest Atlantic	0	5	low	high
	West Tropical Atlantic	0	1		
UK St. Helena	East Tropical Atlantic	63	2	low	mod
	Southeast Atlantic	107	34		
Venezuela	East Tropical Atlantic	358	1	low	mod
	West Tropical Atlantic	5,316	29		
Cooperating Noncontracting Parties					
Chinese Taipei (Taiwan)	Atlantic unclassified	25	10	high	mild
	East Atlantic	27	3		
	East Tropical Atlantic	16	18		
	West Atlantic	13	3		
	West Tropical Atlantic	9	20		
Noncontracting Parties					
Argentina	Southwest Atlantic	88	24	low	mod
Benin	East Tropical Atlantic	13	22	low	mod
Bulgaria	East Tropical Atlantic	7	1	high	mild
Cayman Islands	East Tropical Atlantic	706	3	high	mild
Colombia	West Tropical Atlantic	1,482	3	low	mod
Congo	East Tropical Atlantic	98	16	low	mod
Cuba	East Tropical Atlantic	193	20	low	mod
	West Tropical Atlantic	1,475	31	low	mod

Table E.4
(continued)

Flag	Area	Average	No. of years	Flexibility	Vulnerability
Dominica	Northwest Atlantic	33	3	low	mod
	West Tropical Atlantic	47	13		
Dominican Republic	West Tropical Atlantic	148	27	low	mod
Grenada	Northwest Atlantic	12	1	low	mod
	West Tropical Atlantic	15	27		
Jamaica	West Tropical Atlantic	62	1	low	mod
NEI (ETRO)	East Tropical Atlantic	8,334	24	high	mild
Netherlands Antilles	East Tropical Atlantic	9,070	9	high	mild
	West Tropical Atlantic	38	23		
Romania	East Tropical Atlantic	106	6	high	mild
St. Vincent and Grenadines	Atlantic unclassified	93	1	low	mod
	East Atlantic	1	1		
	Northwest Atlantic	54	15		
	West Atlantic	206	1		
	West Tropical Atlantic	80	6		
St. Lucia	West Tropical Atlantic	85	36	low	mod
Total		128,428	36		

Notes: Average = average of available data from 1970 to 2005; no. of years = number of years with data from 1970 to 2005; flexibility = "low" if areas with majority of harvest are contiguous to a national EEZ and "high" otherwise. "By-catch" indicates that the species is not directly targeted by this fleet. Vulnerability = "high" if highly vulnerable, "grad" if gradually vulnerable, "mod" if moderately vulnerable, "mild" if mildly vulnerable, and "opp" if opportunistic. NEI = not elsewhere included, NEI catch is estimated in several different ways, depending on the stock, fleet, and area covered. Because some overlap may exist between different measures of NEI harvests, these entries are not additive and so are reported separately under the names used in the ICCAT database. ETRO = East Tropical Atlantic.
Sources: ICCAT 2007d.

Table E.5
Average Landings of Atlantic Swordfish for 1970–2005 by Area

Flag	Area	Average	No. of years	Flexibility	Vulnerability
Contracting Parties					
Algeria	Mediterranean Sea	746	32	low	mod
Angola	Southeast Atlantic	189	7	low	mod
Barbados	North Atlantic	10	1	low	mod
	Northwest Atlantic	16	7		
	West Tropical Atlantic	14	2		
Brazil	Northwest Atlantic	117	1	low	mod
	Southwest Atlantic	1,648	36		
Canada	Northwest Atlantic	1,215	33	low	high
	Northwest Central Atlantic	15	2		
China, P.R.	Northeast Atlantic	33	1	high	mild
	North Atlantic	119	12		
	Northwest Atlantic	304	1		
	Southeast Atlantic	5	1		
	South Atlantic	318	7		
	Southwest Atlantic	24	1		
Croatia	Mediterranean Sea	15	2	low	mod
EC Cyprus	Mediterranean Sea	88	31	low	high
EC Denmark	Northeast Atlantic	0	1	low	opp
EC Spain	Canary Islands area	3	18	high	grad
	Mediterranean Sea	1,076	36		
	Northeast Atlantic	4,319	36		

Table E.5
(continued)

Flag	Area	Average	No. of years	Flexibility	Vulnerability
	Northwest Atlantic	11	1		
	Northwest Central Atlantic	1,984	17		
	Southeast Atlantic	3,008	19		
	Southwest Atlantic	3,636	17		
EC France	Mediterranean Sea	15	4	low	high
	Northeast Atlantic	79	20		
EC Greece	Mediterranean Sea	1,319	25	low	high
EC Ireland	Northeast Atlantic	32	10	low	high
	Northwest Atlantic	2	2		
EC Italy	Ligurian Sea	149	9	low	high
	Mediterranean Sea	5,492	30		
	North Ionian Sea	187	10		
	Northwest Atlantic	8	1		
	South Adriatic Sea	273	8		
	South Ionian Sea	1,051	8		
	Sardinia area	148	8		
	Tyrrhenian Sea	2,361	18		
EC Lithuania	Southeast Atlantic	794	1	high	mild
EC Malta	Mediterranean Sea	160	36	low	mod
EC Poland	Northwest Atlantic	36	3	low	mild
EC Portugal	Azores Islands area	256	24	low	high
	Cape Verde area	20	1	(high 1995–2005)	(grad 1995–2005)

Country/Group	Region				
	East Atlantic	118	1		
	Madeira Islands area	26	36		
	Mediterranean Sea	45	6		
	Northeast Atlantic	546	20		
	North Atlantic	25	2		
	Northwest Atlantic	151	6		
	Northwest Central Atlantic	82	4		
	Southeast Atlantic	186	12		
	South Atlantic	84	1		
	Southwest Atlantic	201	10		
EC United Kingdom	Northeast Atlantic	4	7	low	opp
	Southwest Atlantic	0	1		
European Community					
Equatorial Guinea	Southeast Atlantic	2	1	high	grad
Fr. St. Pierre and Miquelon	Northwest Atlantic	24	4	low	mod
Gabon	Southeast Atlantic	9	1	low	mod
Ghana	Southeast Atlantic	149	26	low	mod
Ivory Coast	Southeast Atlantic	20	22	low	mod
Iceland	Northeast Atlantic	1	1	low	mod
Japan	Mediterranean Sea	4	27	low	opp
	Northeast Atlantic	900	11	by-catch	mild
	North Atlantic	842	25		
	Northwest Atlantic	71	11		
	Northwest Central Atlantic	328	7		
	Southeast Atlantic	2,288	14		
	South Atlantic	1,452	23		
	Southwest Atlantic	948	13		

Table E.5
(continued)

Flag	Area	Average	No. of years	Flexibility	Vulnerability
Korea, Republic of	Northeast Atlantic	35	4	by-catch	mild
	North Atlantic	169	24		
	Northwest Atlantic	51	1		
	Northwest Central Atlantic	34	4		
	Southeast Atlantic	186	12		
	South Atlantic	320	23		
	Southwest Atlantic	325	7		
	West Tropical Atlantic	12	1		
Libya	Mediterranean Sea	7	5	low	mod
Mexico	Gulf of Mexico	27	11	low	mod
	Northwest Atlantic	3	4		
Morocco	Mediterranean Sea	1,471	32	low	mod
	Northeast Atlantic	144	36		
Namibia	Southeast Atlantic	575	7	low	mod
Norway	Northeast Atlantic	300	2	low	opp
Panama	North Atlantic	55	8	low	mod
	Northwest Atlantic	17	1		
	Southeast Atlantic	18	1		
	South Atlantic	97	8		
	Southwest Atlantic	87	1		
Philippines	Northeast Atlantic	5	2	high	mild
	Northwest Atlantic	12	4		
	Southwest Atlantic	3	5		

S. Tome and Principe	Southeast Atlantic	14	3	low	mod
Senegal	Northeast Atlantic	38	6	low	mod
South Africa	Southeast Atlantic	113	25	low	mod
Trinidad and Tobago	North Atlantic	84	2	low	mod
	Northwest Atlantic	106	11		
	West Tropical Atlantic	107	10		
Tunisia	Mediterranean Sea	256	27	low	mod
Turkey	Mediterranean Sea	218	36	low	mod
United States	Gulf of Mexico	600	28	low	high
	Northwest Atlantic	1,943	36		
	Northwest Central Atlantic	843	28		
	Southwest Atlantic	152	9		
	West Tropical Atlantic	679	22		
USSR	Northeast Atlantic	22	16	high	mild
	Northwest Atlantic	1	1		
	Southeast Atlantic	128	16		
UK Bermuda	Northwest Atlantic	2	11	low	high
UK British Virgin Islands	North Atlantic	4	2	low	high
UK St. Helena	Southeast Atlantic	12	2	low	mod
Uruguay	Southwest Atlantic	659	25	low	mod
Vanuatu	Northwest Atlantic	32	2	low	mod
	Southeast Atlantic	11	1		
Venezuela	Northwest Atlantic	50	36	low	mod

Table E.5
(continued)

Flag	Area	Average	No. of years	Flexibility	Vulnerability
Cooperating Noncontracting Parties					
Chinese Taipei (Taiwan)	Mediterranean Sea	2	4	high	mild
	North Atlantic	268	36		
	South Atlantic	1,061	36		
Noncontracting Parties					
Albania	Mediterranean Sea	13	4	low	mod
Argentina	Southwest Atlantic	97	26	low	mod
Belize (foreign obs.)	Southeast Atlantic	9	3	high	mod
Benin	Southeast Atlantic	28	18	low	mod
Bulgaria	Southeast Atlantic	3	1	low	mild
Cambodia	Southeast Atlantic	6	1	high	mild
Cuba	North Atlantic	228	30	low	mod
	Northwest Central Atlantic	10	1		
	South Atlantic	370	28		
Dominica	Northwest Atlantic	0	2	low	mod
	West Tropical Atlantic	1	1		
Faroe Islands	Northeast Atlantic	5	2	low	opp
Grenada	Northwest Atlantic	27	14	low	mod
	West Tropical Atlantic	64	2		
Honduras (foreign obs.)	Southeast Atlantic	5	5	high	mod
Liberia	Northeast Atlantic	24	11	low	mod
	Southeast Atlantic	26	7		

		Average	No. of years	Flexibility	Vulnerability
Mixed flags (Fr. + Spain)	Southeast Atlantic	4	1	high	mild
NEI (ETRO)	Northeast Atlantic	302	2	high	mild
	Southeast Atlantic	648	2		
	West Tropical Atlantic	57	2		
NEI-2	Mediterranean Sea	873	13	high	mild
	West Tropical Atlantic	80	9		
Nigeria	Southeast Atlantic	41	4	low	mod
Romania	Northwest Atlantic	1	1	high	mild
Seychelles	Northwest Atlantic	10	1	high	mild
	Southeast Atlantic	6	1		
Sierra Leone	Northeast Atlantic	2	2	low	mod
St. Vincent and Grenadines	Northwest Atlantic	7	15	low	mod
St. Lucia	Northwest Atlantic	0	3	low	mod
	West Tropical Atlantic	2	2		
Togo	Southeast Atlantic	14	11	low	mod
Total		33,589	36	low	mod

Notes: Average = average of available data from 1970 to 2005; no. of years = number of years with data from 1970 to 2005; flexibility = "low" if areas with majority of harvest are contiguous to a national EEZ and "high" otherwise. "By-catch" indicates that the species is not directly targeted by this fleet. Vulnerability = "high" if highly vulnerable, "grad" if gradually vulnerable, "mild" if moderately vulnerable, "mild" if mildly vulnerable, and "opp" if opportunistic. NEI = not elsewhere included, NEI catch is estimated in several different ways, depending on the stock, fleet, and area covered. Because some overlap may exist between different measures of NEI harvests, these entries are not additive and so are reported separately under the names used in the ICCAT database. ETRO = East Tropical Atlantic.
Sources: ICCAT 2007d.

Table E.6
Average Landings of Atlantic Blue Marlin for 1970–2005 by Area

Flag	Area	Average	No. of years	Flexibility	Vulnerability
Contracting Parties					
Barbados	Northwest Atlantic	59	25	by-catch	mild
	West Tropical Atlantic	22	2		
Brazil	Northwest Atlantic	15	1	by-catch	mild
	Southwest Atlantic	164	36		
Canada	Northwest Atlantic	1	2	by-catch	mild
China, P.R.	North Atlantic	44	12	by-catch	mild
	South Atlantic	43	12		
EC Spain	Northeast Atlantic	6	20	by-catch	mild
	North Atlantic	5	1		
	Northwest Central Atlantic	6	14		
	Southeast Atlantic	36	15		
	Southwest Atlantic	27	16		
EC France	West Tropical Atlantic	776	1	by-catch	mild
EC Portugal	Azores Islands area	8	11	by-catch	mild
	Cape Verde area	4	1		
	East Atlantic	3	3		
	Madeira Islands area	2	24		
	Mediterranean Sea	1	1		
	Northeast Atlantic	11	8		
	Northwest Atlantic	7	4		

	Southeast Atlantic	1	5		mild
	South Atlantic	2	1		mild
	Southwest Atlantic	7	4		mild
European Community					
Gabon	Southeast Atlantic	5	2	by-catch	mild
Ghana	Southeast Atlantic	349	26	by-catch	mild
Ivory Coast	Southeast Atlantic	139	22	by-catch	mild
Japan	North Atlantic	351	36	by-catch	mild
	South Atlantic	402	36		
Korea, Republic of	North Atlantic	136	28	by-catch	mild
	Southeast Atlantic	1	2		
	South Atlantic	189	29		
Mexico	Gulf of Mexico	40	13	by-catch	mild
Morocco	Northeast Atlantic	12	1	by-catch	mild
Panama	North Atlantic	63	8	by-catch	mild
	Northwest Atlantic	3	1		
	South Atlantic	79	8		
	Southwest Atlantic	38	1		
Philippines	North Atlantic	22	2	by-catch	mild
	Northwest Atlantic	38	1		
	South Atlantic	18	2		
Russian Federation	East Tropical Atlantic	1	1	by-catch	mild
S. Tome and Principe	Southeast Atlantic	21	2	by-catch	mild
Senegal	Northeast Atlantic	4	6	by-catch	mild
South Africa	Southeast Atlantic	2	2	by-catch	mild

Table E.6
(continued)

Flag	Area	Average	No. of years	Flexibility	Vulnerability
Trinidad and Tobago	North Atlantic	17	2	by-catch	mild
	Northwest Atlantic	20	19		
	West Tropical Atlantic	28	2		
United States	Atlantic unclassified	1	1	by-catch	mild
	Gulf of Mexico	35	26		
	North Atlantic	10	9		
	Northwest Atlantic	162	36		
	Northwest Central Atlantic	11	18		
	Southwest Atlantic	12	4		
	West Tropical Atlantic	24	27		
USSR	Northeast Atlantic	6	10	by-catch	mild
	Southeast Atlantic	16	15		
UK Bermuda	Northwest Atlantic	7	31	by-catch	mild
UK St. Helena	Southeast Atlantic	0	1	by-catch	mild
UK Turks and Caicos	North Atlantic	0	0	by-catch	mild
	Northwest Atlantic	0	1		
Uruguay	Southwest Atlantic	23	1	by-catch	mild
Vanuatu	Northwest Atlantic	1	2	by-catch	mild
	Southeast Atlantic	0	1		
Venezuela	Northwest Atlantic	114	36	by-catch	mild

Cooperating Noncontracting Parties					
Chinese Taipei (Taiwan)	North Atlantic	175	36	by-catch	mild
	South Atlantic	361	36		
Noncontracting Parties					
Benin	Southeast Atlantic	6	18	by-catch	mild
Cuba	Atlantic unclassified	41	5	by-catch	mild
	North Atlantic	175	27		
	Northwest Atlantic	34	1		
	South Atlantic	118	23		
	West Tropical Atlantic	12	1		
Dominica	Northwest Atlantic	52	3	by-catch	mild
Dominican Republic	Atlantic unclassified	115	2	by-catch	mild
	West Tropical Atlantic	40	4		
Grenada	Northwest Atlantic	45	24	by-catch	mild
	West Tropical Atlantic	43	2		
Jamaica	Northwest Atlantic	24	1	by-catch	mild
Liberia	Atlantic unclassified	111	8	by-catch	mild
Mixed flags (France and Spain)	Atlantic unclassified	114	31	by-catch	mild
NEI (ETRO)	North Atlantic	91	5	by-catch	mild
	South Atlantic	103	5		
Netherlands Antilles	Northwest Atlantic	46	23	by-catch	mild
St. Vincent and Grenadines	Atlantic unclassified	4	1	by-catch	mild
	North Atlantic	15	1		
	Northwest Atlantic	1	8		
	South Atlantic	1	1		

Table E.6
(continued)

Flag	Area	Average	No. of years	Flexibility	Vulnerability
St. Lucia	Northwest Atlantic	7	5	by-catch	mild
	West Tropical Atlantic	19	2		
Ukraine	Northeast Atlantic	15	1	by-catch	mild
Total		3,039	36		

Notes: Average = average of available data from 1970 to 2005; no. of years = number of years with data from 1970 to 2005; flexibility = "low" if areas with majority of harvest are contiguous to a national EEZ and "high" otherwise. "By-catch" indicates that the species is not directly targeted by this fleet. Vulnerability = "high" if highly vulnerable, "grad" if gradually vulnerable, "mod" if moderately vulnerable, "mild" if mildly vulnerable, and "opp" if opportunistic. NEI = not elsewhere included, NEI catch is estimated in several different ways, depending on the stock, fleet, and area covered. Because some overlap may exist between different measures of NEI harvests, these entries are not additive and so are reported separately under the names used in the ICCAT database. ETRO = East Tropical Atlantic.
Sources: ICCAT 2007d.

Table E.7
Average Landings of Atlantic White Marlin for 1970–2005 by Area

Flag	Area	Average	No. of years	Flexibility	Vulnerability
Contracting Parties					
Barbados	Northwest Atlantic	35	11	by-catch	mild
	West Tropical Atlantic	29	2		
Brazil	Northwest Atlantic	1	1	by-catch	mild
	Southwest Atlantic	139	36		
Canada	Northwest Atlantic	4	13	by-catch	mild
China, P.R.	North Atlantic	6	12	by-catch	mild
	South Atlantic	7	12		
EC Spain	Mediterranean Sea	0	6	by-catch	mild
	Northeast Atlantic	33	19		
	North Atlantic	8	1		
	Northwest Central Atlantic	11	15		
	Southeast Atlantic	8	15		
	Southwest Atlantic	14	14		
EC France	Northeast Atlantic	0	1	by-catch	mild
EC Portugal	Atlantic unclassified	1	1	by-catch	mild
	Azores Islands area	1	3		
	Cape Verde area	2	1		
	Northeast Atlantic	2	2		
	Northwest Atlantic	19	2		
	Southeast Atlantic	7	1		
	Southwest Atlantic	0	1		
European Community				by-catch	mild

Table E.7
(continued)

Flag	Area	Average	No. of years	Flexibility	Vulnerability
Gabon	Southeast Atlantic	203	2	by-catch	mild
Ghana	Southeast Atlantic	23	26	by-catch	mild
Ivory Coast	Southeast Atlantic	2	10	by-catch	mild
Japan	North Atlantic	135	36	by-catch	mild
	South Atlantic	44	36		
Korea, Republic of	Atlantic unclassified	3	1	by-catch	mild
	North Atlantic	60	28		
	Northwest Atlantic	4	1		
	Southeast Atlantic	11	5		
	South Atlantic	88	27		
	Southwest Atlantic	2	1		
Mexico	Gulf of Mexico	15	12	by-catch	mild
Panama	North Atlantic	16	8	by-catch	mild
	South Atlantic	28	8		
Philippines	North Atlantic	2	2	by-catch	mild
	South Atlantic	5	2		
S. Tome and Principe	Southeast Atlantic	24	2	by-catch	mild
South Africa	Southeast Atlantic	2	1	by-catch	mild
Trinidad and Tobago	North Atlantic	4	2	by-catch	mild
	Northwest Atlantic	7	3		

United States	Atlantic unclassified	1	1	by-catch	mild
	Gulf of Mexico	22	26		
	North Atlantic	4	7		
	Northwest Atlantic	61	36		
	Northwest Central Atlantic	5	19		
	Southwest Atlantic	10	4		
	West Tropical Atlantic	5	20		
USSR	Northeast Atlantic	1	4	by-catch	mild
	Southeast Atlantic	7	9		
UK Bermuda	Northwest Atlantic	1	22	by-catch	mild
Uruguay	Southwest Atlantic	14	13	by-catch	mild
Vanuatu	Northwest Atlantic	0	1	by-catch	mild
Venezuela	Northwest Atlantic	117	36	by-catch	mild
	West Tropical Atlantic	62	1		
Cooperating Noncontracting Parties					
Chinese Taipei (Taiwan)	North Atlantic	116	35	by-catch	mild
	South Atlantic	370	36		
Noncontracting Parties					
Argentina	Southwest Atlantic	19	11	by-catch	mild
Belize (foreign obs.)	Southeast Atlantic	1	4	by-catch	mild
Cambodia	Southeast Atlantic	1	1	by-catch	mild
Costa Rica	Atlantic unclassified	6	3	by-catch	mild
Cuba	North Atlantic	147	21	by-catch	mild
	Northwest Atlantic	7	1		
	South Atlantic	76	23		

Table E.7
(continued)

Flag	Area	Average	No. of years	Flexibility	Vulnerability
Grenada	Atlantic unclassified	14	1	by-catch	mild
	Northwest Atlantic	8	3		
	West Tropical Atlantic	22	2		
Honduras (foreign obs.)	East Tropical Atlantic	0	1	by-catch	mild
	Southeast Atlantic	0	3		
Mixed flags (France and Spain)	Atlantic unclassified	18	31	by-catch	mild
NEI (ETRO)	North Atlantic	49	5	by-catch	mild
	South Atlantic	54	5		
St. Vincent and Grenadines	North Atlantic	0	1	by-catch	mild
	Northwest Atlantic	44	1		
	West Tropical Atlantic	1	3		
Total		1,396	36		

Notes: Average = average of available data from 1970 to 2005; no. of years = number of years with data from 1970 to 2005; flexibility = "low," if areas with majority of harvest are contiguous to a national EEZ and "high" otherwise. "By-catch" indicates that the species is not directly targeted by this fleet. Vulnerability = "high" if highly vulnerable, "grad" if gradually vulnerable, "mod" if moderately vulnerable, "mild" if mildly vulnerable, and "opp" if opportunistic. NEI = not elsewhere included, NEI catch is estimated in several different ways, depending on the stock, fleet, and area covered. Because some overlap may exist between different measures of NEI harvests, these entries are not additive and so are reported separately under the names used in the ICCAT database. ETRO = East Tropical Atlantic.
Sources: ICCAT 2007d.

Table E.8
Average Landings of Atlantic Bluefin Tuna for 1970–2005 by Area

Flag	Area	Average	No. of years	Flexibility	Vulnerability
Contracting Parties					
Algeria	Mediterranean Sea	707	35	low	mod
Brazil	Southwest Atlantic	4	14	low	mod
Canada	Northwest Atlantic	550	36	low (by-catch pre-1979)	high (mild pre-1979)
Cape Verde	Azores Islands area	6	2	low	mod
China, P.R.	East Atlantic	38	5	high	mild
	Mediterranean Sea	94	4		
	Northeast Atlantic	89	3		
Croatia	Mediterranean Sea	1,088	15	low	mod
EC Cyprus	Mediterranean Sea	31	26	low	high
EC Denmark	Northeast Atlantic	3	19	low	high/opp
EC Spain	Canary Islands area	335	36	low	high
	Mediterranean Sea	1,444	36	(by-catch pre-1980)	(by-catch pre-1980)
EC France	Northeast Atlantic	3,048	36	low	high
	Mediterranean Sea	4,854	36	(by-catch pre-1980)	(mild pre-1980)
	Northeast Atlantic	552	36		
EC Germany	Northeast Atlantic	4	7	low	high/opp

Table E.8
(continued)

Flag	Area	Average	No. of years	Flexibility	Vulnerability
EC Greece	East Tropical Atlantic	5	1	low	high
	Mediterranean Sea	427	21		
EC Ireland	Northeast Atlantic	15	9	low	high
EC Italy	Adriatic Sea	1,312	28	low	high
	Ligurian Sea	1,208	29	(by-catch pre-1980)	(by-catch pre-1980)
	Mediterranean Sea	3,634	8		
	North Ionian Sea	42	11		
	South Ionian Sea	288	11		
	Sardinia area	102	11		
	Tyrrhenian Sea	2,963	31		
EC Malta	Mediterranean Sea	172	32	low	mod
EC Poland	East Tropical Atlantic	100	2	high	mod/opp
	Northwest Atlantic	3	2		
EC Portugal	Azores Islands area	43	26	low	high
	Cape Verde area	0	1		
	East Tropical Atlantic	60	1		
	Madeira Islands area	37	30		
	Mediterranean Sea	171	13		
	Northeast Atlantic	97	24		
	Northwest Atlantic	31	2		
EC Sweden	Northeast Atlantic	3	9	low	high/opp

Country	Region				
EC United Kingdom	Northeast Atlantic	2	7	low	high/opp
	Southwest Atlantic	0	1		
European Community					high
Fr. St Pierre and Miquelon	Northwest Atlantic	4	5	low	mod
Guinea Conakry	East Atlantic	330	1	low	mod
Iceland	Northeast Atlantic	10	3	low	opp
Japan	Mediterranean Sea	487	34	high	grad
	Northeast Atlantic	1,844	36		
	Northwest Atlantic	1,100	36		
Korea, Republic of	East Atlantic	54	13	high	mild
	Mediterranean Sea	579	7	(by-catch pre-1980)	(by-catch pre-1980)
	Northwest Atlantic	1	1		
	Southeast Atlantic	3	2		
	West Atlantic	10	7		
Libya	Mediterranean Sea	660	36	low	mod
	Northeast Atlantic	469	6		
Mexico	Gulf of Mexico	12	10	low	mod
	Northwest Atlantic	24	11		
Morocco	Mediterranean Sea	345	32	low	mod
	Northeast Atlantic	942	36	(by-catch pre-1980)	(mild pre-1980)
Norway	East Tropical Atlantic	246	4	low	opp
	Northeast Atlantic	305	17	(by-catch pre-1980)	(mild pre-1980)

Table E.8
(continued)

Flag	Area	Average	No. of years	Flexibility	Vulnerability
Panama	East Atlantic	89	17	high	mild/IUU
	Mediterranean Sea	685	11	(by-catch pre-1980)	(by-catch pre-1980)
Trinidad and Tobago	West Atlantic	44	8		
	West Tropical Atlantic	1	1	low	mod
Tunisia	Mediterranean Sea	968	35	low	mod
Turkey	Mediterranean Sea	1,498	36	low	mod
United States	Gulf of Mexico	94	23	low	high
	Northeast Atlantic	5	1	(by-catch pre-1979)	(by-catch pre-1979)
	Northwest Atlantic	1,735	36		
	Northwest Central Atlantic	22	9		
	West Tropical Atlantic	1	4		
UK Bermuda	Northwest Atlantic	1	8	low	high
Uruguay	Southwest Atlantic	3	13	low	mod
Cooperating Noncontracting Parties					
Chinese Taipei (Taiwan)	East Atlantic	50	20	high	mild
	Mediterranean Sea	317	13	(by-catch pre-1980)	(by-catch pre-1980)
	Northeast Atlantic	154	4		
	West Atlantic	8	17		

Noncontracting Parties		Average	No. of years	Flexibility	Vulnerability
Argentina	Southwest Atlantic	2	8	low	mod
Cuba	Northwest Atlantic	137	2	low	mod
Faroe Islands	East Atlantic	64	2	low	opp
	Northeast Atlantic	54	3		
Israel	Mediterranean Sea	14	1	low	high
NEI (combined)	Mediterranean Sea	662	10	high	mild
NEI (ETRO)	Mediterranean Sea	578	9	high	mild
	Northeast Atlantic	15	7		
	Northwest Atlantic	18	6		
NEI (flag related)	East Atlantic	66	1	high	mild
	Mediterranean Sea	469	7		
	Northeast Atlantic	141	7		
	Northwest Atlantic	188	4		
NEI-2	Mediterranean Sea	39	3	high	mild
Serbia and Montenegro	Mediterranean Sea	3	3	low	mod
Seychelles	Southeast Atlantic	2	1	high	mild
Sierra Leone	Northeast Atlantic	105	2	low	mod
St. Lucia	Northwest Atlantic	11	10	low	mod
Yugoslavia Fed.	Mediterranean Sea	646	21	low	mod
Total		29,329	36		

Notes: Average = average of available data from 1970 to 2005; no. of years = number of years with data from 1970 to 2005; flexibility = "low" if areas with majority of harvest are contiguous to a national EEZ and "high" otherwise. "By-catch" indicates that the species is not directly targeted by this fleet. Vulnerability = "high" if highly vulnerable, "grad" if gradually vulnerable, "mod" if moderately vulnerable, "mild" if mildly vulnerable, and "opp" if opportunistic. NEI = not elsewhere included, NEI catch is estimated in several different ways, depending on the stock, fleet, and area covered. Because some overlap may exist between different measures of NEI harvests, these entries are not additive and so are reported separately under the names used in the ICCAT database. ETRO = East Tropical Atlantic.
Sources: ICCAT 2007d.

Appendix F

Delineating High-Flex and Low-Flex Phases for Gradually Vulnerable Countries

Global production of the species in question was utilized to determine when a gradually vulnerable country entered the "low-flex" phase. These data were obtained from the FAO's World Capture Production 1950–2005 Databas (FAO 2007b). As a rule of thumb, countries were considered to be low-flex once their global harvests of a species peaked. In some cases, such as the early yellowfin case, two peaks were evaluated because of an important break in the fishery. The following figures show this information for the gradually vulnerable countries in the cases. Figure F.1 provides world production of bigeye and yellowfin tunas by Japan, which is gradually vulnerable and targets both with longlines now, although they also had a large baitboat fleet targeting small tropical tunas until the 1980s. Note that both data sets peak first in the 1960s, then decline until about 1976, which is when the fishery for yellowfin started to expand away from coastal areas.

Almost all of Canada's history with tropical tunas is captured in figure F.2. High catches of both yellowfin and skipjack in the 1970s signal the prevalence of purse seine fleets, which quickly exited after a peak around 1978. Later, longlines began targeting bigeye, but this coastal fleet is highly vulnerable. In contrast, U.S. harvests of skipjack and yellowfin (mostly purse seines) remained quite high until the turn of the century, peaking once in 1976 and again in 1987 (figure F.3). Targeting all of the tropical tunas together, French and Spanish fleets were late starters and did not peak until the mid-1990s (figures F.4 and F.5, respectively). As figure F.6 shows, Spanish landings of swordfish had a double peak, first in 1995 and then again in 2004. Finally, figure F.7 provides the data on Japanese landings of the three species of bluefin tuna, which reached an apex in 1961 but began a steep decline in 1981. These double peaks made selection of the "high-flex" divider a bit difficult, but usually I went with the earliest, or, as in the yellowfin case, reported both.

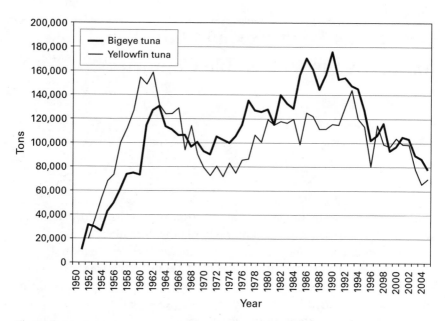

Figure F.1
Global harvests of bigeye and yellowfin tunas by Japan. Source: FAO 2007b.

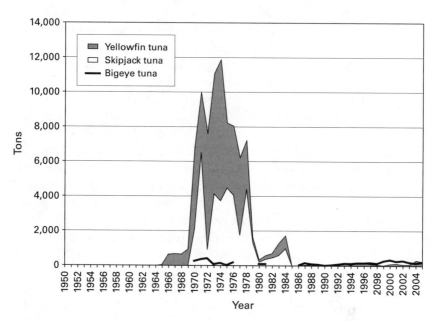

Figure F.2
Global harvests of tropical tunas by Canada. Source: FAO 2007b.

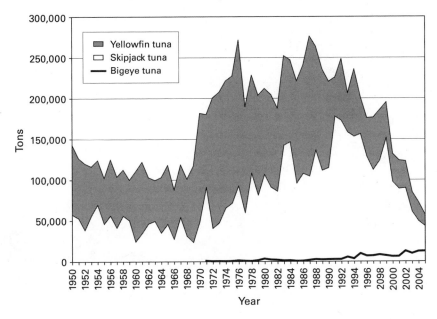

Figure F.3
Global harvests of tropical tunas by the United States. Source: FAO 2007b.

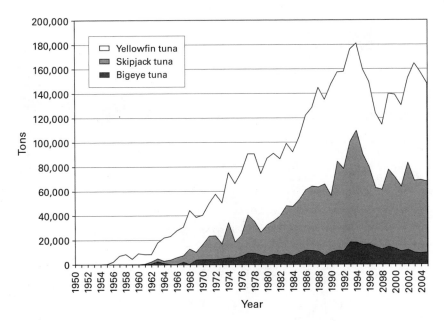

Figure F.4
Global harvests of tropical tunas by France. Source: FAO 2007b.

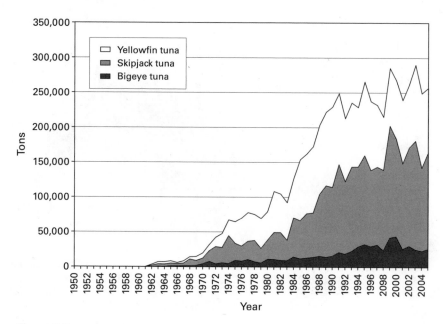

Figure F.5
Global harvests of tropical tunas by Spain. Source: FAO 2007b.

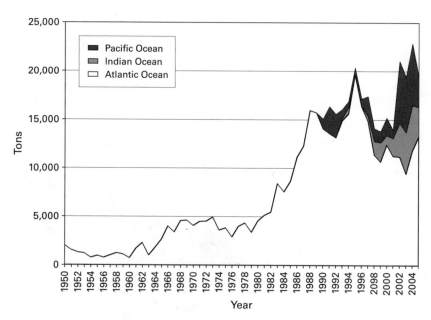

Figure F.6
Global harvests of swordfish by Spain. Source: FAO 2007b.

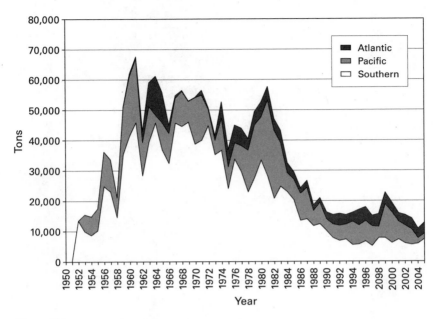

Figure F.7
Global harvests of bluefin tuna by Japan. Source: FAO 2007b.

Notes

Chapter 1

1. Data from 2005. Fishing entities include representative multilateral organizations, such as the European Community, as well as territories and other semi-autonomous governments.

2. The use of the expression "regional fisheries organization" here can be misleading to students of international relations. As used in international parlance, it refers to the entirety of an international fisheries regime, not just the secretariats of the various commissions, which are actually organizations, as defined by Young (1982, 18).

3. Explanations for these failures abound, ranging from the political science perspectives of DeSombre (1999, 2000, 2005) and Peterson (1995) to the economic approaches exemplified by Bjorndal et al. (2000), Hannesson (1997), McKelvey, Sandal, and Steinshamn (2003), and Munro, Van Houtte, and Willmann (2004).

4. Western bluefin was the major exception—although the only recommendation was to maintain or implement those regulations that were adopted early in the decade.

5. Assessments are all based on historical catch and effort levels, so a systemic change that shifts the underlying dynamics would not be captured until after it manifests.

6. Young and Levy (1999) provide an excellent discussion of these difficulties.

7. A time-area closure is simply a prohibition on fishing in specific areas during certain periods. Capacity limits restrict the level of fishing effort by reducing the number or size of vessels permitted to target the stock.

8. There are seventeen separate qualifying items listed in the 2001 allocation criteria. These range from membership or cooperating status at ICCAT to the needs of coastal fishing communities to the historical catches of qualifying participants.

9. See Kubler (2001) for a good model of norm entrepreneurship.

10. Military force is no longer considered to be a legitimate means of obtaining access to international resources. There have been a few minor skirmishes over

international fisheries resources, notably the cod wars between Iceland and Britain in the 1950s and 1970s and the turbot war between Canada and Spain in 1995. However, these "wars" consisted of little more than the firing of warning shots and impounding of vessels (Juda 1996, 171–180, 267–273).

11. New research on consensus using the International Regimes Database suggests that, in general, it is not as impermeable a barrier to effective environmental management as previously thought (Breitmeier, Young, and Zurn 2006, 114–153).

12. ICCAT did impose trade sanctions on Honduras the year after that country joined the commission. However, no representatives from Honduras were present at that meeting to utilize their ability to block consensus. In addition, when representatives attended the next annual meeting, sanctions were lifted without much commotion (ICCAT 1995–2007a: 2001; 2002).

13. Under the current World Trade Organization regime, unilateral sanctions are not acceptable even when they are used as a punitive measure to ensure protection of some commons resource. However, several findings by the WTO's appellate body have established that multilateral sanctions are permitted to enforce binding regulations that have been adopted by a recognized international body (DeSombre and Barkin, 2002; Knox, 2004).

14. The social practice classification was delineated by Young (2002, 30–31).

15. See also Griffin (1992), DeSombre (1999), Joyner and Tyler (2000), and DeSombre and Barkin (2002).

16. See also Iudicello, Weber, and Wieland (1999) for a good discussion of the costs and benefits of different types of management.

17. The seminal example would be March and Simon (1958) or the most recent edition, March and Simon (1993).

Chapter 2

1. This also allows an investigation of the common assumption that decision makers are most strongly influenced by their domestic commercial fishing industries. This general assertion can be found in many economic and political analyses of international fisheries—as opposed to marine mammal or sea turtle issues. See DeSombre (2000) for an in-depth look at the role of domestic interests in the formulation of U.S. fisheries policies. Similar analyses are available for other major fishing countries, but this analysis focuses on the international level and therefore greater simplification is necessary.

2. There are many books and articles that describe these processes within different countries. These include Christy and Scott (1965), Durrenberger and King (2000), and Royce (1987), which provide overviews for a variety of countries; Bergin and Haward (1996), which is a good review of Japanese fisheries governance; Conceição-Heldt (2004) and Lequesne (2004) on EU fisheries management; and Weber (2002) on U.S. governance of marine fisheries.

3. Indeed, satisficing models in the literature on organizations have been referred to as "garbage can" models by their own creators (March and Simon 1993).

4. See Alker (1974) for more on the benefits of these attributes in theoretical approaches to international relations.

5. Keohane and Nye (2001) characterize the level of interdependence in an international system as a mix between the vulnerability (degree of impact) and sensitivity (ability to recover from an impact) of elements within the system to each other.

6. In developed and developing countries alike, individuals engaged in the fisheries sector tend to be isolated socially, geographically, and in terms of marketable skills. McGoodwin (1990), Crean and Symes (1996), and Apostle et al. (1998) cover social aspects of fishing communities and fisheries management. See also Lawson (1984, 158–162). Fishing capital tends to be tied up in industry-specific equipment such as boats and gear that are specifically designed for catching certain types of fish. Alterations to target different stocks or for non-fisheries utilization are usually costly.

7. The authors are more interested in unilateral versus multilateral engagement in this piece, but the logic can be translated into the multilateral context.

8. Creation of a continuous vulnerability space, allowing countries to be placed more specifically in relation to each other, is one possibility. However, because there are so many combinations of factors that affect the independent variables (domestic costs of production and opportunity costs of alternatives), it is necessary to carefully formulate whatever indices are used to determine such placement.

9. See Sahrhage and Lundbeck (1992) for an excellent review of the history of fishing.

10. See subsection 2.5.1 for more on the proxies used to determine competitiveness and flexibility.

11. Servicing by smaller transshipment vessels has allowed some distant-water fleets to stay out for years at a time.

12. The United States does have a distant-water tuna fleet in the western Pacific Ocean, but has never managed the huge, multiocean fleets harbored by Japan, France, and Spain.

13. It is interesting that domestic management can also emerge owing to competition at the local level. For instance, disparate demands on stocks of northern Atlantic groundfishes led to the creation of the first national fisheries management organization in the United States (Weber 2002, 3–4).

14. See Clark (1990) and almost any other basic bioeconomic text for the theoretical links among open-access exploitation, stock levels, and economic competition.

15. The unsustainability of fishery subsidies is well known and can even be found in introductory texts such as Iudicello, Weber, and Wieland (1999) and Tietenberg (2003) as well as advanced bioeconomics books like Clark (1990).

16. There can be conflicts between coastal and distant-water fleets within the same country over policies that affect them differently. This was especially clear during the period in which exclusive economic zones (EEZs) were being established since distant-water fleets feared that coastal enclosure would cut them off from valuable harvests in foreign waters. Similar issues still exist, but they are much less contentious than in the past (Weber 2002, 64–67).

17. It is possible for states to move between the vulnerability categories if there is a change in one of the underlying factors. For instance, a moderately vulnerable state could invest in distant-water technology, moving the state into the mildly vulnerable category. However, for the reasons described earlier, this does not happen often when scarcity rents are already diminished (Lawson 1984, 173).

18. Also, in some organizations like the International Commission for the Conservation of Atlantic Tunas, recent attempts to block consensus have met with a temporary return to voting procedures.

19. Strategically, however, Taiwan is hobbled in some RFMOs by the Chinese refusal to recognize this country's existence and their insistence on excluding Taiwan from full membership in most of the tuna commissions.

20. U.S. fleets in the Atlantic and eastern Pacific are only coastal, so it is highly vulnerable there. Some distant-water boats from the United States also operate in the western Pacific Ocean, making them gradually vulnerable there (Joseph 1983).

21. See Tolba (1998) for a more detailed description of international environmental negotiations and Bemelmans-Videc, Rist, and Vedung (1998) for more on threats, side payments, and other negotiating tactics.

22. Specific expectations will be developed retrospectively in the cases because changes in bioeconomic factors, such as an exogenous price increase or the adoption of a new fishing technology, can change the distribution of competitiveness within a fishery, affecting political response.

23. A simple majority is 50% of the members present, assuming there is a quorum (two-thirds of the contracting parties; ICCAT 1966, art. III para. 3).

24. There is probably an apex in this curve somewhere—a point at which the domestic fleet becomes so small that it no longer can influence policy and so the state would simply exit the commission. However, there are few examples of such dropouts, particularly among the more vulnerable yet historically dominant countries.

25. Panel 3 includes southern bluefin tuna (*Thunnus orientalis*), which is primarily managed by the Commission for the Conservation of Southern Bluefin Tuna. Cases for albacore have not yet been compiled, owing to lack of time and space.

26. Any limit from $12,000 to $17,000 could have been chosen without substantively affecting the analysis.

27. The European Community is a pillar within the European Union structure that has been given the task of negotiating international treaties and regulations on behalf of EU member states. The EC became a member of ICCAT in 1997,

replacing individual EU members such as France, Spain, and Portugal (ICCAT 1995–2007a: 1998, 5).

28. For strategic reasons, membership in the Group of 18 is rather nebulous, but a list of possible members is given in appendix A.

29. The author attended the ICCAT meetings as an official observer from 2001 to 2006. This allowed her to sit in on all sessions of the meetings except for those of the heads of delegation and any informal drafting exercises. The author was also an observer at the 2001 meeting of the Indian Ocean Tuna Commission and the 2003 meeting of the Inter-American Tropical Tuna Commission and various related meetings.

30. Realizing that every person contacted regarding ICCAT had their own perspective and their own objectives, the author took all these communications with a grain of salt. In the case studies, every private communication is corroborated with as much physical evidence as possible and all assertions rely on information obtained from multiple sources.

Part I

1. There are other tropical tuna species in the Atlantic, but these are the only three that have been managed by ICCAT.

2. Actually, the decline in prices for skipjack reflects the overall decline in the value of tunas caught for canning purposes. The per-unit value of yellowfin is higher in aggregate because it includes the sale of longline-caught adult fish for high-end consumption as well as surface-caught small fish sold for canning. The same is true for bigeye, but its much larger value is due to the much higher prices for unprocessed fish.

3. The UN Food and Agriculture Organization provides great descriptions of these fishing technologies. See http://www.fao.org/fi/website/FISearch.do?dom =factsheets and type in one of these terms to get a fact sheet with details and images (FAO, 2007a).

Chapter 3

1. The 1996 estimates of bigeye biomass ranged from 60 to 80% of B_{MSY} and continued at this low level until 2002 when several years of reduced fishing effort facilitated an increase in biomass to 80–90% of B_{MSY} (ICCAT 1995–2007b: 1997, 22–24; 2003, 26–27).

2. Because numerous countries are involved in this fishery, many of which seldom enter a statement regarding their policy positions on the official ICCAT record, the list in figure 3.2 has been condensed to cover only those that frequently express their opinions or make proposals. While selected countries were listed in figure 3.2 for ease of reference, the predictions presented here apply to all countries in each category as per table B.1. Those who would like a full list of all

countries involved in this fishery, which also includes the year of ICCAT membership and dominant gear type for each national fleet, can refer to table B.1 in appendix B. A similar format is used in the rest of the cases.

3. The EC comprises one of the biggest fishing entities in the Atlantic and around the world. Surface fisheries in the Atlantic are dominated by two EC member states, France and Spain. With its fingers in many pies, the EC has multiple sources of linkage with developing and industrialized countries alike. There is also the significant threat of defection posed by such a large fishing entity (Lequesne 2004, 146–147).

4. Taiwan, or Chinese-Taipei as the Chinese insist on calling it, cannot be a member of the United Nations or its subsidiary bodies under current international law and therefore cannot be a member of ICCAT. Special cooperating status was developed for Taiwan, but its power is still extremely limited.

5. Brazil is the most productive country in the moderately vulnerable category, with 6% of longline landings of bigeye tuna in 2002. None of the other developing coastal states come close to that mark. The majority, like Venezuela (0.08%) and Uruguay (0.15%), capture less than 0.2% of the total longline harvests of bigeye (ICCAT 2007d).

6. Japan has taken in almost 100% of all bigeye imports over the recorded history of the fishery. At the peak of the market in 1999, Japanese imports of bigeye were valued at upward of US $950,000 (FAO 2007c). The current analysis focuses solely on commercial fishing interests as determinants of national policy, but it is likely that its interest in maintaining the availability of bigeye for domestic consumption has increased governmental concern somewhat in Japan.

7. As shown in table 3.1, Iceland and Norway are also coastal producers with high costs of production; however, their harvests are opportunistic, made by coastal fleets that target other species most of the time but that will switch to bigeye if any of the species happen to swim that far north. From 1970 on, Norway reported only 60 tons of bigeye harvest in 1988 and Iceland reported only 1 ton in 1999 (ICCAT 2007d).

8. The commercial value of U.S. swordfish landings from the Atlantic and Gulf of Mexico peaked at US $30.8 million in 1988 and quickly dropped to US $20.6 million by 1992. The decline continued until 1998, and the annual gross revenues from U.S. landings of Atlantic swordfish have varied around US $10 million since then (NMFS 2007).

9. The first serious limits on western bluefin tuna were adopted in 1992 (ICCAT 2007a, rec. 91-1). The first limits for North Atlantic swordfish were adopted in 1994 (ICCAT 2007a, res. 94-4).

10. Catch limits on western bluefin and North Atlantic swordfish were specified for Canada as well as the United States. Canada became especially interested in bigeye tuna when the stock shifted northward, making it more accessible to coastal Canadian fleets in the late 1990s (ICCAT 1995–2007a: 2000, 177). Therefore, it is not expected to be vocal as early on as the United States.

11. There is a common norm in international fisheries that the countries with fleets targeting a stock should have proportional influence on its management according to their economic dependence and share of the total catch. References to this norm were often made by both large and small fishing states, as I observed at multiple meetings of regional fisheries organizations.

12. The SCRS estimated that the stock was fully exploited in 1994 and somewhat overexploited in 1996 (ICCAT 1971–1994: 1991, 154; 1995–2007b: 1995, 168; 1997, 23; 2000, 26). There is evidence to suggest that the stock was depleted even more quickly than is reflected in the ICCAT reports, owing to a high level of unreported catch by noncontracting parties and others using flags of convenience.

13. See chapters 4 and 5. They chronicle the adoption of size limits for yellowfin tuna, then the most valuable highly migratory species in the Atlantic, and the subsequent adoption of size limits for bigeye tuna to prevent misreporting of undersized yellowfin.

14. The Gulf of Guinea is a major fishing ground for tropical tunas, including bigeye. It is also the only region in which Ghana's coastal fleets can operate. As will be seen in chapter 5, this plays an important role in the protection of juvenile bigeye.

15. This failure has been noted in almost every annual report of the SCRS since the measure was adopted.

16. Ghana had begun to push against FADs in 1992, but by 1994 its fleets had begun using the technology. China had not yet begun targeting bigeye in the Atlantic, so it was not yet active at ICCAT.

17. Before the EC became a member of ICCAT, individual EC member states represented themselves at the commission. It is interesting that Portugal, with its small fishery targeting bigeye, agreed with Japan on FADs. However, since the consolidation of EC membership, the interests of the two largest fishing countries, France and Spain, have dominated positions taken by the EC.

18. Reported landings were 31,000 tons above the highest estimate of MSY (ICCAT 2007d).

19. The commission did formally move bigeye from panel 4 to panel 1 in recognition of its close interactions with yellowfin and skipjack tunas in tropical waters. Also, panel 4 was getting overworked, with two important species, swordfish and bigeye, while panel 1 was relatively unencumbered since there was little controversy surrounding yellowfin and skipjack. Moving bigeye would redistribute the workload more evenly (ICCAT 1995–2007a: 1997, 48).

20. Since reported landings remained above 100,000 tons in 1996 and effort was up to 150–200% of the optimal level, it was clear that the 1995 resolution had not been effective. Nor was there improvement in the application of the 1979 size limit, since 70% of the total catch was <3.2 kg (ICCAT 1995–2007b: 1996, 22–24). Because the biomass was already below the level that could support MSY, catches of that magnitude would continue to deplete the stock until it was rebuilt.

In order to get the stock back to a size that would support MSY, the commission would have to reduce fishing mortality to a level below the replacement yield (60,000–80,000 tons). On the positive side, revised historical data from Taiwan led to the upward revision of MSY to 70,000–90,000 tons (ICCAT 1995–2007b: 1998, 31). Replacement yield is the amount of fish that can be caught without reducing the biomass of the stock. It is basically equal to the surplus production of the stock. MSY is itself a replacement yield when the biomass is at a level high enough to support such a yield.

21. This reduction requirement was instituted because Taiwan's landings of bigeye had rocketed from 1,000 tons in 1989 to 25,000 tons in 1996. Of course, Taiwan expressed severe reservations regarding the resolution, but could do little more at official levels because it is not a member of ICCAT. Although it has one of the largest fleets in the Atlantic, Taiwan has been unable to join the commission because of objections from China regarding its status as an independent state (ICCAT 1995–2007a: 1998, 151).

22. Cooperating noncontracting parties are hard to define. The term was originally developed to provide a place for Taiwan, but other countries have since tried to fit under this umbrella. The commission itself is still trying to decide how to deal with the issue.

23. A few ancillary measures were taken in 1998 as well. To facilitate the new capacity restrictions, another binding recommendation was adopted that amended the previous year's "white list" to require annual reporting of vessels of more than 24 meters' length that were licensed to target bigeye. The 1998 recommendation went further by also requesting contracting parties and cooperating noncontracting parties to provide the secretariat with any information they might have regarding unlisted vessels observed catching bigeye (ICCAT 2007a, rec. 98-2).

24. The SCRS had been able to revise landings data using Japanese trade statistics to calculate estimates of unreported landings and now recognized that catches had been well above MSY since 1991 rather than 1994 (ICCAT 1995–2007b: 2000, 26).

25. On a positive note, the proportion of undersized fish in the catch had gone down to an average of 55% per year over the period from 1996 to 1998, and Taiwan had complied with its established quota of 16,500 tons.

26. Owing to lags in data reporting, the commission was not yet aware of the exceptionally high catches reported in 1999, nor could the SCRS provide detailed rebuilding plans for the fishery because of a lack of basic biological data. Given that the Bigeye Year Program had finally begun in 1998, with substantially less funding than had originally been requested, some countries felt that ICCAT should wait to see what effect the 1998 vessel limit had on landings and give the SCRS time to collect and analyze data before taking new measures.

27. The working group was put together in response to conflicts that had arisen in the context of two other ICCAT stocks—bluefin tuna and Southern Atlantic swordfish. Landings of both species were already limited by quota systems, and it was the criteria for setting each state's allotment of the total allowable catch

that had caused friction among contracting parties. Members that had historically high catch levels, such as the United States, Japan, and the EC, believed that quota allocations should be based on past catch levels. On the other hand, countries that were still trying to develop fisheries for highly migratory species, like Brazil, Venezuela, and South Africa, believed that other criteria should be considered. They wanted recognition for coastal states' rights of access as well as economic and nutritional dependence on a given stock, and were willing to block management measures until their concerns were addressed.

28. Recommendation 00-1 established effort limits for only a single year, but similar recommendations have been adopted every year since.

29. The 2004 assessment also showed that fishing mortality was at 73–101% of the level that would produce maximum sustainable yield.

30. In fact, a combination of increased competition and economic troubles at home led to the almost complete cessation of South Korean longlining for bigeye in the Atlantic by 1991 (ICCAT 1971–1994: 1993, 141).

31. Fleets in the NEI categories are not represented at the commission, and therefore have no direct impact on management. However, as long as these countries contribute to the level of competition in a fishery, they speed up vulnerability response. Furthermore, excluding NEI fleets carries little to no negotiation costs because they have no power at the commission.

32. Coined in the late 1990s, the commission generally uses the term IUU to refer to any fishing activity that takes place in contravention of ICCAT recommendations, or that is misreported to the secretariat.

33. The states sanctioned were Belize, Cambodia, Honduras, and St. Vincent and the Grenadines.

34. For instance, China officially objected to the recommendation in 2000 that limited its landings of bigeye to 4,000 tons, setting its own autonomous quota at 7,300 tons for 2001 (ICCAT 1995–2007a: 2002, 323–325).

35. Sanctions were lifted from Honduras in 2002, the year after that country joined the commission (ICCAT 2007a, rec. 02-18). For all other countries, membership was denied until after sanctions were lifted.

36. Currently, members are protected from enforcement mechanisms by their ability to block consensus or formally object to management measures. It is unlikely that these aspects of the contractual environment will change any time soon.

37. An economic recession in Japan contributed to falling prices for bigeye around the turn of the millennium. This served to increase competitiveness in the fishery (FAO 2007c).

Chapter 4

1. ICCAT (1995–2007b: 2007, 14–15) provides the most recent description of the changes in the Atlantic yellowfin fisheries. Similar information can be found in all previous reports of the SCRS.

2. The calculation of optimum size at first capture is based on a model in which only fish above a certain size are removed from the stock. The idea is to optimize the reproductive capacity of younger fish by leaving them in the water long enough to at least replace themselves. The optimum varies among stocks, depending on the recruitment rate, age at recruitment, age at first reproduction, and other factors.

3. At the same time, Canada began expressing concern regarding bluefin tuna, which was important to some of their coastal communities. It may be that it was using yellowfin as leverage or trying to set an example that could be followed for bluefin (see chapter 8).

4. A plenary session is a meeting of the entire commission in which the measures adopted in the various panels are approved (or not).

5. The 3.2-kg lower boundary was based on size limits already in place in some West African countries, including Ghana and the Ivory Coast. Fish as small as 1 kg were being taken in fisheries for both species.

6. If all mortality of small fish is avoided, then those fish survive to reproduce and may be caught when they have grown to a larger size, so that actual production increases. However, if those fish are simply discarded dead (and most don't survive capture), then they do not reproduce nor are they utilized in any other way, compounding the loss in utility.

7. Most yellowfin were captured in the eastern Atlantic when ICCAT was formed, but the rapid growth of South American fleets and improvements in the range of vessels increased the area of exploitation.

8. This was down from an estimate of 80% the year before (ICCAT 1971–1994: 1993, 138).

9. In 1995 the commission did pass a nonbinding resolution stating that in 1996 members would put together more specific management measures to implement the 1993 recommendation, but nothing ever came of it (ICCAT 2007a, res. 95-6).

10. The SCRS suggested further limits partly because new technologies were increasing catches of small fish. Also, if effective effort had indeed increased, then any growth in the stock biomass would result in higher catches, much as was observed in 2002, when reported landings exceeded the 1992 catch by about 5,000 tons. That's not much in percentage terms, but the SCRS did point out that continued catches of that magnitude would cause the biomass of yellowfin to decline further below that which would support MSY.

11. In addition, it was difficult to determine whether catches were below the 1992 landings mark because effort had declined or because the catch per unit effort was down, making it difficult to judge the overall change in effort.

Chapter 5

1. Most of the earlier increase was in captures by purse seines using FADs. From 1991 to 1998, 70% of all skipjack was caught with FADs (ICCAT 1995–2007b: 2000, 33).

2. Until 2001, the SCRS evaluated skipjack based on a two-stock assumption, with one stock in the east and one in the west. Since then, the stock structure of skipjack has been called into question because of conflicting data from FAD fisheries (ICCAT 1995–2007b: 2002, 35). However, in their few discussions, the commission treats skipjack as a single management unit and therefore it is treated as a single stock in the case.

3. A more comprehensive list of the countries in each vulnerability category is provided in table B.4 in appendix B. These predictions apply to all countries, including those that were omitted from figure 5.4 to make it more accessible.

4. If a country had very low catches using one type of gear and large catches using another type of gear, then the latter was assumed to be the dominant source of political response. Countries in italics had high reported landings from both surface and longline gears.

5. A more comprehensive list of countries in each category can be found in table B.5 in appendix B. These predictions apply to all countries, including those that were omitted from figure 5.5 to make it more accessible.

6. South Korea had seven baitboats working in the Gulf of Guinea in the late 1970s. Interestingly, Panama also had four. All were based out of Tema, like the sixteen Japanese baitboats that were operating in the gulf at the time (ICCAT 1971–1994: 1978, 256). Korean vessels were up somewhat from the early 1970s, but Japanese boats were down from twenty-three in 1973–74 (ICCAT 1971–1994: 1976, 180).

7. Many ICCAT delegates informed me that South Korea tends to defer to Japan at commission meetings, an assertion that is generally confirmed by the record.

8. In retrospect, the global trend in harvests of tropical tunas by French and Spanish fleets looks relatively flat through the 1970s (FAO 2007b).

9. At least two such moves are recorded for EC fleets. Fleet growth continued over these periods as well, so that more vessels were left behind after each movement, and crowding occurred in all three oceans.

10. In 1997, the EC replaced its component members at the commission. As will be seen, the community did not veer far from the interests of its two biggest tuna fishing states, France and Spain.

11. ICCAT (2007a, rec. 98-1) placed a moratorium on the use of FADs in the Gulf of Guinea from November 1, 1999 through January 31, 2000.

12. The Ghanaians started using FADs in 1999 (ICCAT 1995–2007a: 2000, 167).

13. Harvests in the not elsewhere included category decreased somewhat after the implementation of the time-area closure, but landings by the flag-of-convenience country, Panama, virtually disappeared (ICCAT 2007d).

14. By adopting FAD technology, Ghana and several other small African states had significantly increased their catches of tropical tunas in their coastal waters.

15. For instance, if the nursery area singled out for a closure were located in the western Atlantic, the EC would have faced much stronger opposition from

members of the Group of 18. Alternatively, for many stocks, nursery areas have not yet been identified, so a closure would not be a viable option.

16. See Sahrahage and Lundbeck (1992, 192) and Joseph (1983, 131–133) regarding these impacts on distant-water fleets. Also see Juda (1996) or Schrijver (1997, chap. 7) for the broader history of the development of exclusive economic zones and current international law covering the oceans.

17. Axelrod (1997), Lempert, Popper, and Bankes (2003), and Miller and Page (2007) provide accessible descriptions of this type of modeling.

18. Readers who would like to see this for themselves can compare tables B.4 and B.5 in appendix B (lists of countries in each category for each period) with the overview of evidence in table C.3, appendix C.

19. By 1984, the SCRS could report that undersized fish of both species were still being caught in large numbers, which was far above the stipulated 15% tolerance level, but data had also improved and misreporting was less of a problem (ICCAT 1971–1994: 1985, 122).

Part II

1. There is some disagreement among marine biologists regarding the placement of swordfish. Some put it in the billfish category but others contend that it is too distinct. I decided to go with the former because ICCAT refers to swordfish and marlins together as "billfish," both in management and in science.

2. The sale of swordfish was banned in these countries in the 1970s owing to concern about high levels of mercury in the fish.

3. There are two other billfishes in the Atlantic: sailfish (*Istiophorus albicans*) and spearfish (*Tetrapturus pfluegeri*). Unfortunately, there has not been enough scientific evidence to provide a foundation for management recommendations on the species and therefore they have not been included in this set of cases.

4. Individual values for the different species of marlin were unavailable. Therefore the data presented here cover all marlins, including black marlin and striped marlin, which are not found in the Atlantic. Unfortunately, Atlantic-only values were not available either. The international value is probably higher than that for the Atlantic alone because, except for artisanal sources, marlin is not consumed much in Atlantic coastal countries and is too cheap to be transported to those places where it is in demand.

5. Executive summaries of stock assessments (ICCAT 1971–1994, 1995–2007b) provide information on technical aspects of the fisheries.

6. Some Indo-Pacific marlins are commercially targeted, largely for sale in Taiwan and other parts of east Asia.

7. Scientists could not calculate biological parameters for Mediterranean swordfish because there are not yet enough data available. Nevertheless, the SCRS did suggest that the catch levels (14,000–15,000 tons) for South Atlantic and Mediterranean swordfish should be maintained until better information emerges.

Chapter 6

1. That is, southern Atlantic and Mediterranean swordfish. See figure II.2.

2. Estimates ranged from 41 to 100%.

3. Estimates ranged from 87 to 127%.

4. For administrative purposes, Atlantic swordfish are divided into two stocks at the 5° north latitude line. However, since this is a temperate stock, the largest concentration of fish is found much farther north (ICCAT 1971–1994: 1989, 131).

5. Spain has harvested the lion's share of EC landings of northern Atlantic swordfish (80–100%) over the entire data set for the stock. Portugal captured most of the remainder, but its fleets are coastal and were technologically unable to move south with Spanish longliners in the early 1990s (ICCAT 2007d). Labor costs are high for large-scale European vessels that bring in most of the swordfish harvest because they pay their workers minimum wage, which is not high relative to U.S. wages but is considerably higher than wages paid in many other fleets (Lequesne 2004, 6).

6. Spanish swordfish landings declined from 1995 to 2001, then increased again as their fleets expanded into the Indian and Pacific Oceans. However, the volume of landings from those oceans is quite small compared with the Atlantic, and the expansion did not raise harvests much above the 1995 peak. Even so, it may be that the EC was not low-flex until 2002, when their total harvests leveled off again (FAO 2007b).

7. Portugal is the second-largest EC producer of northern Atlantic swordfish (0–20%) but Spain still dominates production, not just in the northern Atlantic, but in many other areas as well (ICCAT 2007d; FAO 2007b). Also, the Portuguese acquired distant-water capacity about 1995, which allowed their longline fleet to start targeting southern swordfish (ICCAT 1971–1994: 1994, 375; 2007d).

8. Until 2000, northern Atlantic swordfish were equal to roughly 6% of the Japanese landings of bigeye in the area. These landings dried up when the Japanese banned retention of swordfish by fleets in the Atlantic. More on this can be found in section 6.3.

9. Countries like Venezuela, Mexico, and Brazil seldom catch more than 100 tons of northern Atlantic swordfish a year. In fact, annual landings of the stock are often closer to 30 or 40 tons for these countries. Of the developing countries known to harvest northern swordfish on the western side, only Trinidad and Tobago consistently topped 100 tons until recent actions by ICCAT forced a reduction. On the eastern side, Morocco is the only major developing country, with landings that can fluctuate between 100 and more than 500 tons per year (ICCAT 2007d).

10. The nomenclature is somewhat misleading. Although the Group of 18 did originally have 18 members, that number has increased with the recent influx of developing countries joining the commission. Because this is an informal group,

no official list of members in the group is available. See appendix A for more information.

11. See figure II.2. Estimates of fishing mortality remained around twice the MSY level until the adoption of regulations in the late 1990s. This suggests that fishing effort was actually increasing since mortality remained stable while biomass was declining. Although it is counterintuitive to most economists, this pattern of increasing effort with decreasing prices is common for open-access fisheries (Clark, 1990).

12. In 1987, a peak production year for northern Atlantic swordfish, Spain caught 53%, the United States caught 28%, and Japan and Canada combined caught only 9% of reported landings (ICCAT 1971–1994: 1988, 139).

13. Countries without a quota or by-catch tolerance were instructed to limit their catches to 1993 levels.

14. The commission requested estimates of the total allowable catches that would provide a 50% chance of rebuilding the biomass to MSY level in 5-, 10-, and 15-year periods.

15. During the 1995 meeting of panel 4, a few countries, notably South Korea and Brazil, complained about the lack of room in the sharing arrangement for small developing countries to build domestic capacity. They requested that the share allotted for the others category be increased to 10% but were denied because the agreement among the five major fishing states was so tenuous that reopening discussions might have destroyed the recommendation altogether.

16. Technically, ICCAT had already adopted four enforcement measures on swordfish with the 1995 Swordfish Action Plan. However, the trade-restrictive measures set up in the plan were not used until 1999. Furthermore, monitoring was problematic until the adoption of the statistical document program for swordfish in 2001.

17. Quotas for the contracting parties were established as per the 1995 sharing arrangement outlined in table 6.2.

18. Future allocations to Bermuda would be decided at the next annual meeting.

19. The sharing arrangement was maintained as per the 1995 recommendation except that the shares for Spain and Portugal were combined with a small portion of the others category to give the newly joined European Community a 49.85% allotment. The "others" share was reduced to an allocation of only 4.9%. Ireland and a few other EC member states had been harvesting swordfish under the "others" quota. During its first 3 years, the 10-year rebuilding plan that was adopted in 1999 was only modified once, in 2001, to correct a technical error in the quota designation for Trinidad and Tobago. (ICCAT 2007a, res. 01-3).

20. Landings data are usually not known until the year after fish are harvested. If Japan had known about the increase in its landings of northern swordfish in 1996, it might not have agreed to the recommendation so readily.

21. The charge of hypocrisy has regularly been used as a defense tactic by countries that are under pressure to conform to ICCAT regulations that they deem to be unfair. Taiwan and China often lobbed such accusations at Japan when they were pressed to curb their fishing effort in the Atlantic.

22. The amount of the transfer was not specified.

23. The regulation was designed to prevent fishers from killing swordfish brought to their boats alive. After the ban on all landings of swordfish, Japanese fishers no longer had any incentive to keep live swordfish to sell along with the bigeye they targeted. Dead discards were still counted against the Japanese quota, but because live fish were released, Japan was able to cut its landings in half. Because many fish are not alive when the lines are hauled in, dead discards of northern Atlantic swordfish more than doubled in a singled year, but live discards ensured that Japanese landings from the stock were reduced to zero.

24. Landings for Japan were 161 tons in 2000; the discard regulation was not quite fully effective in its first year. The total Japanese catch (landings plus dead discards) was 741 tons that year (ICCAT 1995–2007b: 2004, 96–97, SWO-table 1).

25. The dead discards allowance was reinstated, but at the low level of 100 tons and only for 2003. Any discards above the allotment would be counted against the contracting parties' catch quotas.

26. As part of this program, Japan also agreed to place observers on its vessels and to participate in a scientific study of the stock structure and mixing of Atlantic swordfish.

27. Large historical fishers preferred individual quotas for the others category because small fishing countries would be more accountable for their overages.

28. See chapter 7 and appendix A for more on the Group of 18.

29. Table C.4 in appendix C provides a summary of the case, with countries grouped by the policy positions they expressed.

Chapter 7

1. Shifts to the Pacific and Indian Oceans did reinvigorate EC landings of swordfish from 2000 on, but they never matched the volume of production in the Atlantic (FAO 2007b).

2. Although it should be noted that the observer from Uruguay had mentioned their concerns regarding the southern stock the year before.

3. The range of estimates for biomass is 82–118%. The range of estimates for fishing mortality is 94–193% (ICCAT 1995–2007b: 1997, 66).

4. The Canadian proposal also included a precautionary reduction in the TAC for northern swordfish (ICCAT 1995–2007a: 1997, 138).

5. This regulation was not very effective (ICCAT 1995–2007b: 1999, 94).

6. Since it does not harvest southern swordfish, Canada was not at the intersessional meeting. In fact, the only countries represented at this meeting were Brazil, Spain, the United States, Japan, Portugal, the United Kingdom, Uruguay, Venezuela, and Argentina (observer; ICCAT 1995–2007a: 1998, 190–192).

7. The allocation criteria were finally adopted in 2001 (ICCAT 2007a, oth. 01-25).

8. Specifically, the SCRS shifted from a hard recommendation of 13,000 tons to a nebulous suggestion of a TAC that was less than replacement yield, which was estimated at around 14,600 tons for 1996. The reasons for this shift are not completely clear. The 1997 SCRS report does not provide any explanation, nor was this directly questioned by any of the commission participants (ICCAT 1995–2007b: 1997, 68; 1998, 93).

9. Their shares came out of the quota set aside for noncontracting parties (NCP).

10. The South African proposal was aimed at curbing the substantial increases in harvests of southern swordfish by the Taiwanese fleet targeting bigeye tuna. As figure 7.2 shows, the Taiwanese catch went up almost fivefold from 1990 to 1994 and remained around that level until 1998. South Africa was also concerned about Chinese harvests of southern swordfish, which had just begun in 1997. Although it was much smaller than Taiwan's, the Chinese fleet had considerable potential to increase its production. See chapter 3 on bigeye tuna.

11. Essentially, by-catch of southern swordfish had declined while effort had not. Normally this would indicate a reduction in the size of the stock, but because fleets targeting bigeye tuna had taken measures to avoid incidental landings of swordfish, this interpretation might be incorrect. Since the trends in catch per unit effort for fleets targeting swordfish directly had been optimistic in 1999, the SCRS had chosen to assume that the true abundance should be estimated using a combination of these two data sets (ICCAT 1995–2007b: 2000, 87).

12. Japanese landings of southern swordfish were less than 300 tons in 2005 (ICCAT 2007d).

13. In 2003 there was some discussion of quota transfer protocol. As part of a larger move to obtain compliance from Taiwan, Japan expressed its intent to transfer about 100 tons of its southern swordfish quota to that country. Other contracting parties insisted that such transfers needed to be approved by the entire commission. Also in 2003, Uruguay, which had not been present for the division of quota in 2002, requested a larger allotment, but was denied. There were no discussions on southern swordfish in 2004 or 2005 (ICCAT 1995–2007a: 2004, 26, 212–213; 2005, 175; 2006, 200).

Chapter 8

1. Biomass estimates ranged from 25 to 60% of B_{MSY}. Fishing mortality was at between 250 and 600% of the level acceptable for management at MSY.

2. Biomass estimates ranged from 6 to 25% of B_{MSY}. Fishing mortality was at between 450 and 1,580% of the level acceptable for management at MSY.

3. U.S. recreational landings of Atlantic marlins peaked in the late 1970s at around 400 tons. Since then, they have declined to less than 50 tons per year. This seems to be due to the growing practice of catch and release, a reduction in availability as stocks decline, and domestic U.S. regulations protecting marlins. Minor recreational landings of Atlantic marlins have also been reported by Brazil, Canada, Portugal, Gabon, Senegal, Trinidad and Tobago, the UK Overseas Territories (Bermuda), Venezuela, and St. Lucia (ICCAT 2007d; see section 8.2).

4. The main obstacle to scientifically assessing by-catch as opposed to commercially targeted stocks is the ability of fishers to discard landings of by-catch at sea with little opportunity forgone, as opposed to commercial stocks, which could not be discarded without a large loss of revenue. Thus, unless effective monitoring is undertaken at sea, fishers can easily misreport incidental catches.

5. Cuba was a member of the commission from 1975 to 1991. Before it could be approved, the ERBP proposal was sent to ICCAT's Standing Committee on Finance and Administration to determine the amount of funds that could be allocated to the program. Although members of the commission did sometimes express concern about the costs of research programs on other species, including skipjack and bigeye tuna, their objections were never as vociferous as on the ERBP.

6. Recreational fishers had been involved in the U.S. policy-making process for many years and had also engaged in scientific tag-and-release efforts since the mid-1970s (ICCAT 1971–1994: 1978, 147).

7. In contrast, swordfish biomass had never fallen below 58% of B_{MSY} and bigeye biomass was not allowed to fall below 60% of B_{MSY}.

8. A cynical observer of the 1997 meeting might notice that a few other U.S. proposals, including a 20% reduction of bigeye catches and a compliance recommendation on catches of small fish, had been laid aside with little complaint from their originator. Since the United States doesn't catch much bigeye tuna and has been quite successful at minimizing its landings of small fish in accordance with ICCAT regulations, these proposals seem designed to affect members like Japan and the EC. However, because such negotiations are carried on behind closed doors, one can only speculate about the tradeoffs that were made to reach consensus on the billfish proposition.

9. As part of a larger marine conservation movement, the Sustainable Fisheries Act of 1996 requires that all fish stocks, commercial or otherwise, be managed at an optimal yield that is less than or equal to maximum sustainable yield. Implementation of this act included requiring commercial longliners to discard all marlins, dead or alive, and the creation of several time-area closures within the U.S. EEZ in 2001 (ICCAT 1995–2007b: 2004, 75). In addition, the Endangered Species Act of 1990 caused U.S. fishers to be more responsive to SCRS reports on the level of biological depletion of marlins because listing of either stock as an

endangered species could result in a complete closure of the U.S. longline fishery in the Atlantic. White marlin was especially important in this regard because it does not exist in any other ocean (ICCAT 1995–2007a: 2001, 219; Webster 2006).

10. Bigger fishing operations give states more power in terms of the ability to defect as well as national legitimacy under the norm of conservation for use that places socioeconomic concerns above all other reasons for regulation. It is evident throughout the recorded history of ICCAT negotiations that socioeconomic arguments are used for validation by all states, no matter what their position on management measures. In this instance, the United States frequently pointed out the economic importance of its domestic recreational fisheries when pleading for protection of marlins. Other members like Japan and the EC countered that their commercial fishing interests would be too severely damaged by the marlin regulations proposed by the United States. As of yet, commercial considerations override recreational interests from the perspective of most ICCAT members.

11. Such a listing would eliminate all trade in white marlins and could also have domestic repercussions, even in countries with low susceptibility to environmental interests, owing to the high levels of publicity associated with the endangered species label.

12. The 2000 marlins rebuilding plan has been revised twice in the past 3 years. First, in 2001, at the instigation of Japan, the reference point for reduction of landings was changed to account for compliance, or lack thereof, with the 1997 recommendation to reduce catches of both species by 25% by 1999. As Japan pointed out, some countries had complied with the 1997 regulation, reducing their catches in 1999, while others had not. To make things more equitable, the rebuilding plan was modified so that countries could choose to reduce their landings of blue marlin and white marlin relative to either 1999 or 1996 landings, whichever was higher. Owing to an overload of work for the SCRS, the blue marlin assessment was postponed until 2003, and the terms of the rebuilding plan were extended for that species (ICCAT 2007a, res. 01-10). Similarly, in 2002, the landings and size limits in the rebuilding plan were extended for both species for three more years and assessments were also postponed until 2005 (ICCAT 2007a, rec. 02-13).

13. Based on the stated affiliations of delegation members in the list of participants for each annual meeting of the commission. See also ICCAT (1995–2007b: 1996, 46).

14. This is the compliance measure that gave Japan such difficulties when it was unable to control its by-catch of northern swordfish in the late 1990s. A few other contracting parties were having some trouble with overharvests as well, so in 1999, the compliance recommendation was amended to provide 2 years in which to remedy any overage. The amendment also permitted contracting parties to roll over any underharvests of northern swordfish, applying any unused quota to catch limits over the next 2 years. This gave contracting parties a little more leeway to adjust their effort levels to highly variable economic and environmental

conditions (ICCAT 2007a, res. 99-13). The recommendation was extended in 2001, as per ICCAT (2007a, rec. 01-13).

15. The import ban on swordfish from Honduras was lifted in 2001 when that country chose to join the commission (ICCAT 2007a, rec. 01-15). Trade-restrictive measures against Belize have also ended pursuant to a 2002 recommendation that stipulated that the import ban would be lifted in 2004 pending a 2003 review of measures taken to comply with ICCAT regulations (ICCAT 2007a, rec. 02-16).

16. Of course, a different method would need to be found to deter countries that do not engage in discarding but consistently report excessive landings of under-sized fish. Theoretically, catches of small fish could be counted in some ratio against a national quota, making them more expensive in terms of the allowed catch.

17. Lower-value fish are simply discarded to make room if the haul of the tar-geted stock is ample.

18. This can be seen clearly by comparing the "positions expressed" and "actions taken" sections of the overview provided in appendix C, table C.6.

19. As before, representation is measured by the stated affiliations of delegates as recorded in the list of participants for each annual meeting of the commission.

20. The United States did implement some strategic time-area closures to protect marlins in its own EEZ in 2001 (ICCAT 1995–2007b: 2003, 75).

21. The dolphin-tuna controversy that disrupted the Inter-American Tropical Tuna Commission for more than a decade springs to mind as an example. See DeSombre (1999).

Part III

1. The UN Food and Agriculture Organization provides great descriptions of these fishing technologies. Go to http://www.fao.org/fi/website/FISearch.do?dom =factsheets and type in one of these terms to get a fact sheet with details and images (FAO, 2007a).

Chapter 9

1. Atlantic bluefin is one of the longest-lived of the tuna species and its stock structure is still not well understood. However, because these fish take so long to reach sexual maturity, the SCRS uses spawning stock biomass rather than overall biomass as a better benchmark for MSY. Also, this estimate is contingent on the assumption that historical recruitment (survival of juvenile fish) has been similar to that of recent years (ICCAT 1995–2007b: 2007, 53).

2. The sudden decline in Japanese harvests in the late 1960s is attributed to a de-crease in fishing effort and catch, dispersion of the fleet to higher latitudes, and a

change in the target species (ICCAT 1971–1994: 1971, 93). This probably refers to the decline of bluefin by-catch in the tropical Atlantic and the expansion of the fishery targeting adults in the temperate northern zone that was facilitated by the installation of freezers in fishing vessels in the 1960s.

3. The United States and Canada were the first contracting parties to express concern about bluefin tuna in 1973 (ICCAT 1971–1994: 1974, 39, 57, 61–62).

4. They also noted that fewer catches of small fish did not indicate lower mortality because small fish can be discarded without reporting.

5. Canada was actually one of the first countries to develop bluefin farming techniques in the 1970s, but its operations closed down in the 1980s owing to a lack of fish (Oceanic Development et al. 2005, 32).

6. My thanks to John Mark Dean and Michael Orbach for pointing this out to me.

7. In 1975, Canada proposed more stringent measures but instead the size limit was extended indefinitely and the limit on fishing effort was extended for another 2 years. Again, Morocco requested lenience for its incidental harvest (ICCAT 1971–1994: 1976, 66, 71–72). In 1977, the United States and Canada again pushed for stronger measures, but no changes were made (ICCAT 1971–1994: 1978, 63–65, 72).

8. The size limit was only proposed in 1978.

9. A year later the SCRS approved an increase in the minimum size limit, but only after it was suggested by the United States and Canada (ICCAT 1971–1994: 1980, 133).

10. The ineffectiveness of size limits was discussed in chapters 4 and 5. The 1974 freeze on fishing mortality also made little difference to by-catch fleets as long as they were not required to report dead discards (which was the practice at the time).

11. See chapter 10 for the vulnerability matrix on eastern bluefin.

12. The United States and Canada did make references to the more pessimistic biological findings of their national scientists when justifying their positions.

13. Brazil also expressed some reservations regarding the measures because they might limit the country's future ability to exploit bluefin. However, because of the geographic exclusion described earlier, this statement is probably a reflection of Brazil's broader concern about access for developing coastal countries.

14. ICCAT (2007d). In spite of these cuts, total landings missed the 800-ton mark set in 1981 by more than 600 tons.

15. While their main aim is recreation, sportfishers may sell their catches.

16. It is interesting that in the 1982 discussions, delegates from the major western bluefin countries got a bit sloppy in their use of the term, leaving out the "scientific" qualifier. Both France and Spain made a point of correcting them, stating that the idea of regular quotas for such a heavily depleted stock was antithetical to the spirit of the commission (ICCAT 1971–1994: 1983, 78–79).

17. Cuba was granted an exception in 1983 (ICCAT 1971–1994: 1984, 85–86).

18. The SCRS has yet to be able to estimate B_{MSY} for western bluefin, largely because there are insufficient data. Disagreements among scientists—particularly those from the United States and Canada on the one hand and Japan on the other—also contributed to the growth of uncertainty in the 1980s.

19. At half the current harvest, the 1994 stock of large bluefin had a 74% chance of being below the 1992 levels. The odds were split in 1995, with a 47% chance of the stock increasing above the 1992 level and a 27% chance that it would still be lower, depending on the recruitment of the 1987 year class (ICCAT 1971–1994: 1992, 121–122).

20. This has not yet happened. Sanctions have only been applied to members when they failed to send a delegation to the annual meeting.

21. It was estimated that a TAC of 3,000 tons would give the western stock a 75% chance of rebuilding to B_{MSY} by 2018. The pessimistic model showed that a 3,000-ton TAC would have only a 36% chance of rebuilding to MSY levels and that the analogous figure for the current TAC of 2,500 tons was only 47% (ICCAT 1995–2007b: 2001, 50–53).

22. Prior to 1981, the SCRS frequently claimed that it did not have enough information to fully assess western bluefin.

23. The leverage of a possible CITES listing could not be maintained in subsequent years. No country could be convinced to propose listing of bluefin tuna after 2001 because of heavy pressure from fishing countries.

24. The TAC adopted in 1998 was 500 tons above the level recommended by the SCRS. This was at the behest of Japan, which cited more optimistic science as a rationale for the decision (ICCAT 1995–2007a: 1999, 143–144).

25. As an economist would say, the growth rate of the stock is lower than the social discount rate, so that even a perfectly rational decision maker would chose to allow the stock to be fished out. On the other hand, these countries have made attempts to slow down depletion, which seems to negate that hypothesis.

Chapter 10

1. The commission prohibited the landing or sale of western bluefin of less than 30 kg in 1998 (ICCAT 2007a, rec. 98-7).

2. This finding is contested. It is possible that the exceptionally large increase in landings in the early 1990s was due to overreporting in expectation of management measures. Because allocation is usually based on historical catch levels, countries have incentives to overreport before the adoption of regulations so as to increase their share in multilateral quota arrangements. Lower reported landings in the late 1990s may be attributed to underreporting after management measures were put into place. The overall increase could be an average over these two periods (personal commication from Peter Miyake, Federation of Japan Tuna Fisheries Co-operative Associations, April 12, 2007).

3. Norway did have a commercial fishery for bluefin until the fish disappeared from their waters in the early 1960s. The reasons for this disappearance are not clear, but may be associated with increases in fishing mortality to the south (ICCAT 2007d).

4. These estimates were based on assumptions regarding the availability of small fish and were therefore highly uncertain.

5. The 85% estimate for the Mediterranean was based on research data rather than data on reported landings.

6. Ironically, interpreted as a limit on landings with 1974 as the year of reference, "recent levels" would require a total catch reduction of about 5,000 tons and would give the lion's share of the residual to Italy as opposed to either France or Spain. Earlier reference years would have resulted in even lower catch levels (see figure 10.2). Of course, it can always be argued that these countries had held their effort down and that increases in national landings were due to greater abundance of the resource. This is a common loophole in effort-based management where monitoring of actual effort is incomplete.

7. Catch limits for the central Atlantic were renewed for one more year. Spain again insisted that the measure was only temporary and that its fleets might demand access in the future (ICCAT 1995–2007a: 1995, 60).

8. Figure 10.1 contains revised data and therefore does not match the information available at the time (ICCAT 1995–2007b: 1995, 157; 1996, 37). It is possible that this jump reflects overreporting rather than actual catches. Because the reference year for the reduction mandated by recommendation 94-11 was the higher of 1993 or 1994 landings, overreporting in 1994 would provide leeway to maintain or even increase harvests while seeming to comply with the regulation (ICCAT 2007a; Peter Miyake was kind enough to point this possibility out to me in a personal communication on April 12, 2007). That said, current estimates of fishing capacity suggest that actual landings have risen to the levels reported in 1994.

9. After several statements on this in Panel 2, which has jurisdiction over Atlantic bluefin, discussions were moved over to the Permanent Working Group for the Improvement of ICCAT Statistics and Conservation Measures (PWG), which is in charge of compliance by noncontracting parties.

10. Because there is no record of the initial EC proposal, it is impossible to document any changes in quota allocations to placate Morocco or Libya. In other circumstances when such side payments have been made, there is usually some record of gratitude in the discussion, even if the original proposal is not available. Since no such entries are found here, it is likely that the cooperation of these countries was obtained through unofficial channels.

11. The discrepancy in percentage reduction is actually worse for most other reference periods.

12. A copy of the original draft proposal is available on request.

13. Copies of notes are available on request.

14. Copies of notes are available on request.

15. Copies of the EC proposal are available upon request.

Chapter 11

1. Chapter 2 describes those literatures that were utilized when formulating the secondary assumptions.

2. Technically, the EC fit into the highly vulnerable niche for eastern bluefin, although their fleets were more flexible than most others in that category.

3. See Webster (2006) for more specifics on the U.S. politics surrounding Atlantic marlins.

4. Scientists and members of ICCAT were already concerned about these species at the outset of the commission.

5. In the skipjack tuna and eastern bluefin tuna cases, actions were taken during the period of concern largely because of mixing with other stocks.

6. The vast majority of all bigeye imports are received by Japan and in recent years about two-thirds of bigeye production entered the international market-place annually (FAO 2007c).

7. Pulse fishing occurs when a fleet overfishes one stock and then moves on to another while allowing the first stock to rebuild. This can lead to a cyclical pattern of overfishing and rebuilding between two or more stocks of fish (see Berkes et al. 2006 for a recent discussion of this problem). The term I have coined here, *pulse management*, refers to a situation in which regional fisheries organizations allow the temporary overexploitation of one stock in order to cushion the effects of cutbacks required to rebuild another stock. This strategy may not be obvious or even intentional on the part of the entire organization, but it can result when one or more powerful members have coordinated policy processes that transcend geographic and species boundaries. For instance, the EC began backtracking on management of eastern bluefin tuna and other stocks in the northern Atlantic the same year that groundfish fisheries in the region were closed because of heavy overexploitation. Considering that the same people, in fact the same man, developed the EC policy for both types of species, it is not inconceivable that the intention was to mitigate some of the negative repercussions of the groundfish closure by redirecting fishing effort toward highly migratory species.

8. An exception would be the 1977 Skipjack Year Program, but this was aimed at increasing skipjack production rather than managing the fishery (ICCAT 1971–1994: 1978, 44, 151–152).

9. Tversky and Kahneman (1991) present a cognitive model of risk assessment that is reference dependent with loss aversion and diminishing sensitivity. Peter Haas (1994, 42) discusses such cognitive learning among policy makers in international cooperative environmental management. See also Ernst Haas (1990).

10. Although the United States still had a quota for western Atlantic bluefin, it was allotted to the small fleet of purse seines, rather than longlines. A similar

learning situation occurred when Japan staunchly pursued trade measures on bigeye tuna because of what it had learned from its experience trying to control IUU fishing of bluefin tuna. South Africa also displayed learning in its attempts to obtain sharing arrangements on southern albacore and southern swordfish to prevent overexploitation of those stocks.

11. For one thing, loss aversion plays out differently for most developing fishing states since they are more concerned with the ability to increase their fishing activities rather than to maintain a certain level of exploitation. There are also availability issues, in that domestic decision makers that have not experienced recession in the fisheries sector may not believe that similar problems will occur in their country, even when they have heard accounts from elsewhere. See Kahneman et al. (1982) on decision heuristics. It will be interesting to see whether more widespread experience of recession in the fisheries sector linked to biological depletion might lead to information cascades that could alter current perceptions of risk. See Kuran and Sunstein (1999).

12. For instance, the Group of 18 has become much more adept at manipulating its numerical advantage to obtain concessions from more vulnerable countries by learning from previous experience. This is partially illustrated in the comparison between management of northern swordfish and bigeye tuna.

13. See Ernst Haas (1990, 41) for a definition of epistemic communities in the context of organizational learning; especially important is the common acceptance of the legitimacy of a proposed solution to whatever problem is at hand.

14. Young (1999, 2002) adroitly addresses this general problem.

15. See Lempert, Popper, and Bankes (2003).

16. See Joseph (1983) for a good overview of the development of global tuna fisheries.

17. Membership lists for each organization are readily accessible through their official web sites, which can in turn be accessed at http://www.tuna-org.org/.

References

The following abbreviations are used in text references:

FAO   Food and Agricultural Organization of the United Nations
IATTC   Inter-American Tropical Tuna Commission
ICCAT International Commission for the Conservation of Atlantic Tunas
IOTC   Indian Ocean Tuna Commission
IMF   International Monetary Fund
NMFS   National Marine Fisheries Service

Alker, Hayward. 1974. Are there structural models of voluntaristic social action? *Quality and Quantity* 8: 199–246.

———. 1996. *Rediscoveries and Reformations*. Cambridge: Cambridge University Press.

Ando, Amy Whritenour. 1999. Waiting to be protected under the Endangered Species Act: The political economy of regulatory delay. *Journal of Law and Economics* 42 (April): 29–60.

Apostle, Richard, Gene Berrett, Petter Hom, Svein Jentoft, Leigh Mazany, Bonnie McCay, and Knut H. Mikalsen. 1998. *Community, State, and Market on the North Atlantic Rim*. Toronto: University of Toronto Press.

Axelrod, Robert. 1997. *The Complexity of Cooperation*. Princeton, NJ: Princeton University Press.

Axelrod, Robert and Robert Keohane. 1985. Achieving cooperation under anarchy: Strategies and institutions. *World Politics* 38 (October): 226–254.

Baldwin, David A., ed. 1993. *Neorealism and Neoliberalism: The Contemporary Debate*. New York: Columbia University Press.

Barkin, J. Samuel and Elizabeth R. DeSombre. 2000. Unilateralism and multilateralism in international fisheries management. *Global Governance* 6: 339–360.

Barkin, J. Samuel and George Shambaugh. 1999a. *Anarchy and the Environment*. Albany: State University of New York Press.

———. 1999b. Hypotheses on the international politics of common pool resources. In J. Samuel Barkin and George Shambaugh, *Anarchy and the Environment*. Albany: State University of New York Press, 1999, pp. 1–25.

Barrett, Scott. 2001. International cooperation for sale. *European Economic Review* 45: 1835–1850.

Bemelmans-Videc, Marie-Louise, Ray C. Rist, and Evert Vedung, eds. 1998. *Carrots, Sticks and Sermons*. New Brunswick, NJ: Transaction Publishers.

Bergin, Anthony and M. G. Haward. 1996. *Japan's Tuna Fishing Industry*. Commack, Canada: Nova Science Publishers.

Berkes, F. T. P. Hughes, R. S. Steneck, J. A. Wilson, D. R. Bellwood, B. Crona et al. 2006. Globalization, roving bandits, and marine resources. *Science* 311 (March): 1557–1558.

Bestor, Theodore C. 2000. How sushi went global. *Foreign Policy* no. 121: 54–63.

Bjorndal, Trond, Veijo Kaitala, Marko Lindros, and Gordon R. Munro. 2000. The management of high seas fisheries. *Annals of Operations Research* 94: 183–196.

Breitmeier, Helmut, Oran R. Young, and Michael Zurn. 2006. *Analyzing International Environmental Regimes*. Cambridge, MA: MIT Press.

Cacaud, Philippe. 2005. *Fisheries Laws and Regulations in the Mediterranean: A Comparative Study, Studies and Reviews No. 75*. Rome: Food and Agriculture Organization of the United Nations.

Central Intelligence Agency. 2007. CIA World Factbook Online, Langley, VA: Central Intelligence Agency. https://www.cia.gov/library/publications/the-world-factbook/fields/2004.html.

Christy, Francis T., Jr. and Anthony Scott. 1965. *The Common Wealth in Ocean Fisheries*. 2nd ed., Baltimore: Johns Hopkins University Press.

Clark, Colin W. 1990. *Mathematical Bioeconomics: The Optimal Management of Renewable Resources*. 2nd ed., New York: Wiley.

Conceição-Heldt, Eugénia. 2004. *The Common Fisheries Policy in the European Union*. New York: Routledge.

Crean, Kevin and David Symes, eds. 1996. *Fisheries Management in Crisis*. Cambridge, MA: Fishing News Books.

Crowder, L. B., G. Osherenko, O. R. Young, S. Airame, E. A. Norse, N. Baron et al. 2006. Resolving mismatches in US ocean governance. *Science* 313 (August): 617–618.

De Leiva Moreno, J. I. and J. Majkowski. 2005. Status of the tuna stocks of the world. In W. H. Bayliff, J. I. De Leiva Moreno, and J. Majkowski, eds., *Proceedings of the Second Meeting of the Technical Advisory Committee of the FAO Project, Management of Tuna Fishing Capacity: Conservation and Socioeconomics* (pp. 58–114). FAO Fisheries Proceedings 2. Rome: Food and Agriculture Organization of the United Nations, http://www.fao.org/docrep/008/y5984e/y5984e0a.htm#bm10 (accessed July 25, 2006).

DeSombre, Elizabeth R. 1995. Baptists and bootleggers for the environment. *Journal of Environment and Development* 4 (1): 53–75.

———. 1999. Tuna fishing and common pool resources. In Samuel J. Barkin and George Shambaugh, *Anarchy and the Environment*. Albany: State University of New York Press, 1999, pp. 51–69.

———. 2000. *Domestic Sources of International Environmental Policy*. Cambridge, MA: MIT Press.

———. 2005. Fishing under flags of convenience: Using market power to increase participation in international regulation. *Global Environmental Politics 5* (4): 73–94.

———. 2006. *Flagging Standards: Globalization and Environmental, Safety and Labor Regulations at Sea*. Cambridge, MA: MIT Press.

DeSombre, Elizabeth R. and J. Samuel Barkin. 2002. Turtles and trade: The WTO's acceptance of environmental trade restrictions. *Global Environmental Politics* 2 (1): 12–18.

Durrenberger, Paul E. and Thomas D. King, eds. 2000. *State and Community in Fisheries Management: Power, Policy, and Practice*. Westport, CT: Bergin and Garvey.

European Commission. 2007. Eurostat DS-016890—EU27 Trade Since 1995 by CN8 Database. Brussels: European Commission. http://epp.eurostat.ec.europa .eu/portal/page?_pageid=0,1136217,0_45571467and_dad=portaland_schema =PORTAL (accessed May 2, 2007).

Food and Agriculture Organization of the United Nations. 2002. *The State of World Fisheries and Aquaculture 2002*. Rome: FAO Fisheries Department.

———. 2006. *The State of World Fisheries and Aquaculture 2004*. Rome: FAO Fisheries Department. Retrieved July 26, 2006 from http://www.fao.org/ DOCREP/007/y5600e/y5600e00.htm#TopOfPage.

———. 2007a. FI Fact Sheets. Rome: FAO Fisheries Department, Fishery Information, Data, and Statistics Department. http://www.fao.org/fi/website/FISearch .do?dom=factsheets (accessed June 13, 2007).

———. 2007b. FAO Capture Production 1950–2005 Database. Rome: FAO Fisheries Department, Fishery Information, Data, and Statistics Department. http://www.fao.org/fi/website/FIRetrieveAction.do?dom=topicandfid=16062 (for use with FishStat Plus, Universal software for fishery statistical time series. Version 2.3. 2000; accessed February 13, 2007).

———. 2007c. FAO Commodities Production and Trade 1976–2005 Database. Rome: FAO Fisheries Department, Fishery Information, Data, and Statistics Department. http://www.fao.org/fi/website/FIRetrieveAction.do?dom=topicandfid =16062 (for use with FishStat Plus, Universal software for fishery statistical time series. Version 2.3. 2000; accessed February 13, 2007).

Griffin, Rodman D. 1992. Marine mammals vs. fish. *CQ Researcher* 2 (32): 739–758.

Haas, Ernst B. 1990. *When Knowledge Is Power*. Berkeley: University of California Press.

Haas, Peter M. 1994. Regime patterns for environmental management. In Peter M. Haas, Helge Hveem, Robert O. Keohane, and Arid Underdal, eds., *Complex Cooperation*. Oslo: Scandinavian University Press, 1994, 35–63.

Haas, Peter M. and Ernst B. Haas. 1995. Learning to learn: Improving international governance. *Global Governance* 1 (3): 255–284.

Haas, Peter M., Robert O. Keohane, and Marc A. Levy, eds. 1995. *Institutions for the Earth*. Cambridge, MA: MIT Press.

Hannesson, Rognvaldur. 1997. Fishing as a supergame. *Journal of Environmental Economics and Management* 32: 309–322.

Hersoug, Bjorn. 1996. Social Consideration in Fisheries Planning and Management—Real Objectives or a Defence of the Status Quo? in Kevin Crean and David Symes, eds., *Fisheries Management in Crisis*. Cambridge, MA: Fishing News Books, 1996, pp. 19–24.

Hilborn, R., J. M. Orensanz, and A. M. Parma. 2005. Institutions, incentives, and the future of fisheries. *Philosophical Transactions of the Royal Society* 360: 47–57.

Hirschman, Albert O. 1970. *Exit, Voice, and Loyalty: Responses to Decline in Firms, Organizations, and States*. Cambridge, MA: Harvard University Press.

Inter-American Tropical Tuna Commission. 2006. *Tunas and Billfishes in the Eastern Pacific Ocean in 2005*. La Jolla, CA: Inter-American Tropical Tuna Commission. http://www.iattc.org/FisheryStatusReportsENG.htm (accessed March 22, 2007).

International Commission for the Conservation of Atlantic Tunas. 1966. *International Convention for the Conservation of Atlantic Tunas*. Rome: Food and Agriculture Organization of the United Nations.

———. 1971–1994. *Annual Report*. Madrid: International Commission for the Conservation of Atlantic Tunas (Publication occurs the year after each meeting is held. Until 1994 the annual report included the proceedings of the commission as well as its Standing Committe on Research and Statistics.)

———. 1995–2007a. *Annual Report of the Commission*. Madrid: International Commission for the Conservation of Atlantic Tunas (Publication occurs the year after each meeting is held. Prior to 1995 the proceedings of the commission were published in combination with the proceedings of the Standing Committe on Research and Statistics.)

———. 1995–2007b. *Annual Report of the Standing Committe on Research and Statistics*. Madrid: International Commission for the Conservation of Atlantic Tunas (Publication occurs the year after each meeting is held. Prior to 1995 the proceedings of the Standing Committe on Research and Statistics were published in combination with the proceedings of the commission.)

———. 2007a. *Compendium of Management Recommendations and Resolutions Adopted by ICCAT for the Conservation of Atlantic Tunas and Tuna-like Species*. Madrid: International Commission for the Conservation of Atlantic Tunas. http://www.iccat.es/RecsRegs.asp (accessed June 13, 2007).

————. 2007b. List of Contracting Parties. Madrid: International Commission for the Conservation of Atlantic Tunas. http://www.iccat.es/contracting.htm (accessed May 3, 2007).

————. 2007c. Report of the Inter-Sessional Meeting of Panel 2 to Establish an Allocation Scheme for Eastern Atlantic and Mediterranean Bluefin Tuna, Tokyo, Japan, January 29–31, 2007. Madrid: International Commission for the Conservation of Atlantic Tunas.

————. 2007d. ICCAT Reported Landings 1950–2005 Database. International Commission for the Conservation of Atlantic Tunas. http://www.iccat.es/accesingdb.htm (accessed February 19, 2007). Madrid: International Commission for the Conservation of Atlantic Tunas.

International Monetary Fund. 2006. IMF World Economic Outlook Database. Washington, DC: International Monetary Fund. http://www.imf.org/external/pubs/ft/weo/2006/02/data/download.aspx (accessed September 19, 2006).

Indian Ocean Tuna Commission. 2005. *Resolutions*. Victoria, Seychelles: Indian Ocean Tuna Commission. http://www.iotc.org/English/resolutions.php?PHPSESSID=4972501739b2c1151c2019d938fdfa49 (accessed July 21, 2005).

Iudicello, Suzanne, Michael Weber, and Robert Wieland. 1999. *Fish, Markets and Fishermen*. Washington, DC: Island Press.

Johnston, Douglas M. 1965. *The International Law of Fisheries: A Framework for Policy-Oriented Inquiries*. New Haven, CT: Yale University Press.

Joseph, James. 1983. International tuna management revisited. In Brian J. Rothschild, ed., *Global Fisheries: Perspectives for the 1980s*. New York: Springer-Verlag, 1983, pp. 123–150.

Joyner, Christopher C. and Zachary Tyler. 2000. Marine conservation versus international free trade: Reconciling dolphins with tuna and sea turtles with shrimp. *Ocean Development and International Law* 31 (1–2): 127–150.

Juda, Lawrence. 1996. *International Law and Ocean Use Management: The Evolution of Ocean Governance*. New York: Routledge.

Kahneman, Daniel, Peter Slovic, and Amos Tversky, eds. 1982. *Judgment Under Uncertainty: Heuristics and Biases*. Cambridge: Cambridge University Press.

Keohane, Robert O. and Joseph S. Nye. 1977. *Power and Interdependence*. Boston: Little, Brown.

————. 2001. *Power and Interdependence*. 3rd ed. New York: Longman.

Knox, John H. 2004. The judicial resolution of conflicts between trade and the environment. *Harvard Environmental Law Review* 28: 1–78.

Kubler, Dorothea. 2001. On the regulation of social norms. *Journal of Law, Economics, and Organization* 17 (2): 449–476.

Kuran, Timur and Cass R. Sunstein. 1999. Availability cascades and risk regulation. *Stanford Law Review* 51 (4): 685–768.

Lawson, Rowena. 1984. *Economics of Fisheries Development*. New York: Praeger.

Lempert, R. J., S. W. Popper, and S. C. Bankes. 2003. *Shaping the Next One Hundred Years: New Methods for Quantitative, Long-Term Policy Analysis.* Santa Monica, CA: RAND.

Lequesne, Christian. 2004. *The Politics of Fisheries in the European Union.* New York: Manchester University Press.

Litfin, Karen. 1998a. The greening of sovereignty: An introduction. In Karen Litfin, *The Greening of Sovereignty in World Politics.* Cambridge, MA: MIT Press, pp. 1–27.

———, ed. 1998b. *The Greening of Sovereignty in World Politics.* Cambridge, MA: MIT Press.

Ludwig, Donald, Ray Hilborn, and Carl Walters. 1993. Uncertainty, resource exploitation, and conservation: Lessons from history. *Science* 260 (5104): 17–18.

Majkowski, Joseph. 2005. *Tuna Resources, Fisheries and their Management.* Rome: Food and Agriculture Organization of the United Nations. ftp://ftp.fao .org/FI/excerpt/tuna_resources/tuna_resources.pdf (accessed July 13, 2005).

March, James G. and Herbert A. Simon. 1958. *Organizations.* New York: Wiley.

———. 1993. *Organizations,* 2nd ed. Cambridge, MA: Blackwell.

March, James G. and Johan P. Olsen. 1998. The institutional dynamics of international political orders. *International Organization* 52: 943–969.

McGoodwin, James R. 1990. *Crisis in the World's Fisheries.* Stanford, CA: Stanford University Press.

McKelvey, Robert W., Leif K. Sandal, and Stein I. Steinshamn. 2003. Regional fisheries management on the high seas: The hit-and-run interloper model. *International Game Theory Review* 5: 327–345.

Miller, John H. and Scott E. Page. 2007. *Complex Adaptive Systems: An Introduction to Computational Models of Social Life.* Princeton, NJ: Princeton University Press.

Munro, G., A. Van Houtte, and R. Willmann. 2004. *The Conservation and Management of Shared Fish Stocks: Legal and Economic Aspects.* FAO Fisheries Technical Paper 465. Rome: Food and Agriculture Organization of the United Nations.

National Marine Fisheries Service. 1989. *US ICCAT Advisory Committee Report.* Prepared by Rebecca S. Rootes. Silver Spring, MD: U.S. Dept. of Commerce, NOAA, National Marine Fisheries Service.

———. 2007. Annual Commercial Landings Statistics Database. Silver Spring, MD: National Marine Fisheries Service. http://www.st.nmfs.noaa.gov/st1/ commercial/landings/annual_landings.html (accessed March 15, 2007).

Oceanic Development, Poseidon Aquatic Resource Management Ltd., and Megapesca. 2005. *The European Tuna Sector: Economic Situation, Prospects and Analysis of the Impacts of the Liberalization of Trade. Final Report.* Coneameau, France: Oceanic Development.

Opsomer, J.-D. and J. M. Conrad. 1994. An open-access analysis of the northern anchovy fishery. *Journal of Environmental Economics and Management* 27: 21–37.

Peterson, M. J. 1995. International fisheries management. In Peter M. Haas, Robert O. Keohane, and Marc A. Levy, eds., *Institutions for the Earth*. Cambridge, MA: MIT Press, 1995, pp. 249–305.

Powell, Walter W. and Paul J. DiMaggio. 1991. *The New Institutionalism in Organizational Analysis*. Chicago: University of Chicago Press.

Putnam, Robert D. 1988. Diplomacy and domestic politics: The logic of two-level games. *International Organization* 42 (3): 427–460.

Rosenau, James N. 1993. Environmental Challenges in a Global Context. In Sheldon Kamieniecki, ed. 1993. *Environmental Politics in the International Arena*. New York: State University of New York Press, pp. 257–274.

Royce, William F. 1987. *Fishery Development*. New York: Academic Press.

Sahrhage, D. and Johannes Lundbeck. 1992. *A History of Fishing*. New York: Springer-Verlag.

Schelling, Thomas C. 1978. *Micromotives and Macrobehavior*. New York: Norton.

Schrijver, Nico. 1997. *Sovereignty over Natural Resources: Balancing Rights and Duties*. Cambridge: Cambridge University Press.

SFI Bulletin. 1974. Conservation of Northern Bluefin Tuna, no. 256 (July): 1–3.

Simon, Herbert A. 1955. A behavioral model of rational choice. *The Quarterly Journal of Economics* 69: 99–118.

Sprinz, Detlef and Tapani Vaahtoranta. 1994. The interest-based explanation of international environmental policy. *International Organization* 48 (1): 77–105.

Stokke, O. S., L. G. Anderson, and N. Mirovitskaya. 1999. The Barents Sea fisheries. In O. Young, ed., *The Effectiveness of International Environmental Regimes*. Cambridge, MA: MIT Press, 1999, pp. 91–154.

Sydnes, A. K. 2001. Regional fishery organizations: How and why organizational diversity matters. *Ocean Development and International Law* 32 (4): 349–372.

Tietenberg, Tom. 2003. *Environmental and Natural Resource Economics*. 6th ed. Boston: Addison Wesley.

Tolba, Mostafa Kamal. 1998. *Global Environmental Diplomacy: Negotiating Environmental Agreements for the World, 1973–1992*. Cambridge, MA: MIT Press.

Tversky, Amos and Daniel Kahneman. 1991. Loss aversion in riskless choice: A reference-dependent model. *Quarterly Journal of Economics* 106 (4): 1039–1061.

U.S. Congress. 1975. *Atlantic Tunas Convention Act of 1975*. Public Law 94-70, U.S. Code 16. http://www.access.gpo.gov/uscode/title16/chapter16a_.html (accessed July 16, 2005).

Weber, Michael L. 2002. *From Abundance to Scarcity: A History of U.S. Marine Fisheries Policy*. Washington, DC: Island Press.

Webster, D. G. 2006. The marlin conundrums: Turning the tide for by-catch species. *Bulletin of Marine Science* 79 (3): 561–576.

Wendt, Alexander. 1999. *Social Theory of International Politics*. Cambridge: Cambridge University Press.

World Bank. 2006. World Development Indicators. Online Database. Washington, DC: World Bank. http://devdata.worldbank.org/dataonline/old-default.htm (accessed September 19, 2006).

Worm, B., E. B. Barbier, N. Beaumont, J. E. Duffy, C. Folke, B. S. Halpern et al. 2006a. Impacts of biodiversity loss on ocean ecosystem services. *Science* 314 (5800): 787–790.

Worm, B., E. B. Barbier, N. Beaumont, J. E. Duffy, C. Folke, B. S. Halpern et al. 2006b. Response to Comments on "Impacts of biodiversity loss on ocean ecosystem services." *Science* 316 (5829): 1285.

Young, Oran R. 1982. *Resource Regimes*. Los Angeles: University of California Press.

———, ed. 1999. *The Effectiveness of International Environmental Regimes*. Cambridge, MA: MIT Press.

———. 2002. *The Institutional Dimensions of Environmental Change: Fit, Interplay, and Scale*. Cambridge, MA: MIT Press.

Young, Oran R. and Marc A. Levy. 1999. The effectiveness of international environmental regimes. In Oran Young, ed. 1999, pp. 1–32.

Zahran, Sammy, S. D. Brody, H. Grover, and A. Vedlitz. 2006. Climate change vulnerability and policy support. *Society and Natural Resources* 19: 771–789.

Zeidberg, Louis D. and Bruce H. Robison. 2007. Invasive range expansion by the Humboldt squid, *Dosidicus gigas*, in the eastern North Pacific. *Proceedings of the National Academy of Sciences of the United States* 104 (31): 12948–12951.

Index

Global Environmental Accord: Strategies for Sustainability and Institutional Innovation
Nazli Choucri, series editor